MAO ZEDONG

www.royalcollins.com

MAC
ZED

A TRUE STORY

ONG

LI JIE

Mao Zedong: A True Story

By Li Jie

First published in 2025 by Royal Collins Publishing Group Inc.
Groupe Publication Royal Collins Inc.
550-555 boul. René-Lévesque O Montréal (Québec) H2Z1B1 Canada

10 9 8 7 6 5 4 3 2 1

Copyright © Li Jie, 2024
Original edition © People's Publishing House
This English edition is authorized by People's Publishing House.

All rights reserved. Without limiting the rights under copyright reserved above, no part of this publication may be reproduced, stored in or introduced into a retrieval system, or transmitted in any form or by any means (electronic, mechanical, photocopying, recording, or otherwise), without the prior written permission of both the copyright owner and the above publisher of this book.

ISBN: 978-1-4878-1269-0

To find out more about our publications, please visit www.royalcollins.com.

Contents

	Introduction	1
Chapter 1	"A Startling Emergence"	3
Chapter 2	Initial Show of Strength	19
Chapter 3	Pioneering a New Path	39
Chapter 4	Difficult Days	61
Chapter 5	"The Red Army Fears No Difficult Expedition"	79
Chapter 6	The National War of Resistance and the Protracted War	105
Chapter 7	Independent and Autonomous Guerrilla Warfare Behind Enemy Lines	123
Chapter 8	Marxism Must Also Be Adapted to China	145
Chapter 9	Confrontation and Negotiation	169
Chapter 10	Carrying the Revolution to the End	191
Chapter 11	The World Has Changed	209

Chapter 12	Resisting US Aggression and Aiding Korea to Protect the Homeland	227
Chapter 13	Establishing a Socialist System	251
Chapter 14	"Using the Soviet Union as a Reference"	273
Chapter 15	The Great Leap Forward	295
Chapter 16	Reflections After Calming Down	321
Chapter 17	The Struggle with Khrushchev	333
Chapter 18	Launching the "Great Cultural Revolution"	349
Chapter 19	Opening the Door to Normalizing China-US Relations	371
Chapter 20	Unfulfilled Aspirations	393
	Notes	413
	Index	445

Introduction

On September 9, 1976, a great leader passed away. The entire nation mourned, and a grand memorial service was held in Tiananmen Square. A few days later, the United Nations General Assembly observed a moment of silence in his honor before officially convening.

This great leader was Mao Zedong.

Nearly half a century has passed, and today, at the Chairman Mao Memorial Hall at the southern end of Tiananmen Square in Beijing and Mao Zedong's former residence in Shaoshan, Xiangtan City, Hunan Province, there are still endless streams of people coming to pay their respects. Among these are officials of various levels, workers, farmers, students, and international friends. Some newlyweds even come here, following their parents' teachings, to express their gratitude and respect.

Who was he? How did he become a revolutionary? What extraordinary achievements did he accomplish?

We say that people are shaped by their times, and the outstanding figures of these times can deeply influence them in return. So, how did the times shape Mao Zedong? And how did Mao Zedong influence the course of the 20th century?

Let us trace Mao Zedong's life journey to unravel these questions.

CHAPTER 1

"A Startling Emergence"

I view the Russian Revolution as a desperate measure when all other means have failed. It is not that a better method was available and ignored in favor of this terrifying approach.

MAO ZEDONG,
"A Letter to Cai Hesen" (December 1, 1920)

After initiating his career as a revolutionary, Mao Zedong began this journey by founding the Communist Party of China (CPC).

Like many revolutionaries in China, they were not born dissenters or revolutionaries. Numerous factors fostered their path to revolution. Before the establishment of the CPC, how did Mao Zedong gradually become a revolutionary?

Born on December 26, 1893, in Shaoshan Chong (韶山冲), a small inland village south of the Yangtze River in Hunan Province, Mao Zedong's early life was rooted deeply within China's rural heartlands. Many place names in China relate to the local topography, geomorphology, or geographical location, and the *chong* (冲) in Shaoshan Chong, where Mao's hometown was situated in a gentle area among hills, derives from this tradition.

Mao was the quintessential farmer's son. From his ancestors to his father, the family subsisted on agriculture. His father embodied many virtues of the Chinese peasant: hardworking, frugal, and astute. Under his management, the Mao family was considered relatively prosperous locally. His mother, a devout Buddhist, was charitable and empathetic toward people with low incomes, epitomizing the traditional virtues of Chinese women.

In line with the emphasis on education prevalent in many Chinese families, Mao's father also sent him to study in a private school. Yet, his greatest hope was for Mao to dedicate himself to farming and household management, ensuring the continuation of the Mao lineage.

However, China was undergoing significant social upheaval following the defeat in the First Sino-Japanese War. The Japanese victory over the mighty Qing Empire (AD 1616–1911), demanding territorial concessions and indemnities, was a profound humiliation for the Chinese. The subsequent invasion by the Eight-Power Allied Forces and the flight of Empress Dowager Cixi and the Qing Emperor from Beijing's Forbidden City, followed by the signing of the Xinchou Treaty, led many Chinese intellectuals to fear for the nation's survival.

By the time Mao began to remember his studies, China had entered the 20th century, and its feudal autocratic regime was teetering—"like a clay Buddha crossing a river, hardly able to save itself." Against this backdrop, new ideas on national salvation proliferated.

Mao started his education at nine, initially studying traditional texts such as the *Three Character Classic*, *Tales from the Children's Knowledge Treasury*, and *Four Books and Five Classics*. By fourteen or fifteen, he left school to work in the fields during the day and keep accounts for his father at night. Around this time, a book rekindled his waning interest in study. This book was *Words of Warning to a Prosperous Age* by the reformist Zheng Guanying, written in the 1890s.

Mao borrowed *Words of Warning to a Prosperous Age* from his cousin, Wen Yunchang. The book advocated for the establishment of a parliamentary system, the development of commerce, the promotion of agricultural studies, and the founding of schools to unify society's efforts, fully utilize human talent, and optimize the use of resources. It attributed China's weakness to its need for Western technologies like railways, telephones, telegraphs, and steamships. According to what Mao later told Edgar Snow, "*Words of Warning to a Prosperous Age* stimulated in me a desire to resume my studies."[1]

In the autumn of 1909, as Mao Zedong returned to school, the Xinhai Revolution was imminent. A new teacher, Li Shuqing, arrived in Shaoshan, advocating for patriotic reforms and suggesting that temples be converted into schools. The villagers had mixed reactions, but Mao admired and supported Li's ideas.

Another significant event occurred in April 1910. A severe famine in Hunan led to protests in Changsha Chong, where hungry citizens demanded relief from the provincial governor. The governor's unreasonable response incited the protesters to storm his office, break flagpoles, and scare him away. The uprising was brutally suppressed, and many were killed or arrested. Mao and his classmates discussed the event for days. Mao later recalled that this incident "influenced my whole life." "I felt that there with the rebels were ordinary people like my own family and I deeply resented the injustice of the treatment given to them."[2]

"These incidents, occurring close together, made lasting impressions on my young mind, already rebellious. In this period also I began to have a certain amount of political consciousness, especially after I read a pamphlet telling of the dismemberment of China. I remember even now that this pamphlet opened with the sentence 'Alas, China will be subjugated!' It told of Japan's occupation of Korea and Formosa, of the loss of suzerainty in Indochina, Burma, and elsewhere. After I read this, I felt depressed about the future of my country and began to realize that it was the duty of all the people to save it."[3]

From concerns about the country's peril to anger over the rebels' suppression and the realization that "the rise and fall of the nation is the responsibility of every individual," Mao's desire to leave his small village and understand the wider world grew stronger.

In the autumn of 1910, Mao Zedong left Shaoshan Chong for the first time to attend Dongshan Higher Primary School in Xiangxiang County. Before leaving, he wrote a note to his father, expressing his grand ambitions through a modified poem.

Determined is the child to go out of his hometown,
And the pledges not to come back without studying to the fame.
A land of mulberry and Chinese catalpa is not necessary for burying bone,
And human life sees nowhere without a green mountain.

Dongshan Higher Primary School was a modern school, a stark contrast to the traditional private school Mao had received. Here, he learned about the deaths of Emperor Guangxu and Empress Dowager Cixi. For the first time, he saw Liang Qichao's *Journal of the New Citizen*, which had ceased publication three years earlier.

As often happens, the more knowledge one gains, the less satisfied one becomes and the more one yearns to explore larger worlds.

In the spring of 1911, Mao Zedong was recommended to attend the Xiangxiang Provincial Middle School, located in Changsha, the capital of Hunan Province. There, he witnessed the outbreak of the Xinhai Revolution and the Changsha Uprising firsthand. Resolutely, Mao abandoned his studies to join the revolutionary army, becoming a soldier in the new Hunan Army.

Mao later recalled as follows:

Many students were now joining the army. A student army had been organized and among these students was Tang Shengzhi. I didn't like the student army, I considered the basis of it too confused. I decided to join the regular army instead, and help complete the revolution. The Qing Emperor had not yet abdicated, and there was a period of struggle. My salary was seven yuan a month—which is more than I get in the Red Army now, however—and of this I spent two yuan a month on food. I also had to buy water. The soldiers had to carry water in from outside the city, but I, being a student, could not condescend to carrying, and bought it from the water-peddlers. The rest of my wages were spent on newspapers, of which I became an avid reader. Among the journals then dealing with the revolution was the *Xiangjiang Daily News*. Socialism was discussed in it, and in those columns I first learned the term. I also discussed socialism, really social-reformism, with other students and soldiers. I read some pamphlets written by Jiang Kanghu about socialism and its principles. I wrote enthusiastically to several of my classmates on the subject, but only one of them responded in agreement.[4]

After the success of the Xinhai Revolution led by Sun Yat-sen, the term "revolutionary party" became popular. At that time, like many Chinese inclined toward revolution, Mao Zedong considered himself part of the revolutionary party, although he did not understand the true meaning of revolution. He served in the new army for only six months. On February 12, 1912, the last Qing Emperor Puyi abdicated. On March 10, Yuan Shikai became the provisional president of the Republic of China. Believing the revolution was over, Mao left the army and decided to return to school.

Soon after, Mao Zedong ranked first in the entrance exam to Hunan Provincial High School (later renamed The First Provincial Middle School). However, he quickly realized that he did not like the school. Coincidentally, a Chinese literature teacher lent him a book, *Chronicles with Imperial Commentaries*. This was an official historical compilation from the Qianlong era, covering history from ancient times to the late Ming dynasty (AD 1368–1644), with annotations by Emperor Qianlong. "After reading *Chronicles with Imperial Commentaries*, I had also come to the conclusion that it would be better for me to read and study alone."[5]

Mao Zedong created a self-education plan and spent his days at the Hunan Provincial Library at the ancient Dingwang Platform in Changsha. He recalled to Edgar Snow: "I went to the library in the morning when it opened. At noon I paused only long enough to buy and consume two rice cakes, which were my daily lunch. I stayed in the library every day reading until it closed."[6]

During this period of self-education, Mao read extensively, learning about world geography and history. He saw a world map for the first time and studied it with great interest. He also read Adam Smith's *The Wealth of Nations*, Darwin's *Origin of Species*, and John Stuart Mill's *A System of Logic*. He read works by Rousseau, Spencer's *Logic*, and Montesquieu's *The Spirit of Laws*. "I mixed poetry and romances, and the tales of ancient Greece, with serious study of history and geography of Russia, America, England, France, and other countries."[7]

The six months of self-education at the Hunan Provincial Library were eye-opening for Mao and instilled in him a lifelong habit of reading. He told Snow: "I was very regular and conscientious about it, and the half year I spent in this way I consider to have been extremely valuable to me."[8]

However, his strict father threatened to cut off his financial support, forcing Mao to continue his formal education. In the spring of 1913, he enrolled in the preparatory course at the Fourth Provincial Normal School of Hunan. In March of the following year, the school merged with the Hunan Provincial First Normal School, where Mao studied for five years, becoming a normal student.

Mao chose to attend a normal school not out of a desire to become a teacher but because these schools had special appeal for students from less affluent backgrounds—they charged no tuition and had low room and board costs. Later in life, Mao came to value the teaching profession highly. He once told Snow in his later years: "What 'four greats'?[9] It's annoying! Someday they will all be gone, leaving only one: Teacher. Because I have always been a teacher, and I still am. I will resign from everything else."[10]

During Mao Zedong's time at the Hunan Provincial First Normal School, it had a significant impact on his later revolutionary path and the beginning of his revolutionary career. Mao summarized his time at the Hunan Provincial First Normal School as follows: "I was a student in the normal school for five years, and managed to resist the appeals of all future advertising. Finally I actually got my degree. Incidents in my life here, in the Hunan Provincial First Normal School, were many, and during this period my political ideas began to take shape. Here also I acquired my first experiences in social action."[11]

For Mao Zedong, who had an intense thirst for knowledge, being able to study at the Hunan Provincial First Normal School was a stroke of luck. The school boasted a group of teachers who were not only genuinely knowledgeable but also held progressive ideas, such as Yang Changji, Xu Teli, Yuan Zhongqian, Li Jinxi, Wang Jifan, and Fang Weixia. The school offered many courses, but those that attracted Mao the most were philosophy, history and geography, and literature.

The teachers who had the most profound influence on Mao Zedong were Yang Changji and Xu Teli. Yang Changji taught subjects like pedagogy and ethics, and he was not only Mao's mentor but later also became his father-in-law. Mao praised his teacher as follows:

> The teacher who made the strongest impression on me was Yang Changji, a returned student from England, with whose life I was later to become intimately related. He taught ethics; he was an idealist and a man of high moral character. He believed in his ethics very strongly and tried to imbue his students with the desire to become just, moral, virtuous men, useful in society. Under his influence, I read a book on ethics translated by Cai Yuanpei and was inspired to write an essay which I entitled "The Energy of the Mind." I was then an idealist, and my essay was highly praised by Professor Yang Changji, from his idealist viewpoint. He gave me a mark of 100 of it.[12]

Mao Zedong also left a deep impression on Yang Changji. In his diary entry dated April 5, 1915, Yang wrote as follows:

> Mao Zedong said that his hometown lies at the border between Xiangtan and Xiangxiang, separated only by a mountain, yet the dialects of the two places are different. The area is among high mountains, where people live in large family groups, mostly engaged in farming, which makes it easy to accumulate wealth. Wealthy families often buy land in Xiangxiang. The customs are simple and honest, with little smoking or gambling. Mao's father used to farm but is now a trader; his younger brother is still a farmer, and his maternal family in Xiangxiang are also farmers. Mao himself is exceptionally talented, which is rare. I encouraged him by citing examples of Zeng Guofan[13] and Liang Qichao,[14] who also came from farming backgrounds. Mao had farmed for two years and served as a soldier for six months during the revolution. These experiences are quite interesting.[15]

Xu Teli, who taught pedagogy, various teaching methods, and self-cultivation, also greatly influenced Mao Zedong with his rigorous scholarship. Later, on January 30, 1937, Mao wrote a letter to Xu Teli from Yan'an to celebrate his 60th birthday. In Chinese culture, turning 60 signifies having experienced a *jiazi* (甲子),[16] garnering respect from others for one's rich life experiences.

In his letter, Mao wrote: "You were my teacher twenty years ago, you are still my teacher now, and you will definitely remain my teacher in the future."[17]

This deeply expressed the bond between teacher and student.

Two major events during his time at the Hunan Provincial First Normal School significantly influenced Mao Zedong's life.

First, through the introduction of Yang Changji, Mao Zedong, Cai Hesen, and others became avid readers of *New Youth*, a magazine founded by Chen Duxiu, and were greatly influenced by it. The magazine was first published on September 15, 1915, originally named *Youth Magazine*. It was well-received by young scholars and became a beacon of the New Culture Movement. That year, Mao was a vigorous 22-year-old. Mao said: "Most of these societies were organized more or less under the influence of *New Youth*, the famous magazine of the New Culture Movement, edited by Chen Duxiu. I began to read this magazine while I was a student in the normal college and admired the articles of Hu Shi and Chen Duxiu very much. They became for a while my models, replacing Liang Qichao and Kang Youwei, whom I had already discarded."[18]

Second, just before graduating, in April 1918, Mao Zedong participated in founding the Xinmin Institute. Mao and Zou Dingcheng drafted the society's charter, which stated its purpose as "reforming academics, cultivating character, and improving customs." The charter also established five rules: "(1) No hypocrisy. (2) No laziness. (3) No waste. (4) No gambling. (5) No visiting prostitutes."[19] The society elected Xiao Zisheng as the general secretary, with Mao Zedong and Chen Shunong as officers. Shortly after, Xiao Zisheng went to France, and Mao took over the management of the society. Many members went on to become prominent figures in modern Chinese history, such as Cai Hesen, He Shuheng, Li Weihan, Xia Xi, Guo Liang, Xiao San, Luo Zhanglong, and Yi Lirong.

During the May Fourth Movement, the Xinmin Institute played a crucial role in the work-study movement in France and in the founding of the CPC. It was the first progressive youth organization Mao Zedong joined, greatly influencing his political thoughts and social experiences. Many members of the society became revolutionaries and maintained strong ties with Mao.

During this period, Mao also developed the habit of reading newspapers. He recalled: "During my years in normal school in Changsha I had spent, altogether, only 160 yuan—including my numerous many registration fees. Of this amount I must have used a third for newspapers, because regular subscription cost me one about one yuan a month, and I often bought books and journals on the news-stands. My father crushed me for this extravagance. He called it wasted money on wasted paper. But I had acquired the newspaper-reading habit, and from 1911 to 1927, when I climbed up Jinggangshan, I never stopped reading the daily newspapers of Beijing, Shanghai, and Hunan."[20]

Edgar Snow noted Mao's recollection and added an annotation to "acquired the newspaper-reading habit": "Modern newspapers were then still a novelty in China, and many people, particularly officials, looked upon them with extreme repugnance, as indeed they do today! (In the 1930s when Snow was writing.)"

Reflecting on the political thoughts he formed at the Hunan Provincial First Normal School, Mao said: "At this time my mind was a curious mixture of ideas of liberalism, democratic reformism, and utopian socialism. I had somewhat vague passions for 'nineteenth-century democracy,' Utopianism, and old-style liberalism, and I was definitely anti-militarist and anti-imperialist. I entered the normal college in 1912 and was graduated in 1918."[21]

In June 1918, Mao graduated from the Hunan Provincial First Normal School, ready to embark on a broader journey.

At that moment, a new ideological storm was brewing in Beijing, the birthplace of the New Culture Movement. The Russian October Revolution showed advanced Chinese intellectuals like Li Dazhao and Chen Duxiu the power of organized workers and peasants and the promise Marxism held for China.

In July 1918, Li Dazhao published three articles that caused a significant stir among Chinese intellectuals and young scholars: "A Comparative Review of the French and Russian Revolutions," "The Victory of the Common People," and "The Victory of Bolshevism." He praised the Russian October Revolution as a "socialist revolution," a "victory for labor," and "the precursor of world revolution in the 20th century." On New Year's Day 1919, he published another article, "The New Epoch," advocating that China should follow the path of the October Revolution.

Many historical influences occur intentionally or unintentionally. At the time, Mao Zedong was unaware of these influences, which would later significantly impact his revolutionary path. Facing the practical problem of securing future living expenses, Mao found guidance from Yang Changji.

Yang Changji had by then begun teaching at Peking University, which had become a vibrant hub of talent and ideas under President Cai Yuanpei. Around this time, France was recruiting Chinese laborers, and Cai Yuanpei and Li Shizeng initiated the work-study program in France. Recognizing Mao's situation, Yang saw this as a good opportunity and sent the news back to the Hunan Provincial First Normal School. Mao, Cai Hesen, and Xiao Zisheng saw it as a viable path and mobilized the Xinmin Institute members for the program, with Cai Hesen going to Beijing first to make arrangements.

On June 30, Cai Hesen wrote from Beijing: "I left on the 23rd, took the train in Hankou on the 24th, and arrived in Beijing on the evening of the 25th after three days and nights of travel, with mixed weather. I have discussed your situation in detail with Professor Yang, who hopes you can enter Peking University. I believe it is necessary for the three of us (referring to Mao Zedong, Cai Hesen, and Xiao Zisheng) to enter the university, and if we do, we will have a solid and lasting foundation here."[22]

On August 15, 1918, Mao Zedong and a group of like-minded students set out for Beijing.

Upon arriving in Beijing, making a living was Mao's primary concern: "Beijing seemed very expensive to me. I had reached the capital by borrowing money from friends, and when I arrived, I had to look for work at once. Yang Changji, my former ethics teacher at the normal school, had become a professor at Peking National University. I appealed to him for help in finding a job, and he introduced me to the university librarian. This was Li Dazhao, who later became a founder of the CPC, and was afterward executed by Chang Tso-lin. Li Dazhao gave me work, as assistant librarian, for which I was paid the generous sum of eight yuan a month."[23]

The "assistant librarian" position Mao Zedong referred to was actually that of a library clerk, typically a role for new hires responsible for registering new periodicals and the names of readers.

While working at the Peking University Library, Mao was keen on two activities. First, he participated in the Peking University Philosophy Research Society and the Journalism Research Society to audit lectures at the university. The president of the Journalism Research Society was Cai Yuanpei. Mao said: "In the Journalism Society, I met fellow-students like Chen Gongbo, who is now a high official at Nanjing, Tan Pingshan, who later became a Communist and still later a member of the so-called 'Third Party,' and Shao Piaoping. Shao, especially, helped me very much. He was a lecturer in the Journalism Society, a liberal, and a man of fervent idealism and fine character. He was killed by Chang Tso-lin in 1926."[24]

The second activity was preparing for the work-study program in France, the main purpose for Mao and the Xinmin Institute members coming to Beijing.

With the help of Yang Changji, Cai Yuanpei and Li Shizeng agreed to set up preparatory classes for the students from Hunan. These classes were held at Peking University and in Baoding and Li County, Hebei. Later, another half-work, half-study preparatory class was established at the Changxindian locomotive and car plant. Subsequently, except for Luo Zhanglong, who was admitted to Peking University, and Mao Zedong, who worked in the library, the other members of the Xinmin Institute, including Cai Hesen, went to these preparatory classes. Mao shuttled between these classes, coordinating and organizing.

Mao Zedong was enthusiastic about the work-study program in France but did not plan to go abroad immediately. He said: "I accompanied some of the Hunan students to Beijing. However, although I helped organize the movement, and it had the support of the Xinmin Institute, I did not want to go to Europe. I felt that I did not know enough about my own country, and that my time could be more profitably spent in China. Those students who had decided to go to France studied French from Li Shizeng, who is now president of the Sino-French University, but I did not. I had other plans."[25]

At this time, Mao already possessed some of the qualities that would play important roles throughout his life: sharpness, decisiveness, independence, and a refusal to go with the flow.

Mao lived in Beijing for just over six months. In March 1919, news of his mother's serious illness reached him, and Mao, being the eldest son and a devoted one, could no longer remain in Beijing.

On March 12, 1919, Mao left Beijing. On March 14, he arrived in Shanghai. He chose to go via Shanghai to send off a group of Hunan students going to France for the work-study program. After staying in Shanghai for half a month, he returned to Changsha on April 6.

Thus ended Mao Zedong's first trip to Beijing. Although the time was short, the gains were unprecedented.

The greatest gain for Mao Zedong during his time in Beijing was intellectual. He said: "My interest in politics continued to increase, and my mind turned more and more radical. I have told you of the background for this. But just now, I was still confused, looking for a road, as we say I read some pamphlets on anarchy, and was much influenced by them. With a student named Zhu Qianzhi, who used to visit me, I often discussed anarchism and its possibilities in China. At that time I favored many of its proposals."[26]

Another significant gain was personal. Mao frequently visited his mentor Yang Changji's home in Beijing, located near the Drum Tower on Doufuchi Alley. Initially, he visited to seek guidance and discuss issues with his teacher. Gradually, he developed feelings for Yang Changji's daughter, Yang Kaihui. At the time, Mao was 25 and Yang Kaihui was 18. Their shared fate and common ideals drew them together. Mao later recalled: "And here also I met and fell in love with Yang Kaihui. She was the daughter of my former ethics teacher, Yang Changji, who had made a great impression on me in my youth, and who afterward was a genuine friend in Beijing."[27]

Beijing left a profound impression on Mao. He described his experience there as a mix of hardship and beauty.

> My own living conditions in Beijing were quite miserable, and in contrast the beauty of the old capital was a vivid and living compensation. I stayed in a place called Three-Eyes Well, in a little room which had seven other people.

When we were all packed fast on the *kang* [炕 a traditional heated bed], there was scarcely room enough for any of us to breathe. I used to have to warn people on each side of me when I wanted to turn over. But in the parks and the old palace grounds, I saw the early northern spring, and the white plum blossoms flower while the ice still held solid over the Beihai. I saw the willows over Beihai with the ice crystals hanging from them and remembered the description of the scene by the Tang poet Cen Chen, who wrote about Beihai's winter-jeweled trees, looking "like ten thousand peach-trees blossoming." The in trees innumerable trees in Beijing aroused my wonder and admiration.[28]

As a newcomer from the south, the scenery of the north gave Mao a novel impression. In August 1936, he reminisced about his travels to and from Beijing with Edgar Snow: "I walked on the ice of the Gulf of the Beihai. I walked round the Dongting Lake, and I circled the walls of Baodingfu. I walked round the wall of Xuzhou, famous in the *Three Kingdoms*, and round Nanjing's wall, also famous in history. Finally, I climbed Mount Tai and visited Confucius's grave. These seemed to me traveling then achievements worth adding to my adventures and walking tours in Hunan."[29]

Life is full of coincidences. Shortly after Mao returned to Changsha, the May Fourth Movement erupted. The relationship and influence between Peking University, the birthplace of the movement, and distant Hunan became extraordinary due to Mao and the Xinmin Institute. Changsha became a significant center of the May Fourth Movement, alongside Beijing, Shanghai, and Tianjin.

After the movement broke out, the Beijing Student Union sent Deng Zhongxia to Hunan to establish contact with Mao Zedong, He Shuheng, and others. Subsequently, Mao and the Xinmin Institute members mobilized and established the new Hunan Student Union, with member Peng Huang as its president. On June 2, the Hunan Student Union held a general meeting and decided that students from all schools in the province would go on strike starting June 3.

Starting from June 3, Shanghai workers began striking and joining the May Fourth Movement, marking a new stage where the movement was no longer just about patriotic students. On the same day, students from twenty schools in Changsha, including the First Provincial Normal School, Xiangya Medical School, and the Commercial School, went on a general strike. Their strike declaration published in *Ta Kung Pao* of Changsha stated: "Diplomatic failures, internal strife, the nation is on the brink of ruin, urgent rescue is needed," adding more fuel to the May Fourth Movement.

Mao Zedong understood that for the student movement to be sustainable, it needed broad support from all sectors of society. With his efforts, the Hunan General Union was established on July 9, using the "Ten Men Rescue Society" as the grassroots organization. Later, the Hunan Ten Men Rescue Society Federation was formed, providing significant support to the student movement. Mao's talent for organizing mass movements began to show.

As the May Fourth Movement gained momentum in Hunan, Mao added more fuel to the fire by launching the *Xiangjiang Review* on July 14. Although the magazine was nominally the organ of the Hunan Student Union, Mao was its chief editor and main contributor.

In the manifesto of the first issue, Mao sharply raised critical questions: "What is the biggest problem in the world? The problem of food is the biggest. What is the strongest force? The united strength of the masses is the strongest. What should not be feared? Do not fear heaven, do not fear ghosts, do not fear the dead, do not fear bureaucrats, do not fear warlords, do not fear capitalists." He concluded that the world trend was a call for "world revolution" and a vigorous advance in the "movement for human liberation." The manifesto reviewed changes from the Renaissance to the Reformation, summarizing them as "gaining freedom from authoritarianism." As for how to overthrow authoritarianism, he advocated "the masses united in a continuous 'advice movement' toward the powerful, implementing a 'voice revolution'—the voice for bread, the voice for freedom, the voice for equality—a 'bloodless revolution.'"[30]

Like many publications that emerged during the May Fourth period, *Xiangjiang Review* focused on "promoting the latest ideas." It featured sections such as reviews of major events in the East and West, global commentary, local news from Xiangjiang, and new literature. Starting with the second issue, Mao's "The Great Union of the Popular Masses" was serialized under the pen name "Zedong." He argued: "The country has reached an extreme state of decay; humanity is suffering to the extreme, and society is in extreme darkness. The remedy and reconstruction method is the great union of the masses. Historically, there have been unions of the powerful, unions of the nobility, and unions of capitalists, but the most formidable is the great union of the masses." Among various mass unions, Mao particularly praised the Russian October Revolution and the May Fourth Movement. He emphasized: "We have awakened! The world belongs to us. The country belongs to us. Society belongs to us. If we don't speak up, who will? If we don't act, who will? The urgent and necessary great union of the masses must be actively pursued!" To achieve the great union of the masses, Mao suggested starting with small unions and promoting liberation in various areas such as thought, politics, economy, gender, and education. He predicted: "The Chinese nation has great potential! The deeper the oppression, the longer it has been stored, the faster it will erupt. I dare say that the future reform of the Chinese nation will be more thorough than that of any other nation. The society of the Chinese nation will be brighter than that of any other nation. The great union of the Chinese nation will be the first to succeed ahead of any other region or nation."[31]

This grand and powerful article, written with sharp insight, clear reasoning, and compelling language, quickly spread and was reprinted by newspapers in Beijing, Shanghai, Chengdu, and other places, having a significant impact on progressive thought at the time. In issue 36 of Beijing's *Weekly Review*, Hu Shi wrote in the "Introduction to New Publications" section that this article "has a broad vision and lively discussions and is indeed important literature of the present time."

At this time, Mao Zedong's thoughts clearly exhibited contradictions. On the one hand, he increasingly valued the power of the grassroots masses, firmly believing that China needed a fundamental social upheaval and that strong powers had to be eradicated. On the other hand, his overall tendency was still to imagine achieving revolutionary goals through "bloodless revolution" and various petition movements. This phenomenon was not just a personal perception but was widespread during that era. Under the long-term influence of Confucian thought, even in deeply troubled modern China, becoming a thorough revolutionary was not easy.

The *Xiangjiang Review* only published four issues. In mid-August, Hunan's military governor Zhang Jingyao dispatched military police to suddenly surround the Hunan Student Union and raided the Xiang-E Printing Company, confiscating and destroying all copies of the freshly printed fifth issue of *Xiangjiang Review*. This forced Mao Zedong to resolve to unite people from various sectors to drive out warlord Zhang Jingyao from Hunan through strikes, petitions, and other methods.

CHAPTER 2

Initial Show of Strength

The revolutionary party is the guide of the masses. In the course of the revolution, no revolution ever succeeds if the revolutionary party leads it astray. For our revolution to avoid mistakes and ensure success, we must pay close attention to uniting with our true friends to attack our true enemies.

MAO ZEDONG,
Analysis of the Classes in Chinese Society (December 1, 1925)

On December 6, 1919, 13,000 students from various schools in Changsha went on strike. The newly reestablished Hunan Student Union issued a national proclamation: "As long as Zhang Jingyao remains in Hunan, students will not return to school." Thus began a massive campaign to expel Zhang Jingyao.

On December 18, Mao Zedong led the Hunan Petition Delegation to Beijing, making Beijing the headquarters of the Hunan campaign to expel Zhang Jingyao. This was Mao Zedong's second visit to Beijing.

In Beijing, Mao Zedong organized several petition activities. On one occasion, he met with the adjutant of Jin Yunpeng, the Premier of the Beiyang Government, to present the demands for expelling Zhang.

To build momentum, Mao Zedong organized the establishment of the Citizen News Agency and appointed himself as the director. He issued daily news reports to newspapers in Beijing, Tianjin, Shanghai, and Wuhan, denouncing Zhang Jingyao's crimes in Hunan and reporting on the expulsion campaign. He also personally wrote a petition titled "The Hunan People's Struggle to Secure Mines and Factories," addressed to the Presidential Office, State Council, and the Ministries of Foreign Affairs, Finance, and Agriculture and Commerce, under the name of "Hunan Citizens in Beijing." These publicity efforts, combined with the petition activities, once again showed Mao Zedong the power of mobilizing the masses.

Despite the large scale of the expulsion campaign and the pressure it put on the Beiyang Government and warlord Zhang Jingyao, it ultimately could not resolve the issue. In early April 1920, Mao Zedong gathered Hunan representatives in an alley on Jingshan East Street to discuss ending the campaign in Beijing, deciding to leave a few people in Beijing while the rest moved to other places to continue their activities. In June of the same year, Zhang Jingyao was defeated in a warlord conflict. He was replaced in Changsha by Tan Yankai, the Commander-in-Chief of the Hunan Army and Governor of Hunan Province.

The expulsion campaign ended without achieving its goal, but Mao Zedong gained something else. The biggest gain from his second trip to Beijing was seeing the dawn of truth.

Shortly after arriving in Beijing for the expulsion campaign, on January 4, 1920, Mao Zedong met with his teacher and close friend from the Hunan Provincial First Normal School, Li Jinxi, at the Citizen News Agency located at 99 Beichang Street. Li Jinxi recalled, "When I visited him, Chairman Mao was sitting behind the incense table in the middle of the main hall. The long incense table had an oil printing machine and news manuscripts on the left, indicating that some of the manuscripts might have been written, engraved, and printed by the Chairman himself. On the right was a large pile of new books and periodicals on socialism, and it was here that I first read the full text of *The Communist Manifesto*."[1]

Mao Zedong was a man who deeply valued faith. His pursuit of faith aimed to solve fundamental global issues and find a total solution to human problems, as well as to address the problem of saving and preserving China. With this in mind, from leaving his hometown to entering Changsha, he quickly underwent a transformation in thought, moving from being deeply influenced by reformists Kang Youwei and Liang Qichao to being influenced by Sun Yat-sen's revolutionary faction. From entering the Hunan Provincial First Normal School, to his first trip to Beijing, to leading the May Fourth Movement and the expulsion campaign in Hunan, he began another search for truth. He studied, advocated, and even tried various forms of socialism, from Western bourgeois enlightenment thought to reformism to anarchism, but he still could not solve a perplexing question in his mind.

Mao Zedong later accurately expressed this process of exploration in his essay "On the People's Democratic Dictatorship," written when the founding of the new China was imminent: "At that time, progressive Chinese people read any Western book that contained new ideas. The number of students sent to Japan, Britain, the United States, France, and Germany reached an astonishing level. The domestic abolition of the imperial examination system and the establishment of schools were like bamboo shoots after a spring rain, with a vigorous effort to learn from the West. In my youth, I also studied these things. These were the cultures of Western bourgeois democracy, the so-called new learning. This was the situation of Chinese people learning from foreign countries from the 1840s to the early 20th century."

"Imperialist aggression shattered the Chinese dream of learning from the West. Strangely, why do teachers always invade students? Chinese people learned a lot from the West, but it did not work out, and ideals were never realized. Multiple struggles, including national-scale movements like the Xinhai Revolution, all failed. The country's situation worsened day by day, and the environment forced people into a desperate situation. Doubts arose, grew, and developed."[2]

This was roughly Mao Zedong's mindset when he first read *The Communist Manifesto*. However, at this time, he had not yet determined his faith; he wanted to continue a serious comparison. Yet, among the various ideologies he compared, he began to delve into Marxism. This was the biggest difference from his previous trip to Beijing and his greatest intellectual gain.

The second trip to Beijing was not only a period when Mao Zedong was extensively active in the campaign to expel Zhang Jingyao but also a time when he voraciously read books in search of the truth to save the country. In several letters to members of the Xinmin Institute, Mao discussed his plans to continue seeking the truth.

In February 1920, Mao Zedong wrote to Tao Yi (who was teaching at Zhou Nan Girls' School in Changsha): "I feel that we need to form a group of noble, pure, and courageous comrades who strive for progress. He Shuheng wants to study in France, but I persuaded him not to go to France but rather to go to Russia. My own plan is to go to Shanghai in a week. Once the Hunan issue is settled, I will return to Changsha and form a 'Society for Free Study' (or simply call it a self-study university) with my comrades. I expect that within one or two years, we will have a clear understanding of the general outline of both ancient and modern Chinese and foreign scholarship, which will serve as a tool for studying abroad (otherwise, we cannot study abroad). Then, we will form a group to go to Russia for work-study." He also said: "For this matter, my mind is full of joy and hope."[3] From these ideas, the influence of the Russian October Revolution on Mao Zedong is evident.

Subsequently, on March 14, Mao Zedong detailed his new ideas in a letter to Zhou Shizhao. Discussing his plan to systematically study various doctrines from ancient and modern times, both domestic and foreign, he said as follows:

> I plan not to go abroad for the time being but to stay in the country to study various academic outlines. I feel that staying in the country temporarily has the following benefits:
>
> (1) Reading translations is much faster than reading the original texts, allowing us to acquire more knowledge in a shorter time.
> (2) World civilization is divided into Eastern and Western streams, with Eastern civilization occupying a significant position within world civilization. Eastern civilization can essentially be considered Chinese civilization. It seems appropriate to first study the main ideas and systems of our country's ancient and modern scholarship before studying abroad to have something to compare.

(3) If we want to contribute even a little in today's world, we cannot ignore the "China" context. It is essential to conduct on-site investigations and research the situation within our country.

Regarding his future plans to travel to Russia, he said: "Russia is the first civilized country in the world. I think we should organize a group to visit Russia in two or three years." Speaking about the plan for a self-study university, he expressed: "I think we should create a new way of life in Changsha, inviting comrades to rent a house and run a self-study university (a term coined by Mr. Hu Shi). We will practice a communal life in this university." In the letter, Mao discussed his beliefs: "Honestly, I do not yet have a clear understanding of various doctrines and theories. I intend to extract the essence from translations and contemporary newspapers and magazines to form a clear concept of both ancient and modern Chinese and foreign ideas."[4]

The "communal life" mentioned in the letter refers to the work-study mutual aid movement. Mao Zedong experimented with this idea after arriving in Shanghai in early May. He rented a few rooms in Minhou Nanli, Shanghai, and lived a simple life with his classmate Zhang Wenliang from Hunan Provincial First Normal School, working and studying together, sharing meals and clothing. However, this experiment was not successful. On June 7, he admitted in a letter to Li Jinxi: "The work-study group is unreliable. We have decided to stop the initiative and establish a self-study society to engage in part-time work and study."[5]

In the June 7 letter, Mao also discussed his self-study progress with Li Jinxi: "Recently, I have been focusing on three subjects: English, philosophy, and newspapers. In philosophy, I started with 'The Three Great Modern Philosophers' and gradually moved on to various schools of thought; in English, I read a short lesson from the most basic textbooks every day; in newspapers, I carefully read them daily, cutting out good materials." He expressed his desire to study philology, linguistics, and Buddhism. He also emphasized the importance of learning foreign languages: "A foreign language is like a gateway that must be opened. I read a bit of English every day, and with persistence, I can make some progress." He also reflected on his weaknesses: "I am too emotional and suffer from the flaw of being easily moved, which prevents my mind from being calm and makes it hard to maintain lasting effort. Because I am easily driven by emotions, it is difficult to lead a disciplined life."[6]

According to Li Jinxi, who worked in the Ministry of Education in Beijing at the time, Mao Zedong frequently visited his home to discuss various socialist theories and modern philosophical schools, particularly those of French philosopher Henri Bergson, British philosopher Bertrand Russell, and American philosopher John Dewey.[7] It was through this process of reading, thinking, practicing, rethinking, and reading again that Mao Zedong increasingly gravitated toward Marxism.

During Mao Zedong's second trip to Beijing, two events directly related to him occurred. First, on January 17, 1920, his esteemed teacher Yang Changji passed away due to illness at the German Hospital in Beijing. Second, on January 23, his father Mao Yichang died in his hometown.

Before Yang Changji passed away, he wrote a letter to Zhang Shizhao. In the letter, he said, "I earnestly tell you, these two young men are talents within the nation, with bright futures ahead. If you do not speak of saving the country, so be it, but if you do, you must first value these two."[8] The "two young men" referred to in the letter were his prized students, Mao Zedong and Cai Hesen. After Yang Changji's death, Mao Zedong, along with Yang Kaihui and Yang Kaizhi, kept vigil beside his coffin. Together with Cai Yuanpei, Fan Yuanlian, Zhang Shizhao, Yang Du, Li Jinxi, Zhu Jianfan, and others, they issued a notice in the *Peking University Daily*, stating: "Mr. Yang was of pure conduct, dedicated to learning, uninterested in wealth and fame, and supported himself through his salary."

When his father, Mao Yichang, died, Mao Zedong was busy with the campaign to expel Zhang Jingyao in Beijing and was unable to return to Hunan for the funeral. This became a lifelong regret for him.

In July 1920, Mao Zedong returned to Changsha and began initiating and promoting the Hunan autonomy movement. This was his final effort toward a "bloodless revolution" before ultimately choosing Marxism.

He wrote numerous articles and commentaries for the *Ta Kung Pao* in Changsha, advocating for Hunan's autonomy. The titles of some of these articles give a glimpse into his views: "The Fundamental Issue of Hunan's

Development: The Hunan Republic," "Breaking the Groundless Construction of a Great China and Starting Many Chinas from Hunan," "Absolutely Supporting 'Hunanism,'" "The 'Hunan Autonomy Movement' Should Be Initiated," "'Hunan People Govern Hunan' and 'Hunan People Autonomous,'" and "A Respectful Appeal to the 300,000 Citizens of Changsha for Hunan Autonomy."

This Hunan autonomy movement, however, could only end in failure under the rule of various warlords in China. After Hunan warlord Tan Yankai used "public opinion" as a pretext to establish official autonomy, Mao Zedong withdrew from the movement in late October of that year and devoted himself to founding the Cultural Book Society.

On November 25, he expressed his disappointment in a letter to Xiang Jingyu, a member of the Xinmin Institute in France: "The political arena is deeply mired in decay and corruption, and there is absolutely no hope for political reform. We can only disregard everything, carve out a new path, and create a new environment."[9]

On the same day, in a letter to Luo Zhanglong, he emphasized the importance of ideology, determined to use it to change China's corrupt atmosphere and transform the Xinmin Institute into an ideological union. He wrote, "Ideology is like a flag. Once the flag is raised, everyone has something to aspire to and a direction to follow."[10]

Mao Zedong had already made up his mind about the ideology he referred to. On December 1, in reply to Cai Hesen, he clearly stated that he had chosen Marxism and the path of the Russian October Revolution.

Earlier, in July 1920, members of the Xinmin Institute in France held a meeting in Montargis, proposing "reforming China and the world" as the society's guideline. However, there were differing opinions on how to achieve this goal. In his reply, Mao Zedong expressed his views. He agreed with the idea of "reforming China and the world" as the society's guideline but emphasized the method of doing so. He supported Cai Hesen's opinion that the Russian approach should be used to reform China and the world. He said, "I see the Russian-style revolution as an inevitable measure when all other paths are blocked, not because there are better methods that we abandon in favor of this one." "Therefore, in my current view, absolute liberalism, anarchism, and democracy are all just theoretically appealing but practically unachievable." Here, he was summarizing his half year of reading, thinking, and choosing. At the end of the letter, Mao Zedong asserted, "The great task of reforming China and the world is definitely not something that can be monopolized by a few people."[11]

At this moment, Mao Zedong firmly decided that only by believing in Marxism and following the path of the Russian October Revolution could China's problems be fundamentally solved. Among the progressive group influenced by the May Fourth Movement, Mao Zedong's establishment of Marxist beliefs was not early, but as he himself said, "Three books especially deeply carved my mind, and built up in me a faith in Marxism, from which, once I had accepted it as the correct interpretation of history, I did not afterward waver."[12]

It was also during this winter that Mao Zedong married Yang Kaihui, the daughter of his admired teacher Yang Changji.

On New Year's Day in 1921, the city was covered in snow, the sun was radiant, and the scenery was refreshing. The New Year's meeting of the Xinmin Institute was held at the Cultural Book Society on Chaozong Street in Changsha. The meeting was chaired by He Shuheng and lasted for three consecutive days. More than ten people, including Mao Zedong, Peng Huang, Zhou Shizhao, Xiong Jinting, Tao Yi, Chen Shunong, and Yi Lirong, attended the meeting.

This meeting was essentially a continuation of the Montargis meeting held by the members of the Xinmin Institute in France. The meeting mainly discussed three issues: (1) What should be the common purpose of the Xinmin Institute? (2) What methods should be used to achieve this purpose? (3) How should these methods be implemented immediately? Mao Zedong first introduced the results of the Montargis meeting in France regarding these three issues. Subsequently, the participants discussed these issues one by one.

When discussing the methods to achieve the purpose, Mao Zedong, to facilitate the discussion, listed various propositions: (1) Social policy, (2) Social democracy, (3) Radical communism (Leninism), (4) Moderate communism (Russellism), (5) Anarchism.

Regarding these ideologies, Mao Zedong clearly stated: "Social policy is a patchwork policy and is not feasible. Social democracy uses parliament as a tool for reform, but in reality, the legislation of parliament always protects the interests of the propertied class. Anarchism denies power, and this ideology is likely never to be realized. Moderate communism, as advocated by Russell, which promotes extreme freedom and laissez-faire capitalism, is also impossible to achieve. Radical communism, the so-called labor and peasant ideology, uses the method of class dictatorship and is expected to be effective, making it the most suitable to adopt."[13] Mao Zedong's opinion was supported by the majority.

After this meeting, on January 21, Mao Zedong replied to Cai Hesen. Cai Hesen's letter, written on September 16 of the previous year, detailed the situation of the working class parties in various countries, especially the Russian Bolshevik Party, and discussed the starting point of the Russian social revolution as the materialist conception of history. Mao Zedong stated in his reply, "Your letter is very insightful, and I agree with every word." Speaking about establishing the Communist Party, Mao Zedong told Cai Hesen, "Regarding the party, Mr. Chen Duxiu and others are already organizing it. As for publications, you should be able to get *The Communist* published in Shanghai. It truly lives up to the phrase 'clear banner and definite stand' (the manifesto was written by Chen Duxiu)."[14]

By this time, the conditions for creating the CPC were largely in place. Under the guidance of the Comintern, the First National Congress of the CPC was secretly held from July 23 to early August 1921, first at No. 3, Shudeli Road, Rue Amiral Bayle (now No. 76 Xingye Road) in the French Concession of Shanghai and later on a boat on South Lake in Jiaxing, Zhejiang, to evade the secret police. Mao Zedong participated in this historic congress from start to finish. The two founders, Li Dazhao and Chen Duxiu, were unable to attend the meeting. The meeting was chaired by Zhang Guotao, with Mao Zedong and Zhou Fohai serving as recorders. The congress adopted the Party's program, established the Party's name as the CPC, elected Chen Duxiu, Zhang Guotao, and Li Da to form the Central Bureau, with Chen Duxiu as the secretary, and determined that the central task of the Party after its establishment would be to organize trade unions and lead the workers' movement.

To unify the leadership of the Chinese labor movement, the Chinese Labor Secretariat was established on August 11 in Shanghai, the city with the highest concentration of workers, following the conclusion of the congress. Branches were also set up in various locations. Mao Zedong was appointed head of the Hunan branch.

At this time, Mao Zedong had become a full-fledged professional revolutionary. His first significant task was to initiate, organize, and lead the Hunan labor movement. His earliest experiences in this area were gained while leading the campaign to expel Zhang Jingyao.

From December 1921 to September 1922, Mao Zedong deeply engaged with workers at the Anyuan Coal Mine in Pingxiang, Jiangxi, the Shuikoushan lead-zinc mine in Changning, Hunan, and the railway in Yuezhou (now Yueyang), among other locations. He mobilized the workers, nurtured key activists, and established workers' organizations. From September to November 1922, under Mao Zedong's leadership, a massive strike involving 17,000 workers erupted at the Anyuan Coal Mine. This strike was followed by a wave of strikes in Changsha, including strikes by sewing workers, carpenters, barbers, pen workers, and printers. The strike at the Shuikoushan lead-zinc mine also ended in victory.

After the tragic February 7 Massacre in 1923, where workers along the Beijing–Hankou Railway were brutally suppressed, the nationwide labor movement entered a low period. Mao Zedong suggested a strategy of "bending the bow and waiting to release the arrow," observing the situation and deciding whether to strike based on the development of the situation. Under his guidance, Anyuan only held a demonstration with modest economic demands, which were quickly accepted by the mining bureau, avoiding unnecessary losses and instead achieving some progress.

In June 1923, the Third National Congress of the CPC was held at No. 31 Xuguyuan Backstreet, Dongshan, Guangzhou. This congress decided that Communist Party members could join the Kuomintang (KMT) in their personal capacity to achieve cooperation between the two parties through "intra-party cooperation." After the congress, Mao Zedong began working in the Central Bureau, serving as the secretary of the Central Bureau, assisting Chen Duxiu in handling daily Party affairs.

Following this, Mao Zedong's focus, apart from internal Party affairs, was largely on promoting cooperation between the KMT and the CPC, taking on several important roles.

In January 1924, at the First National Congress of the KMT held in Guangzhou, Mao Zedong was elected as an alternate member of the Central Executive Committee of the KMT and was appointed to the Regulations Review Committee. After the congress, he was assigned to work in the KMT's Shanghai Executive Department.

In February of the same year, the KMT's Shanghai Executive Department was officially established, overseeing Jiangsu, Zhejiang, Anhui, Jiangxi, and Shanghai. Shao Yuanchong was appointed head of the Documentation Department, but before he took office, Mao Zedong acted on his behalf. The head of the Organization Department was Hu Hanmin, and Mao Zedong served as his secretary. Mao also directly participated in organizing the KMT's Hunan branch.

Amid the unpredictable revolutionary activities, Mao Zedong always missed Yang Kaihui, whom he had left behind. By this time, Yang Kaihui was a mother of two, living with her mother in Bancang, Changsha County, Hunan. In June of that year, after securing a relatively stable residence, Mao Zedong brought his mother-in-law, Xiang Zhenxi, Yang Kaihui, Mao Anying, and Mao Anqing from Bancang, Changsha, to Shanghai. They lived in Jiaxiuli, Muerming Road (now 583 Weihai Road) in the British Concession. Besides managing household chores, Yang Kaihui also assisted Mao Zedong in organizing materials and copying manuscripts.

Regarding the issue of cooperation between the KMT and the CPC, Mao Zedong quickly developed differences of opinion with Chen Duxiu. Due to overwork and illness, he requested leave from the Central Committee and, at the end of December of the same year, returned to Hunan with his wife and children.

For Mao Zedong, the Chinese New Year of 1925 was particularly warm and peaceful. He spent this New Year at his mother-in-law's home in Bancang. Soon after, he returned to Shaoshan with Yang Kaihui, Mao Anying, and Mao Anqing.

In Shaoshan, while recuperating, Mao Zedong conducted in-depth rural investigations and worked on mobilizing and organizing the peasants. He organized secret peasant associations in the Shaoshan area, established peasant night schools, and in mid-June, founded the Shaoshan branch of the CPC. Shortly thereafter, he also established the Seventh District Party Branch of the KMT.

This visit to Shaoshan was particularly significant in Mao Zedong's revolutionary career. Although he was born and raised there and was familiar with every blade of grass and tree, the enormous revolutionary potential hidden among these simple peasants was something he had never realized before. This realization became especially strong after the failure of leading the labor movement. This experience prompted Mao Zedong to shift his focus from the workers' movement to the peasant movement.

Mao Zedong later recalled: "Formerly I had not fully realized the degree of class struggle among the peasantry, but after the May 30 Incident (1925), and during the great wave of political activity which followed it, the Hunanese peasantry became very militant. I left my home, where I had been resting, and began a rural organizational campaign. In a few months we had formed more than twenty peasant unions, and had aroused the wrath of the landlords, who demanded my arrest. Chao Hêng-t'i sent troops after me, and I fled to Canton!"[15]

On his way from Shaoshan to Guangzhou, Mao Zedong passed through Changsha. He held a special affection for Changsha, where he formed his initial political thoughts, led the Hunan May Fourth Movement and the campaign to expel Zhang Jingyao, and after the founding of the CPC, led the labor movement there. All these memories and associations came together, inspiring his timeless poem, "*Qinyuanchun* · Changsha."

> In autumn cold stand I,
> Of Orange Islet at the head,
> Where Xiangjiang River northward goes by.
> I see the hill on hill all in red,
> And wood on wood in a deep dye;
> The river green down to the bed,

In speed a hundred barges vie.
Far and wide eagles cleave the blue,
Up and down fish in shallows glide,
All creatures strive for freedom under frosty skies.
Lost in immensity,
I wonder who,
Upon this boundless earth,
Decide all beings' fall and rise?
With many friends I oft came here,
How thick with salient days the bygones times appear.
When, students in the flower of our age,
Our spirit bright was at its height;
Full of the scholar's notable rage,
We criticized with all our might.
Pointing to stream and hill,
Writing in blame or praise,
We treat d like dirt all mighty lords of old days.
Do you remember still,
Swimming mid-stream, we struck waves to impede,
That boats which passed at flying speed?

The Guangzhou period marked a peak for Mao Zedong before he embarked on an independent path to explore China's revolutionary road. During this time, at a critical moment when Sun Yat-sen had just passed away, and the struggle within the KMT-CPC cooperation camp was becoming increasingly apparent, Mao published *Analysis of the Classes in Chinese Society* on December 1, 1925. This article not only clearly posed the fundamental revolutionary question, "Who are our enemies? Who are our friends?" but also incisively analyzed the economic and social positions and attitudes toward the revolution of various classes, including the landlord class and comprador class, the middle class, the petty bourgeoisie, the semi-proletariat (semi-self-employed farmers, poor peasants, small handicraftsmen, shop assistants, and peddlers), the proletariat, and the lumpenproletariat. This article was a scientific conclusion drawn from Mao's long-term research and observation of Chinese society and became the basic basis for his subsequent land revolution in the countryside.

Shortly after arriving in Guangzhou, Mao Zedong was appointed Acting Head of the Publicity Department of the Central Executive Committee of the KMT. The position was originally held by Wang Jingwei, who resigned due to his busy schedule with the National Government. After taking office, Mao founded the *Political Weekly* on December 5, which played an important role in the struggle against the KMT rightists like Dai Jitao.

Once settled in Guangzhou, Mao Zedong brought Yang Kaihui, his mother-in-law Xiang Zhenxi, and his sons Mao Anying and Mao Anqing from Hunan to Guangzhou. They lived at 38 Miaoqian West Street, Dongshan. Yang Kaihui once again became Mao Zedong's capable assistant, helping him edit the *Political Weekly*.

On March 20, 1926, Chiang Kai-shek orchestrated the Zhongshan Warship Incident, using it as a pretext to accuse the CPC of plotting a coup by commandeering the Zhongshan Warship. Subsequently, Chiang proposed the "Party Affairs Reorganization Case" at the Second Plenary Session of the Second Central Executive Committee of the KMT held from May 15 to 22. This led to all CPC members holding ministerial positions in the KMT, including Mao Zedong, being forced to resign. This incident deepened Mao Zedong's resentment toward Chen Duxiu's rightist capitulationism and the Soviet advisors' appeasement of the new right-wing faction within the KMT.

Mao later recalled: "On the basis of my study and of my work in organizing the Hunan peasants, I wrote two pamphlets, one called *Analysis of the Classes in Chinese Society*, and the other called *The Class Basis of Chao Hêng-t'i and the Tasks Before Us*. Chen Duxiu opposed the opinions expressed in the first one, which advocated a radical land policy and vigorous organization of the peasantry, under the Communist Party, and he refused it publication in the Communist central organs. It was later published in the *Peasant Monthly* of Canton, and in the magazine *Chinese Youth*. The second thesis was published as a pamphlet in Hunan. I began to disagree with Chen's Right opportunist policy about this time, and we gradually drew further apart, although the struggle between us did not come to a climax until 1927."[16]

After resigning from his position as Acting Head of the Publicity Department of the Central Executive Committee of the KMT, Mao Zedong focused his efforts on directing the sixth session of the Peasant Movement Training Institute in Guangzhou from May to September 1926. Although the institute was still officially run under the name of the KMT, it was effectively controlled by the CPC. Over 300 students from more than 20 provinces attended, and they played crucial roles in uprisings and base-building after the failure of the Great Revolution. Mao Zedong served as the principal, with Xiao Chunü as the director of academic affairs and Gao Yuhan as the political training director. The curriculum included peasant movement theory, research on peasant issues, and military training, which accounted for one-third of the courses. Mao Zedong personally lectured on "The Chinese Peasant Question" and "Rural Education Issues" and even taught geography. He led students on field trips to Shaoguan and Haifeng, the latter under the leadership of Peng Pai.

Mao also guided teachers and students in compiling the *Peasant Issues Series*, planning to publish 52 volumes, of which 26 were actually published. In the preface "National Revolution and Peasant Movement," Mao wrote: "The peasant question is the central issue of the national revolution. Without the participation and support of the peasants, the national revolution will not succeed. The feudal class in the economically backward semi-colonial countryside is the sole solid foundation of the domestic ruling class and foreign imperialism. Without shaking this foundation, it is impossible to shake the superstructure built upon it. Overthrowing this exploitative regime (referring to the landlord regime) is essential for the peasant's position; this is the most significant feature of the current Chinese peasant movement."[17]

In November 1926, Mao Zedong was appointed secretary of the Central Committee of the Peasant Movement, requiring him to reside in Shanghai. This separation from his family meant that Yang Kaihui and her mother, Xiang Zhenxi, returned to Changsha with Mao Anying and Mao Anqing.

The establishment of the sixth session of the Peasant Movement Training Institute coincided with the Northern Expedition Army's victories, supported by the workers' and peasants' movements in Guangdong, Hunan, and Jiangxi. However, many officers in the Northern Expedition Army were from wealthy families, and the rising tide of the workers' and peasants' movement, especially actions against local tyrants and evil gentry, generated hostility toward the movement among these officers. Chiang Kai-shek and other new right-wing members of the KMT exploited this sentiment to secretly organize and expand an anti-Communist alliance. Meanwhile, within the CPC and society, there were sharply contrasting views on the peasant movement, with some praising it highly and others criticizing it severely.

To address various questions, from January 4 to February 5, 1927, Mao Zedong spent 32 days conducting an on-site investigation in the five counties of Xiangtan, Xiangxiang, Hengshan, Liling, and Changsha in Hunan. He subsequently wrote the "Report on an Investigation of the Peasant Movement in Hunan." The report listed numerous facts to demonstrate: "The national revolution needs a significant rural upheaval. The Xinhai Revolution failed because it lacked this upheaval. Now, with this upheaval, it is a crucial factor for the revolution's success. The theory that things are 'terrible' clearly stands from the landlord's perspective to suppress the peasantry, is an attempt by the landlord class to preserve the old feudal order and obstruct the establishment of a new democratic order and is a counter-revolutionary theory. Every revolutionary comrade should not blindly follow such nonsense." He also proposed a famous saying: "A revolution is not a dinner party, or writing an essay, or painting a picture, or doing embroidery; it cannot be so refined, so leisurely and gentle, so temperate, kind, courteous, restrained, and magnanimous. A revolution is an insurrection, an act of violence by which one class overthrows another."[18]

Mao Zedong's investigation report was clear-cut, with no room for compromise, and it carried a distinct Maoist style. Unfortunately, Mao's opinions expressed at this critical moment of the Great Revolution were not adopted by the Central Committee led by Chen Duxiu. Mao recalled: "In Hunan I inspected peasant organization and political conditions in five places—Changsha, Liling, Xiangtan, Hengshan, and Xiangxiang—and made my report to the Central Committee, urging the adoption of a new line in the peasant movement. Early next spring, when I reached Wuhan, an interprovincial meeting of peasants was held, and I attended it and discussed the proposals of my thesis, which carried recommendations for a widespread redistribution of land. At this meeting were Peng Pai, Fang Zhimin and two Russian Communists, York and Volen, among others. A resolution was passed adopting my proposal for submission to the Fifth Conference of the Communist Party. The Central Committee, however, rejected it."[19]

Mao's opinions received strong support from Qu Qiubai, a senior official in the CPC. In April of the same year, the Changjiang Bookstore in Hankou published Mao's investigation report under the title *The Hunan Peasant Revolution (Part One)*, with a preface by Qu Qiubai praising it: "All Chinese revolutionaries must speak and act on behalf of the 390 million peasants and fight on the front lines. Mao Zedong has merely begun. Every Chinese revolutionary should read Mao Zedong's book, just as they should read Peng Pai's *Haifeng Peasant Movement*."[20]

Through the trials from the founding of the Party to the Great Revolution, Mao Zedong became more mature and resolute and began to form his own independent views. He was sharp in handling matters, good at thinking, adept at summarizing, and particularly focused on combining "books with words" (classic works) and "books without words" (investigations and research). He also had excellent organizational and publicity skills. These qualities later gave him a rare advantage in opening up new prospects. At the same time, he was emotionally sensitive and intolerant of any compromise. A few years earlier, Mao Zedong had expressed in a letter to a friend: "I believe that we can only have ideological disputes, not personal disputes. Ideological disputes arise from necessity, and what is contested is ideology, not personal matters. Personal disputes are common in the world and are generally negotiable."[21] This became his lifelong creed.

In the spring of 1927, Mao Zedong visited the old site of Yellow Crane Tower. Gazing at the rolling waters of the Yangtze River, countless thoughts surged through his mind, inspiring him to write the poem "*Pusaman* · Yellow Crane Tower."

> Wide, wide flow the nine streams through the land,
> Dark, dark threads the line from south to north.
> Blurred in the thick haze of the misty rain,
> Tortoise and Snake hold the great river locked.

The yellow crane is gone; who knows whither?
Only this tower remains a haunt for visitors.
I pledge my wine to the surging torrent,
The tide of my heart swells with the waves.

He later explained, "In 1927, on the eve of the Great Revolution's failure, I felt desolate, not knowing what to do. This was in the spring of that year. By summer, on August 7, the Party's emergency meeting decided on armed resistance, which provided a way out."[22]

At this moment, the first cooperation between the KMT and the CPC had broken down, and the separation between Mao Zedong and Chiang Kai-shek was historically inevitable.

For the CPC, whether it was founding the Party, leading the labor movement, or collaborating with Sun Yat-sen and the KMT in the national revolution, the goal was always the liberation of the working masses, the most oppressed class in Chinese society. The Party's standpoint was consistently on the side of the working people. As a result, the CPC grew from over 50 members at its founding in 1921 to over 50,000 members by 1927, organizing more than ten million workers and peasants.[23] At that time, its influence was second only to the KMT, becoming a major threat to anti-Communist forces within the KMT, including Chiang Kai-shek.

The KMT had long been a loose coalition of various political factions, primarily composed of the socially affluent middle and upper classes, including many political opportunists. Especially after Sun Yat-sen's death, the KMT split into left, center, and right factions over whether to continue the policies of "alliance with Russia, cooperation with the Communist Party, and assistance to workers and peasants." Chiang Kai-shek was known for his political maneuvering within the KMT. Initially presenting himself as a "leftist," he later positioned himself as a "centrist" on the eve of the Northern Expedition, gaining benefits from both sides. During the Northern Expedition, the KMT's power center rapidly shifted to "military power," making Chiang Kai-shek a pivotal force capable of determining the KMT's fate. This prompted Chiang to preemptively strike against the Communists. Before the complete victory of the Northern Expedition, he launched a brutal purge of the Communists, issuing arrest warrants for CPC leaders such as Qu Qiubai, Zhou Enlai, and Mao Zedong. Statistics show that from March 1927 to mid-1928, over 26,000 Communists were killed by the KMT.[24]

Despite suffering significant losses, the CPC was neither intimidated nor eradicated. The Communists stood up again, wiped the blood from their bodies, buried their comrades, and continued the fight.

CHAPTER 3

Pioneering a New Path

The peasants and workers, called to the uprising,
With sickles and axes, they make their stand.
From the peaks of Lushan, they move straight to Hunan,
With determination to fight and win.
Landlords oppress with countless hands,
The peasants united in hatred rise.
Autumn harvest time, clouds hang low,
A thunderclap—the uprising starts.

MAO ZEDONG,
"*Xijiangyue* · The Autumn Harvest Uprising" (September 1927)

This poem, "*Xijiangyue* · The Autumn Harvest Uprising," was written by Mao Zedong on September 9, 1927, during the launch of the Autumn Harvest Uprising on the Hunan-Jiangxi border. This uprising marked a new beginning for Mao Zedong's revolutionary career.

"Heroes are made by the times." Chen Duxiu's erroneous leadership ruined the favorable situation brought about by the first cooperation between the KMT and the CPC, leading to reflections among many party leaders. Mao Zedong admitted with some self-reproach, "I always believed the opinions of the leading comrades were correct, so I did not insist on my own views."[1] By this time, Mao Zedong had matured through many trials, especially the bloody storms following the failure of the Great Revolution, and had begun to think independently, make his own judgments, and decisions. The circumstances at the time also provided Mao Zedong with the opportunity to act independently. After the failure of the Great Revolution, the central leadership was forced to go underground, communication with various regions became difficult, and the connection between the Comintern and the CPC also became more challenging. Additionally, the leadership of the Central Committee of the CPC was significantly weakened by the KMT's massacres, necessitating greater reliance on leaders in the frontline struggles. In this context, Mao Zedong was given considerable space to independently demonstrate his talents.

Under the white terror, organizing the peasants to launch a successful uprising was no easy task. The first issue Mao Zedong faced was which banner to raise.

As early as the founding of the CPC, Mao Zedong had said, "An ideology is like a banner; once the banner is raised, people will follow. An ideology is like a flag; once the flag is raised, everyone will have hope and know where to go."[2] When the CPC was founded, it raised its own banner. During the period of cooperation between the KMT and the CPC, the banner of the National Government was often raised. However, when Chiang Kai-shek and Wang Jingwei withdrew from cooperation and began to massacre Communists and workers and peasants revolutionaries, the question arose as to whether they should continue to raise the banner of the National Government and the left wing of the KMT.

Before Mao Zedong led the Autumn Harvest Uprising on the Hunan-Jiangxi border, the Nanchang Uprising, initiated by Zhou Enlai and others on August 1, still raised the banner of the left wing of the KMT. Although it was beneficial in uniting a group of progressive members of the KMT, it was not conducive to deeply mobilizing the workers and peasants.

Mao Zedong was someone who paid great attention to drawing lessons from history. In a letter to the Central Committee written on behalf of the Hunan Provincial Committee of the CPC, he stated: "The Comintern representative, Mayak, came to Hunan and mentioned the new directive from the Comintern, advocating for the immediate establishment of workers' and peasants' soviets in China. This made me leap with excitement." "Due to this new directive from the Comintern, it influenced my views on the KMT during the time of the workers' and peasants' soviets, we should no longer raise the banner of the KMT. We should raise the banner of the CPC high, to oppose the KMT banners raised by warlords like Chiang (Kai-shek), Tang (Shengzhi), Feng (Yuxiang), and Yan (Xishan). The KMT's banner has become a warlord's banner; only the CPC's banner is the people's banner. I didn't quite realize this while in Hubei, but after coming to Hunan and seeing Tang Shengzhi's provincial party department and the people's reaction to it, I can conclude that the KMT's banner can no longer be raised; if we raise it again, we will surely fail again."[3]

Previously, in his speech at the "August 7" Central Emergency Meeting, Mao Zedong emphasized, "In the future, we must pay great attention to military affairs. It must be understood that political power comes from the barrel of a gun."[4] After the meeting, his political supporter Qu Qiubai hoped Mao Zedong would go to work at the Central Office in Shanghai. However, Mao Zedong expressed his reluctance to live in the high-rise buildings of the big city and his desire to go to the countryside, to the mountains, to make friends with the outlaws.[5] This marked the beginning of Mao Zedong's independent pursuit of his career.

On September 9, 1927, the Autumn Harvest Uprising on the Hunan-Jiangxi border, led by Mao Zedong, erupted. Before the uprising, he specifically asked He Changgong to design a red military flag adorned with a sickle and hammer. Mao Zedong named this force of over 5,000 people the First Division of the First Army of the Workers' and Peasants' Revolutionary Army. In his capacity as the Secretary of the Front Committee of the Hunan Provincial Committee of the CPC, he led the entire uprising.

For a period, the situation resembled the description in "*Xijiangyue* · The Autumn Harvest Uprising": "From the peaks of Lushan, they move straight to Hunan."

The uprising army, primarily composed of peasants, was large but lacked strong combat effectiveness. The task they undertook was doomed to fail given the significant disparity in strength between the enemy and themselves. Before they could attack Changsha, they suffered a severe setback in Liuyang County.

A series of defeats posed a brutal question to the uprising army: What should they do if they failed? Should they continue with the original plan to attack Changsha or immediately relocate?

In the prevailing atmosphere, advancing meant bravery and fearlessness of death, while relocating signified "escape." This dilemma was placed before Mao Zedong, who had to handle it rationally without dampening the revolutionary enthusiasm of the uprising army. He would encounter similar situations many times later in his revolutionary and building career. This was a country where small-scale peasant farmers were the overwhelming majority, creating a unique historical process.

September 19 was a decisive day for the uprising army. On this day, the Autumn Harvest Uprising troops, commanded by Mao Zedong, assembled in Wenjiashi, Liuyang. By then, the total strength of the uprising army had decreased from 5,000 to just over 1,500.

That night, Mao Zedong presided over a meeting of the Front Committee at Liren School to discuss the next direction of the army's actions. Different opinions emerged at the meeting. Commander Yu Sadu and others insisted on continuing "directly attacking Changsha from Liuyang," while Mao Zedong advocated abandoning the attack on Changsha and shifting to rural and mountainous areas where the enemy's control was weaker, seeking a foothold to preserve strength and plan for future development. After intense debate, Mao Zedong's proposal was supported by the General Commander of the Front Committee, Lu Deming, and was passed.

On the same day, the Central Committee in Shanghai issued an order for the uprising army to attack Changsha again. However, this order could no longer be executed. Later, Mao Zedong was labeled with "gun-barrelism" and "escapism," was reprimanded, and was removed from his position as an alternate member of the Political Bureau. Nearly 30 years later, he recalled as follows:

During the Jinggang period, a false rumor spread that the Central Committee had expelled me from the Party, which meant I could not participate in Party activities and could only serve as a division commander. I couldn't even attend branch meetings. Later, it was said that this was a rumor and that I was expelled from the Political Bureau, not from the Party. Ah, I was relieved! At that time, they gave me a label called "gun-barrelism" because I said, "Political power grows out of the barrel of a gun." They argued that political power does not come from the barrel of a gun. Marx never said that, and there was no such phrase in any of the books. Therefore, they said I was wrong and labeled me "gun-barrelism."[6]

The next morning, on the playground of Liren School in Wenjiashi, Liuyang, Mao Zedong announced to the uprising army the decision to change the course of action. He candidly admitted that the armed uprising had suffered setbacks but said that victory and defeat are common in military operations. He emphasized that their current strength was still small, and they could not attack the heavily fortified large cities. Instead, they should first move to the countryside where the enemy's control was weak, preserve their strength, and mobilize the peasant revolution. He compared their current situation to a small stone, while Chiang Kai-shek's reactionary forces were like a big water tank. But he confidently asserted that one day, their small stone would definitely shatter Chiang Kai-shek's big water tank.

Listening to Mao Zedong's speech while perched on the school wall were two students in their teens. The two were cousins, one named Yang Yong, the other Hu Yaobang. Inspired by Mao Zedong's words, they later resolved to join the Red Army and became known as the "Red Youths" within the army.

Wenjiashi in Liuyang is located to the east of Changsha, at the northern end of the Luoxiao Mountains. The troops rested there for another day. On September 21, Mao Zedong led the troops southward along the Luoxiao Mountains, passing through places such as Pingxiang in Jiangxi.

Pingxiang was not unfamiliar to Mao Zedong. Shortly after the founding of the CPC, Mao Zedong visited Pingxiang multiple times to mobilize the workers' movement at the Anyuan Coal Mine, even descending into the mine to talk with the workers. In September 1922, under Mao Zedong's guidance, the famous Anyuan Coal Mine strike occurred and was successful. Even after the peak of the workers' movement was suppressed, the workers' movement there continued to thrive, earning the place the nickname "Little Moscow of China." Mao Zedong's outstanding performance in mobilizing the workers' movement in Hunan was recognized by Chen Duxiu, who was the General Secretary of the Central Committee at that time. As a result, Mao Zedong was elected Secretary of the Central Bureau at the Third National Congress of the CPC in June 1923, assisting Chen Duxiu in his work. This marked Mao Zedong's first entry into the central leadership of the Party.

Mao Zedong's exceptional leadership in the workers' movement earned him the attention of Chen Duxiu. However, differences arose later over the peasant movement, leading to disagreements between Mao and Chen. Despite this, Mao Zedong always remembered that it was Chen Duxiu and Li Dazhao who had led him to participate in the founding of the Party, and it was Chen Duxiu who guided him in establishing the early Party organization in Hunan.

Mao Zedong's previous visit to Anyuan was just before the launch of the Autumn Harvest Uprising on the Hunan-Jiangxi border. He held a military meeting at Zhangjiawan in Anyuan, conveyed the spirit of the August 7 Central Emergency Meeting, officially established the First Division of the First Army of the Workers' and Peasants' Revolutionary Army, and made deployments for the uprising. Therefore, this time, choosing to pass through Pingxiang was a familiar and relatively assured route.

However, during the revolutionary downturn, anything could happen. Along the way, in places like Luxi and Lianhua, they repeatedly suffered heavy blows from the enemy. One of Mao Zedong's capable and steadfast generals, General Commander Lu Deming, heroically sacrificed himself to cover the main force's retreat.

Internal disagreements within the revolutionary army resurfaced. Non-combat attrition increased steadily. By the time they reached Sanwan Village in Yongxin County, Jiangxi Province, the troops were reduced to about a thousand men. At this point, the leadership positions within the army were still largely held by mid- and low-level officers of the National Revolutionary Army from the period of the Great Revolution. While they had revolutionary ideas, their methods of leading troops in battle were outdated and influenced by warlordism. Clearly, continuing in this manner would make it difficult to sustain the army.

At this time, Mao Zedong's foot injury worsened, causing him great pain. Although the soldiers wanted him to ride on a stretcher, he insisted on walking with them. This injury occurred just before the launch of the Autumn Harvest Uprising, when he was traveling alone from Anyuan to the command post in Tonggu. He injured his foot while hurrying along a road at night to escape the escort of the local militia. In times of peril, Mao Zedong's spirit of enduring hardships alongside everyone else inspired the entire army. From then on, whenever the soldiers saw Mao Zedong's presence, their confidence surged.

Twenty days after the start of the Autumn Harvest Uprising, on September 29, the troops arrived at Sanwan Village in Yongxin County. This small village, surrounded by mountains, had a dirt road passing in front of it that connected the Hunan-Jiangxi border.

When the troops arrived, the villagers had already fled. Historically, there was a saying in China that "soldiers and bandits are one and the same," causing the common people to fear the troops. Mao Zedong instructed the soldiers to split up and go into the mountains to call out to the hiding villagers, reassuring them and encouraging them to return to the village. This action set a precedent for the People's Army, being both a combat force and a publicity team.

That night, Mao Zedong convened an expanded meeting of the Front Committee, where he proposed the reorganization plan that had been brewing for days. First, reduce the target size and reorganize the structure, downsizing from a division to a regiment. Second, establish Party branches at the company level, with Party groups in squads and platoons, and Party branches in companies. Above the company level, appoint Party representatives and establish Party Committees at the battalion and regiment levels. The entire army would be uniformly led by the Front Committee of the CPC, with Mao Zedong as the secretary. This system of Party leadership over the military was later adopted by various Red Army forces and continues to this day. Third, abolish the warlord system and establish an internal democratic system, setting up soldiers' committees at all levels from company to regiment. Under the influence of the feudal system, which had lasted for over a thousand years, soldiers were treated like the officers' "domestic servants," subject to arbitrary punishment. The establishment of soldiers' committees gave the soldiers the right to express their opinions equally, breaking this tradition.

The troops stayed in Sanwan Village for several days, during which they completed the "Sanwan Reorganization" as decided by the Front Committee. Thus, a new type of People's Army unprecedented in Chinese history was born.

With the major reorganization settled, the issue of finding a base was also resolved. Mao Zedong established contacts with Long Chaoqing, the Party Secretary of Ninggang County, and local armed forces leader Yuan Wencai. Shortly thereafter, they received assistance from Yuan Wencai and Wang Zuo, who agreed to allow the revolutionary army to move into the Jinggang Mountains area. Thus, the initial problem of establishing a rural base in the Jinggang Mountains was solved.

On October 3, the newly reorganized revolutionary army set out from Sanwan Village. Before departure, Mao Zedong announced a few simple rules of discipline to the troops: First, speak politely. Second, conduct fair trade. Third, do not take even a single sweet potato from the masses. Mao Zedong knew that without strict discipline, the army would not succeed. These simple rules later evolved into the famous "Three Main Rules of Discipline and Eight Points for Attention" of the People's Army, which are still strictly followed today.

From October 1927, when Mao Zedong led the uprising army to the Jinggang Mountains, to January 1929, when Mao Zedong and Zhu De led the main forces of the Fourth Red Army down from the Jinggang Mountains, Mao Zedong spent a year and three months at the revolutionary base in the Jinggang Mountains. When they went up the mountain, the total strength was less than 1,000 men. When they came down, the main force had grown to over 3,600 men.

In this way, Mao Zedong used tactical retreats to gain strategic initiative, marking a historic turning point in the exploration of China's revolutionary path. From then on, the Chinese revolution had its first stable rural revolutionary base, bringing vitality and hope to the Chinese revolution amid the vast white terror.

However, whether this base could withstand repeated enemy "encirclement and suppression," whether it could sustain the consumption of so many troops, and whether it could resist the enemy's strict blockade were still unresolved issues.

With these questions in mind, under the dim oil lamp, Mao Zedong wrote the "Resolution of the Second Congress of the CPC on the Hunan-Jiangxi Border" (October 5, 1928). This document addressed a common question within the Red Army: "How long can the red flag last?" Using the Marxist-Leninist "Theory of Uneven Development," Mao Zedong focused on analyzing the reasons and five conditions for the emergence and existence of the Chinese Red political power.

First, China was an economically backward semi-colonial country under indirect imperialist rule. The semi-feudal local agricultural economy and the imperialist policy of dividing China into spheres of influence created conditions for continuous division and war among the white regimes, allowing small areas of Red political power to emerge and exist. Second, the places where Red political power first emerged and could exist for a long time were areas influenced by the first Great Revolution, such as Hunan, Guangdong, Hubei, and Jiangxi provinces. Third, as long as the national revolutionary situation continued to progress, the long-term existence of small Red political powers was beyond doubt. Fourth, the existence of a relatively strong formal Red Army was a necessary condition for the existence of Red political power. Fifth, the strength of the Communist Party organization and the correctness of its policies were crucial conditions.

The most important theoretical contribution of this resolution was the first proposal of the idea of "armed separation of workers and peasants," which contrasted with the "urban center theory" advocated by the Comintern and the Central Committee in Shanghai. The first part of this resolution was later known as Mao Zedong's famous essay "Why Can China's Red Political Power Exist?"

The sister essay to this famous work was "The Struggle in the Jinggang Mountains," written on November 25, 1928. This was a report from Mao Zedong, on behalf of the Front Committee of the Fourth Red Army, to the Central Committee. The report summarized the experience of the armed separation of workers and peasants in the Jinggang Mountains and further elaborated on the idea. One of its significant contributions was addressing, through practice, the questions of how rural revolutionary bases could survive and develop. It proposed the integration of the Party's leadership, armed struggle, land revolution, and the construction of revolutionary bases. The correct leadership of the Party guaranteed the conduct of armed struggle, land revolution, and the construction of revolutionary bases; without revolutionary armed struggle, there could be no effective land revolution and development of revolutionary bases; without the land revolution, the Red Army could not gain the support of the masses, and the revolutionary bases could not be consolidated and developed; without the construction of revolutionary bases, there would be no rear support for the armed struggle, and the gains of the land revolution could not be maintained.

The peak period of the Jinggang Mountains base was after the meeting of Zhu De and Mao Zedong's troops in April 1928.

Mao Zedong and Zhu De had long anticipated this meeting. For Mao Zedong, he had been closely monitoring the situation of the remnants of the Nanchang Uprising led by Zhu De and Chen Yi, hoping for a strong-armed force to strengthen the struggle in the Jinggang Mountains base. He even sent He Changgong, who had studied in France, to try to establish contact with Zhu De. For Zhu De, the long expedition and hiding in the ranks of his old schoolmate Fan Shisheng's troops made him acutely aware of the difficulties without a stable base. He had also been following Mao Zedong's struggle in the Jinggang Mountains and sent Mao Zedong's brother, Mao Zetan, to the Jinggang Mountains to contact Mao Zedong.

These efforts were not in vain. After several twists and turns, around April 24, 1928, the troops led by Zhu De and Chen Yi successfully met with the First Regiment of the Workers' and Peasants' Revolutionary Army led by Mao Zedong in Longshi, Ninggang.

On that day, Mao Zedong, Zhu De, and Chen Yi met at Longjiang Academy and decided to establish the Fourth Army of the Workers' and Peasants' Revolutionary Army. Based on Mao Zedong's suggestions, they determined to use the central section of the Luoxiao Mountains as their base, to mobilize the masses, carry out land reforms, and adopt the strategy of developing northward and conducting guerrilla warfare southward.

On May 4, 1928, a grand ceremony was held in Longshi, Ninggang, to celebrate the merger of the two armies and formally establish the Fourth Army of the Workers' and Peasants' Revolutionary Army. Zhu De was appointed as the army commander, and Mao Zedong as the Party representative. The entire army, consisting of over 10,000 people, abolished the division structure and was reorganized into six regiments.

Zhu De's arrival significantly enhanced the combat effectiveness of the Fourth Red Army, enabling it to repeatedly defeat the KMT's "encirclement and suppression" campaigns on the Hunan-Jiangxi border. Notably, after the great victory at Longyuankou in June of that year, the Jinggang Mountains base area expanded to include the entire counties of Ninggang, Yongxin, and Lianhua, extending into parts of Ji'an, Anfu, Suichuan, and Lingxian, covering an area of more than 7,200 square kilometers with a population of over 500,000. Mao Zedong referred to this period as the "peak of the border region."[7]

During this period, Mao Zedong and Zhu De continually refined and shaped the Red Army's combat principles, which became known as the "Sixteen-Character Formula."[8] Mao Zedong described this development process as follows:

> Our war began in the autumn of 1927, at a time when we had no experience. The Nanchang Uprising and the Guangzhou Uprising both failed, and the forces from the Autumn Harvest Uprising on the Hunan-Jiangxi border also suffered several defeats, eventually moving to the Jinggang Mountains area. In April of the following year, the remaining troops from the Nanchang Uprising also moved to the Jinggang Mountains via southern Hunan. However, by May 1928, the basic principles of guerrilla warfare that suited the situation at the time had already been formed. "When the enemy advances, we retreat; when the enemy camps, we harass; when the enemy is tired, we attack; when the enemy retreats, we pursue." This Sixteen-Character Formula was recognized by the Central Committee before the Li Lisan line. Later, our combat principles further developed.[9]

During the Jinggang period, Mao Zedong's personal life also saw developments. In late June 1928, in Tangbian, Yongxin County, he married He Zizhen, becoming lifelong comrades in arms. He Zizhen later recalled, "Although our material life was poor, our spiritual life was rich. Mao Zedong read extensively. Late at night, when he was tired from writing, he would tell me stories from his readings and recite his poems. His words transported me into a colorful world. Often, one of us would be talking, the other listening, and we would unknowingly welcome a new day."

During this period, many future prominent figures gathered under Mao Zedong and Zhu De's command, such as Chen Yi, Lin Biao, Luo Ronghuan, Xiao Ke, Tan Zheng, Tan Zhenlin, He Changgong, Chen Bojun, Jiang Hua, Zeng Zhi, Lai Chuanzhu, Zhang Zongxun, Tan Guansan, and Yang Lisan. Jinggang Mountains was like a university of the Chinese revolution.

In December 1928, Peng Dehuai and Teng Daiyuan led the Fifth Red Army to meet the Fourth Red Army in Longshi and Xincheng, Ninggang. The Fifth Red Army was reorganized into a regiment of the Fourth Red Army, with Peng Dehuai and Teng Daiyuan appointed as deputy army commander and regiment commander, and deputy Party representative and regiment Party representative, respectively. This was Mao Zedong's first meeting with Peng Dehuai, and they had a heartfelt conversation. Mao Zedong discussed his views on the Chinese revolutionary path and its prospects, the necessity of establishing revolutionary bases, the unique reasons for the existence of Red political power in China, and the relationship between the current democratic revolution and the future socialist revolution. This conversation left a lifelong impression on Peng Dehuai.

The rapid growth of the Zhu-Mao Red Army alarmed Chiang Kai-shek, who vowed to eliminate this threat. On November 7, 1928, he appointed He Jian as the acting commander-in-chief of the "encirclement and suppression" in the two provinces, with Jin Handing as the deputy commander-in-chief. On January 1, 1929, the command headquarters for the "encirclement and suppression" of Hunan and Jiangxi provinces was formally established in Pingxiang, Jiangxi, commanding approximately 30,000 troops in six brigades from the two provinces, planning the third "encirclement and suppression" campaign against the Jinggang Mountains revolutionary base.

This was the most severe "encirclement and suppression" campaign the Jinggang Mountains revolutionary base had encountered since its establishment. Given the current strength of the Red Army, it was impossible to risk a head-on confrontation. Mao Zedong decided to change their previous tactics and split the forces into two. One force would stay behind to defend Jinggang Mountains, under the unified command of Peng Dehuai and Teng Daiyuan. The other force, the main force of the Fourth Red Army, led by Mao Zedong and Zhu De, would strike south into southern Jiangxi. They adopted a strategy of combining static defense with mobile offense, internal and external line operations. They hoped to emulate the Warring States tactic of "besieging Wei to rescue Zhao" by attacking Ganzhou or Ji'an with the main force, aiming to force the KMT forces to split up and retreat to relieve the siege on Jinggang Mountains. Later, due to changing circumstances, the Jinggang Mountains revolutionary base quickly fell, and the "besieging Wei to rescue Zhao" plan could not be realized. However, this provided an opportunity to break the deadlock and open up a new, larger base.

On January 14, 1929, Mao Zedong and Zhu De led the main force of the Fourth Red Army, 3,600 strong, to leave the Jinggang Mountains revolutionary base, which they had managed for a year and three months and marched toward southern Jiangxi via Suichuan.

This move, like the ascent to the Jinggang Mountains, was of decisive significance in Mao Zedong's career. Under the white terror, without retreating to the mountains, they could not preserve the living forces of the revolution or open up a new revolutionary path. In an improving revolutionary situation, without descending from the mountains, they could not gain the broader space needed for the development and expansion of revolutionary forces, nor could they advance the revolutionary path.

From descending the mountains in January until achieving a complete victory in the Battle of Dabaidi in February, the Zhu-Mao Red Army was constantly pursued and driven by the enemy. They broke through from Suichuan, passed through Shangyou and Chongyi counties, were attacked by the enemy in Dayu, detoured through Nanxiong in northern Guangdong, and then entered southern Jiangxi, passing through Xinfeng, Anyuan, and Xunwu. In Zhenxia Village, Xunwu, they were again attacked, and Zhu De and Mao

Zedong were separated. Mao Zedong later described this situation in a report to the Central Committee: "Along the way, there were no Party organizations or mass bases. Five enemy regiments pursued closely, with reactionary militias bolstering their strength. This was the most difficult time for our army." Mao Zedong once considered dispersing the troops, but quickly abandoned this plan as dispersal might lead to the enemy defeating them in detail. After reuniting, Mao Zedong and Zhu De led the troops to continue advancing toward Ruijin.

The Nanchang Uprising forces had passed through Ruijin when advancing toward the Chaoshan region, fighting battles there and establishing a certain mass base. At this moment, the KMT forces, eager for accolades, divided their forces and advanced rashly, hoping to quickly eliminate the Zhu-Mao Red Army in this area. The main force of the Fourth Red Army utilized the narrow terrain near Dabaidi to set up an "ambush pocket."

On February 10, 1929, as soon as the two regiments of Liu Shiyi's brigade entered the "ambush pocket," the Zhu-Mao Red Army launched an attack. As usual, Commander Zhu De led the charge, and Mao Zedong, who rarely handled firearms, also took up a rifle and led the guard platoon in a charge against the enemy positions. The battle continued until the afternoon of the next day, resulting in the capture of over 800 officers and soldiers, including the regimental commander and deputy commander, and seizing more than 800 rifles. The remnants of Liu Shiyi's brigade were forced to abandon their "pursuit and suppression" and retreat to Ganzhou.

This was the first major victory for the main force of the Fourth Red Army since descending from Jinggang Mountains, opening the gateway to southern Jiangxi and western Fujian. Chen Yi described the significance of this victory in a report to the Central Committee: "In this battle, our army, after repeated defeats, made a final effort to defeat a strong enemy. When ammunition was exhausted and reinforcements were cut off, officers and soldiers struggled in a sea of blood using tree branches, stones, and empty rifles, finally achieving victory. This was the most honorable battle since the establishment of the Red Army."[10]

Four years later, when Mao Zedong passed by Dabaidi, he composed a poem, titled "*Pusaman* · Dabaidi."

Red, orange, yellow, green, blue, indigo, violet,
Who's dancing with a colored band in the sky fire-lit?
After the rain the sinking sun is seen,
The mountain pass exhales floods of deep green.
A furious battle raged then on this spot,
The village walls are still riddled with shots.
Dotted today with these traces of war,
The mountain pass looks fairer than before.

After the Battle of Dabaidi, the Zhu-Mao Red Army established a foothold in southern Jiangxi and twice entered Fujian for operations, initially opening up two revolutionary bases in southern Jiangxi and western Fujian. The strength of the Fourth Red Army grew stronger with each battle, and the revolutionary influence continued to expand.

At this time, the Central Committee's "February Letter" arrived, causing a stir within the Fourth Red Army.

The February Letter from the Central Committee, dated February 7, 1929, was addressed to Mao Zedong and Zhu De and forwarded to the Special Committee on the Hunan-Jiangxi Border. This directive emphasized the importance of urban work and offered a pessimistic analysis of the Red Army's prospects in the countryside. It suggested dividing the Fourth Red Army into smaller units and proposed that "Comrades Zhu and Mao may need to leave the army temporarily." It instructed them, upon receiving the Central Committee's decision, to "decisively leave the army and quickly come to the Central Committee."

After receiving the letter on April 3, Mao Zedong convened a meeting of the Front Committee on April 5 to discuss it. Mao immediately drafted a reply from the Front Committee of the Fourth Red Army to the Central Committee, refuting the February Letter with reasoned arguments. This also demonstrated the unique and independent character Mao Zedong had forged through the practice of establishing the Jinggang Mountains base. Without such character, one could not accomplish great feats and achievements.

In the reply from the Fourth Red Army's Front Committee, Mao Zedong pointed out: "The Central Committee's letter is too pessimistic in its assessment of the objective situation and subjective strength." He continued, "We feel that the Party made significant errors of adventurism in the past, but now there is a considerable tendency toward opportunism in some places. In the places we have been in western Fujian and southern Jiangxi, the spirit of combat among the Party branches is very weak, and many opportunities for struggle have been easily passed by. The masses are vast and revolutionary, but the Party stands by and does not lead. The examples of western Fujian and southern Jiangxi make us think this phenomenon might exist in other places as well."

He summarized the tactics they had used against the enemy over the past few years.

> The tactics we have developed through struggle over the past three years are different from those of ancient and modern times, both at home and abroad. Using our tactics, the development of the masses' struggle expands day by day, and no matter how strong the enemy's forces, they cannot defeat us. Our tactics are guerrilla tactics, which can be summarized as "dividing forces to mobilize the masses, concentrating to deal with the enemy." "When the enemy advances, we retreat; when the enemy camps, we harass; when the enemy tires, we attack; when the enemy retreats, we pursue." "Holding fixed areas, advancing in waves." "When pursued by strong enemies, use a circling strategy." "Using very short times and good methods to mobilize the masses." These tactics are like casting a net, which must be opened at times to catch the masses and closed at times to deal with the enemy.

Mao Zedong never attended a military academy. His unique approach was to "learn to swim by swimming" and "learn warfare through warfare." Through the trials of leading the Autumn Harvest Uprising on the Hunan-Jiangxi border, establishing the Jinggang Mountains base, and advancing the wars in southern Jiangxi and western Fujian, Mao Zedong was no longer the "scholar pointing out rivers and mountains and stirring words" of the past, but a revolutionary leader who could both strategize and command.

In his reply, Mao Zedong politely rejected the Central Committee's suggestion, stating: "The Central Committee's demand to divide our forces into very small units scattered across the countryside, with Zhu and Mao leaving the main force to avoid large targets, aims to preserve the Red Army and mobilize the masses. This is an ideal. We have planned and implemented this approach multiple times since the winter before last, and all have failed."

He emphasized that the current strategy of combining large-scale operations with guerrilla tactics was more effective and that the suggestions from the Central Committee did not align with the practical realities they faced. Mao Zedong's ability to critically assess and adapt strategies based on real-world experiences underscored his leadership qualities and the revolutionary principles that would guide the Red Army in its subsequent struggles.

In the conclusion of the reply, Mao Zedong wrote: "Since coming to southern Jiangxi and western Fujian, the mail route has been very convenient. Every day, we can read newspapers from Nanjing, Shanghai, Fuzhou, Xiamen, Zhangzhou, Nanchang, and Ganzhou. In Ruijin, we can even see He Jian's official newspaper, the *Republic Daily* from Changsha. It is truly like seeing clear skies after the clouds part, and the joy is indescribable." "We hope that the Central Committee will send us a letter every month," and "We also hope that the Central Committee's publications can be sent to us."[11] The words revealed Mao Zedong's urgent desire to receive timely external information to judge the situation and determine the direction of actions, also highlighting the significant inconvenience caused by the information blockade during the Jinggang period.

Subsequently, the Central Committee sent another directive, with a much milder tone, but still insisting that Zhu De and Mao Zedong leave the troops. If they could not come to the Central Committee immediately, they were asked to send a capable comrade to report on their work and participate in discussions.

As one wave subsided, another arose. In early May, the Central Committee sent Liu Angong to the Fourth Red Army to serve as the director of the Political Department and interim military committee secretary. Liu Angong had just returned from the Soviet Union and was not familiar with the actual situation but was determined to implement the spirit of the Central Committee's "February Letter." After arriving at the Fourth Red Army, he arbitrarily criticized Mao Zedong's correct propositions and spread rumors that there were two factions among the leaders of the Fourth Red Army: one supporting the Central Committee and the other opposing it. This sparked a debate within the Fourth Red Army regarding the principles of army building.

These internal disagreements within the Fourth Red Army had existed for a long time. Although many were part of the revolutionary army, the negative influences of old military ideas, habits, and systems persisted. They preferred "the commander's word is final," believed "the Party interferes too much," and thought "Party representatives have too much power." They advocated that "the headquarters should handle external matters" while the Political Department should only "handle internal matters." These sentiments were temporarily hidden during successful developments but became more apparent due to frustrations and setbacks during the initial phase of advancing into southern Jiangxi and western Fujian. Liu Angong's arrival undoubtedly bolstered this resistance. Additionally, non-proletarian thoughts such as purely military viewpoints, bandit mentality, extreme democratization, and remnants of warlordism also resurfaced in the debates.

This situation caused considerable pressure on Mao Zedong, who at one point considered resigning as secretary of the Front Committee. To him, this was not a matter of personal grievances but a significant issue concerning the principles of army building. In a letter to Lin Biao, Commander of the First Column, dated June 14, he wrote: "The current debate is not a personal or temporary issue; it concerns the entire Party of the Fourth Army and the long-term struggle over the past year. Previously, it was concealed due to various reasons, but it has now surfaced. In fact, the previous concealment was wrong, and the current exposure is correct. The occurrence of debates within the Party signifies progress, not regression. Only by hastily reconciling and brushing the issue aside, reducing it to trivial matters, would we be regressing."[12] Since the issue had arisen and fully surfaced, Mao Zedong believed in taking the opportunity to resolve it thoroughly, a principle he adhered to throughout his life.

Mao Zedong recognized that the debate within the Fourth Red Army was "not a personal or temporary issue" but a long-standing principled issue. What exactly were the issues that sparked the debate? Mao Zedong listed these issues in a checklist: "(1) Personal leadership versus Party leadership, (2) Military viewpoint versus political viewpoint, (3) Sectarianism versus anti-sectarianism, (4) Bandit mentality versus anti-bandit mentality, (5) Governance in the central section of the Luoxiao Mountains, (6) Local armed forces issue, (7) Urban policy and Red Army discipline issue, (8) Estimation of the current situation, (9) The failure in southern Hunan, (10) Issues of scientification and regularization, (11) Military technology of the Fourth Army, (12) Formalism versus pragmatism, (13) Decentralization versus centralization, (14) Other corrupt thoughts."[13]

Most of these issues were later thoroughly and satisfactorily resolved at the Ninth Congress of the Fourth Red Army of the CPC.

This debate naturally also involved Mao Zedong and Zhu De. According to Fu Baicui, Commander of the Fourth Column, "Zhu and Mao also had disagreements on certain issues. Along the way, to resolve these issues, several large and small meetings were held, and debates were conducted within the Party. Zhu and Mao also responded to criticisms in small meetings. I remember in June 1929, while the troops were resting in Xinquan, two meetings of the Front Committee of the Fourth Red Army were held, and Zhu and Mao responded to the criticisms raised."[14]

The situation continued to evolve. On June 22, after the third capture of Longyan, a key town in western Fujian, the Fourth Red Army held its Seventh Congress. In the atmosphere of "everyone striving to debate," the congress resolution essentially negated Mao Zedong's correct propositions, and Mao Zedong was not re-elected as the secretary of the Front Committee. This position was taken over by Chen Yi. After the congress, Mao Zedong left the Fourth Red Army and went to western Fujian to both recuperate and guide local work as assigned by the Front Committee. Accompanying him were Cai Xiemin, Tan Zhenlin, Jiang Hua, Zeng Zhi, and others who staunchly supported Mao Zedong's ideas in this debate.

Mao Zedong's temporary departure from the Fourth Red Army was not an act of defiance but a strategic move to await an opportunity for the ultimate resolution of the debate. As he predicted in his letter to Lin Biao: "Since the Party's ideological differentiation and struggle have begun, it will not stop achieving victory just because I leave."[15]

At this time, seeing the rapid growth of the Fourth Red Army in western Fujian, Chiang Kai-shek ordered the KMT armies of Fujian, Guangdong, and

Jiangxi provinces to launch an "encirclement and suppression" campaign against the Fourth Red Army and the western Fujian Soviet area. To thwart this campaign, Zhu De, Chen Yi, and others rushed to Mao Zedong's residence in Jiaoyang, Shanghang County. On July 29, an emergency meeting of the Front Committee of the Fourth Red Army was held there, deciding on strategies to repel the enemy. The meeting also, based on the Central Committee's April letter, assigned Chen Yi to go to Shanghai to report to the Central Committee, with Zhu De temporarily acting as the secretary of the Front Committee.

Earlier, Mao Zedong had attended the First Congress of the CPC in western Fujian at Wenchang Pavilion in Jiaoyang, Shanghang County. During the later stages of the meeting, he contracted malaria. After the Front Committee meeting, due to his severe malaria, Mao Zedong went to Sujiapo, Dayangba, and Niugupu, Hexi, in Yongding County to recuperate. Despite the lack of medical supplies, Mao Zedong's condition gradually improved thanks to the treatment by a doctor. He remarked: "It seems I have a strong fate, and I have managed to get through this 'gate of hell.'"

After Mao Zedong's departure, Zhu De led the main force of the Fourth Red Army and eventually crushed the KMT Army's "encirclement and suppression" campaign after bitter fighting. However, during the battles and marches, the troops suffered significant losses. In late September, Zhu De, taking advantage of a break in the fighting, convened the Eighth Congress of the Fourth Red Army to address some unresolved issues from the Seventh Congress. Mao Zedong received the notification of the meeting but replied: "I cannot return casually if the rights and wrongs within the Fourth Red Army Party are not resolved."

The meeting lasted three days, with no results as everyone held their ground. The situation made everyone realize that "the entire army has lost its political leadership center" after Mao Zedong's departure. They jointly wrote a letter inviting Mao Zedong to return and lead the work of the Front Committee. Zhu De also welcomed Mao Zedong's return. Upon hearing this, Mao Zedong traveled on a stretcher to the meeting, but by the time he arrived, the meeting was over. Seeing his weak and swollen condition, everyone advised him to continue recuperating.

At this time, Chen Yi had arrived in Shanghai. The Central Committee had already understood the debate within the Fourth Red Army and Liu Angong's actions. After a detailed report from Chen Yi on August 29, the Central Committee decided to form a committee of Li Lisan, Zhou Enlai, and Chen Yi, chaired by Zhou Enlai, to draft a directive letter.

On September 28, the Central Committee issued a directive letter to the Front Committee of the Fourth Red Army (the "September Letter"), drafted by Chen Yi and reviewed by Zhou Enlai. The directive essentially affirmed Mao Zedong's exploration since the creation of the Jinggang Mountains rural revolutionary base, stating: "First the rural Red Army, then the urban political power. This is a feature of the Chinese revolution, a product of China's economic foundation."[16] The directive also affirmed Mao Zedong's insistence on the Party's absolute leadership over the army, the concentration of all Party powers in the Front Committee's guiding body and emphasized that this was correct and could not be shaken. It criticized the use of the term "patriarchal system" to weaken the guiding body's power under the guise of extreme democratization. The directive stressed that the Front Committee should resolutely combat various erroneous notions within the Red Army. It criticized the resolutions of the Seventh Congress of the Fourth Red Army and the actions of the expanded Front Committee meeting, urging the Front Committee to promptly correct these errors. "After the Front Committee meeting, Comrades Zhu and Mao should sincerely accept the Central Committee's directives, with Comrade Mao resuming his role as the secretary of the Front Committee and ensure that all comrades in the Red Army understand and accept this."[17]

The Central Committee's September Letter provided clear direction for resolving the long-standing debate on the principles of army building within the Fourth Red Army.

CHAPTER 4

Difficult Days

For those injustices and grievances, for those inappropriate punishments and mistakes, such as being labeled as an "opportunist," being dismissed from one's position, or being transferred, there are two possible attitudes. One attitude is to become passive, angry, and dissatisfied; the other is to view it as a beneficial education and a form of training.

MAO ZEDONG,
"On the Election of the Eighth Central Committee" (September 10, 1956)

On November 18, 1929, Chen Yi conveyed the Central Committee's "September Letter" and Zhou Enlai's oral instructions to the Front Committee of the Fourth Red Army. Prior to this, Zhu De had led the main force of the Fourth Red Army to advance to the Dongjiang area of Guangdong, attacking Mei County with severe losses, reducing the force by one-third. The arrival of the Central Committee's "September Letter" was like a timely rain, greatly boosting morale and stabilizing the army. Zhu De, a person of broadmindedness and great righteousness, was praised by Mao Zedong as having "a capacity as vast as the ocean and a will as firm as steel." He clearly expressed his firm support for the Central Committee's instructions and welcomed Mao

Zedong back to the Front Committee. Subsequently, Chen Yi sent the Central Committee's "September Letter" to Mao Zedong.

Seeing that the long-awaited opportunity to fundamentally resolve the principles of army building had arrived, Mao Zedong, despite just recovering from a severe illness and being physically weak, immediately rushed to Changting to reunite with the Fourth Red Army, resuming his role as the secretary of the Front Committee. On November 28, he presided over an expanded meeting of the Front Committee of the Fourth Red Army, deciding to conduct reorganization and training of the army in preparation for the Ninth Congress of the Fourth Red Army of the CPC. Subsequently, Mao Zedong, Zhu De, and Chen Yi conducted investigations within the troops, and Mao Zedong drafted eight resolutions totaling over 30,000 characters for the congress.

From December 28 to 29, the Ninth Congress of the Fourth Red Army of the CPC was held in an ancestral hall in Gutian Town, Shanghang County, Fujian. The congress heard Mao Zedong's political report and Zhu De's military report, and Chen Yi conveyed the Central Committee's instructions. The congress unanimously adopted the eight resolutions drafted by Mao Zedong, collectively known as the "Resolutions of the Ninth Congress of the Fourth Red Army of the CPC," which later became known as the "Gutian Conference Resolutions." The congress elected Mao Zedong, Zhu De, Chen Yi, Luo Ronghuan, Lin Biao, Wu Zhonghao, Tan Zhenlin, and others as members of the Front Committee of the Fourth Red Army, with Mao Zedong re-elected as the secretary.

The "Gutian Conference Resolutions" included resolutions on correcting erroneous thoughts within the Party, organizational issues, internal education, Red Army publicity work, political training of soldiers, abolishing corporal punishment, preferential treatment of wounded soldiers, and the relationship between the military and political systems of the Red Army. These resolutions not only fundamentally resolved the long-standing disputes within the Fourth Red Army but also provided fundamental guidelines for the construction of the People's Army and the Party. The Gutian Conference was a milestone in the history of the Red Army's development. The formation of the "Gutian

Conference Resolutions" significantly accelerated the construction of the People's Army, a type of army unprecedented in Chinese history.

The internal debate within the Fourth Red Army over the principles of army building was thus satisfactorily resolved. Both Zhu De and Mao Zedong engaged in self-criticism. The Central Committee's special envoy, Tu Zhennong, wrote in his report to the Central Military Commission:

> Comrade Zhu De frankly stated that he unconditionally accepted the Central Committee's instructions. He admitted that he was wrong in the past debates. Comrade Mao Zedong also acknowledged the incorrectness of his work style and attitude and identified the reasons for his mistakes. The previous poor relationship between the military and political aspects was due to the opposition between political and military personnel and the lack of active political leadership. It should also be noted that although there were debates within the Fourth Army Party, they were conducted openly in Party meetings, and despite differing opinions, there were no factional organizations. It was purely a personal debate among comrades, not a factional struggle.[1]

After this, Mao Zedong and Zhu De formed a close relationship, and "Zhu-Mao" became a nickname for the highest leaders of the Chinese Workers' and Peasants' Red Army. Later, American journalist Agnes Smedley used the term "China's Twin Stars" to describe their relationship. Through this debate, Mao Zedong gradually learned the art of patience, waiting, and unity. He once told Chen Yi: "Patience in everything, think more about one's shortcomings, and improve what one lacks. Take care of the overall situation, as long as it does not harm major principles, and forgive others. Patience is the hardest, but as a politician, one must practice patience."[2] After the founding of the People's Republic of China, when discussing the qualifications of successors for the proletarian cause, he also mentioned: "They must be able to unite the majority. This includes those who previously opposed and wronged them, regardless of which faction they belonged to. Do not hold grudges; it cannot be 'one dynasty's officials replace another's.'"[3] This is Mao Zedong's experience gained through long-term practice.

Because of such trials, Mao Zedong grew from a regional revolutionary leader into a trusted leader of the Party, capable of navigating complex situations and uniting diverse forces.

It was these experiences that made Mao Zedong deeply appreciate a passage from *Mencius · Gaozi II*: "When heaven is about to place a great responsibility on a man, it always first frustrates his spirit and will, exhausts his muscles and bones, exposes him to hunger and poverty, and confounds his endeavors. In this way, his patience and endurance are developed, and his weaknesses are overcome."

In October 1930, the revolutionary base areas in southern Jiangxi and western Fujian, established by Mao Zedong and Zhu De, faced a severe test.

Prior to this, the Zhu-Mao Red Army had taken advantage of the conflict between Chiang Kai-shek and the Guangxi warlords to establish revolutionary bases in southern Jiangxi and western Fujian. Following the Gutian Conference, they further expanded during the warlord conflicts between Chiang Kai-shek and the warlords Yan Xishan and Feng Yuxiang in the Central Plains, as well as during the border conflicts involving Li Zongren and Zhang Fakui.

In March 1930, the governments of the Southwestern Jiangxi Soviet and the Western Fujian Soviet were successively established. These bases, with a combined population of two million, formed the largest strategic area for the Red Army at the time, providing ample manpower and strategic depth. In June, the Fourth Red Army, the Sixth Red Army, and the Twelfth Red Army were reorganized into the First Red Army, soon renamed the First Red Army Corps, with Zhu De as the commander and Mao Zedong as the political commissar. The Red Army forces in southern Jiangxi and western Fujian transitioned from guerrilla warfare to mobile warfare. In August, the First Red Army Corps merged with the Third Red Army Corps, led by Peng Dehuai, to form the First Front Army of the Chinese Red Army. Zhu De became the commander-in-chief, and Mao Zedong served as the political commissar. The Chinese Workers' and Peasants' Revolutionary Committee was also established, with Mao Zedong as its Chairman, overseeing both the Red Army and local governments. The First Front Army had grown to 80,000 troops, a significant increase from the Jinggang period. Mao

Zedong's prediction that "a single spark can start a prairie fire" was nearing realization.

In October of that year, after ending the warlord conflicts, Chiang Kai-shek saw the Zhu-Mao Red Army growing in strength and immediately mobilized 100,000 troops to launch a major offensive against the revolutionary base areas in southwestern Jiangxi, starting in November with a "drive straight in, divide and conquer" strategy.

In December, the First Front Army held a mobilization meeting in Xiaobu, Ningdu County. Mao Zedong wrote a couplet for the meeting: "When the enemy advances, we retreat; when the enemy camps, we harass; when the enemy tires, we attack; when the enemy retreats, we pursue. In guerrilla warfare, we hold the initiative. We advance and retreat in large steps, luring the enemy in deep, concentrating our forces, and destroying them one by one. In mobile warfare, we annihilate the enemy."[4]

Assessing the enemy's aggressive advance, Mao Zedong decided to avoid their sharp edge and adopted the strategy of "luring the enemy in deep" for the first counter-campaign against the encirclement and suppression. He noticed that Zhang Huizan's and Tan Daoyuan's divisions, under the command of Lu Diping, had advanced to Longgang and Yuantou, close to the main forces of the First Front Army. He then resolved to "break through the center" and first strike at Longgang. Mao Zedong later recalled, "In our first battle, we decided to attack and successfully captured two brigades and one division headquarters of Zhang Huizan's main force, capturing 9,000 men, including the division commander, without losing a single person or horse. This victory scared Tan Daoyuan's division into fleeing to Dongshao and Xu Kexiang's division to Toupi. We pursued Tan Daoyuan's division and annihilated half of it. In five days, we fought two battles (from December 30, 1930, to January 3, 1931), causing the enemy in Futian, Donggu, and Toupi to retreat in fear, thus ending the first encirclement and suppression."[5]

In February 1931, Chiang Kai-shek appointed He Yingqin, the Minister of Military and Political Affairs of the KMT Government, as the Director of the Nanchang Headquarters and Commander-in-Chief of the Army, Navy, and Air Force. Learning from the previous "encirclement and suppression" campaign's mistake of advancing too quickly, they adopted a strategy of "steady advance, securing every step" and mobilized 200,000 troops to launch another "encirclement and suppression" campaign in April.

Chiang Kai-shek, eager to annihilate the Zhu-Mao Red Army, initiated one "encirclement and suppression" campaign after another, each larger than the last. However, Mao Zedong remained calm and, amid the tense preparations, composed a poem, titled "*Yujiaao* · Against the First 'Encirclement' Campaign."

> Forests blaze red beneath the frosty sky,
> The wrath of Heaven's armies soars to the clouds.
> Mist veils Longgang, its thousand peaks blurred,
> All cry out in unison,
> Our van has taken Zhang Huizan.
> The enemy returns to Jiangxi two hundred thousand strong,
> Fumes billowing in the wind in mid-sky.
> Workers and peasants are wakened in their millions,
> To fight as one man,
> Under the riot of red flags round the foot of Buzhou.

The first half of the poem describes the first counter-campaign against "encirclement and suppression" by the Red Army. The second half speaks of the second counter-campaign. At the end of the poem, Mao Zedong references an ancient Chinese legend: "In ancient times, Gonggong fought with Zhuanxu to become emperor. In his anger, he struck the Buzhou Mountain, breaking the pillar of the sky and tearing the earth's cords. The sky tilted to the northwest, causing the sun, moon, and stars to move; the earth sank in the southeast, causing water and dust to gather there."[6] He later explained that "Gonggong is a victorious hero," comparing the Red Army and the workers and peasants under the CPC to the legendary Gonggong.

During the Jinggang period and the establishment of the Central Soviet Area, Mao Zedong wrote many such poems filled with romantic and inspiring allusions to boost morale. These poems spread widely and were collected and published in the first issue of *Poetry Periodical* in 1957 after the founding of the People's Republic of China. Mao Zedong gave these poems a romantic name, calling them "Poems Hummed on Horseback."

In the midst of the life-and-death struggles of the war, Mao Zedong uniquely had the elegance to compose poems and songs, turning them into battle horns.

At this time, significant changes occurred within the Party. In January 1931, the CPC held the Expanded Fourth Plenary Session of the Sixth Central Committee in Shanghai, marking the beginning of the "leftist" dogmatic rule represented by Wang Ming (Chen Shaoyu). Dogmatism involved blindly copying Soviet experiences and rigidly applying the directives of the Comintern, using "big hats" to intimidate people.

While Mao Zedong was leading the First Front Army to victory in the first counter-campaign against "encirclement and suppression," on January 15, 1931, the Central Bureau of the Soviet Area was established by the CPC, with Zhou Enlai appointed as secretary (though he had not yet assumed his position). Xiang Ying, sent from the Central Committee in Shanghai, was appointed as acting secretary. The General Front Committee of the First Front Army of the Red Army, headed by Mao Zedong, was abolished. The Central Revolutionary Military Commission, led by the Central Bureau of the Soviet Area, was established with Xiang Ying as chairman and Zhu De and Mao Zedong as vice chairmen. The Chinese Workers' and Peasants' Revolutionary Committee, chaired by Mao Zedong, was also abolished. Consequently, Mao Zedong was no longer the primary leader, neither in the Party leadership nor in military command.

Around the same time, on November 14, 1930, Yang Kaihui was executed by the KMT outside the Liuyang Gate in Changsha. Mao Zedong was deeply grieved when he later learned of her death, writing to her relatives, "Kaihui's death is beyond atonement, even if I were to die a hundred times."[7]

After the founding of the People's Republic of China, Mao Zedong met Li Shuyi, the wife of his early comrade Liu Zhixun. She asked Mao for some of his old poems. Mao responded, "The one Kaihui mentioned is not good; let's not write it. I have one called 'You Xian' as a gift." The poem he referred to is "*Dielianhua* · Reply to Li Shuyi."

I lost my proud Poplar and you your Willow,
Poplar and Willow soar to the Ninth Heaven.
Wu Gang, asked what he can give,
Serves them laurel brew.
The lonely moon goddess, spreads her ample sleeves,
To dance for these loyal souls in infinite space.
Earth suddenly reports the tiger subdued,
Tears of joy pour forth falling as mighty rain.

In this poem, the "proud poplar" symbolizes Yang Kaihui, and the "willow" symbolizes Liu Zhixun. Mao uses the ancient Chinese legend of "Chang'e flying to the moon" to express his deep longing for Yang Kaihui and others. When a friend, Zhang Shizhao, asked Mao about the meaning of "proud poplar," Mao replied, "A woman who sacrifices her *yuan* for the revolution,[8] how could she not be proud?"

Mao Zedong's resilience and inner strength were unparalleled. He was undeterred by various blows and fully committed himself to winning the second counter-campaign against "encirclement and suppression."

During the discussion of battle strategies within the Central Bureau of the Soviet Area, three different proposals emerged. One proposed "dividing forces to repel the enemy," and another suggested withdrawing from the Central Soviet Area. Mao Zedong firmly advocated for continuing the effective strategy of "luring the enemy in deep," which eventually gained the support of Xiang Ying and other comrades. The Central Bureau also agreed with Mao's suggestion to launch the first battle of the counter-campaign in the Futian area.

Why was the first battle chosen to be in Futian? From his own experience, Mao Zedong had learned the principle of avoiding the enemy's sharp edge and ensuring a victory in the initial battle. The Fifth Route Army of the KMT forces, led by Wang Jinyu, had recently arrived from the north and was unfamiliar with the southern terrain, making them less combat-effective. The left-wing forces of Guo Huazong and Hao Mengling were similarly inexperienced. Additionally, starting the campaign in Futian allowed the Red Army to sweep eastward, expanding the base area into the regions of Jianning,

Lichuan, and Taining along the Fujian-Jiangxi border. This would facilitate resource collection and better prepare for breaking the next "encirclement and suppression" campaign. Advancing from the east to the west, however, would be constrained by the Gan River, limiting further strategic opportunities. This strategy proved to be effective.

According to Mao Zedong's recollection, "When attacking Wang Jinyu, we were between two enemy forces, Cai Tingkai and Guo Huazong, about ten *li* from Guo and over forty *li* from Cai. Some said we were 'drilling into a cow's horn,' but in the end, we drilled through. This was mainly because of the favorable conditions in the base area and the lack of coordination among the enemy forces. After Guo's division was defeated, Hao's division fled back to Yongfeng overnight, thus avoiding disaster." Mao continued, "After the victory, we immediately attacked Guo (Huazong), Sun (Lianzhong), Zhu (Shaoliang), and Liu (Heding). In fifteen days (from May 16 to May 31, 1931), we marched seven hundred *li*, fought five battles, captured over twenty thousand guns, and decisively broke the 'encirclement and suppression.'"[9]

Mao Zedong's command of the First Front Army's two victories in countering the "encirclement and suppression" campaigns demonstrated that "luring the enemy in deep" was an effective strategy for the relatively weaker Red Army. The key to victory was to concentrate forces and first strike the weaker enemy, ensuring a win in the initial battle. In reality, achieving this required exceptional courage and the willingness to take risks that ordinary people would not dare. Mao recalled, "During the first counter-campaign, we initially planned to attack Tan Daoyuan, but since the enemy did not leave their advantageous position at Yuantou, our forces advanced twice but retreated both times. A few days later, we found a more favorable target in Zhang Huizan. In the second counter-campaign, our forces advanced to Donggu, but waited for Wang Jinyu to leave his fortified position at Futian. Despite the risk of leaking information, we rejected all suggestions for a hasty attack and waited for 25 days to meet our objective."[10]

Despite Chiang Kai-shek's failure in the first two "encirclement and suppression" campaigns, he quickly organized a third one. This time, four significant changes were made: First, Chiang Kai-shek personally took command as the overall commander of the "encirclement army," with He Yingqin as the frontline commander. Second, in addition to the original 200,000 miscellaneous troops surrounding the Central Soviet Area, he brought in 100,000 elite troops. Third, military advisers from Britain, Japan, and Germany were hired to participate in planning. Fourth, the strategy shifted to "drive straight in," aiming to annihilate the main force of the First Front Army.

The third "encirclement and suppression" campaign began on July 1, 1931. As the enemy's 300,000 troops advanced, the First Front Army was still dispersed and had not received necessary rest and reinforcements, unprepared for the enemy's rapid renewed offensive.

Faced with the relentless and swift advance of the enemy, Mao Zedong remained calm. He organized forces to delay the enemy's progress while directing the main force of the First Front Army to regroup and relocate, avoiding the enemy's vanguard. They maneuvered through a thousand *li*, secretly returning to southern Jiangxi from northwestern Fujian.

By late July, despite the enemy's frantic search for over twenty days, they failed to locate the main force of the First Front Army. Learning that the main force was concentrated in the Xingguo area, Chiang Kai-shek and He Yingqin speculated that they might cross the Gan River to the west and concentrated nine divisions to advance rapidly toward Xingguo.

Seeing an opportunity, Mao Zedong decided to adopt the strategy of "avoiding the main enemy force and attacking its weaknesses." He first attacked from the flanks, breaking through at Futian from Xingguo via Wan'an, and then swept from west to east along the enemy's rear communication lines, rendering the enemy's main force deep in southern Jiangxi ineffective. As the main enemy force turned north, they would be exhausted, providing a chance to strike at their weakest points.

However, this time, the enemy was indeed highly vigilant. "As our army advanced toward Futian, we were discovered by the enemy. Chen Cheng and Luo Zhuoying's divisions rushed to the area. I had to change the plan and return to Gaoxingwei in the western part of Xingguo. At this time, we had only this market town and the surrounding area, covering dozens of square miles, to concentrate our forces. After concentrating for one day, we decided to move eastward toward Liantang in eastern Xingguo County, Liangcun in southern Yongfeng County, and Huangpi in northern Ningdu County. On the first night, we passed through a forty-*li* gap between the forces of Jiang Dingwen and those of Jiang Guangnai, Cai Tingkai, and Han Deqin, and arrived at Liantang. On the second day, we encountered the vanguard of Shangguan Yunxiang's forces (Shangguan commanded his own division and Hao Mengling's division). On the third day, we fought Shangguan's division as our first battle, and on the fourth day, we fought Hao Mengling's division as our second battle. After three days of marching, we reached Huangpi and fought Mao Bingwen's division as our third battle. We won all three battles, capturing over ten thousand guns. At this point, the main enemy forces advancing west and south turned eastward, focusing their attention on Huangpi, advancing rapidly in a dense formation to encircle us. Our army then slipped through a twenty-*li* gap between the forces of Jiang Guangnai, Cai Tingkai, Han Deqin, Chen Cheng, and Luo Zhuoying, and returned to Xingguo from the east. By the time the enemy discovered our movement and advanced westward again, we had already rested for half a month, while the enemy was exhausted and demoralized, finally deciding to retreat."[11]

By mid-September 1931, the third counter-campaign against "encirclement and suppression" had been won. Following this victory, Mao Zedong directed the Red Army to continue expanding its achievements, linking the revolutionary bases in southern Jiangxi and western Fujian into one contiguous area. The central revolutionary base area was further expanded to include 21 counties and a population of 2.5 million, entering a period of great prosperity.

Through leading the Zhu-Mao Red Army's advance into southern Jiangxi and western Fujian and directing three counter-campaigns against "encirclement and suppression," Mao Zedong's understanding of the art of command in the Chinese revolutionary war greatly deepened. This was reflected in the transformation of the revolutionary forces from a single army to an army corps and then to a full front army, the shift in warfare from primarily guerrilla tactics to mobile warfare, and the expansion of operational space from a single province to a multi-province area and then to the entire Central Soviet Area.

He later recalled, "By the time of the first counter-campaign in the Jiangxi base area, the strategy of 'luring the enemy in deep' was proposed and successfully applied. By the time we defeated the enemy's third 'encirclement and suppression,' the overall principles of the Red Army's combat strategy were formed. This period marked a new stage in the development of military principles, with significantly enriched content and many changes in form, surpassing the simplicity of earlier times. However, the basic principles remained encapsulated in the Sixteen-Character Formula: 'When the enemy advances, we retreat; when the enemy camps, we harass; when the enemy tires, we attack; when the enemy retreats, we pursue.' This formula encompassed the basic principles of countering 'encirclement and suppression,' covering both strategic defense and strategic offense, as well as strategic retreat and strategic counterattack during the defense phase. Later developments were merely extensions of this foundation."[12]

During this period, the practical experiences were crucial for Mao Zedong's later writing of the military strategy masterpiece "Problems of Strategy in China's Revolutionary War." At the same time, it established his leadership authority among the officers and soldiers of the First Front Army. In the minds of most people, where Mao Zedong was, victory was assured.

For Mao Zedong, the severe tests were far from over. Before he could ultimately become the leader of the entire Party, he had to endure many more hardships.

After the Expanded Fourth Plenary Session of the Sixth Central Committee of the CPC, the Central Committee's organs in Shanghai suffered significant destruction. In September 1931, since less than half of the Political Bureau of the Central Committee members and Central Committee members were in Shanghai, a provisional Political Bureau of the Central Committee (commonly referred to as the "Provisional Central") was established. It was headed by Bo Gu (Qin Bangxian), Luo Pu (Zhang Wentian), and Lu Futan (who later defected), with Bo Gu taking overall responsibility. Subsequently, Wang Ming went from Shanghai to Moscow, and in December, Zhou Enlai went to the Central Soviet Area.

From November 1 to 5, 1931, the first CPC Congress of the Soviet Area was held in Ruijin, Jiangxi. Unusually, this congress was presided over by the Central Delegation. The congress passed documents such as the "Political Resolution," which criticized the work of the First Front Army and the Central Soviet Area under Mao Zedong's leadership without naming him. Mao's correct opposition to dogmatism was accused of being "narrow empiricism"; the principle of "taking from the rich to help the poor" was criticized as the "rich peasant line"; and the Red Army was accused of "not completely abandoning guerrilla traditions" and neglecting "positional warfare" and "urban warfare." The meeting particularly emphasized concentrating efforts against rightist tendencies. Clearly, in this atmosphere, it was difficult for Mao Zedong to continue his leadership role in the Party, government, and military in the Central Soviet Area.

This exclusion continued to escalate.

From November 7 to 20, 1931, the First National Congress of the Soviet Republic of China was held in Ruijin. The congress proclaimed the establishment of the Soviet Republic of China and passed the *Constitution Outline*, *Land Law*, *Labor Law*, and others. Mao Zedong was elected Chairman of the Central Executive Committee and the People's Committee of the Soviet Republic of China. The title "Chairman Mao" originated from this.

However, in the subsequent appointments announced by the Central Executive Committee regarding the Central Revolutionary Military Commission (hereafter referred to as the "Central Military Commission"), Mao Zedong was only a member, with Zhu De as chairman, and Wang Jiaxiang and Peng Dehuai as vice chairmen. It was also decided to abolish the positions of General Commander and General Political Commissar of the First Front Army. Thus, Mao Zedong's military leadership was stripped away.

From March to September 1932, Mao Zedong led the Eastern Route Army into Fujian for combat as Chairman of the Provisional Central Government and a member of the Central Military Commission and participated in directing the fourth counter-campaign against "encirclement and suppression." However, due to differing opinions from the central directives during the operations in Fujian and serious conflicts with the Central Bureau of the Soviet Area during the fourth counter-campaign, Mao further angered leaders who were staunchly implementing Wang Ming's "leftist" dogmatic errors.

In early October 1932, a plenary meeting of the Central Bureau of the Soviet Area was held in Ningdu. The attendees included Ren Bishi, Xiang Ying, Gu Zuolin, and Deng Fa from the rear, and Zhou Enlai, Mao Zedong,

Zhu De, and Wang Jiaxiang from the front. The meeting was chaired by Zhou Enlai, the Secretary of the Central Bureau. During the meeting, "a struggle against tendencies within the Central Bureau that had never been before"[13] was launched. The focus of the debate was the strategy for frontline combat. In the end, the opinions of the Central Bureau members from the rear prevailed. The meeting implemented the "leftist" dogmatic offensive line of the Provisional Central, criticizing the frontline comrades for "focusing on preparation, with Mao Zedong showing this most prominently." The meeting focused its criticism on Mao Zedong, accusing him of "passively undermining" the policy of "seizing key cities" and labeling his opposition to attacking Ganzhou and other key cities as "purely defensive." Mao's strategy of "luring the enemy in deep" was accused of being the "main danger of rightist deviation." The meeting approved Zhou Enlai's proposal that Mao Zedong "remain at the front to assist" while also approving Mao's "temporary sick leave, to be taken when necessary."[14]

During the fourth counter-campaign against "encirclement and suppression," Mao Zedong was appointed as the General Political Commissar of the First Front Army in August 1932, on Zhou Enlai's recommendation. However, by late October, the CPC Provisional Central Committee appointed Zhou Enlai to concurrently serve as the General Political Commissar of the First Front Army. Thus, Mao Zedong's recently restored military leadership position was once again stripped away.

Mao Zedong left the front lines and arrived at the Gospel Hospital in Changting, western Fujian, in mid-October 1932 to recuperate. The Gospel Hospital was a church-run hospital, and its director, Fu Lianzhang, had graduated from the Yashengdun Medical Hall at the Gospel Hospital in Tingzhou. Fu Lianzhang sympathized with the revolution and had previously treated the wounded soldiers of the Nanchang Uprising who passed through Changting. Chen Geng, Xu Teli, and others had received treatment at the Gospel Hospital. In 1929, when the Fourth Red Army advanced into western Fujian, he actively treated the Red Army's wounded. Mao Zedong had a good impression of him.

Under Fu Lianzhang's arrangement, Mao Zedong stayed at the Old Gujing Hospital sanatorium—a two-story garden house. Upon arriving at the hospital, Mao immediately visited his wife, He Zizhen, who was giving birth there.

Mao Zedong stayed here for four months. To recuperate well, he followed Fu Lianzhang's advice and took regular walks on Wolong Mountain behind the hospital.

At the same time, Zhou Yili, Chen Zhengren, and others who had been sidelined and persecuted by Wang Ming's line were also staying there. Zhou Yili was a member of the Central Executive Committee of the Provisional Central Government and the People's Commissar for Internal Affairs. He was also the chief writer for the Provisional Central Government's newspaper, *Red China*, and had supported Mao Zedong during Li Lisan's "leftist" adventurism. Chen Zhengren had long worked in the Southwestern Jiangxi Special Committee and the Jiangxi Provincial Committee and was a steadfast supporter of Mao Zedong. The three of them gathered almost daily to discuss various issues openly. Mao Zedong spoke candidly about his views on many issues at the time.

Soon after Mao arrived at the Gospel Hospital, he met Luo Ming, the Acting Secretary of the Fujian Provincial Committee, who was about to be discharged. Mao Zedong had a good understanding of Luo Ming and shared his views with him. He particularly emphasized that, like Jiangxi, Fujian should intensify the broad-based local guerrilla warfare to support the main Red Army's mobile warfare. This would enable the main Red Army to concentrate superior forces, select the enemy's weak points, and annihilate their vital forces, thus crushing the fourth "encirclement and suppression." He also suggested that Luo Ming develop guerrilla warfare in the old revolutionary base areas of Shanghang, Yongding, and Longyan to contain and attack the KMT 19th Route Army stationed in Zhangzhou and the forces of Chen Jitang in Guangdong.

After being discharged, Luo Ming presided over a meeting of the Fujian Provincial Committee in Changting, where he conveyed Mao Zedong's views, which were widely endorsed. The Provincial Committee immediately decided to appoint Luo Ming as a special commissioner to further develop guerrilla warfare in Shanghang, Yongding, and Longyan. Once there, Luo Ming assessed the local situation and wrote "Some Opinions on the Work" to the

Provincial Committee. He proposed that the Red Army should develop in areas where the enemy was weak to consolidate and expand the base area in western Fujian. He also suggested that the expansion of the Red Army should be planned and step by step, avoiding the excessive weakening of local armed forces to "rapidly expand the Red Army." This later became considered the so-called "ironclad evidence" of the "Luo Ming Line."

Mao Zedong stayed at the Gospel Hospital in Changting until mid-February 1933. Before leaving, he suggested to Fu Lianzhang that the hospital be transformed into the Central Red Hospital and relocated to Ruijin. Fu Lianzhang readily agreed.

Shortly after, Fu Lianzhang, his family, and the hospital moved to Ruijin. During a visit, Mao Zedong said to Fu Lianzhang: "This hospital is our first hospital, and you will be the director. The hospital has a heavy responsibility. To be a good director, you must prioritize serving the wounded and sick. Besides treating the Red Army, the hospital should also treat the common people." He added, "Prevention and treatment of diseases must be combined, and everyone should be educated about hygiene."

China's rural areas had long lacked adequate medical care, and farmers suffered greatly from diseases. Mao Zedong understood the importance of the hospital. His bond with Fu Lianzhang not only transformed Fu into a loyal revolutionary but also provided the Red Army and the Central Soviet Area with their own hospital.

By January 1933, Bo Gu and others arrived in the Central Soviet Area from Shanghai. They quickly began to eliminate Mao Zedong's influence in the Central Soviet Area, starting with the criticism of the "Luo Ming Line" without explicitly naming Mao. First, they removed Luo Ming from his position as acting secretary of the Fujian Provincial Committee, followed by the removal of Tan Zhenlin, Commander of the Fujian Provincial Military District, and Zhang Dingcheng, Chairman of the Fujian Provincial Soviet Government. This struggle expanded to Jiangxi, targeting central county secretaries like Deng Xiaoping, Mao Zetan, Xie Weijun, and Gu Bo as representatives of the Jiangxi "Luo Ming Line."

From the Ningdu Conference to the early stages of the Long March, Mao Zedong endured the most challenging and trying two years of his life as

Chairman of the Provisional Central Government of the Soviet Republic of China.

Mao later recalled, "They blindly followed the international line, believed in capturing large cities, and revered foreign political, military, organizational, and cultural policies. We opposed these excessively 'leftist' policies. We had some Marxist principles, but we were isolated. I, a once effective figure, became ineffective. They dunked me, a wooden Buddha, into a cesspool and then took me out, making me stink. At that time, not a single person, not even a ghost, would come to see me."[15]

During these difficult days, He Zizhen remained by Mao's side, providing him with immense emotional support. As a devoted couple, He Zizhen not only accompanied Mao through the physical pain caused by illness but also through mental anguish.

With extraordinary faith and perseverance, Mao Zedong withstood various pressures. While actively participating in the work of the Provisional Central Government of the Soviet Republic of China, he used his recuperation time to diligently read the works of Marx, Engels, and Lenin, contemplating and summarizing revolutionary experiences.

In April 1932, after leading the Eastern Route Army to capture Zhangzhou, Mao found a collection of Marxist-Leninist classics. These included Marx's *Capital*, Engels' *Anti-Dühring*, and Lenin's *Two Tactics of Social-Democracy in the Democratic Revolution* and *Left-Wing Communism: An Infantile Disorder*. These books accompanied him through this challenging period. Peng Dehuai recalled that in the autumn of 1933, "I received a book from Chairman Mao titled *Two Tactics*, with a pencil note on it that read (paraphrased): 'If this book had been read during the Great Revolution, mistakes wouldn't have been made.' Shortly thereafter, he sent me another book, *Left-Wing Communism: An Infantile Disorder* (both of these books were obtained during the capture of Zhangzhou Middle School). He also wrote on the book: 'If you read the previous book, you would know one but not the other; reading *Left-Wing Communism* will make you understand that both the left and the right can be harmful.'"[16]

Mao Zedong himself recalled as follows:

> I have never eaten Western bread, never been to the Soviet Union, nor studied abroad in any other country. When I proposed establishing a red political power centered on the Jinggang Mountains base area, implementing the red regime theory, and developing guerrilla warfare based on the "Sixteen-Character Formula" and the tactic of encircling the enemy, those who had eaten Western bread did not trust me, believing that Marxism could not emerge from the mountains. In the autumn of 1932, when I was out of work, I collected books from Zhangzhou and other places, gathering all the relevant works by Marx, Engels, Lenin, and Stalin. If there were any missing or incomplete, I borrowed from comrades. I immersed myself in reading Marxist-Leninist works almost all day long, switching from one book to another, sometimes alternating between them. I diligently studied for two years. The later writings of "On Contradiction" and "On Practice" were formed during these two years of reading Marxist-Leninist works.[17]

Mao Zedong never got discouraged. He firmly believed that his ideas were correct and drew even more confidence and courage from these classic works. He patiently waited for the responsible comrades of the Central Committee to awaken, convinced that this day would inevitably come.

Indeed, that day eventually came.

CHAPTER 5

"The Red Army Fears No Difficult Expedition"

The enemy's headquarters possesses a certain strategic vision. Only by training ourselves to be superior can we achieve strategic victory.

MAO ZEDONG,
"Problems of Strategy in China's Revolutionary War" (December 1936)

Under Wang Ming's "leftist" dogmatic leadership, the fifth counter-campaign against "encirclement and suppression," which began in September 1933, was doomed to failure by April 28, 1934, when Guangchang, the northern gateway to the Central Soviet Area, fell. After a period of preparation and with the Comintern's approval, the main force of the Central Red Army, numbering over 86,000, embarked on a long strategic retreat in October of the same year. No one anticipated that this journey would last an entire year and that the destination would be the remote northern Shaanxi. To outmaneuver and evade the enemy, the Red Army covered a distance of 25,000 *li* (approximately 12,500 kilometers).

On October 18, 1934, Mao Zedong left Yudu with the central column to begin the Long March. Accompanying him were Zhang Wentian and Wang Jiaxiang.

The Long March represented both a severe test and a rare opportunity for Mao Zedong. Reflecting on his emotions before and during the Long March, he later said: "In 1934, the situation was critical, and as we prepared for the Long March, my mood was one of depression. The Long March covered ten thousand *li* with countless twists and turns, with far more difficulties than successes, and my mood was heavy. After crossing the Min Mountains, I felt a sudden sense of clarity and transformation. It was like finding a bright village amid the dark willows."[1]

The phrase "a sudden sense of clarity and transformation" aptly encapsulates the significance of the Long March in Mao Zedong's revolutionary career.

According to the original plan, the Central Red Army's strategic transfer was to join forces with the Second and Sixth Army Corps in northwest Hunan. At this time, Chiang Kai-shek had established four blockade lines on the Red Army's westward path. Sticking to the original plan would mean walking straight into the enemy's trap. However, Bo Gu (Qin Bangxian) and others stubbornly adhered to the set plan. The brave Red Army, with immense sacrifice, broke through the four blockade lines, protecting the Central Committee, the Central Military Commission, and the massive logistics convoy. On December 1, they successfully escorted the Central Committee, the Central Military Commission, and affiliated agencies across the Xiangjiang River. By this point, the Central Red Army's numbers had drastically decreased from 86,000 to over 30,000.

The failure of the fifth counter-campaign, especially the heavy losses incurred while breaking through the four blockade lines, prompted the Red Army officers and soldiers to start thinking independently. They vividly recalled how Mao Zedong had led them to establish the Central Soviet Area and successfully repelled the enemy's three previous "encirclement and suppression" campaigns, contrasting sharply with the current central leadership under Bo Gu and others.

Around this time, Mao Zedong began using every opportunity to work on Wang Jiaxiang and Zhang Wentian. Both of them had returned from the Soviet Union to take on significant leadership roles, trusted by the Comintern and Wang Ming, but they were now beginning to have doubts. Mao explained and analyzed the military errors of Li De (Otto Braun) and Bo Gu during the fifth counter-campaign. Wang Jiaxiang was the first to support Mao's views, believing that to reverse the critical situation of the Party and the Red Army, it was necessary to convene a Political Bureau of the Central Committee meeting to change the central leadership. Zhang Wentian soon accepted Mao's ideas and began to resist the erroneous military commands within the Political Bureau. Subsequently, Mao also spoke with Zhou Enlai and Zhu De, garnering their support. After crossing the Xiangjiang River, Mao proposed to the Central Committee that they discuss the issue of military failures.

On December 18, 1934, the Political Bureau of the Central Committee held a meeting in Liping, Guizhou, to reconsider their strategic direction. After intense debate, Mao Zedong's views were adopted, resulting in a resolution that stated: "The previous decision to establish a new Soviet base in western Hunan is now impossible and inappropriate" and "the new base area should be in the Sichuan-Guizhou border region, initially centered around Zunyi."[2]

In his book *Chronicles of China*, Li De recalled: "Before reaching Liping, we held an impromptu meeting to discuss future combat plans. ... I asked everyone to consider: Should we allow the forces pursuing us along parallel routes or rushing westward to strategic locations to overtake us, and then turn north behind them to link up with the Second Army Corps? ... And we can create a large Soviet area in the triangular border region of Hunan, Guizhou, and Sichuan." Mao Zedong, however, firmly rejected this suggestion, insisting on continuing westward into the interior of Guizhou. This time, he not only had the support of Zhang Wentian and Wang Jiaxiang but also of Zhou Enlai, who was beginning to side with the 'Central Troika.' Consequently, Mao's proposal was approved."

Just after New Year's Day in 1935, good news arrived: The Red Army had captured Zunyi, a major town in northern Guizhou.

From January 15 to 17, the Political Bureau of the Central Committee held an expanded meeting in a unique two-story building that had been the private residence of Bai Huizhang, Commander of the Second Division of the KMT 25th Army. The meeting was held in a rectangular room on the second floor, with a long rectangular table in the center and a circle of wooden folding chairs with rattan seats around it. It was the middle of winter, and there was an old charcoal brazier under the table.

For a long time, there was much speculation about the purpose of the Zunyi Conference and who attended, due to a lack of historical documents. It wasn't until the later discovery of the summary of the Zunyi Conference written by Chen Yun shortly after the meeting that a definitive account emerged. The *Summary of the Expanded Political Bureau Meeting in Zunyi* states as follows:

> The convening of the expanded Political Bureau meeting in Zunyi was decided by the Liping Political Bureau meeting based on various debates in southern Hunan and Tongdao. The purpose of this meeting was (1) to decide and review the decision made at the Liping meeting to temporarily establish a Soviet base area centered on northern Guizhou, and (2) to review the experiences and lessons of military command in the fifth counter-campaign and the westward expedition. The expanded Political Bureau meeting commenced immediately after the Red Army occupied Zunyi. Besides the formal and alternate members of the Political Bureau, attendees included the corps commanders and political commissars of the First and Third Army Corps, Lin Biao, Nie Rongzhen, Peng Dehuai, and Yang Shangkun, as well as the political commissar of the Fifth Army Corps, Li Zhuoran, Li Fuchun, the director of the General Political Department, and Chief of Staff Liu Bocheng. After three days, the meeting concluded with its resolutions.[3]

The term "westward expedition" mentioned here would later become commonly known as the Long March. At the time, the Political Bureau members attending the meeting included Mao Zedong, Zhang Wentian, Zhou Enlai, Zhu De, Chen Yun, and Bo Gu, with Bo Gu, Zhang Wentian, and Zhou Enlai being the Political Bureau Standing Committee members. Alternate Political Bureau members included Wang Jiaxiang, Liu Shaoqi, Deng Fa, and He Kequan (Kai Feng). Also present was Deng Xiaoping, who served as the central secretary-general.

The meeting focused on the military strategy of the fifth counter-campaign against "encirclement and suppression." Bo Gu first delivered a report summarizing the fifth counter-campaign, followed by a supplementary report from Zhou Enlai. Then, Zhang Wentian, Mao Zedong, and Wang Jiaxiang spoke, sharply criticizing the purely defensive strategy adopted by Bo Gu and others during the fifth counter-campaign. In his speech, Mao Zedong specifically pointed out that Bo Gu and others had replaced decisive defense with a purely defensive strategy, substituting positional and fortress warfare for mobile warfare. They supported the purely defensive strategic line with the so-called "short and swift attacks" tactical principle, which led to the Red Army's defeat by the enemy's protracted warfare and fortress tactics, causing significant losses to the Red Army. He emphasized that this strategy was completely contrary to the basic principles of the Red Army's successful strategic and tactical approaches.

These views were supported by the majority of the attendees. The meeting entrusted Zhang Wentian with drafting the "Central Resolution on the Summary of the Fifth Counter-Campaign Against the Enemy."

The meeting also adjusted the central leadership structure. Mao Zedong was elected as a member of the Political Bureau Standing Committee, the "Central Troika" was abolished, and Bo Gu and Li De's supreme military command was revoked. It was decided that the military would continue to be led by Zhu De and Zhou Enlai, with Zhou Enlai being the final decision-maker on military command within the Party. After the meeting, two important decisions were made: First, during the Central Red Army's mobile operations, the Political Bureau Standing Committee decided on February 5 that Zhang Wentian would replace Bo Gu as the overall leader of the Central Committee and that Mao Zedong would assist Zhou Enlai in military command. Second, in mid-March, a new "Central Troika" was formed, consisting of Zhou Enlai, Mao Zedong, and Wang Jiaxiang, with Zhou Enlai as the leader. This became the most crucial military leadership body of the Central Committee.

This series of organizational adjustments marked significant changes in the central leadership structure since the establishment of the CPC Provisional Central Political Bureau in September 1931. First, Bo Gu and others' military command was revoked. Second, Mao Zedong became a member of the Political Bureau Standing Committee, gaining decision-making power on major issues. Third, through the Zunyi Conference, a new internal unity formed around Mao Zedong with Zhang Wentian, Zhou Enlai, Zhu De, Chen Yun, and Wang Jiaxiang. This established a new central leadership represented by Mao Zedong.

The Zunyi Conference set a precedent for independently resolving significant internal Party issues and provided an exemplary model. Following Mao Zedong's suggestion, the meeting focused on military strategy without delving into the political line issues from Wang Ming's period. Therefore, Chen Yun's *Summary of the Expanded Political Bureau Meeting in Zunyi* also stated, "The expanded meeting generally considered the Party's overall political line at the time to be correct."[4] This approach addressed the most urgent and life-and-death critical issue while avoiding endless internal debates, ensuring Party unity. Mao Zedong knew well that without unity, there would be no victory in the Long March.

According to He Zizhen's recollections, after the Zunyi Conference, Mao Zedong once sighed to her, "To accomplish anything, you need a majority!" She clearly felt that after the Zunyi Conference, Mao Zedong had undergone significant changes. He became more composed, experienced, and thorough in his thinking, and he was especially better at uniting people.

The Zunyi Conference was held at a time when communication with the Comintern had been lost. However, Mao Zedong did not forget to send someone to report to the Comintern when the opportunity arose. The person chosen for this task was Political Bureau member Chen Yun.

After the Central Red Army successfully crossed the Dadu River and captured Luding, Chen Yun secretly left the troops, traveled to Shanghai, and then made his way to Vladivostok, arriving in Moscow in early September of the same year. On October 15, he reported to the Comintern Executive Committee Secretariat about the Red Army's westward expedition and the Zunyi Conference. The report was attended by Secretariat members Manuilsky and alternate secretary Florin. When discussing the Zunyi Conference, Chen Yun emphasized: "At this meeting, we corrected the errors of the military leaders during the final stage of the fifth counter-campaign and the initial stage of the westward expedition. As everyone knows, the military leaders made a series of mistakes during this period. Now, these errors have been thoroughly rectified. A strong leadership team has been established to replace the previous leaders. The Party's leadership over the army has been strengthened. We have replaced the 'strategists who command with pencils' and elected Comrade Mao Zedong as the leader." In his conclusion, Chen Yun also stated: "Our Party is capable of and proficient in flexibly and correctly leading the civil war. Military leaders like Mao Zedong and Zhu De have matured."[5]

The successful convening of the Zunyi Conference and the critique of the erroneous military line filled Mao Zedong with confidence in the flexible and mobile strategic and tactical principles that the Red Army had accumulated through long-term experience:

> Starting in January 1932, after the Party's resolution containing serious principled errors about striving for first victories in one or several provinces following the crushing of three "encirclement and suppression" campaigns, "left" opportunists fought against the correct principles, ultimately abolishing a set of correct principles and establishing another set of so-called "new principles" or "regular principles," which were contrary to the former. From then on, what was previously considered correct was no longer "regular"; it was the "encirclement and suppression" that should be negated. The "encirclement and suppression" atmosphere dominated for three years. Its first stage was military adventurism, the second stage shifted to military conservatism, and finally, the third stage became escapism. It wasn't until the Party's expanded Political Bureau meeting in Zunyi, Guizhou, in January 1935, that this erroneous line was declared bankrupt, and the correctness of the previous line was re-acknowledged. This came at an enormous cost![6]

After the Zunyi Conference, Mao Zedong returned to a leadership position in the Party and the Red Army. At this time, Zhang Wentian replaced Bo Gu as the overall leader of the Central Committee. Military command was jointly held by Zhou Enlai, Mao Zedong, and Wang Jiaxiang. This arrangement allowed Mao Zedong's opinions to quickly become collective decisions and be implemented. The political environment within the Party was vastly different from before.

At this time, the more than 30,000-strong Central Red Army was still surrounded by hundreds of thousands of KMT troops, with the encirclement extending from Hunan, Guangdong, Guangxi, Guizhou, Yunnan, and even to Sichuan. Clearly, Chiang Kai-shek was determined to annihilate the Central Red Army, personally overseeing the battle from Nanchang, Guiyang, and Kunming.

From late January to April 1935, Mao Zedong engaged in a strategic battle of wits and courage with the KMT "pursuit and suppression" forces, employing flexible and mobile tactics to maneuver the enemy along the banks of the Chishui River. This included the masterful military actions of crossing the Chishui River four times, threatening Guiyang and Kunming, and skillfully crossing the Jinsha River.

As Mao Zedong later recalled, the strategic masterpiece of crossing the Chishui River four times was sparked by a failed operation: "I have made mistakes in battles. For instance, I commanded the defeat at Gaoxingwei, the defeat at Nanxiong, the battle of Tucheng during the Long March, and the battle at Maotai." The battle of Tucheng, referred to here, is generally known as the battle of Qinggangpo, a heavily costly battle commanded by Mao Zedong after the Zunyi Conference.

After the Zunyi Conference, following the strategy of crossing the Yangtze River to join forces with the Fourth Front Army, Mao Zedong, along with Zhu De, Zhou Enlai, and Liu Bocheng, decided to annihilate the pursuing Sichuan army led by Guo Xunqi in the area east of Tucheng and Qinggangpo. On January 28, the Cadre Regiment of the Military Commission Column, the Third Red Army Corps, the Fifth Red Army Corps, and part of the First Red Army Corps launched a fierce attack on the enemy at Qinggangpo from the north and south, fighting intensely throughout the day but ultimately suffering a defeat. At this point, two additional brigades of Sichuan reinforcements arrived quickly, and two brigades of Sichuan troops stationed at Wanglongchang also attacked the Central Red Army from the flanks, creating a highly perilous situation.

There is no general who wins every battle, but the key is whether one can remain unflinching and turn danger into safety. At this moment, Mao Zedong once again demonstrated his exceptional abilities. He proposed convening a meeting of the main leaders of the Political Bureau of the Central Committee, deciding to immediately withdraw from the battle, and directed the combat troops and the Military Commission Column to quickly cross the Chishui River lightly armed and head west, abandoning the original decision. This initiated the famous "four crossings of the Chishui River" during the Long March.

Mao Zedong once likened war to a stage, saying, "A military strategist cannot seek victory in war beyond the limits of material conditions, but within those limits, a military strategist can and must strive for victory. The stage for a military strategist's activities is built on objective material conditions, but with this stage, a military strategist can direct many lively, powerful, and magnificent dramas."[7] In the perilous environment of the Long March, Mao Zedong perfectly embodied this principle.

During the command of the "four crossings of the Chishui River," Mao Zedong skillfully exploited Chiang Kai-shek's fear of the Red Army crossing the river to join forces with the Fourth Front Army. He misled the enemy, maneuvering tens of thousands of KMT "pursuit and suppression" troops in circles along the Chishui River, and then unexpectedly crossed the Wu River to the south, pressing toward Guiyang. This caught the enemy off guard and threw them into disarray.

Liu Bocheng, then the Chief of Staff of the Red Army, recalled as follows:

> At that time, Chiang Kai-shek was personally directing the battle in Guiyang, hurriedly mobilizing warlord troops from Yunnan to "protect" him, and ordered Xue Yue and Hunan troops to defend Yuqing and Shiqian to prevent our army from moving east to join forces with the Second and Sixth Army Corps. During the planning of this operation, Chairman Mao said, "As long as we can draw out the Yunnan troops, it will be a victory." Sure enough, the enemy acted entirely according to Chairman Mao's direction. Our army surrounded Longli City southeast of Guiyang with the First Army Corps, creating a false impression to confuse the enemy. The main forces crossed the Xiangqian Highway, heading toward Yunnan, moving in the opposite direction of the reinforcements to Guiyang. Once again, Chairman Mao successfully used flexible tactics, creating the illusion of being east of Guiyang, causing

the enemy to make mistakes, and allowing our army to seize the opportunity to suddenly head west. ... Once we crossed the highway, we left the enemy behind, and the troops moved swiftly, covering 120 *li* in one day. Along the way, we captured the counties of Dingfan (now Huishui), Guangshun, and Xingyi and crossed the Beipan River. By late April, we had advanced into Yunnan in three directions: one detachment, the Ninth Army Corps, remained north of the Wu River to contain the enemy, defeating five enemy regiments and occupying Xuanwei before crossing the Jinsha River through Huize; the other two main forces captured Zhanyi, Malong, Xundian, and Songming, advancing directly toward Kunming. At this time, the main Yunnan forces had all been deployed eastward, leaving the rear defenseless. Our army's entry into Yunnan frightened Long Yun, causing him to concentrate militia forces in Kunming to defend the city, while our army feigned an attack and then swiftly advanced northwest toward the Jinsha River.[8]

During the rapid advance into Yunnan, Mao Zedong's wife, He Zizhen, was severely injured. At that time, the cadre rest regiment she was with was attacked by enemy aircraft. She was severely wounded while shielding the injured. When she regained consciousness, she told Mao Zemin and his wife, who had rushed to her side, "Please don't tell Chairman Mao about my injury for now. He is very busy commanding battles at the front line and should not be distracted. Please leave me with the local villagers. We will meet again when the revolution is victorious." Later, when Mao Zedong arrived, she said, "Runzhi, leave me here, and you all move forward!" Mao Zedong replied, "Zizhen, don't think that way. My comrades and I will never leave you here alone!"[9] Mao Zedong later recalled that he rarely shed tears in his life, but this time he did.

The hardships of the Long March were not only due to the continuous battles against the well-trained and well-equipped KMT forces, which outnumbered the Red Army by more than ten to one, and the hundreds of skirmishes and battles they had to endure. The Red Army also faced severe shortages of supplies, often going hungry and cold, and suffered from natural disasters. Many soldiers perished crossing snow-capped mountains and marshlands, never to rise again.

Another significant challenge of the Long March was managing internal party conflicts.

After the Central Red Army crossed the Jinsha River and shook off all pursuing KMT forces, they finally met with the main force of the Fourth Front Army in June of the same year. The expectation was that the two armies would march north together, but they unexpectedly encountered the warlordism of Zhang Guotao.

By this time, four years had passed since the Japanese invasion began with the September 18 Incident in 1931, leading to their occupation of the northeast and their growing ambition to conquer China, threatening North China and Beijing. The nationwide sentiment for resistance against Japanese aggression was rising, and the national conflict had become the primary social contradiction.

Mao Zedong consistently opposed the slogan "Armed Defense of the Soviet Union" proposed by Wang Ming, Bo Gu, and others, advocating instead for seizing the opportunity to raise the banner of resistance against Japanese aggression and unite all possible domestic forces. At this moment, he explicitly put forward the proposal of "marching north to resist against Japan."

After the First Red Army and the Fourth Red Army joined forces, Mao Zedong and others repeatedly sent telegrams to Zhang Guotao, earnestly urging him to recognize the greater good and join in the "marching north to resist against Japan." However, Zhang Guotao evaded the issue by proposing to develop westward instead.

On June 26, 1935, the Political Bureau of the Central Committee held a meeting at Lianghekou in Maogong County. The meeting discussed the strategic direction after the meeting of the First and Fourth Front Armies. Zhou Enlai presented a report proposing a strategy of rapid mobile warfare to attack Songpan and Hu Zongnan's forces, with the goal of moving north to establish a base area in Sichuan, Shaanxi, and Gansu; and emphasized the need for unified command under the Military Commission. Zhang Guotao, however, stressed that the situation north of Songpan had not been thoroughly investigated and that moving to southern Gansu would not be sustainable. He insisted on moving south toward Chengdu, believing the local enemies were not a significant problem.

Mao Zedong, in his speech, agreed with Zhou Enlai's report and added five points:

(1) The Chinese Red Army should exert all efforts to develop a new base area. Establishing a base in Sichuan, Shaanxi, and Gansu could lay a more solid foundation for the Soviet movement. This is a forward-moving strategy. It is essential to explain this to comrades in the Fourth Front Army, who are aiming to attack Chengdu. After the First and Fourth Front Armies meet, there is the possibility of advancing north.
(2) The nature of the war is not decisive defense nor retreat but offensive. Base areas are developed through offensives. We need to cross the mountains, defeat Hu Zongnan, capture southern Gansu, and rapidly advance north to establish a new base area.
(3) We must identify the critical points where Chiang Kai-shek is vulnerable and break them first. High mobility is required, which involves selecting the best route for northward development to seize the initiative.
(4) Concentrate forces on the main attack, such as attacking Songpan. If Hu Zongnan engages us in field battles, we can handle it with our twenty regiments; if he resorts to fortifications, we must break his strongholds to pin down his forces. We should quickly defeat Hu's forces and advance to capture Songpan. The decision must be made today, and action taken tomorrow. Given the sparse population and harsh conditions, we should strive to break through by June and proceed through Songpan to our designated area.
(5) Task the Standing Committee and the Military Commission with resolving the issue of unified command.[10]

After three days of discussion, the meeting approved the strategic plan to move north and establish a base area in Sichuan, Shaanxi, and Gansu.

Songpan was the gateway to southern Gansu, and Chiang Kai-shek had specifically assigned his trusted general Hu Zongnan and the KMT First Army to guard it. Therefore, the key to the northward advance was the immediate capture of Songpan. At this time, it was still early summer in the northwest.

Missing this window of opportunity would make the attack even more difficult as the weather turned colder.

At the meeting, Zhang Guotao saw that the central faction had more people and their opinions were unanimous, so he found it inconvenient to continue opposing them. However, once he returned to the Fourth Front Army, he came up with various excuses to refuse the implementation of the decisions made at the Lianghekou meeting.

Zhang Guotao first proposed the promotion of new cadres, suggesting that some could be assigned to work at the Military Commission. His plan was to control the Central Red Army, which only had 30,000 troops, by promoting and transferring cadres from the Fourth Front Army, which, including local forces, had 80,000 troops.

To unite with Zhang Guotao and advance northward, the Standing Committee of the Political Bureau of the Central Committee of the CPC agreed at its July 18 meeting to replace Zhou Enlai with Zhang Guotao as the General Political Commissar of the Red Army. On the same day, the Central Revolutionary Military Commission issued a notice: "Comrade Zhu De will continue to serve as Chairman of the Central Revolutionary Military Commission and Commander-in-Chief, and Comrade Zhang Guotao is appointed as General Political Commissar." On the 21st, a Forward Command Headquarters was organized, with Xu Xiangqian as General Commander, Chen Changhao as Political Commissar, and Ye Jianying as Chief of Staff. Prior to this, Zhang Guotao had been appointed as Vice Chairman of the Central Revolutionary Military Commission, with Xu Xiangqian and Chen Changhao as members of the Military Commission.

Seeing that his objective had been achieved, Zhang Guotao took the opportunity to confiscate the cipher books of each army corps under the pretext of centralized command, intending to cut off communication between the Central Committee and the Central Red Army. Peng Dehuai recalled: "After completing my mission and returning to the Luhua headquarters, the Military Commission's staff confiscated the cipher books used for inter-corps communication, including those used for communications between the First and Third Army Corps, the Military Commission, and Chairman Mao.

From then on, we could only communicate with the Forward Command Headquarters. We were cut off from the Central Committee and the First Army Corps."[11]

Due to Zhang Guotao's repeated delays, the opportunity to attack Songpan was missed. In early August, the Red Army Headquarters revised the "Xiatao Campaign Plan," dividing the Red Army into left and right routes to move north. The main leaders, including Commander-in-Chief Zhu De, General Political Commissar Zhang Guotao, and Chief of Staff Liu Bocheng, moved with the Left Route Army, while central leaders such as Zhang Wentian, Mao Zedong, Zhou Enlai, and Wang Jiaxiang moved with the Right Route Army led by Xu Xiangqian and Chen Changhao.

Peng Dehuai recalled the situation of the Right Route Army.

> During this northward advance, the Third Army Corps was at the rear of the right-wing column, with the First Army Corps at the front, followed by the Fourth Front Army's Fourth, Thirtieth, and Ninth Army Corps, and the Forward Command Headquarters. At that time, I felt that Zhang Guotao had ambitions, but it seemed the Central Committee had not noticed. Chairman Mao and Zhang Wentian were with the Forward Command Headquarters, which arrived at Shangxia Baozuo a day or two before the Third Army Corps reached Axi and Baxi, about fifteen to twenty *li* away from the Forward Command Headquarters. When I arrived at the camp, I immediately went to the Forward Headquarters and Chairman Mao's place. In reality, I went to the Forward Headquarters just to see Chairman Mao. At that time, Zhou Enlai and Wang Jiaxiang were both ill and staying at the Third Army Corps. We stayed in Baxi for four or five days, and I visited the Forward Headquarters every day, secretly stationing the Eleventh Regiment near Chairman Mao's residence as a precaution.[12]

Zhang Guotao initially hoped that after the two armies united, the Central Committee would follow his command. However, he encountered a formidable opponent in Mao Zedong. The central leadership, including Zhang Wentian, Zhou Enlai, Zhu De, Wang Jiaxiang, Bo Gu, and Li De, all firmly supported Mao, leaving Zhang Guotao no opportunity to assert his influence.

In despair, Zhang Guotao issued an order on September 9 for the Right Route Army, which was advancing north, to turn south and "thoroughly carry out the internal Party struggle." To avoid conflict, Mao Zedong commanded the Central Red Army units within the Right Route Army to continue moving north overnight. Xu Xiangqian, who was with the Fourth Front Army, also declared at this critical moment, "How can the Red Army fight the Red Army?"

On September 10, before setting off northward, the Central Committee issued Mao Zedong's "Letter from the Central Committee to Comrades on Implementing the Northward Policy," which stated as follows:

> Since we crossed the snow-capped mountains and traversed the grasslands, we achieved victory as soon as we arrived at Baozuo, annihilating the 49th Division of the White Army. The current situation is entirely favorable to us. We should follow the correct strategic policy of the Central Committee, continue advancing north, and massively eliminate the forces of Chiang Kai-shek and Hu Zongnan to establish a new Soviet area in Sichuan, Shaanxi, and Gansu. Under no circumstances should we retreat along our original path, cross the snow-capped mountains again, traverse the grasslands, and return to areas inhabited by ethnic minorities who have completely fled. Marching south is a dead end.[13]

After arriving in northern Shaanxi, Mao Zedong summarized: "Zhang Guotao's policy did not believe that we could establish our base area in the Tibetan and Hui regions. It was only after encountering failure that he realized this."[14] This instance proved the foresight of the "Letter from the Central Committee to Comrades on Implementing the Northward Policy."

On September 12, the Political Bureau of the Central Committee held an expanded meeting at E'jie, passing the "Resolution on Comrade Zhang Guotao's Errors." It was also decided to reorganize the First Red Army, the Third Red Army, and the Military Commission Column into the Shaanxi-Gansu Detachment of the Chinese Workers' and Peasants' Red Army, totaling over 8,000 people. Peng Dehuai was appointed commander, and Mao Zedong was appointed political commissar. A five-member group was formed to lead military operations, consisting of Mao Zedong, Zhou Enlai, Wang Jiaxiang, Peng Dehuai, and Lin Biao.

Subsequently, the Central Committee led the Shaanxi-Gansu Detachment swiftly northward, breaking through the dangerous Lazikou Pass and opening the passage into southern Gansu.

As they crossed the Min Mountains and victory of the Long March was in sight, Mao Zedong composed the poem "*Qi Lü* · The Long March."

The Red Army fears not the trials of the Long March,
Holding light ten thousand crags and torrents.
The Five Ridges wind like gentle ripples,
And the majestic Wumeng roll by, globules of clay.
Warm the steep cliffs lapped by the waters of Golden Sand,
Cold the iron chains spanning the Dadu River.
Min Mountain's thousand li of snow joyously crossed,
The three Armies march on, each face glowing.

On October 19, 1935, Mao Zedong led the main forces of the Central Red Army to Wuqi Town in the Shaanxi-Gansu base area, successfully concluding the year-long, 25,000-*li* Long March.

From November 21 to 24, the Central Red Army, reorganized as the First Army Corps of the First Front Army, fought alongside the Fifteenth Army Corps, achieving a major victory in the Battle of Zhiluo Town. They annihilated one division and one regiment of the Northeastern Army, thwarting Chiang Kai-shek's third "encirclement and suppression" campaign against the Shaanxi-Gansu base area and delivering a severe blow to Zhang Xueliang and Yang Hucheng.

From December 17 to 25, the Political Bureau of the Central Committee held a meeting in Wayaobu, establishing the strategic policy of the Chinese United Front Against Japanese Aggression in response to the new wave of national resistance.

After the meeting, on December 27, Mao Zedong delivered a report titled "On the Tactics Against Japanese Imperialism" at the Wayaobu Party

Activists' Meeting. In his speech, he passionately reflected on the recently concluded Long March.

> What is the significance of the Long March? We say the Long March is the first of its kind in history. The Long March is a manifesto, a publicity force, and a seeding machine. Since the beginning of the world, from Pangu's creation to the present day, has there ever been a Long March like ours in history? In twelve months, with dozens of planes bombing and reconnoitering us daily, with hundreds of thousands of enemy troops encircling and pursuing us, encountering countless hardships and obstacles along the way, we managed to march over 20,000 *li* across eleven provinces. Has there ever been a Long March like ours in history? No, never. The Long March is also a manifesto. It declares to the world that the Red Army is a group of true heroes, while the imperialists and their lackeys, like Chiang Kai-shek, are utterly useless. The Long March proclaimed the failure of the encirclement, pursuit, and blockade by the imperialists and Chiang Kai-shek. The Long March is also a publicity force. It announced to approximately 200 million people across eleven provinces that only the path of the Red Army could liberate them. Without this grand endeavor, how could such a vast population quickly learn that there is a Red Army and the truth it represents? The Long March is also a seeding machine. It spread many seeds across eleven provinces, which will germinate, grow leaves, blossom, and bear fruit, promising future harvests. In summary, the Long March concluded with our victory and the enemy's defeat. Who made the Long March victorious? It was the Communist Party. Without the Communist Party, such a Long March would be unimaginable. The CPC, its leadership, its cadres, and its members do not fear any hardship. Anyone who doubts our ability to lead the revolutionary war will fall into the quagmire of opportunism. With the end of the Long March, a new era has begun. The Battle of Zhiluo Town symbolized the unity between the Central Red Army and the Northwestern Red Army, crushing the traitor Chiang Kai-shek's "encirclement" of the Shaanxi-Gansu border region and laying the foundation for the Central Committee to establish the national revolutionary base in the northwest.[15]

In world history, there have been expeditions, such as Hannibal's march, that are renowned for their achievements. However, the 25,000-*li* Long March led by Mao Zedong and the Chinese Workers' and Peasants' Red Army surpassed all previous expeditions in terms of difficulty and profound impact.

The Long March, originally a passive strategic retreat following the failure of the fifth counter-campaign against the encirclement, was transformed under Mao Zedong's leadership into a positive expedition carrying the banner of "marching north to resist against Japan." The endpoint of this expedition was strategically chosen in the northwest, the region most favorable for launching proactive resistance against the Japanese frontlines. This shift not only gained the CPC support for their stance on resisting Japan but also caused Chiang Kai-shek to lose ground due to his insistence on continuing the civil war against the Communists. Generals Zhang Xueliang and Yang Hucheng, who were on the frontlines of Chiang's "encirclement and suppression" campaign in the northwest, clearly recognized this. Consequently, after the failure of the "encirclement" campaign, they resolved to build alliances with Mao Zedong, Zhou Enlai, and others.

On April 9, 1936, Zhou Enlai, sent by the Central Committee, held talks with Zhang Xueliang, leader of the Northeast Army, in a church in Yan'an. While Mao Zedong was commanding the main forces of the First Front Army in the Eastern Expedition in Shanxi, he also guided this meeting.

Three days before the meeting, on April 6, Mao Zedong sent a telegram through Wang Yizhe, Commander of the 67th Army of the Northeast Army, to Zhang Xueliang: "Our representative Comrade Zhou, along with Kenong, will come to Fushi as agreed on the 8th to discuss the national salvation plan with Mr. Zhang Xueliang." He outlined the issues to be discussed as follows: "(1) Cease all internal conflicts and unite the national army, regardless of Red or White, to resist against Japan and save the country. (2) Concentrate all Red Army forces in Hebei to first resist the advance of Japanese imperialism. (3) The specific steps and political program for organizing a national defense government and a resistance against-Japanese coalition army. (4) The issue of forming an alliance with the Soviet Union and first sending representatives to Moscow. (5) The preliminary agreement between your side and ours on non-aggression and economic and trade matters."[16]

The talks on April 9 lasted from that evening until 4 a.m. the next day. The results were summarized in Zhou Enlai's telegram to Zhang Wentian, Mao Zedong, and Peng Dehuai: Regarding the first point, "Cease all internal conflicts," Zhou reported, "He completely agrees with ceasing internal conflicts and uniting to resist against Japan, but before openly resisting Japan, he cannot avoid obeying Chiang's orders to station troops in the Soviet area. If he does not advance, he cannot respond to Chiang (who has reprimanded him by telegram, and transmitted Yan's telegram accusing him of watching the fire from the other side of the river)." Regarding the second point, "Concentrate all Red Army forces in Hebei," Zhou conveyed, "If the Fourth Front Army moves north, he can make Shaanxi-Gansu troops give way. The Second and Sixth Armies need the Central Army's consent to move north, and he is willing to work on this matter." Regarding the third point, "Organize a national defense government," Zhou noted, "He believes that the only way to resist against Japan is through this path, and he is willing to consider it. He will review the Ten Major Programs and provide feedback." On the issue of Chiang Kai-shek, Zhou reported, "He believes there is division within Chiang's ranks, and that Chiang is at a crossroads. He feels that opposing Chiang is unfeasible. If Chiang truly steps down, he will leave him." On the fifth point, "Economic and trade matters," Zhou detailed, "Regarding regular purchases, we can set up shops within his defensive area to purchase supplies ourselves. He can help with radio equipment, medicines, and even provide ammunition. Both sides will send reliable agents disguised as scouts to maintain communication. Additionally, we will appoint individuals with political acumen and not overly conspicuous backgrounds to operate in other areas (Kenong, being too well-known, is unsuitable for such tasks)."[17]

There is another telegram related to this meeting, sent by Mao Zedong and Peng Dehuai to Lin Biao and Nie Rongzhen on April 11. At the time, Lin Biao and Nie Rongzhen were leading the First Red Army Corps in the Eastern Expedition in Shanxi. The telegram stated as follows:

> Vice Chairman Zhou entered Fushi City at 8 p.m. on the 9th and left the city at 4 a.m. on the 10th after an all-night discussion with Zhang Xueliang. The results were as follows:

(1) Zhang believes that a national defense government and a resistance against-Japanese coalition army are the only way out. He will review the Ten Political Programs and provide his feedback.

(2) Zhang supports the concentration of the Red Army in Hebei and the Fourth Front Army moving into Gansu. His troops can give way, but the Second and Sixth Army Corps will need the Central Army's consent, and he is willing to mediate this.

(3) Regarding sending representatives to the Soviet Union, his representatives will go from Europe, while ours will be protected by Zhang and go via Xinjiang.

(4) He fully agrees to cease internal conflicts, adding that if the Red Army engages the Japanese army, the national ceasefire movement will gain more strength.

(5) Before openly expressing his resistance against-Japanese stance, he cannot avoid obeying Chiang's orders to occupy the Soviet area.

(6) On trade issues, for regular goods, we can set up shops to purchase supplies ourselves, and for military supplies, he will handle procurement, including providing ammunition.

(7) Representatives will be exchanged to stay permanently on both sides.

(8) Zhang suggests that the Red Army's movement into Hebei might be disadvantageous and that it might also be difficult to establish a foothold in Shanxi. He recommends focusing on Suiyuan, but if the Red Army decides to move into Hebei, he can inform Wan Fulin's troops not to attack us.[18]

Wan Fulin was the commander of the 53rd Army of the Northeast Army. During the talks, Zhang Xueliang also raised the question: if we can unite to resist against Japan, how should we treat Chiang Kai-shek? Zhou Enlai expressed his willingness to hear Zhang Xueliang's opinion. Zhang Xueliang believed that Chiang Kai-shek still had the potential and intention to resist against Japan, but the problem was his insistence on the "anti-Communist" policy. Therefore, the most critical issue at present was to find a way to turn Chiang's incorrect policy around and truly achieve a ceasefire and united resistance against Japanese aggression. After listening, Zhou Enlai agreed with

Zhang Xueliang's opinion and stated that this was an important policy issue. He promised to take this opinion back to the Central Committee for careful consideration before making a final response. Zhang Xueliang happily said, "You apply pressure from the outside, and I'll persuade from the inside; together, we can exert internal and external pressure on Chiang Kai-shek and definitely turn him around."

Mao Zedong attached great importance to Zhang Xueliang's suggestion. On April 9, the same day the talks ended, he telegraphed Zhang Wentian, who was in charge of the Central Committee in the rear, suggesting, "At present, we should not issue a declaration against Chiang but rather a proclamation to the people and a telegram." "Our fundamental slogan should not be a declaration against Chiang but a declaration to resist against Japan."[19] On May 5, after the Eastern Expedition concluded, Mao Zedong, as Chairman of the Central Government of the Soviet Republic of China, and Zhu De, as Chairman of the Chinese People's Red Army Revolutionary Military Commission, issued a "Telegram Calling for a Ceasefire and United Resistance Against Japanese Aggression." The telegram stated, "In the face of national calamity, a decisive battle between the two sides, regardless of the victor, would be a loss to China's national defense capabilities and a source of joy for Japanese imperialism." "We are willing to implement a ceasefire and negotiate peace within one month with all armed forces attacking the resistance against-Japanese Red Army to achieve the goal of united resistance against Japan." This telegram used the term "Mr. Chiang Kai-shek" for the first time. Four months later, on September 1, the Central Committee officially issued the "Directive on Forcing Chiang to Resist Against Japan," changing the policy from opposing Chiang to compelling him to resist against Japan.

The Eastern Expedition commanded by Mao Zedong and the First Front Army began on February 20, 1936, and ended on May 2, lasting 75 days. It swept through most of Shanxi, expanding the army by more than 8,000 troops, raising over 300,000 yuan, and increasing the influence of the Party and the Red Army, laying the foundation for establishing a solid resistance base area behind enemy lines in Shanxi during the War of Resistance Against Japanese Aggression.

Mao Zedong was very satisfied with the results of Zhou Enlai's talks with Zhang Xueliang. He soon telegraphed Zhou Enlai, deciding that "the relationship with Zhang and Yang's forces should be handled and guided by you. Keep us informed of any developments, but we generally will not engage directly. Externally, we will present a united front, but internally, you will bear full responsibility."[20]

Prior to this, under Mao Zedong's overall planning, an agreement had also been reached with Northwest Army leader Yang Hucheng for united external action and joint resistance against Japanese aggression. Thus, in the half year since the Central Committee established a base in northern Shaanxi, a united front against Japanese aggression had formed in the northwest region with the Red Army, Northeast Army, and Northwest Army forming a tripartite alliance, taking the political initiative in compelling Chiang Kai-shek to resist against Japan.

History favors those who are prepared. The Xi'an Incident on December 12, 1936, occurred when patriotic generals Zhang Xueliang and Yang Hucheng detained Chiang Kai-shek during his campaign against the Red Army, providing the CPC and Mao Zedong with a golden opportunity to end the civil war and prepare for the War of Resistance Against Japanese Aggression.

The CPC and Mao Zedong had no prior knowledge of the Xi'an Incident, and its occurrence was just as sudden for them as for anyone else. It was only after Zhou Enlai and others arrived in Xi'an that they gradually understood the details of the incident and Chiang Kai-shek's changing attitude. Therefore, it is difficult to imagine that after ten years of internal war, during which the KMT and Chiang Kai-shek massacred millions of CPC members and outstanding leaders—including Mao's own wife, Yang Kaihui, and his brother, Mao Zetan—Mao Zedong could immediately propose a peaceful resolution to the Xi'an Incident. As the saying goes, "He who tied the bell must untie it." The enmity between the KMT and CPC, which turned from allies in the first cooperation to complete adversaries, was initiated by none other than Chiang Kai-shek with the April 12, 1927, counter-revolutionary coup.

At the Political Bureau of the Central Committee meeting held on December 13, the day after the Xi'an Incident, Mao Zedong proposed: "We should take Xi'an as the center and the northwest as the front line for resisting Japan, to influence and lead the whole country and form the center of the resistance against-Japanese front. Around this, we should expose Chiang Kai-shek's crimes to the people, stabilize the Huangpu faction, the CC clique, and push the elder statesmen faction, the Euro-American faction, and other factions to support the Xi'an Incident. Our political slogan should be to convene a National Salvation Congress, with other slogans being subsidiary." Given the context of the time, these proposals were not excessive. He also stated, "We are not directly opposing Chiang Kai-shek, but rather specifically pointing out Chiang Kai-shek's personal mistakes"; and "We should emphasize the banner of resisting Japan and aiding Suiyuan, rather than placing opposing Chiang Kai-shek and resisting Japan on equal footing."[21] This idea of not equating opposition to Chiang with resisting Japan had been Mao's stance since Zhou Enlai's talks with Zhang Xueliang. Zhang Wentian further suggested, "We should strive to gain the legitimacy of the Nanjing government and unite with non-Chiang factions. Militarily, we should adopt a defensive stance, while politically, we should be on the offensive."[22] These strategies were in stark contrast to Chiang Kai-shek's policy of "pacifying the internal threat before resisting the external threat."

In this speech, Mao also suggested sending key comrades to carry out these tasks. After the meeting, Mao Zedong and Zhou Enlai sent a telegram to Zhang Xueliang: "Enlai plans to come to Xi'an to discuss future plans with you. Please send a plane to Yan'an to pick him up."[23]

The work done by Zhou Enlai and his delegation during the Xi'an Incident, along with the crucial information they gathered, played a key role in the CPC's final decision to resolve the Xi'an Incident peacefully. On December 18, Mao Zedong received a telegram from Zhou Enlai in Xi'an addressed to him and the Central Committee. Zhou reported: "The pro-Japanese faction in Nanjing aims to create a civil war; Soong Mei-ling's letter to Chiang Kai-shek stated, 'Better to resist against Japan than to die at the hands of an enemy'; Kung Hsiang-hsi seeks reconciliation; Soong Tse-vung has come to Xi'an with the condition of a ceasefire; Wang Jingwei is returning to the country. Chiang's attitude initially seemed firm but has since shifted toward reconciliation, seeking to regain his freedom. Regarding the Red Army, he neither wishes to surrender nor cooperate, leaving the resolution of the northwest issue and relations with the Red Army entirely to Zhang Xueliang."[24]

On December 19, the Political Bureau of the Central Committee held another expanded meeting to further study the strategy for resolving the Xi'an Incident and to discuss the Central Committee's telegram regarding the incident. In his concluding remarks, Mao Zedong pointed out: "The current camps consist of two sides: the Japanese imperialists and the pro-Japanese faction, and the Communist Party and the resistance against-Japanese faction. There are also wavering and neutral factions in the middle, and we should strive to win over these middle factions. We need to win over Nanjing, and even more so, we need to win over Xi'an. Only by ending the civil war can we resist against Japan. Six forces could potentially end the civil war: first, the Red Army; second, the Northeast Army; third, the friendly forces in Xi'an; fourth, the people; fifth, internal divisions within Nanjing; and sixth, international assistance. We should unite these six anti-civil war forces to end the civil war and transform the domestic war into a resistance against-Japanese war."[25] The meeting approved the "Directive on the Xi'an Incident and Our Tasks," which stated, "We insist on the position of being the organizer and leader of the cessation of the civil war and the united resistance against Japanese aggression, oppose a new civil war, and advocate for a peaceful resolution between Nanjing and Xi'an based on unity in resisting Japan."[26]

Through the joint efforts of Zhou Enlai, Zhang Xueliang, and Yang Hucheng, after repeated negotiations, they forced Chiang Kai-shek to commit to "stopping the anti-Communist campaign and uniting with the Communists to resist against Japan," and reached a nine-point agreement with Soong Tse-vung and Soong Mei-ling.[27] Thus, the Xi'an Incident was peacefully resolved. On December 25, Chiang Kai-shek left Xi'an accompanied by Zhang Xueliang.

Afterward, although the situation remained volatile and Chiang Kai-shek did not fully honor his promises, the trend of stopping the civil war and establishing a national united front for resisting Japan became inevitable. As Mao Zedong said, "The Xi'an Incident ended the civil war, which also marked the beginning of the War of Resistance."[28]

History often shows that situations which seem hopeless to resolve can be swiftly settled once a breakthrough is achieved. Coincidentally, two months before the peaceful resolution of the Xi'an Incident, on October 9 and 22, 1936, the Fourth Front Army and the Second Front Army (composed of the Second Army Corps and the Sixth Army Corps) successfully united with the First Front Army in Huining and Jingning, Gansu (now part of Ningxia Hui Autonomous Region). This long-awaited grand union greatly strengthened the revolutionary forces, achieving an unprecedented level of concentration, reunion, and unity not seen since the failure of the Great Revolution. This laid the groundwork for the CPC and its army to transition from a domestic revolutionary war to a nationwide War of Resistance Against Japanese Aggression.

On January 13, 1937, Mao Zedong led the Central Committee and the Central Revolutionary Military Commission from Bao'an in northern Shaanxi to Yan'an. They would stay there for ten years, a stark contrast to the ten years of constant movement during the civil war.

If the ten years from September 1927, when Mao led the Autumn Harvest Uprising on the Hunan-Jiangxi border, were spent on horseback, the coming ten years would be spent in the caves of Yan'an.

CHAPTER 6

The National War of Resistance and the Protracted War

Think it over carefully, the Japanese are indeed a formidable enemy to China! Despite having vast territories, China has succumbed to a country with only three islands; despite having a population of 400 million, China is on the verge of becoming the slave of 30 million Japanese. If Manchuria and Mongolia are lost, the northern territories will inevitably be threatened, and the enemy can invade the Central Plains at will. Moreover, Shandong has already been lost, and the railway from Kaifeng to Jinan has been seized by the Japanese, thus allowing them to enter Henan at any time. Within twenty years, if we do not fight a decisive battle with Japan, the Chinese nation will find it difficult to survive. However, our compatriots are still in a deep slumber, unaware of the danger, and even fewer are paying attention to the situation in Japan. In my humble opinion, our generation has nothing else to do; if we want to secure ourselves and ensure the well-being of our descendants, we must prepare actively to respond to Japanese aggression.

MAO ZEDONG,
"Letter to Xiao Zisheng" (July 25, 1916)

On July 7, 1937, the Lugou Bridge Incident shocked China. Japan's full-scale invasion of China had begun, and the Chinese nation faced an unprecedented threat of extinction.

On July 13, Mao Zedong personally wrote, "Defend Beiping and Tianjin, defend North China, defend the entire nation, and resolutely fight Japanese imperialism to the end. This is the overarching strategy for today's war against Japan. Mobilization efforts on all fronts are the means to achieve this strategy. Any wavering or passive inaction is unacceptable."[1]

On July 17, Chiang Kai-shek gave a speech in Lushan, expressing his resolve to resist against Japan: "Once war breaks out, it will be a matter of defending the land without distinction between north and south, young and old. Everyone has the duty to defend the soil and resist the war, and all must be prepared to sacrifice everything."[2]

Japan's ambitions to conquer China were vast. They rapidly mobilized troops from Japan and Korea to the Chinese battlefield and accelerated their invasion. By July 29, they had occupied Beiping (now Beijing), and by July 30, they had taken Tianjin. On August 13, they attacked Shanghai, directly threatening the KMT Government's center of power, aiming for a swift and decisive occupation of China.

On August 22, the Central Executive Committee of the KMT held a secret meeting, declaring a state of war and electing Chiang Kai-shek as commander-in-chief of the Army, Navy, and Air Force. They also decided to establish the National Defense Supreme Council.

On the same day, the National Military Council issued orders to reorganize the Red Army. On August 25, the Central Revolutionary Military Commission of the CPC officially announced the reorganization of the Red Army into the Eighth Route Army of the National Revolutionary Army. Zhu De was appointed as the commander, Peng Dehuai as the deputy commander, and Ye Jianying as the chief of staff, comprising the 115th, 120th, and 125th Divisions, totaling nearly 46,000 troops.[3] On September 28, the National Military Council appointed Ye Ting as the commander of the New Fourth Army, reassigning the Red Army and guerrilla forces in southern China into this new unit, comprising over 10,300 troops.[4]

On September 22, the Central News Agency of the KMT broadcast the "Declaration of the CPC on the Cooperation Between the Two Parties." This declaration was handed to Chiang Kai-shek by Zhou Enlai on behalf of the CPC on July 15, just eight days after the Lugou Bridge Incident. On September

23, Chiang Kai-shek gave another speech in Lushan, effectively recognizing the CPC's legal status.

This unprecedented situation had never occurred during the ten years of civil war and was the result of Mao Zedong's continuous efforts since the Central Red Army's arrival in northern Shaanxi.

In response, Mao Zedong published an article on September 29 titled "The Urgent Tasks After the Establishment of the United Front of the KMT and the CPC." In it, he commented as follows:

> The CPC's declaration and Chiang Kai-shek's speech announce the cooperation between the two parties and lay the necessary foundation for their joint effort to save the nation. The CPC's declaration not only sets the guidelines for the unity of the two parties but also becomes the fundamental policy for the unity of the entire nation. Chiang's speech acknowledges the CPC's legal status nationwide and highlights the necessity of unity for national salvation. This is commendable; however, it still reflects the KMT's arrogance and lacks the necessary self-criticism, which we cannot be satisfied with. Nonetheless, the united front of the two parties has been proclaimed. This marks a new epoch in the history of the Chinese revolution and will have a profound impact on defeating Japanese imperialism.[5]

From this commentary, it is evident that while Mao Zedong had some dissatisfaction with Chiang Kai-shek's speech, he also held a great deal of anticipation.

At this moment, Mao Zedong was most concerned with two pressing issues. First, how to conduct the national War of Resistance Against Japanese Aggression based on KMT-CPC cooperation. Second, how the CPC and its army would participate in this national war.

The situation at that time was far from optimistic. Japan, at the peak of its aggression, had amassed a total armed force of over 400,000 troops, more than 2,600 combat aircraft, and 200 large warships before the full-scale invasion of China. Japan's industrial capacity also far surpassed that of China. In 1937, Japan's total industrial output exceeded $5.5 billion, with annual steel production of 5.8 million tons and oil production of 1.6 million tons, supported by a comprehensive military-industrial system.[6] In contrast, the KMT had an army of 1.7 million, which, despite its numerical advantage, suffered from a weak industrial base and the debilitating effects of long-standing warlordism and factionalism, leading to low combat effectiveness. At this time, the Eighth Route Army and the New Fourth Army combined had only about 56,000 troops, equipped solely with conventional light weapons, which were vastly inferior to both Japanese and KMT forces.

In these circumstances, Mao Zedong clearly recognized that both China's national resistance and the CPC's participation in it had to be conducted in ways that suited their strengths and avoided their weaknesses. They could neither passively avoid battle nor recklessly engage the enemy.

On July 23, 1937, Mao Zedong published "The Policy, Methods, and Prospects of Resisting Japan's Invasion," outlining the CPC's approach to the national War of Resistance.

In Mao's view, the key to successful national resistance lay in whether the KMT could abolish its one-party dictatorship and include all political factions willing to resist against Japan. Thus, he emphasized the CPC's eight-point program in this article: (1) General mobilization of the national army; (2) General mobilization of the people; (3) Reform of political institutions; (4) Diplomatic efforts for resistance; (5) Implementation of a program to improve people's lives; (6) National defense education; (7) Fiscal and economic policies for resistance; (8) Uniting all Chinese people, the government, and the army to form a solid Great Wall of national unity.

These policies later evolved into the CPC's "Ten-Point Program for Resisting Japan and Saving the Nation" at the expanded meeting of the Political Bureau of the Central Committee of the CPC held in Luochuan, Shaanxi. The meeting also approved a publicity outline on the current situation and tasks, drafted by Mao Zedong for the Central Publicity Department, titled "Strive to Mobilize All Forces to Win the War of Resistance."

In this publicity outline, Mao did not hide his praise for the KMT's active resistance and his concerns about its limited war policy: "The KMT's progress on the issue of resistance is commendable, which is what the CPC and the entire nation have long hoped for, and we welcome this progress. However, the KMT's policies on mobilizing the masses and political reform have not changed significantly; it still fundamentally refuses to open up the resistance against-Japanese movement to the people, is unwilling to make principled changes to government institutions, and has no program for improving people's lives. Moreover, it has not reached a level of sincere cooperation with the CPC."[7]

Mao straightforwardly pointed out the different outcomes of limited resistance versus full-scale national resistance: "A purely government-led resistance can achieve some individual victories, but it is impossible to thoroughly defeat the Japanese invaders. Only a comprehensive national resistance can achieve complete victory over Japan. However, to achieve full-scale national resistance, the KMT must completely and fundamentally change its policies."[8]

Next, Mao Zedong fully elaborated on the Ten-Point Program in his publicity outline. The main points of the Ten-Point Program are as follows: (1) defeat Japanese imperialism, (2) general mobilization of the national military, (3) general mobilization of the people, (4) reform of political institutions, (5) resistance against-Japanese foreign policy, (6) wartime fiscal and economic policies, (7) improve people's livelihoods, (8) resistance against-Japanese educational policy, (9) eliminate traitors and pro-Japanese factions to consolidate the rear, (10) national unity in the resistance against-Japanese effort.[9]

It can be said that achieving a comprehensive national resistance against Japanese aggression was the goal of Mao Zedong and the CPC in proposing the Ten-Point Program. It was also their answer to the first question, "How to conduct a national War of Resistance Against Japanese Aggression based on KMT-CPC cooperation?" Whether this program could serve as the political foundation for the second KMT-CPC cooperation was key to understanding the contradictions between the two parties throughout the eight-year-long War of Resistance.

While there was relatively unanimous agreement within the CPC regarding the first question, opinions diverged significantly on the second question, namely, "How should the CPC and its army participate in this national war?"

After the occupation of Beiping and Tianjin, the Japanese invasion forces continued their strategic offensive in North China along the Pinghan Railway

(Beijing–Hankou Railway), Pingsui Railway (Beijing–Baotou Railway), and Jinpu Railway (Tianjin–Pukou Railway). By September, the Japanese forces in North China had increased to approximately 370,000 troops.[10] As a result, Shanxi became the main battlefield in North China after Hebei.

At that time, many leaders within the Party believed that, since it was a national united front against Japanese aggression and a cooperative effort between the KMT and the CPC, the CPC's forces should advance to the Shanxi frontline to fight a major battle alongside allied forces and demonstrate their commitment to the entire nation.

Mao Zedong also agreed to assist allied forces and fighting the Japanese to show the CPC's sincerity and to establish the Party's credibility among the people. However, he believed that this sincerity and credibility should be based on the development and strengthening of the Eighth Route Army, avoiding reckless actions that could lead to complete loss. Therefore, he repeatedly emphasized the principle of "independent and autonomous guerrilla warfare in the mountains." By "independent and autonomous," he meant that the deployment and operations of the forces should not be entirely dictated by Chiang Kai-shek. By "guerrilla warfare in the mountains," he meant that in the mountainous terrain of Shanxi, the strategy should be to develop alongside the mountains, engage in battles that could be won, and retreat from those that could not, avoiding attritional and positional warfare whenever possible.

From August 22 to 25, 1937, the Political Bureau of the Central Committee of the CPC held an expanded meeting in a primary school in Fengjia Village, on the outskirts of Luochuan City. This was an important meeting convened by the Central Committee of the CPC after the outbreak of the national War of Resistance.

At the meeting, Mao Zedong delivered a report on military issues and the relationship between the KMT and the CPC. The report stated: "Our most fundamental strategy is a protracted war, not a quick war; the result of a protracted war will be China's victory." Based on this strategy, the report outlined the strategic approach for the Red Army: "independent and autonomous guerrilla warfare in the mountains (including engaging enemy formations under favorable conditions and developing guerrilla warfare in the plains, but with an emphasis on mountainous areas)."

The principles of guerrilla warfare were to "disperse to mobilize the masses, concentrate to annihilate the enemy, engage in battles that can be won, and retreat from those that cannot." The report also outlined five basic tasks for the Red Army: "(1) Create base areas. (2) Pin down and annihilate the enemy. (3) Assist allied forces in combat (strategic support tasks). (4) Preserve and expand the Red Army. (5) Strive for leadership in the national revolutionary war."

Regarding the relationship between the KMT and the CPC, the report stated: The united front is currently maturing, but the KMT is still restricting and undermining us. We should continue to make principled concessions, maintain the independence of the Party and the Red Army, demand freedom, and adopt a policy of non-separation.[11]

Taking into account that Chiang Kai-shek had deployed ten divisions in the Shaanxi-Gansu area, Mao proposed at the meeting that after the main forces moved to the frontline, a unit should be left behind to consolidate the Shaanxi-Gansu-Ningxia base area.

The meeting decided to expand the Central Revolutionary Military Commission to eleven members, with Mao Zedong as the secretary (actually referred to as the chairman) and Zhu De and Zhou Enlai as deputy secretaries (actually referred to as vice chairmen).

In his speech, Zhou Enlai suggested, "Our region is to arrange guerrilla warfare behind enemy lines and, if necessary, concentrate forces to annihilate the enemy."[12] He called this approach "mobile guerrilla warfare," which was somewhat different from Mao Zedong's "independent and autonomous mountain guerrilla warfare." Due to the urgency of the Red Army's departure, this issue was not thoroughly discussed.

After the Luochuan Conference, the main force of the newly reorganized Eighth Route Army crossed the Yellow River from the Hancheng area in Shaanxi Province, advancing north under the cover of the Lüliang Mountains toward the Hengshan Mountain range. At this time, the main force of the Japanese Kwantung Army's Chahar Expeditionary Corps, after occupying Datong in Shanxi on September 13, was moving south along the Datong–Puzhou Railway toward the strategic town of Xinkou in northern Shanxi, aiming directly at Taiyuan. The Japanese North China Area Army's 5th

Division was also advancing south from the eastern section of the Pingsui Railway toward Zhangjiakou. Under such circumstances, if the main force of the Eighth Route Army continued to concentrate on the Hengshan area, the consequences would be dire.

In Yan'an, Mao Zedong closely monitored the movements of both the enemy and allied (KMT) forces on the Shanxi and North China battlefields. On September 17, he sent a telegram to the Eighth Route Army Headquarters and the commanders of the 115th Division, 120th Division, and 129th Division, instructing them to change the original strategic deployment. The telegram stated as follows:

> Based on the Japanese army's offensive situation in North China, the Hengshan Mountain range has become the strategic hub for the enemy to capture Hebei, Chahar, and Shanxi provinces. The enemy is deploying its main forces here, and the armies under Yan Xishan's command have lost their fighting spirit and are retreating step by step. Under these circumstances, the previous plan for the entire Eighth Route Army to create a guerrilla base in the Hengshan Mountain range is fundamentally unsuitable. If we still follow the original plan and all move to the Hengshan Mountain range in northeastern Shanxi, we will place ourselves in a passive position surrounded by the enemy. Therefore, we should change the original deployment to achieve a strategically active position, that is, to deploy on the enemy's flanks, pin down the enemy's offensive toward Taiyuan and further south, assist the Shanxi and Suiyuan Army to avoid excessive losses, truly implement independent and autonomous mountain guerrilla warfare, extensively mobilize the masses, organize volunteer armies, create base areas, support guerrilla warfare in North China, and expand our own forces. It also pointed out that at this time, the Eighth Route Army is in a supporting role, not playing a decisive role in the battle, but if deployed correctly, it can play a decisive role in supporting guerrilla warfare in North China, mainly in Shanxi.[13]

On September 19, Mao sent another telegram to Peng Dehuai, Deputy Commander-in-Chief of the Eighth Route Army, advising him: "The enemy is determined to take Taiyuan, and the current deployment should be farsighted."[14] On the 21st, he sent another telegram to Peng, earnestly stating: "Concentrated battles at this time will yield no results. The current situation is fundamentally different from the past civil war; we cannot reminisce about the past and act the same way now. Today, the Red Army does not play any decisive role in battles but has a unique strength in truly independent and autonomous mountain guerrilla warfare (not mobile warfare). To implement this strategy, we need powerful forces on the enemy's flanks, prioritize creating base areas and mobilizing the masses, and focus on dispersing our forces rather than concentrating them for battles." He also urged Peng to "think from a broad and distant perspective, deeply explain the strategy to any comrades with misunderstandings, and unify the strategic approach."[15]

Regarding the Eighth Route Army's dispersed deployment to complete the strategic spread in Shanxi as soon as possible, Mao proposed in a telegram to Zhu De and Ren Bishi (Political Director of the Eighth Route Army) on September 16: "The 115th Division is to be positioned in northeastern Shanxi, focusing on activities around Wutai, temporarily in Lingqiu and Laiyuan, and gradually moving south to the Taihang Mountain range if conditions are unfavorable. The 120th Division is to be positioned in northwestern Shanxi, focusing on activities in the Guancen and northern Lüliang Mountain ranges. The 129th Division is to be positioned in southern Shanxi, focusing on activities in the Taiyue Mountain range."[16] Shortly afterward, the Eighth Route Army Headquarters issued orders for implementation.

On September 25, the 115th Division of the Eighth Route Army achieved victory in the Battle of Pingxingguan. At the cost of over 400 casualties, they annihilated more than 1,000 troops from the North China Area Army's 5th Division, including the transport regiment and part of the 21st Brigade. This was the first significant victory for the Chinese forces in the national War of Resistance where they actively sought to annihilate Japanese troops. Subsequently, the Eighth Route Army coordinated with the Second War Zone forces of the KMT Army in the Xinkou and Taiyuan battles. After Taiyuan fell on November 8, they shifted to independently establishing resistance base areas behind enemy lines and opening up the North China battlefield.

From October 1937 to the spring and summer of 1938, the various units of the Eighth Route Army completed their strategic deployment in the Jin-Cha-Ji

(Shanxi-Chahar-Hebei), northwest Shanxi, southeast Shanxi, and southwest Shanxi regions, establishing four resistance base areas. Mao Zedong's strategic intentions were successfully realized amid the complex situation of enemy advances, ally retreats, and our progress. By the time the strategic stalemate began in October 1938, the Eighth Route Army and various resistance forces had grown from over 40,000 to more than 150,000 troops. They had engaged in over 1,500 battles and annihilated more than 50,000 Japanese and puppet troops, effectively pinning down the Japanese forces and preventing them from advancing on the main front.[17]

While closely monitoring the development of the Eighth Route Army, Mao Zedong also paid great attention to the overall situation of the resistance war. Following the defeat in the Taiyuan battle and the fall of Taiyuan, the three-month-long Battle of Shanghai ended with the city's fall on November 12. Sensing the changes in the situation, Mao Zedong drafted an outline of the report titled "The Situation and Tasks of the War of the Resistance After the Fall of Shanghai and Taiyuan" on the day Shanghai fell.

In this outline, Mao pointed out: "The current situation is transitioning from partial resistance to total resistance." After the fall of Shanghai and Taiyuan, "in North China, the regular warfare led by the KMT has ended, and guerrilla warfare led by the CPC has taken the primary role. In Jiangsu and Zhejiang, the KMT lines have been broken, and the Japanese are advancing toward Nanjing and the Yangtze River basin. The KMT's partial resistance has shown it cannot last." "Therefore, the transition from partial resistance to total resistance is possible. Striving for this transition is the urgent task of all Chinese Communists, all progressive elements of the KMT, and all Chinese people."

Discussing the situation within the Party, Mao Zedong stated: "After the Lugou Bridge Incident, the primary dangerous tendency within the Party has shifted from 'leftist' sectarianism to rightist opportunism, specifically, to capitulationism. This is mainly because the KMT has already begun resisting Japan. Our united front with the KMT and any other factions is based on implementing a specific program. Without this foundation, there is no united front, and such cooperation becomes an unprincipled action, which is a manifestation of capitulationism. Therefore, the explanation, practice, and adherence to the principle of 'independence and self-reliance within the united front' are central to leading the Resistance Against-Japanese National Revolutionary War to victory."[18]

Mao's words were soon proven true.

On November 29, 1937, Wang Ming (Chen Shaoyu), a former CPC representative to the Comintern, arrived in Yan'an, sent by the Comintern and Stalin. At the time, Mao Zedong had high hopes, personally going to Yan'an airport to greet him, calling it "joy descending from heaven."

From December 9 to 14, the Central Committee of the CPC held a Political Bureau meeting in Yan'an, commonly referred to as the "December Meeting." On the first day, Wang Ming gave a report titled "How to Continue the National Resistance and Achieve Victory." In his report, he comprehensively criticized the CPC's line since the start of the national resistance, particularly the principles of independent action within the united front and independent mountain guerrilla warfare established at the Luochuan Conference. He directly rejected Mao Zedong's proposition in his report outline "The Situation and Tasks of the Resistance War After the Fall of Shanghai and Taiyuan," which suggested that the KMT should be raised to the level of the CPC's Ten Points for National Salvation and comprehensive resistance, rather than lowering the CPC to the KMT's position of landlord-bourgeois dictatorship and partial resistance. Wang Ming accused Mao, saying, "In the united front, which party is the main force? In terms of national power and military strength, we must acknowledge the KMT as the leading force. We cannot demand that the KMT rise to the level of the CPC, nor can the CPC surrender to the KMT; neither party can surrender to the other." He emphasized, "Today's central issue is that everything is for the sake of resistance, everything goes through the national united front for resistance, and everything must obey the cause of resistance. We must use these principles to organize the masses."[19] Wang Ming claimed that his report conveyed instructions from the Comintern and Stalin, which influenced many participants, leading many to make "self-criticisms" regarding the united front work since the Luochuan Conference.

Mao Zedong, Zhang Wentian, and others resisted Wang Ming's views expressed in the report, and the meeting failed to reach a resolution on the united front and the resistance strategy. This limited the impact of Chen Shaoyu's rightist proposals on actual work. Mao Zedong later said, "At that time, I conceded on everything except the principles of protracted war, guerrilla warfare, and independent action within the united front, which I adhered to resolutely."[20]

The meeting decided to form the Yangtze River Bureau, composed of Xiang Ying, Zhou Enlai, Bo Gu, and Dong Biwu, to lead the Party's work in Wuhan; a CPC delegation, including Zhou Enlai, Wang Ming, Bo Gu, and Ye Jianying, was to negotiate with the KMT in Wuhan; Liu Shaoqi and Yang Shangkun were put in charge of the Northern Bureau, while Zhu De and Peng Dehuai were responsible for the North China Military and Political Committee to strengthen the leadership of the guerrilla warfare in North China.

The meeting also assigned responsibilities for handling various telegrams: Zhang Wentian would handle Party work, Mao Zedong would handle military issues, and Wang Ming would handle united front work. Until Wang Ming's return to Yan'an, Zhang Wentian would be in charge of the latter.

To prepare for the Party's Seventh National Congress, the meeting decided to establish a preparatory committee, with Mao Zedong as chairman and Wang Ming as secretary. The Secretariat included Mao Zedong, Wang Ming, Zhang Wentian, Chen Yun, and Kang Sheng. However, this congress was not held until 1945.

During the meeting, on December 13, Nanjing fell. Before this, the political center of the KMT and government had temporarily moved to Wuhan. Shortly after the December Meeting, Wang Ming arrived in Wuhan on December 18 and soon met with Chiang Kai-shek, who requested Wang to "assist in Wuhan."[21] Consequently, Wang Ming changed the decisions made at the December Meeting, deciding to stay in Wuhan and merging the CPC delegation with the Yangtze River Bureau, with himself as secretary and Zhou Enlai as deputy secretary.[22]

After capturing Nanjing, the Japanese invaders committed the horrific Nanjing Massacre and assembled forces to seize Xuzhou from Jinan and Nanjing, aiming to open a strategic corridor to central China.

General Li Zongren of the KMT Army's Fifth War Zone adopted the CPC's suggestions and achieved victory in the Battle of Tai'erzhuang from late

March to early April 1938, at the cost of over 7,500 casualties and missing soldiers, destroying over 10,000 Japanese troops. However, the overall Xuzhou Campaign ended in defeat for the Chinese forces. Xuzhou fell on May 19, and Kaifeng in Henan Province fell on June 6. On June 9, Chiang Kai-shek ordered the destruction of the dikes at Huayuankou near Zhengzhou, Henan, to halt the Japanese advance.

At this time, the Japanese offensive was drawing closer to Wuhan. In China, a sense of pessimism and despair, encapsulated in the "theory of national subjugation," coexisted with the blind optimism and reliance on foreign aid embodied in the "theory of quick victory." Almost a year into the national resistance war, questions arose about the effectiveness of current strategies and how to secure victory in a protracted war. These issues became urgent matters requiring answers.

As the War of Resistance Against Japanese Aggression, Mao Zedong's understanding of the war deepened, ultimately leading to the creation of the seminal document, "On Protracted War." This work, delivered as a speech at the Yan'an Research Society of the Resistance Against-Japanese War from May 26 to June 3, 1938, provided guiding principles for the national resistance.

Prior to this, on May 10, during a report on the Sino-Japanese war situation at a Standing Committee of the Political Bureau meeting, Mao discussed his observations of the current situation: "Now, both Chiang Kai-shek and our estimates consider the War of Resistance as a protracted war. Recently, two editorials in *Ta Kung Pao* changed their stance, suggesting that the war in southern Shandong is a quasi-decisive battle,[23] denying that the Sino-Japanese war is a protracted war. There have been two opinions within our estimates of the Sino-Japanese war. I have always estimated it as a protracted war because China is a large country, and Japan cannot fully conquer China, but China is also weak and needs a protracted war to achieve victory."[24]

The extraordinary aspect of "On Protracted War" is not merely the introduction of the concept of a "protracted war." In fact, the term "protracted war" was already in use before the national resistance broke out. Its significance lies in scientifically predicting the three stages the Chinese War of Resistance would go through and offering unique insights into specific strategies.

Mao Zedong pointed out: "Since the Sino-Japanese war is a protracted war, and the final victory will belong to China, it is reasonable to assume that this protracted war will manifest in three stages. The first stage is the period of the enemy's strategic offensive and our strategic defensive. The second stage is the period of enemy strategic consolidation and our preparation for a counteroffensive. The third stage is our strategic counteroffensive and the enemy's strategic retreat. The specific conditions of these three stages cannot be predicted, but some major trends in the war can be identified under the current conditions." Mao referred to the second stage as the "strategic stalemate stage."[25]

When Mao delivered this speech, the Battle of Wuhan had not yet begun, and there were still five months until the strategic stalemate phase began. The stages he predicted were later confirmed by the entire course of the War of Resistance. At that time, only Mao Zedong could make such a strategic forecast.

Moreover, "On Protracted War" discusses the following issues in detail: the intertwined nature of the war; fighting for lasting peace; the role of initiative in war; war and politics; political mobilization for resistance; the purpose of war; offense within the defense, swift decisions within protracted conflict, and external lines within internal lines; initiative, flexibility, and planning; mobile warfare, guerrilla warfare, positional warfare; attrition warfare, annihilation warfare; the possibility of exploiting enemy weaknesses; the issue of decisive battles in the War of Resistance; and the principle that soldiers and civilians are the foundation of victory. Clearly, these topics encompass almost all the existing and potential issues encountered throughout the entire process of the War of Resistance. Only Mao Zedong could systematically discuss all these issues in a predictive manner while the first stage of the War of Resistance was still unfolding.

"On Protracted War" also showcases Mao Zedong's distinctiveness as both a politician and a military strategist, compared to ordinary military leaders.

A particular emphasis on the impact of thought and psychology on warfare is a hallmark of Mao's strategy for protracted war. He frankly acknowledged: "The strengths of the Japanese army lie not only in their weapons but also in the education of their officers and soldiers—their organization, their confidence formed from never having been defeated, their belief in the emperor and ghosts, their arrogance and self-esteem, and their disdain for Chinese people. These characteristics stem from years of autocratic education by the Japanese militarists and Japan's national customs. The main reason why our army has inflicted heavy casualties on them but captured few prisoners is this. This aspect was underestimated by many in the past. Breaking this will take a long process." How should this be supplemented with ideological publicity and psychological warfare? He pointed out: "The main method of breaking this is political persuasion. For Japanese soldiers, it is not to insult their self-esteem but to understand and guide it, using lenient treatment of prisoners to help them understand the anti-people aggression of the Japanese rulers. On the other hand, we must demonstrate the indomitable spirit and tenacious fighting power of the Chinese army and people before them, which means delivering annihilating blows." He particularly emphasized: "In the world, only cats and cats make friends, not cats and mice."

Another characteristic of Mao Zedong's strategy of protracted warfare was the emphasis on the immense role of the combination of soldiers and civilians in the war. He pointed out, "The financial resources for resisting Japan are very difficult to come by. If the masses are mobilized, then finance is not a problem. How can a country with such vast land and numerous people suffer from financial difficulties? The army must blend with the masses, making the army appear as their own in the eyes of the people. This army will be invincible in the world; a few Japanese imperialists are not enough to contend with. The deepest roots of the power of war lie among the masses. The main reason why Japan dares to bully us is the unorganized state of the Chinese people. Overcoming this flaw will put the Japanese invaders before our hundreds of millions of people standing up, making them like a wild bull charging into a ring of fire. At our command, it will be scared, and this bull will surely be burned to death."

Another feature of this strategy was the particular emphasis on the role of initiative. This was the winning formula for the weak to defeat the strong. Mao Zedong stated, "Those who guide war cannot seek victory beyond the limits permitted by objective conditions. However, they can and must strive to achieve victory within those limits. The stage on which war commanders operate must be built within the bounds of objective conditions, but relying on this stage, they can direct many vivid, grand, and heroic dramas." He metaphorically described this initiative as "the art of swimming in the vast sea of war."[26]

Alongside "On Protracted War," its companion piece "The Strategic Problems of Resistance Against Japanese Guerrilla Warfare" was also published. This essay appeared in the 40th issue of the *Liberation* magazine on May 30.

In the early stages of the War of Resistance Against Japanese Aggression, the Red Army, while being reorganized into the Eighth Route Army advancing to the Shanxi front, was also undergoing a difficult strategic transition in terms of combat style. This transition involved moving from large-scale mobile warfare during the ten years of civil war to primarily guerrilla warfare behind enemy lines. During this process, many inside and outside the CPC underestimated the strategic role of guerrilla warfare, placing their hopes for victory on conventional warfare, especially the operations of the KMT Army. To address this issue, Mao Zedong wrote this essay.

The simultaneous publication of "The Strategic Problems of Resistance Against Japanese Guerrilla Warfare" and "On Protracted War" was not coincidental. This is because, "Throughout the entire War of Resistance, China will not primarily engage in positional warfare; the main and important forms will be mobile warfare and guerrilla warfare."[27] In other words, to effectively conduct protracted warfare, it was necessary to simultaneously address a series of issues related to maintaining resistance against Japanese guerrilla warfare.

Mao Zedong pointed out, "Such extensive and protracted guerrilla warfare is quite a novel occurrence in the entire history of human warfare." Generally, guerrilla warfare is a tactical matter. Why would it rise to the strategic level? This is determined by the peculiarities of the Sino-Japanese War, with the unique characteristics of both sides.

> The enemy occupies a vast area in our large country, but their country is small, and their forces are insufficient, leaving many empty areas in the occupied zones. Therefore, resistance against Japanese guerrilla warfare is mainly

not a matter of supporting regular army operations on the inner lines but of fighting independently on the outer lines. Furthermore, due to China's progress, meaning the existence of a strong army and a broad populace led by the Communist Party, resistance against Japanese guerrilla warfare is not small-scale but large-scale. Thus, concepts such as strategic defense and strategic offense come into play. The protracted and consequently brutal nature of the war dictates that guerrilla warfare must undertake many extraordinary tasks. Hence, issues like the creation of bases and the development of mobile warfare arise. Therefore, Chinese resistance against Japanese guerrilla warfare moves from the tactical realm to knocking on the strategic door, demanding that guerrilla warfare be examined from a strategic perspective.

Mao Zedong based all his arguments on a fundamental principle: "The principle of preserving oneself and destroying the enemy is the foundation of all military principles." He emphasized that "all technical, tactical, operational, and strategic principles are conditions for executing this basic principle." On this foundation, Mao Zedong discussed six specific strategic issues of resistance against Japanese guerrilla warfare in separate chapters. These six issues are "(1) actively, flexibly, and systematically executing offensive battles within defensive warfare, swift battles within protracted warfare, and external operations within internal operations; (2) coordinating with regular warfare; (3) establishing bases; (4) strategic defense and strategic offense; (5) developing into mobile warfare; and (6) proper command relationships. These six items form the comprehensive strategic guidelines for resistance against Japanese guerrilla warfare, necessary for preserving and developing oneself, annihilating and expelling the enemy, coordinating with regular warfare, and ultimately achieving victory."

Notably, when Mao Zedong talked about the inevitable development of guerrilla warfare into mobile warfare, and the gradual transformation of guerrilla units into regular troops capable of executing mobile warfare, he stressed: "The development of guerrilla warfare into mobile warfare does not mean the abolition of guerrilla warfare; rather, within the broadly developed guerrilla warfare, a main force capable of conducting mobile warfare gradually forms. Surrounding this main force, there should still be extensive guerrilla units and guerrilla warfare. These extensive guerrilla units provide a rich support system for this main force and are the continuous source of expansion for this main force."[28]

Here, Mao Zedong effectively outlined the formation of the "guerrilla units + local armed forces + regular army" model of people's armed forces within the context of resistance against Japanese guerrilla warfare. This model not only played a significant role in the War of Resistance Against Japanese Aggression but also had a decisive impact during the subsequent War of Liberation. It can be said that by mastering the laws of guerrilla warfare, Mao Zedong not only opened the door to victory in the Chinese People's War of Resistance Against Japanese Aggression but also found the key to winning the future Chinese People's War of Liberation.

CHAPTER 7

Independent and Autonomous Guerrilla Warfare Behind Enemy Lines

---

Communists must not compete for personal military power (definitely do not compete, never emulate Zhang Guotao), but must strive for the Party's military power and the people's military power. Now, during the total resistance against Japanese aggression by the whole nation, we must also strive for the nation's military power. If we suffer from childish disorders regarding military power, we will certainly gain nothing. Japanese imperialist oppression and the nationwide War of Resistance have pushed the laboring people onto the stage of war. Communists should become the most conscious leaders in this war.

MAO ZEDONG,
"Problems of War and Strategy" (November 6, 1938)

On June 15, 1938, Emperor Hirohito of Japan presided over an imperial conference, formally deciding to attack Wuhan. For this, the Japanese invasion army deployed 250,000 troops, 120 ships, and 300 aircraft.[1] The Chinese army, under Chiang Kai-shek's command, concentrated its efforts on the defense of Wuhan. The Central Committee of the CPC also tasked Zhou Enlai, Dong Biwu, and Ye Jianying with mobilizing and organizing people from all walks of life to support the defense of Wuhan. The Battle of Wuhan lasted four-and-a-half months, inflicting nearly 40,000 casualties on the Japanese, but ultimately, on October 24, the order to abandon Wuhan was given. The KMT Government and military departments relocated to the provisional capital of Chongqing. On October 21, Guangzhou fell.

At this point, total resistance against Japanese aggression by the whole nation entered its most arduous and protracted phase—the strategic stalemate stage.

To prepare thoroughly for this stage, the Expanded Sixth Plenary Session of the Sixth Central Committee of the CPC was held at the Qiaoergou Hall in Yan'an from September 29 to November 6, 1938.

Before the plenary session, from September 14 to 27, a Political Bureau of the Central Committee meeting was held. This meeting was particularly significant for Mao Zedong.

Six months earlier, to enable the Comintern to better understand the situation in China, the Political Bureau of the Central Committee decided at a meeting from February 27 to March 1 to send Ren Bishi to Moscow to report to the Comintern. On April 14 and May 17, the Executive Committee of the Comintern held meetings to hear Ren Bishi's report and, on June 11, passed the "Resolution on the Report of the CPC Representative" and the "Decision of the Executive Committee of the Comintern." Subsequently, Ren Bishi replaced Wang Jiaxiang as the CPC's representative to the Comintern. The task of conveying the latest directives from the Comintern to the CPC fell to Wang Jiaxiang. In early July, the General Secretary of the Executive Committee of the Comintern, Georgi Dimitrov, had a conversation with Wang Jiaxiang and Ren Bishi, explicitly expressing support for Mao Zedong.

At the Political Bureau of the Central Committee meeting on September 14, Wang Jiaxiang conveyed the Comintern's directives and Dimitrov's opinions, emphasizing two key points: First, "The Comintern believes that the CPC's political line is correct, and the CPC has truly applied Marxism-Leninism under complex and difficult conditions." Second, "In the leadership organs, the leadership should be resolved under Mao Zedong, and there should be a close atmosphere of unity among the leaders." Wang Jiaxiang also relayed that "in China, the Chinese united front against Japanese aggression is the key to the Chinese people's resistance, and the unity of the CPC is the key to the united front. The victory of the united front relies on the unity within the Party and among the leaders. This was Dimitrov's parting advice."

Wang Jiaxiang also conveyed the Comintern's opinion on the upcoming Seventh National Congress of the CPC: "The Comintern believes that the Seventh National Congress of the CPC should focus on practical issues, primarily the many practical issues in the War of Resistance and should not spend much time debating the issues of the past decade of civil war. The Comintern believes that summarizing the experiences of the decade-long civil war should be done with special caution."[2]

The Comintern's and Dimitrov's directives dispelled the confusion and doubts brought about within the Party by Wang Ming's (Chen Shaoyu's) return and his criticisms of Mao Zedong's independent and autonomous against Japanese aggression line since the December Meeting. This unified the understanding among the Party's senior leaders, laying the political groundwork for the successful holding of the Expanded Sixth Plenary Session of the Sixth Central Committee of the CPC.

On September 24, Mao Zedong made a lengthy speech at the Political Bureau of the Central Committee meeting. He stated that the Comintern's directives were the guarantee of the meeting's success and would also serve as the guiding principles for the Sixth Plenary Session of the Sixth Central Committee and the Seventh National Congress of the CPC, emphasizing the importance of unity within the Party.

On the last day of the meeting, September 27, Mao Zedong spoke again, stating that the Political Bureau of the Central Committee meeting had achieved great success, thus ensuring the success of the Sixth Plenary Session of the Sixth Central Committee. He suggested adopting a set of Central Committee work rules during the plenary session. The Political Bureau of the Central Committee meeting approved the agenda for the expanded Sixth Plenary Session and decided that Mao Zedong would deliver the political report on behalf of the Central Committee.

The Expanded Sixth Plenary Session of the Sixth Central Committee of the CPC opened on September 29. Attendees included 17 Central Committee members and alternate members, as well as 38 heads of various departments and bases. The plenary session lasted nearly 40 days, concluding on November 6.

At the plenary session, Zhang Wentian delivered the opening speech, and Wang Jiaxiang conveyed the directives from the Comintern and Dimitrov. In the following days, Zhang Wentian reported on the "Chinese United Front Against Japanese Aggression and Party Organization Issues," Zhou Enlai presented the "Report on United Front Work by the CPC Delegation," Wang Ming gave the "Report on Communist Members in the National Political Council," Zhu De presented the "Eighth Route Army Work Report," Xiang Ying reported on the "New Fourth Army Work," Chen Yun discussed "Youth Work," Liu Shaoqi gave the "Party Rules and Regulations Report," and He Long, Yang Shangkun, Guan Xiangying, Deng Xiaoping, Peng Zhen, and Luo Ronghuan presented reports on their respective regional work. Lin Boqu and Wu Yuzhang also spoke at the plenary session.

On the afternoons and evenings of October 12, 13, and 14, Mao Zedong, representing the Political Bureau of the Central Committee, delivered a political report titled "The New Stage of Development in the National War of Resistance Against Japanese Aggression and the Chinese United Front Against Japanese Aggression." On the afternoons of November 5 and 6, he delivered consecutive concluding reports.

In his political report, Mao Zedong proposed that the strategic stalemate was approaching, marking a new stage in the development of the Against Japanese Aggression National War and the Chinese United Front Against Japanese Aggression. He emphasized that the future of China, whether it would become a colony or achieve liberation, depended not on the loss of major cities and transportation lines in the first stage but on the national effort in the second stage. He predicted that "in the new stage, while the main force will be engaged in frontline defense, guerrilla warfare behind enemy lines will temporarily become the primary form of combat. However, during the enemy's strategic stalemate, guerrilla warfare will develop in a new direction."

What is this new direction for guerrilla warfare? Mao identified two scenarios. The first scenario is that guerrilla warfare can still develop widely in vast areas. The second scenario is that in certain important strategic areas, such as North China and the lower Yangtze River, the enemy will launch brutal attacks, making it difficult to maintain large units in the plains, with mountainous areas becoming the main bases. Therefore, Mao proposed: "To prepare for the new stage, guerrilla warfare behind enemy lines should be broadly divided into two types of areas. In areas where guerrilla warfare has fully developed, such as North China, the main focus should be on consolidating the established bases to withstand the enemy's brutal attacks and maintain the bases. In areas where guerrilla warfare has not fully developed or is just beginning, such as Central China, the main focus should be on rapidly developing guerrilla warfare to avoid difficulties when the enemy shifts its forces."[3]

Mao Zedong's judgments were all later confirmed by the developments on the ground. The measures he proposed gave the Eighth Route Army and the New Fourth Army a head start during the strategic stalemate phase.

Based on Mao Zedong's political report, the plenary session adopted the political resolution "On the New Stage of Development in the National Self-Defense War Against Japanese Aggression and the Chinese United Front Against Japanese Aggression." The plenary session approved the line of the Political Bureau of the Central Committee, represented by Mao Zedong, and decided to focus the Party's main work on the war zones and enemy-occupied areas. It also clarified the policy of "consolidating North China and developing Central and South China" to expand guerrilla warfare behind enemy lines. The plenary session also decided to abolish the Yangtze Bureau and establish the Central China Bureau and the Southern Bureau. Wang Ming remained in Yan'an from then on.

As the war entered the strategic stalemate phase, Japan adjusted its strategy, reducing its forces on the front lines, focusing on consolidating occupied areas, establishing the puppet regime of Wang Jingwei, and intensifying political maneuvers to induce the KMT Government to surrender.

Chiang Kai-shek's KMT Government also changed its approach. Militarily, it divided its forces into three parts: one-third remained on the front lines, one-third engaged in guerrilla warfare behind enemy lines, and one-third underwent training. Politically, it adopted the policy of "absorbing, preventing, and limiting the Communists," which later led to a passive stance against Japan and active opposition to the Communists.

These changes, on the one hand, proved the correctness of the CPC's judgment and deployment at the Sixth Plenary Session of the Sixth Central Committee. On the other hand, they also complicated the situation for the guerrilla warfare led by the CPC behind enemy lines.

To achieve the strategic goal of "consolidating North China," the main forces of the Eighth Route Army's 120th Division moved from northwest Shanxi to the resistance base area in central Hebei, the main forces of the 129th Division moved from the Taihang Mountains to the resistance base area in southern Hebei, and the main forces of the 115th Division opened up the resistance base area in southern Shandong. Subsequently, from 1939 to 1940, the resistance base areas in North China successfully repelled repeated "mopping-up" operations by Japanese and puppet troops, achieving a significant victory by killing Major General Abe Norihide, the "Flower of the Japanese Army," and rapidly developing themselves.

The New Fourth Army, tasked with the strategy of "developing Central China," opened up resistance base areas in eastern Anhui, Jiangsu-Anhui, and the Henan-Hubei border from November 1938 to 1940. Together with the Eighth Route Army, they also opened up the resistance base area in northern Jiangsu.

In South China, resistance guerrilla bases were established in Dongjiang and Hainan Island.

In 1940, the domestic political situation became increasingly complex. Starting in the winter of 1939, the KMT Army initiated the first anti-Communist campaign. This drew great attention from Mao Zedong. At the Political Bureau of the Central Committee of the CPC meeting on August 16, he suggested that Japan might attempt to cut off China's southwest transportation routes to force a settlement and that without foreign aid, Chiang Kai-shek could not continue the war. Thus, there was a possibility of peace negotiations and compromise in China's War of Resistance. He stressed the need for mental preparation for significant international and domestic changes, advocating for cautious policymaking.[4]

To counter the wavering and compromising tendencies within the KMT ranks and break Japan's "cage policy" in North China, the Eighth Route Army launched a large-scale offensive against Japanese and puppet troops on August 20. This offensive targeted the main transportation lines in North China.

Approximately 200,000 Japanese troops and 150,000 puppet troops were stationed in the area.[5] These forces, relying on several crisscrossing transportation lines, continually expanded their control over the resistance base areas, severely limiting the bases' size and supply lines. "However, as the enemy penetrated our bases and built fortifications, their forces became dispersed, creating vulnerabilities in the occupied rear areas. The main transportation lines became thinly defended, presenting us with an opportunity."[6]

The offensive lasted a long time, from August 20, 1940, to January 24, 1941. The number of participating troops quickly grew from 22 regiments to 105 regiments (hence the name "Hundred-Regiment Campaign"), involving over 200,000 soldiers. The results were significant: by December 5, 1940, the Eighth Route Army had fought 1,824 battles, at the cost of over 17,000 casualties, inflicting 20,645 casualties on the Japanese and 5,155 on the puppet troops.[7]

Mao Zedong was very pleased with the results of the Hundred-Regiment Campaign. According to Peng Dehuai, the Deputy Commander of the Eighth Route Army, who directed the battle on the front lines, Mao immediately sent him a telegram saying, "The Hundred-Regiment Campaign is truly exciting. Can we organize one or two more such battles?"[8]

At the same time, Mao had certain concerns. On September 11, during a Political Bureau of the Central Committee meeting, he remarked that the Hundred-Regiment Campaign should not be described as a large-scale offensive but rather as a guerrilla counteroffensive.[9] On September 23, in his report "Current Situation and Border Area Issues" delivered at Yangjialing in Yan'an, he referred to the ongoing Hundred-Regiment Campaign as a larger-scale counteroffensive during the enemy's stalemate phase. He described it as "one" such offensive, indicating that there would be more in the future, and "larger-scale" compared to previous large-scale counteroffensives. He emphasized that it was a "counteroffensive against the enemy's encirclement and suppression," meaning it was not a strategic counteroffensive. He also stated that all regions should continue the Hundred-Regiment Campaign while preparing for potential attacks from reactionary elements.[10] These concerns were understandable given the extremely complex and sensitive domestic and international environment at the time.

The ability of the Eighth Route Army to mobilize over 200,000 regular troops for concentrated sabotage operations in a short period greatly shocked the Japanese high command. They hurriedly redeployed forces from the front lines to intensify their "mopping-up" operations against the resistance base areas and the Eighth Route Army in North China. After the outbreak of the Pacific War in December 1941, Japan's total military strength had expanded to 2.4 million soldiers, with 1.3 million of them deployed in China to consolidate strategic rear areas and support their southern expansion strategy. A significant portion of these forces was concentrated on the backstage battlefield, where the Eighth Route Army and the New Fourth Army were operating. From 1941 to 1942, the backstage battlefield led by the CPC endured their most difficult period.

During this time, the Eighth Route Army, the New Fourth Army, and various resistance armed forces grew from fewer than 60,000 troops to 500,000 in just over two years. The backstage battlefield engaged and contained 58% to 62% of the invading Japanese forces and almost all of the puppet troops, causing great concern for Chiang Kai-shek. After the first anti-Communist campaign targeting the Eighth Route Army in North China was repelled, Chiang's group chose the relatively weaker Central China region as the breakthrough point for the second anti-Communist campaign.

Chiang first attempted diplomatic measures, using negotiations and orders to force the New Fourth Army and other resistance forces to withdraw from the south of the Yellow River to the north of the Yellow River. When this failed, he orchestrated a military operation. On January 6, 1941, in the Maolin area of southern Anhui, the KMT Army, which had been lying in ambush, launched an attack on the New Fourth Army headquarters and its 9,000 troops while they were moving north. The New Fourth Army's Commander, Ye Ting, was detained, and Deputy Commander Xiang Ying was killed while breaking through the encirclement. This event, known as the "Southern Anhui Incident," shocked both China and the world. On January 17, Chiang Kai-shek declared the New Fourth Army a "rebel army," pushing the anti-Communist campaign to its peak.

Upon hearing the news, Mao Zedong assessed that Chiang Kai-shek's declaration of the New Fourth Army as "rebels" and his decision to put Ye Ting on trial indicated a determination to break with the CPC. Mao decided to take necessary steps politically, militarily, and organizationally. Politically, the plan was to fully expose Chiang's conspiracy without directly naming him while maintaining a defensive stance and mobilizing the masses under the slogan "Persist in Resisting Japan and Oppose Civil War." Militarily, the strategy was to adopt a defensive posture initially. Organizationally, preparations were made to withdraw the offices.

On January 20, the Central Military Commission of the CPC issued an order drafted by Mao Zedong, appointing Chen Yi as acting commander of the New Fourth Army, Zhang Yunyi as deputy commander, Liu Shaoqi as political commissar, Lai Chuanzhu as chief of staff, and Deng Zihui as director of the Political Department. On January 25, the New Fourth Army headquarters was reestablished in Yancheng, northern Jiangsu. Subsequently, the entire army was reorganized into seven divisions and seven independent brigades, totaling over 90,000 troops, continuing to resist the enemy behind the lines both north and south of the Yangtze River.

On January 20, the Central Military Commission of the CPC, drafted by Mao Zedong, issued a statement to Xinhua News Agency regarding the Southern Anhui Incident. The statement pointed out, "The order issued on January 17 carries serious political implications. The fact that the issuer dared to publicly announce this counter-revolutionary order, defying world opinion, indicates a determination for a complete rupture and total surrender." The statement warned the KMT authorities, "There are still over 90,000 troops of the New Fourth Army in central China and southern Jiangsu, who, despite being attacked by both Japanese invaders and anti-Communist forces, will undoubtedly struggle and remain loyal to the nation to the end. At the same time, their brother forces in the Eighth Route Army will not sit idly by while they are attacked but will take appropriate steps to provide necessary support. This is something we can straightforwardly tell them."

The statement also proposed 12 solutions to the Southern Anhui Incident, including "the cancelation of the reactionary order of January 17," "the release of Ye Ting to continue serving as the commander of the New Fourth

Army," and "the abolition of one-party dictatorship and the implementation of democratic politics."[11]

These solutions were righteous and reasonable, and upon being proposed, they immediately gained support from progressive figures within the KMT, respected members of society, and democratic activists. On January 14, KMT progressives Soong Ching-ling, He Xiangning, Liu Yazi, and Peng Zemin issued a declaration to Chiang Kai-shek and the KMT Central Committee, condemning the party for betraying Sun Yat-sen's teachings and causing fear and concern among the Chinese people and their allies by treating the "extermination of the Communists as an imminent issue."[12] On January 25, the Soviet Union's Ambassador to China, Nikolai Panyushkin, met with Chiang Kai-shek, pointing out that civil war in China would lead to destruction. In February, US President Franklin D. Roosevelt's representative, Lauchlin Currie, visiting China, also informed Chiang Kai-shek that the US could not provide substantial aid to China until the KMT-CPC dispute was resolved. On March 1, the second session of the National Political Council opened in Chongqing, which the CPC representatives unanimously boycotted.

At this time, the Japanese army launched the Southern Henan Campaign in late January 1941, surrounding 150,000 KMT troops east of the Pinghan Railway. This move pushed the already precarious Chiang Kai-shek into a dead end.

Mao Zedong initially judged after the Southern Anhui Incident that "there might be a transitional period from the initial rupture to a complete rupture, the duration of which depends on various domestic and international conditions. Our policy is not to hasten this process, but we must be prepared for its acceleration." However, following the Japanese Southern Henan Campaign, Mao revised his assessment: "This Henan campaign, being the largest since the Yichang campaign, will deal a significant political blow to Chiang Kai-shek regardless of its military outcome, as he has instigated the Southern Anhui Incident, creating a deep rift between the KMT and the CPC, thus allowing the enemy to exploit the situation." He concluded that "the anti-Communist surge may decline, and the Sino-Japanese conflict remains the primary issue."[13]

On March 6, 1941, in a speech at the sixth session of the second meeting of the National Political Council, Chiang Kai-shek, while continuing to attack the CPC, also declared, "There will be no more 'extermination of the Communists' military operations in the future. This is something I can responsibly guarantee to this assembly."[14]

The astute Mao Zedong discerned the underlying message in Chiang Kai-shek's speech. In an internal directive on March 18, he said, "Chiang Kai-shek's anti-Communist speech on March 6 and the anti-Communist resolutions of the National Political Council are like the final battle before the withdrawal in this anti-Communist surge. The situation may temporarily move toward some degree of relaxation." He concluded that "this struggle has highlighted the decline of the KMT's position and the rise of the CPC's position, indicating a shift in the balance of power between the KMT and the CPC. This situation forces Chiang Kai-shek to reconsider his position and attitude."[15]

From this confrontation with Chiang Kai-shek, Mao Zedong drew two conclusions: First, "As long as the contradiction between China and Japan remains acute, even if the entire big landlord class and big bourgeoisie turn traitor and surrender, they can never bring about another 1927 situation, with a repetition of the April 12 and the May 21 Incidents of that year." Second, "Fighting against the KMT's anti-Communist policies requires a comprehensive set of tactics; we must not be careless. Any revolutionary force of the people, if it wants to avoid being annihilated by Chiang Kai-shek and force him to recognize its existence, has no other path but to fight resolutely against his counter-revolutionary policies. However, the struggle must be reasonable, advantageous, and measured; missing any one of these elements will lead to losses."[16]

Although the KMT military's attacks and conflicts were repelled, their economic blockade against the resistance base areas never ceased. Combined with frequent Japanese "mopping-up" operations in North China and Central China, the Eighth Route Army and the New Fourth Army faced significant challenges. Frequent battles and financial difficulties prevented timely rest and replenishment of the troops. By 1942, the Eighth Route Army and the

New Fourth Army had shrunk from 500,000 to over 400,000. The total population of the resistance base areas decreased from 100 million to less than 50 million, and the areas themselves were greatly reduced. Even in the Shaanxi-Gansu-Ningxia Border Region, conditions were very harsh. As Mao Zedong described, "We almost had no clothes to wear, no oil to eat, no paper, no vegetables, soldiers had no shoes or socks, and staff had no bedding in the winter. The KMT tried to starve us by stopping funding and imposing an economic blockade. Our difficulties were indeed enormous."[17]

Globally, 1941 was a pivotal year, facing the severe challenge of fascist forces. On June 22, Germany launched a blitzkrieg against the Soviet Union, initiating the full-scale Soviet-German War. On December 8, Japan attacked the US Navy base at Pearl Harbor, triggering the Pacific War. In this context, on December 28, Mao Zedong drafted instructions for the Central Committee and the Central Military Commission regarding the strategic policy following the outbreak of the Pacific War. The instructions stated as follows:

> In 1941, our base areas suffered significant damage. We should take advantage of the enemy being preoccupied with the Pacific and adopting a strategic defensive posture toward China in 1942 to concentrate on recovering our strength. Resolutely implement the Central Committee's December 13 directive: streamline the army and administration, develop the economy, expand mass movements, increase work in enemy-occupied areas, intensify political offensives against the enemy and traitors, and systematically train cadres. In summary, next year's central task is to accumulate strength, recover vitality, consolidate internally, and strengthen the Party, government, military, and civilian sectors. The primary approach to the enemy and traitors should be political offensives, supplemented by guerrilla warfare. In dealing with the KMT, the primary approach should be to foster unity, while also guarding against its anti-Communist actions.[18]

Subsequent developments proved that this policy of recuperation and consolidation during the War of Resistance Against Japanese Aggression was crucial for the resistance base areas to endure the most difficult period.

Among the various policies adopted at the time, the one Mao Zedong was most concerned with was the Production Campaign. As early as January 2, 1939, Mao had mentioned in a foreword for the *Eighth Route Army Military and Political Magazine*: "One of the most difficult issues during the protracted War of Resistance will be the financial and economic problem. This is a nationwide difficulty as well as a challenge for the Eighth Route Army, and it should be recognized with a high level of importance."[19] In 1942, Mao inscribed "Do it yourself" and "Abundant clothes and food," issuing a mobilization order to the entire Party and all resistance forces to launch the Production Campaign.

The rise of the Production Campaign was also connected to a grievance among the people in Yan'an at the time. Mao recalled: "In 1941, the border region asked the people to deliver 200,000 *dan* (approximately 1.2 million liters) of public grain and to transport salt, which was a heavy burden, causing them to complain. During a meeting of the border region government that year, a thunderstorm caused a collapse that killed County Magistrate Li.[20] Some people said, 'Why didn't the thunder god strike Mao Zedong dead?' After investigating, I found the only reason was the excessive grain levy, which made some people unhappy. Indeed, the public grain levy was too much at that time."[21]

Mao Zedong highly valued the role of the Production Campaign, placing it on par with the Rectification Movement. He said, "Without these two links of rectification and production, the revolutionary wheels cannot move forward, and the Party cannot advance!"[22]

Mao personally took the lead by cultivating a plot of wasteland below his cave dwelling, planting vegetables. Zhu De, Liu Shaoqi, Zhou Enlai, Ren Bishi, and others also participated in the movement.

Mao also adopted Zhu De's suggestion, sending Wang Zhen's 359th Brigade of the Eighth Route Army to Nanniwan to open up land for production, pioneering the practice of military farming among the Eighth Route Army.

From 1942 to 1944, more than two million *mu* (approximately 1.33 million acres) of wasteland were cultivated in the Shaanxi-Gansu-Ningxia Border Region. By 1945, most farmers in the region achieved "three years of farming yields one year's surplus," meaning that after three years of farming, the grain harvested could provide a surplus for one year beyond personal consumption. Starting in 1943, the Party and government organs in the resistance base areas generally managed to be self-sufficient in food and vegetables for two to six months each year. The Production Campaign alleviated the burdens on farmers, improved the relations between the military and the people, and greatly enhanced the ability of various resistance base areas to support a protracted war.

The year 1943 was a year of significant turning points in the global war against fascism. The Allied forces, including the Soviet Union, the United States, and the United Kingdom, achieved major victories in the Battle of Stalingrad, the Guadalcanal Campaign, and the North African Campaign, leading to Italy's surrender. In late November of that year, the Cairo Conference was held in the Egyptian capital, attended by the leaders of the United States, the United Kingdom, and China. The conference resulted in the signing of the Cairo Declaration. The Cairo Declaration stated: "The Three Great Allies are fighting this war to restrain and punish the aggression of Japan. They covet no gain for themselves and have no thought of territorial expansion. It is their purpose that Japan shall be stripped of all the islands in the Pacific which she has seized or occupied since the beginning of World War I in 1914, and that all the territories Japan has stolen from the Chinese, such as Manchuria, Formosa, and the Pescadores, shall be restored to the Republic of China. Japan will also be expelled from all other territories which she has taken by violence and greed."[23]

Against this backdrop, the resistance base areas in North China began to recover and develop from 1943 onwards, and the resistance base areas in other regions also passed through their most difficult periods. In 1944, the Japanese invading forces withdrew large numbers of troops from the occupied areas in China to conduct operations aimed at opening up continental communication lines and to support the Pacific theater. As a result, the number of Japanese troops in the Chinese hinterland significantly decreased. From the spring to the winter of that year, the military and civilian populations of the resistance base areas in North China, Central China, and South China seized the opportunity to launch widespread local counterattacks against the Japanese troops and its puppet forces.

In stark contrast to the localized counterattacks by the resistance military and civilians in the occupied territories, the KMT forces on the frontline suffered a massive defeat in April 1944. This collapse occurred when the Japanese invasion forces launched an offensive to open the north-south transportation lines in China. Over eight months, the KMT lost 146 cities and over 200,000 square kilometers of territory along the transportation lines in Henan, Hunan, and Guizhou provinces. In response to this situation, Mao Zedong made a decisive move in November 1944 by dispatching the main force of the 359th Brigade of the 120th Division of the Eighth Route Army, consisting of over 4,000 troops, to form the Southward Detachment. This unit advanced into the occupied territories of Henan, Hubei, Hunan, and Guangdong provinces, establishing new resistance bases behind enemy lines.

The KMT's significant defeats on the frontline starkly contrasted with the continuous victories in the global war against fascism, leading to growing disappointment with the KMT Government. Democratic activist Huang Yanpei convened a symposium on democratic constitutional issues in Chongqing, presenting the KMT Government with ten demands, including respecting people's freedoms and reforming politics. Zhang Lan and others initiated the establishment of the Democratic Constitutional Promotion Association in Chengdu. Progressive KMT members such as Li Jishen and Liu Yazi also formed the Guilin Cultural Resistance Work Association in Guangxi, advocating for "mobilizing the masses, resolute resistance, and eradicating defeatism."

In response to the rising democratic movement in the rear areas, Mao Zedong and the Central Committee of the CPC decided to reopen negotiations with the KMT Government. To further inform the world of the CPC's positions and proposals, Mao Zedong received a group of Chinese and foreign journalists on June 12 who had braved the KMT's obstructions to visit Yan'an. He answered their questions in detail.

According to Israel Epstein, an American journalist from *Time* magazine who was present, "Mao left us with another profound impression in Yan'an:

his composure and ease." "We, the foreign journalists from Chongqing, couldn't help but notice the stark contrast between Mao and Chiang Kai-shek in terms of demeanor. Chiang was rigid, reserved, nervous, and monotonous, seemingly always under tension."[24]

On July 22, Colonel David D. Barrett, head of the US Army Observation Group, led the first batch of members to Yan'an, where they received a warm welcome from the Central Committee of the CPC. Mao Zedong also rewrote the editorial for the *Liberation Daily*, titled "Welcome to Our American Friends of the Observation Group!" which was published on August 15. The editorial stated: "The group of Chinese and foreign journalists and the US Army Observation Group have both broken through the KMT's blockade line and arrived in Yan'an. This concerns the 450 million Chinese people's resistance against the Japanese invaders and the liberation of China. It concerns the issue of which of the two proposals and two lines is right or wrong. It concerns the allied countries' efforts to defeat a common enemy and establish lasting peace." "Regarding the KMT's ineffective and corrupt war efforts, the foreign and Chinese public opinions over the past half year have reached a consensus. Regarding the true nature of the CPC, most foreigners and people in the rear areas of China are still unclear. The visit of the journalist group and the observation group to Yan'an will mark a new stage in changing this perception."[25]

On August 23, during an extended conversation with John Service, a member of the US Army Observation Group, Mao Zedong expounded on the idea of establishing a coalition government: The KMT Government should promptly convene a temporary (or transitional) National Assembly, inviting representatives from all groups. A practical compromise in the allocation of representatives could be that the KMT occupies about half of the seats, while all other groups occupy the other half, with Chiang Kai-shek recognized as the interim president. This temporary National Assembly would have full authority to reorganize the government and enact new laws, which would remain effective until the adoption of a new constitution. It would oversee elections and subsequently convene the National Assembly.[26]

On September 1, Mao Zedong chaired a presidium meeting of the Seventh Plenary Session of the Sixth Central Committee of the CPC, where they discussed proposals for convening a conference of representatives from various parties to establish a coalition government. On September 4, the Central Committee issued instructions to Lin Boqu and others regarding the proposal to reorganize the KMT Government and its implementation plan. The instructions stated as follows:

> The time is now ripe for our party to propose to the KMT, both domestically and internationally, the reorganization of the government. The plan is to demand that the KMT Government immediately convene a national conference of representatives from all parties, factions, armies, local governments, and mass organizations to reorganize the central government and abolish one-party rule. The new government would then convene a National Assembly to implement constitutional governance, pursue the national policy of resistance, and launch a counteroffensive. This proposal should become the political struggle objective among the Chinese people to oppose the KMT's one-party rule and its intended sham National Assembly and constitution.[27]

On September 15, following the instructions of the Central Committee, Lin Boqu proposed at the National Political Consultative Council: "We hope that the KMT will immediately end the one-party rule situation and that the KMT Government will convene a national conference of representatives from all parties, resistance forces, local governments, and mass organizations to organize a coalition government of all resistance parties."[28] This proposal quickly received enthusiastic support from various sectors, and the CPC's idea of a coalition government gained widespread acceptance and popularity.

One significant reason the US government sent the US Army Observation Group to Yan'an was that the war against Japan was approaching its decisive moment. To minimize future American casualties in the fight on Japanese soil, it was crucial for the Chinese theater to tie down as many Japanese invasion forces as possible. As a result, the strategic importance of the Chinese theater became increasingly significant. Coordinating relations between the KMT and the CPC, preventing the collapse of the KMT Government, and uniting all Chinese forces to defeat Japan became the primary focus of the US policy toward China during this period.

At that time, General Joseph Stilwell, Chief of Staff of the Allied China Theater Command, was in conflict with Chiang Kai-shek. On September 6, 1944, US President Franklin D. Roosevelt's special envoy, Major General Patrick J. Hurley, arrived in China to mediate the relationship between the KMT and the CPC. On November 7, Hurley arrived in Yan'an. Mao Zedong, Zhu De, and Zhou Enlai held four consecutive meetings with Hurley on the mornings and afternoons of November 8 and 9, and the morning of November 10, underscoring the importance Mao attached to this meeting.

During the first meeting, Hurley introduced a document he brought, titled "Basis for Agreement." The document contained five points, primarily requiring the CPC's military to obey and execute orders from the KMT Government and its military committee, and for all officers and soldiers of the CPC's military to accept reorganization by the KMT Government. Only then would the KMT Government recognize the CPC's legitimacy.

In the second meeting, Mao reiterated the CPC's proposal to reorganize the current KMT Government into a coalition National Government that included all resistance parties and non-partisan figures. He also proposed specific amendments to the "Basis for Agreement." The main amendments were as follows: (1) Adding a clause to reorganize the current KMT Government into a coalition National Government that included representatives from all resistance parties and non-partisan political figures, and to reorganize the military command into a joint command that included representatives from all resistance forces. (2) Modifying the original clause that required the CPC's military to obey and execute orders from the KMT Government and its military committee, and for all officers and soldiers of the CPC's military to accept reorganization by the KMT Government, to state that all resistance forces should obey and execute orders from the coalition National Government and its joint command and be recognized by this government and its command. (3) Adding provisions to guarantee various freedoms for the people. (4) Requiring the recognition of the legitimacy of the CPC and all resistance parties.[29]

The third meeting had a relatively harmonious atmosphere. During this meeting, a dialogue occurred that laid the groundwork for the later Chongqing negotiations.

Mao Zedong: If Chiang Kai-shek agrees to the plan we have agreed on, that would be very good.

Hurley: I will do everything in my power to make Chiang accept it. I think this plan is correct.

Hurley: If Mr. Chiang expresses a desire to meet with Chairman Mao, I am willing to accompany Chairman Mao to meet with Chiang to discuss major plans for improving the welfare of the Chinese people, reorganizing the government, and the military, and I guarantee that Chairman Mao and his entourage can safely return to Yan'an after the meeting.

Mao Zedong: I have long wanted to meet with Mr. Chiang. In the past, circumstances did not permit it, and I could not fulfill my wish. Now, with the US mediation and General Hurley's mediation, I will not let this good opportunity pass. I am still unsure whether Mr. Chiang will agree to our five points. If he agrees, I can meet with him. I always think it would be better if there is not much debate when I meet with Mr. Chiang.

Both sides agreed to prepare the document today and sign it tomorrow.[30]

That night, Mao Zedong chaired a plenary session of the Seventh Plenary Session of the Sixth Central Committee of the CPC and reported on the talks with Hurley. Mao stated that after the signing the next day, their work would be done, and the matter would move to Chongqing.

After the fourth meeting, Mao Zedong and Hurley signed the "Agreement Between the Chinese National Government, the KMT, and the CPC," leaving a blank for Chiang Kai-shek's signature. During the meeting, Mao Zedong stated: I cannot go to Chongqing with General Hurley today. We have decided to send Zhou Enlai with you. In short, we fully support the agreement endorsed by General Hurley and hope that Mr. Chiang will also sign it.[31]

However, shortly after Hurley returned to Chongqing, the situation changed drastically. Not only did Chiang Kai-shek refuse to sign the document, but Hurley, who was appointed US Ambassador to China in late November, also changed his previously supportive stance. On April 2, 1945, at a press conference held by the US State Department in Washington, he publicly announced that the US would not cooperate with the CPC. Consequently, Mao Zedong concluded that the US government was implementing a "pro-Chiang, anti-Communist policy."[32]

From April 23 to June 11, 1945, the Seventh National Congress of the CPC was held in Yan'an. Mao Zedong submitted a written political report to the congress, titled "On Coalition Government." The first part of the report, under the title "The Fundamental Demands of the Chinese People," stated: "Whether China should establish a democratic coalition government has become a matter of great concern for the Chinese people and the democratic public opinion of the Allied nations. Therefore, my report primarily discusses these demands."[33] The report elaborated on the CPC's general and specific programs for seizing victory in the War of Resistance and the tasks for the KMT-controlled areas, occupied territories, and liberated areas.

The report particularly proposed a standard for evaluating the politics of Chinese political parties: "The quality and extent of the impact of the policies and practices of all Chinese political parties on the Chinese people fundamentally depend on whether and how much they contribute to the development of the productive forces of China. It depends on whether they constrain or liberate the productive forces. The defeat of the Japanese invaders, the implementation of land reform, the liberation of the peasants, the development of modern industry, and the establishment of a new China that is independent, free, democratic, unified, and prosperous will alone enable the liberation of China's productive forces, and this is what the Chinese people welcome."[34] This standard gave the CPC a moral high ground in its confrontation with the KMT both then and later.

In the opening speech of the Seventh Congress, Mao Zedong used the metaphor of "Two Fates of China" to describe the post-war political situation in China. He believed that the Chinese people faced two paths: a bright path and a dark path, with two potential fates for China: a bright fate and a dark fate. He argued that every effort should be made to strive for a bright future and fate while opposing the dark alternative.

In the closing speech of the congress, Mao used the metaphor of "Yugong Moving the Mountain" to describe the effort required to build a New Democratic China and lead China toward brightness, which necessitated removing the two great mountains of imperialism and feudalism.

These metaphors indicated that, after enduring the long eight-year nationwide War of Resistance, the Chinese people were on the brink of another profound struggle. This struggle would fundamentally alter the historical destiny of the Chinese people since modern times.

CHAPTER 8

Marxism Must Also Be Adapted to China

What we mean by Marxism is the Marxism that plays an effective role in the actual life and struggles of the masses, not a Marxism that exists only in words. When Marxism in words is transformed into Marxism in real life, there will be no sectarianism. Not only can sectarianism be overcome, but many other problems can also be solved.

MAO ZEDONG,
"Talks at the Yan'an Forum on Literature and Art" (May 1942)

The Yan'an period was not only the time when Mao Zedong's military command reached its peak but also when he made significant theoretical advancements.

For a long time after the Zunyi Conference, Mao's military talents were widely recognized within the Party, but his theoretical contributions were not as well acknowledged.

In fact, throughout his life, Mao placed the greatest importance on theory, devoting significant effort to it. Since he joined the first cooperation between the KMT and the CPC, he proposed the theory of class analysis to distinguish between enemies, friends, and ourselves. After the failure of the Great Revolution, he put forward the theory of the armed separation of workers and peasants and explained why red political power could exist based on the uneven economic and political development in China. After the Long March, he proposed the theory of the Chinese united front against Japanese aggression, laying the theoretical foundation for shifting from domestic class warfare to the national War Against Japanese Aggression. However, these practical and effective theories for the Chinese revolution were not considered as theories at the time. During the Central Soviet Area period, some even believed that "Marxism could not come out of the mountain valleys."

This raises a question: What is Marxism? How should we treat Marxism? To open the path for the sinicization of Marxism, Mao Zedong had to answer these questions.

In May 1930, Mao Zedong wrote a short article titled "On Investigation Work."[1] At that time, he was conducting research in Xunwu County, Jiangxi Province. After years of exploration, he deeply understood the importance of investigation and research. Combined with the debates from the Seventh to the Ninth Congresses of the Red Fourth Army, he felt keenly the tendency of dogmatism in treating Marxism, the Comintern's instructions, and the Party's resolutions. Later, when he rediscovered this article, he wrote, "This is an old article written to oppose the dogmatism in the Red Army at that time. We didn't use the term 'dogmatism'; we called it 'bookishness.'"[2]

In this article, Mao proposed a viewpoint: "We say Marxism is correct not because Marx was a 'sage,' but because his theory has been proven correct in our practice and struggles. Our struggle needs Marxism. We welcome this theory without any mystical notions about 'sages.'" He further emphasized, "The 'books' of Marxism need to be studied, but they must be integrated with our country's actual conditions. We need 'books,' but we must correct bookishness that is detached from reality."[3]

Against the backdrop of prevalent dogmatism in the CPC and the deification of Comintern instructions and Soviet experiences, especially when Wang Ming's dogmatism dominated, speaking such words required considerable theoretical courage.

Since actual conditions are more important than what is written in books, how can we understand these conditions? In this article, Mao proposed two principles. First, "The victory of China's revolutionary struggle depends on

Chinese comrades understanding Chinese conditions," meaning that our brains must be on our shoulders, emphasizing the independence and self-reliance Mao continuously stressed. Second, "Without investigation, there is no right to speak."[4] A year later, in the "Notice on Investigating Population and Land Conditions" issued by the General Political Department on April 2, 1931, Mao further stated, "Without correct investigation, there is also no right to speak."[5] He also called for "going among the masses for actual investigation," pointing out that "all conclusions come at the end of an investigation, not at its beginning."[6] This idea essentially includes the concept of the mass line.

These ideas were later ridiculed by some within the Party. During the Yan'an period, Mao once said: "The phrase 'no investigation, no right to speak,' although mocked by some as 'narrow empiricism,' is something I do not regret; not only do I not regret it, I still firmly believe that without investigation, it is impossible to have the right to speak. Our Party has suffered countless times from so-called 'imperial envoys,' who were everywhere."[7] The "imperial envoys" Mao referred to were the special agents sent to various bases during the period of Wang Ming's "leftist" dogmatism.

Despite Mao Zedong's clear call to "oppose bookishness" during the establishment of the Central Soviet Area and his early ideas of seeking truth from facts, the mass line, and self-reliance, he was in a weak position with few supporters, insufficient to reverse the Party's prevailing dogmatism.

History favors those who are prepared. The turning point came with the Zunyi Conference, for which Mao had patiently waited for many years. This experience convinced him that "truth is often in the hands of a few."[8]

From January 15 to 17, 1935, the Political Bureau of the Central Committee of the CPC held an enlarged meeting during the Long March, known as the Zunyi Conference. This marked the Party's successful independent resolution of its internal issues. Before this, whether addressing Chen Duxiu's rightist capitulationism or correcting Qu Qiubai and Li Lisan's leftist adventurism, the actions were directly guided by the Comintern, inevitably leaving various historical consequences.

During the Zunyi Conference, Mao Zedong considered Wang Ming's leftist dogmatism's backing by the Comintern and the actual understanding level of the entire Party. Therefore, he did not raise the issue of political line errors but focused on resolving the most urgent internal organizational and military line issues. This later proved to be a wise move, ensuring Party unity.

In the resolution passed at the Zunyi Conference, titled "The Central Committee's Summary on Opposing the Enemy's Fifth Encirclement and Suppression Campaign," numerous sections deliberately emphasized a comparison between the two military strategies, thereby underscoring the correctness of the military strategic line advocated by Mao Zedong. For example, it pointed out: "Our strategic line should be decisive defense (offensive defense), concentrating superior forces to choose the enemy's weak points, eliminating part or most of the enemy's forces through mobile warfare, and defeating the enemy in piecemeal fashion to completely crush the enemy's encirclement." It also noted: "However, in the war against the fifth encirclement, a purely defensive line (or exclusive defense) replaced decisive defense, positional warfare replaced mobile warfare, and the so-called 'short, swift thrust' tactics supported this purely defensive strategic line. This allowed the enemy's protracted war and fortress warfare to achieve their goals, causing partial losses to our main Red Army and forcing us to leave the Central Soviet Area. It should be noted that this line was entirely contrary to the basic principles of the strategic and tactical principles by which our Red Army achieved victory."

This principle applied to specific strategies and tactics as well. For instance, the resolution pointed out: "Because the enemy is operating from external lines, their strategy involves encirclement and converging attacks, which creates opportunities for us to defeat them one by one. By operating on internal lines strategically, we can gain the advantages of external line operations in battles. This means using part of our forces to pin down one or more enemy columns while concentrating our main strength to surround and annihilate another enemy column. This approach allows us to break the enemy's encirclement by defeating them piecemeal." It further noted: "However, past leaders of the purely defensive line, in an attempt to resist the advance of enemies on all fronts, often dispersed our forces (primarily the First and Third Armies). This dispersal resulted in our forces being weak everywhere, putting us in a passive position and making it easier for the enemy to defeat us one by one."

The Zunyi Conference resolution also emphasized: "The slogan 'not one inch of Soviet territory to be ceded' is politically correct, but its mechanical application to military strategy is entirely wrong and serves only as a cover for the purely defensive line."⁹

Using such language to criticize Wang Ming's leftist dogmatic military line was unimaginable before the Long March. This shift reflected how the Zunyi Conference began to erode the blind faith in those who relied on "foreign dogmas," creating conditions for Mao Zedong to more effectively promote independent thinking and unity.

Even so, some at the Zunyi Conference questioned Mao Zedong's theoretical competence. This included Kai Feng, who was then an alternate member of the Political Bureau of the Central Committee, Secretary of the Central Bureau of the Youth League, and the Central Representative of the Red Ninth Army. Mao recalled: "At the Zunyi Conference, Kai Feng said: 'Your ideas are not particularly brilliant; they are nothing more than a combination of *The Romance of the Three Kingdoms* and *The Art of War* by Sunzi.' I asked him, 'Do you know how many chapters *The Art of War* has? What is the title of the first chapter? Please tell us.' He couldn't answer. I said, 'If you haven't even read it, how can you claim I am familiar with *The Art of War*?' I had read *The Romance of the Three Kingdoms*, but I hadn't read *The Art of War* at that time."¹⁰

After the main force of the Central Red Army successfully reached northern Shaanxi and particularly after arriving in Bao'an in July 1936, the situation in northern Shaanxi began to stabilize, frontline battles became relatively calm, and the central base became more settled. These conditions provided Mao Zedong with better opportunities and more time to concentrate on theoretical research and to summarize the historical experiences of the Agrarian Revolutionary War period.

Compared to the early years of the CPC and the period of the first cooperation between the KMT and the CPC, the Agrarian Revolutionary War period was much richer in experience. Despite the setbacks following the failure of the Great Revolution and three severe defeats due to leftist mistakes, the Party had built a formidable Red Army, gained comprehensive experience in establishing base areas, and developed initial experiences in organizing red political power. Upon first arriving in northern Shaanxi, they also accumulated significant experience in the united front, making the Party much more mature compared to the past. These were unprecedented favorable conditions for Mao Zedong to engage in theoretical work.

Mao Zedong later recalled: "On the eve of the War of Resistance Against Japanese Aggression and during the war itself, I wrote several essays, such as "Problems of Strategy in China's Revolutionary War," "On Protracted War," "On New Democracy," and the "Preface to the First Issue of *The Communist*." I also drafted several central documents on policy and strategy. These were all summaries of revolutionary experience. These essays and documents could only have been produced at that time, not earlier, because we had not yet gone through major upheavals, nor had we had the opportunity to compare two victories and two defeats. We did not yet have sufficient experience to fully understand the laws governing the Chinese revolution."[11]

Mao Zedong's summation of the historical experiences from the agrarian revolutionary period began with issues of military strategy, culminating in the publication of "Problems of Strategy in China's Revolutionary War" in December 1936.

Mao recalled as follows:

In 1936, the Red Army University asked me to lecture on revolutionary strategy. I agreed and began reading reference books, thinking about how to summarize the experiences of the domestic revolutionary war, and writing lecture notes. I read the KMT's military materials, as well as military works from Japan, Russia, and Western Europe, including Clausewitz's military writings. I also looked at some Soviet military materials and ancient Chinese military texts like Sunzi's *The Art of War*. However, the main focus was summarizing the experiences of China's ten-year civil war. The lecture notes were titled 'Problems of Strategy in China's Revolutionary War.' I didn't finish writing them, as the Xi'an Incident occurred, and I didn't have time to continue. There were still issues of strategic offense, political work, and Party work to address.[12]

The "Clausewitz's military writings" mentioned here refer to *On War*. Mao later discussed this with British Field Marshal Bernard Law Montgomery during Montgomery's visit to China. Their conversation went as follows:

Montgomery: "I have read your military writings; they are excellent."

Mao: "I don't think they are particularly good. I learned from your materials. You studied Clausewitz, and I studied him as well. He said that war is a continuation of politics by other means." Montgomery: "I also studied Genghis Khan, who emphasized mobility."

Mao: "You haven't read China's *The Art of War* from over two thousand years ago, have you? It contains many good principles."

Montgomery: "Does it mention more military principles?"

Mao: "Yes, many excellent principles, comprising thirteen chapters in total."[13]

Mao Zedong read Clausewitz's *On War* more than once. In February 1938, Mao organized a study group on Clausewitz's *On War* in Yan'an. Mo Wenhua, the director of the Political Department of the Eighth Route Army Garrison Corps, participated in the study as follows:

> The study sessions were held at Chairman Mao's residence, with discussions taking place once a week, starting at seven or eight in the evening and lasting until eleven at night. … At the time, the translation of *On War* was in classical Chinese and poorly translated, making it difficult to understand. Initially, there was only one copy of the book, which everyone took turns reading. Later, Comrade He Sijing directly translated it from the German original. He translated one chapter at a time, and we introduced and studied each chapter, distributing lecture notes. I remember the most discussed and heated topic was the concentration of forces. Chairman Mao said during these discussions: "Clausewitz did not have much practical experience in command, but his discussions on the concentration of forces were excellent. Napoleon's key principle was also the concentration of forces. When we talk about winning with superior numbers, we mean concentrating five to ten times the enemy's forces at a tactical level."[14]

In addition to Clausewitz's *On War*, Mao also read Japanese military manuals and Soviet books on strategy and combined arms operations, totaling eight books. These readings were all in preparation for writing "Problems of Strategy in China's Revolutionary War."[15]

The exact time when Mao Zedong read these books is now untraceable. Based on a preserved letter, it should have been after October 1936.

On September 7, 1936, Mao Zedong sent a telegram to Liu Ding, who was responsible for liaising with the Northeast Army in Xi'an, asking: "In my previous telegram, I requested you to purchase military books. Have you bought them yet? The Red Army University urgently needs them. Please quickly write to the bookstores in Nanjing and Beiping that sell military books to obtain their catalogs, select the important ones, buy them, and send the catalogs to me."[16]

On October 22, Mao sent another telegram to Ye Jianying and Liu Ding, who were doing united front work in Xi'an, saying: "Most of the military books you bought are not suitable, being mainly about tactics and techniques. What we need are books on campaign command and strategy. Please select and buy accordingly." He specifically instructed: "Also, buy a copy of *The Art of War* by Sunzi."[17]

Of course, to write a military classic like "Problems of Strategy in China's Revolutionary War," merely reading others' works was far from sufficient. It relied more on Mao Zedong's independent thinking. He once said: "Being a teacher has its advantages; it allows one to organize one's thoughts. When they invited me to be a teacher, I had to study, read, think about problems, and summarize experiences."[18]

Like many of his works, in "Problems of Strategy in China's Revolutionary War," Mao Zedong developed his arguments using the "peeling the onion" method. He started with the general laws of war (chapter 1, "How to Study War"), then discussed the relationship between the CPC and the Chinese revolutionary war (chapter 2), and then addressed the particularities of the Chinese revolutionary war (chapter 3, "The Characteristics of China's Revolutionary War"). This argumentative structure closely linked specific laws with general laws, highlighting Lenin's famous saying: "The essence of Marxism, the living soul of Marxism: concrete analysis of concrete conditions."[19] In other words, what is important and decisive are not general principles, but concrete analyses based on specific situations. This implicitly stripped dogmatists of their political capital: "They claim to be Marxist-Leninists, but they haven't learned anything from Marxism-Leninism."[20]

Chapter 4 indicated that the main form of the civil war between the KMT and the CPC was "encirclement and suppression" and anti-encirclement and suppression. This determined the long-term alternation between offensive and defensive operations. The basic characteristic of the "left" opportunist military line was its insistence on attack and "mechanically opposing the use of military defensive means."

Chapter 5 focused exclusively on strategic defense. If the first four chapters primarily discussed "the theory of war" and "the epistemology of war," the fifth chapter systematically examined issues within strategy and operational art. Unlike general war theory works, although this chapter was also categorized by concepts,[21] its starting point was not abstract concepts but concrete facts and vivid battle examples. Therefore, Mao Zedong later referred to his works as "bloody works," meaning "they were written at the cost of bloodshed and sacrifice."[22] These battle examples, from the establishment of the Jinggang Mountains revolutionary base to the failure of the fifth anti-encirclement campaign and the Red Army's forced strategic shift, whether successes or failures, all contained the unique laws of the Chinese revolutionary war. At that time, many people were directly involved in these great events of the Chinese revolution. Among them, only Mao Zedong was able to summarize the regularities and find the path to victory amid the immense joys and sorrows of the revolution.

After summarizing the military line issues from the ten-year civil war, Mao Zedong turned his theoretical focus to the ideological line. This shift was prompted by his deep realization from the struggle against dogmatism that "all major political errors are essentially deviations from dialectical materialism."[23]

Mao Zedong had always been deeply interested in Marxist philosophy. This interest was not only due to the ridicule that "Marxism cannot come out of the mountain valleys," but more importantly because he personally felt that only Marxist philosophy could provide direction amid the vast sea of challenges.

As early as 1929, during the debates around the principles of army building surrounding the Seventh Congress of the Red Fourth Army, Mao Zedong wrote a letter to the Central Committee on November 28, stating: "The theoretical knowledge of Party members is too low; urgent education is necessary. In addition to requesting the Central Committee to send Party publications (e.g., the *Bolshevik*,[24] *Red Flag*, *Outline of Leninism*,[25] *History of the Russian Revolutionary Movement*,[26] etc., none of which we have received), we also ask for a batch of books (approximately 100 yuan worth, with a list of titles to follow)." He added, "We are desperate for books and newspapers. Please do not dismiss this as a trivial matter."[27] On the same day, he wrote to Li Lisan, a member of the Standing Committee of the Political Bureau and Minister of the Central Publicity Department: "I am extremely hungry for knowledge. Please frequently send books and newspapers, and if you can spare the time to write letters of guidance, that would be even better."[28]

During the Central Soviet Area period, Mao Zedong was marginalized. The dogmatists often quoted extensively from texts, intimidating others with grand labels. Mao felt deeply that he knew too little about the classic works of Marxism-Leninism, so he diligently studied all the classics he could find, especially philosophical works. He once said that he learned Marxism-Leninism "on horseback."[29]

In April 1932, after the Red Army captured Zhangzhou, they found a batch of Marxist-Leninist works, including Engels' *Anti-Dühring*, and sent them to Mao Zedong. Mao was so fond of *Anti-Dühring* that he read it multiple times, even during the Long March.

After arriving in Yan'an in January 1937, during a period when the civil war between the KMT and CPC had ceased and the total resistance against Japanese aggression by the whole nation had not yet broken out, Mao had more time to delve into Marxist philosophy.

Based on the books preserved today that Mao Zedong read and annotated, it is evident that he began reading the Chinese translation (third edition) of *Course on Dialectical Materialism* by Soviet philosophers Brokov (then translated as Silokov) and Eisenberg (then translated as Aisenbao) in November 1936, while still in Bao'an. By April 1937, he had read it three or four times and written approximately 12,000 characters of annotations. These notes focused mainly on Marxist epistemology and dialectics, with half of the annotations centered on the law of the unity of opposites. This indicates that Mao was determined to use Marxist epistemology and dialectical views to correct the dogmatism and metaphysics present in the Party. He was not attempting to establish an all-encompassing theoretical system, but rather to use this "microscope and telescope" to clear the obstacles preventing theory from connecting with practice.

In his annotations, he pointed out the dangers of valuing books over practice: "Starting from abstract theoretical propositions rather than concrete reality, both Li Lisanism and the later military adventurism and military conservatism committed this error, which is neither dialectical nor materialistic."[30] Therefore, he titled his two philosophical works "On Practice"[31] and "On Contradiction,"[32] intending to awaken the entire Party, especially senior leaders, to the importance of Marxist epistemology and dialectics. In his own words, he wanted to "shoot the arrow at the target."

Mao Zedong devoted a great deal of effort to writing "On Practice" and "On Contradiction." He recalled as follows:

> Writing "On Practice" and "On Contradiction" was intended for lectures at the Resistance Against-Japanese Military and Political University (Kàngdà). They invited me to lecture, and I was willing to be a teacher. Preparing for a lecture allowed me to summarize revolutionary experiences. Preparing for a two-hour lecture took an entire week, including two all-nighters. After a week of preparation, the two-hour lecture was "sold out." The lectures couldn't just follow the books; that would make the audience drowsy. Preparing on my own, combining theory with practice, and summarizing revolutionary experiences gave the audience enthusiasm.[33]

Mao Zedong took these lectures very seriously, preparing a detailed lecture outline titled "Dialectical Materialism (Lecture Outline)," with "On Practice" and "On Contradiction" being two sections of it. According to the *History of the Resistance Against-Japanese Military and Political University of the Chinese People*: "Every Tuesday and Thursday morning, Mao Zedong lectured at Kàngdà, each time for four hours. In the afternoons, he participated in student discussions, answering their questions. From May until around the time of the 'Lugou Bridge Incident' in July, he lectured for over 110 hours."[34]

In "On Practice," Mao focused on the problem of undervaluing practice, hence the subtitle: "On the Relationship Between Knowledge and Practice, Between Knowing and Doing."[35] The relationship between knowing and doing is an ancient Chinese philosophical concept that dates back at least to the Spring and Autumn and Warring States periods.

"On Practice" opens by stating its basis: "Marxists believe that only social practice can be the criterion of truth." Using his "peeling the onion" method of analysis, Mao delves into the "process of development of knowledge," explaining "how human knowledge arises from practice and serves practice."

He cited contemporary examples, such as the visit of the KMT Government's inspection group to Yan'an, to illustrate the process of knowledge development from perceptual to rational understanding. He then used examples from the proletariat's understanding of capitalism, the Chinese people's understanding of imperialism, people's understanding of war, and the transition from uncertainty to certainty in work to reinforce his points, ultimately proving that "knowledge detached from practice is impossible."

From the close relationship between knowing and doing, and between knowledge and practice, Mao emphasized two points. First, "rational knowledge depends on perceptual knowledge"; second, "knowledge needs to be deepened, and perceptual knowledge must develop into rational knowledge." Emphasizing the former countered dogmatism; emphasizing the latter countered empiricism. In Mao's view, during the agrarian revolutionary period, empiricism often became the captive of dogmatism, posing great harm to the Chinese revolution.

Here, Mao Zedong's unique theoretical creativity is evident. He never pursued the establishment of a textbook-style or encyclopedic theoretical system but focused on the practical usefulness of ideas, ensuring they both originated from and elevated practice.

Mao believed that the mission of practice was not yet complete, nor was the mission of theory. He stressed: "Knowledge begins with practice, and once gained through practice, it must return to practice." This is the process of theory guiding practice and is "the process of testing and developing theory." Emphasizing that any theory must undergo the test of practice effectively broke the rigid, dogmatic thinking about Marxism, sparking a genuine ideological liberation movement.

Later, he further developed this idea. In his May 1963 article, "Where Do Correct Ideas Come From?" Mao proposed: "People's knowledge, after being tested in practice, will undergo another leap. This leap is even greater than the previous one because only this leap can confirm whether the ideas, theories, policies, plans, and methods obtained in the first leap from reflecting the objective external world are correct or not. There is no other way to test the truth. The proletariat's goal in understanding the world is to change it; there is no other purpose."[36]

The conclusion of "On Practice" is thought-provoking: "Marxism-Leninism does not end the pursuit of truth but continually opens up the path to understanding truth in practice. Our conclusion is the concrete, historical unity of the subjective and the objective, of theory and practice, of knowing and doing, opposing all leftist or rightist errors that detach from concrete history."[37]

"On Practice" opposes dogmatism from the perspective of epistemology, while "On Contradiction" opposes it from the perspective of methodology. Mao Zedong begins "On Contradiction" by stating: "Our current philosophical research should aim primarily at eliminating dogmatic thinking."[38]

"On Contradiction" starts with the "two world outlooks," highlighting the opposition between "internal causation" and "external causation" as the fundamental cause of the development of things. At the Zunyi Conference, Bo Gu (Qin Bangxian) emphasized in his summary report on the five "encirclement and suppression" campaigns that the main reason for the failure of the fifth anti-encirclement campaign was the superior strength of the enemy compared to our own.

"On Contradiction" then explains the relationship between the universality and particularity of contradictions, which is the key to the entire work.

Mao pointed out: "The relationship between the universality and particularity of contradictions is the relationship between the general and the specific. However, this generality is contained within all particularities; without particularities, there can be no generality. The principle of the general and the specific, the absolute and the relative, is the essence of the question of contradictions in things. Without understanding this, it is equivalent to abandoning dialectics."[39]

In "On Practice," Mao emphasized that practice is more important than theory. In "On Contradiction," he further emphasized that "without particularities, there can be no generalities." This established the philosophical basis for combining the universal truth of Marxism with the concrete reality of the Chinese revolution, liberating the CPC from the constraints of dogmatizing Marxism and sanctifying Comintern directives.

Mao Zedong delivered his lectures on "On Practice" and "On Contradiction" during the outbreak of the full-scale Japanese invasion of China. Subsequently, he fully committed himself to guiding the total resistance against Japanese aggression by the whole nation. However, he soon encountered various disturbances from the right-wing dogmatism of Wang Ming. This again confirmed a pattern summarized by Mao: leftist errors tend to arise when relations between the KMT and CPC deteriorate, while rightist dangers emerge when these relations improve.

From October 12 to 14, 1938, at the Sixth Plenary Session of the Sixth Central Committee of the CPC, Mao Zedong delivered the report "On the New Stage." This report, without naming names, corrected Wang Ming's rightist capitulationism and comprehensively expounded the political, military, and organizational lines of the CPC, as well as the principle of independence within the Chinese united front against Japanese aggression.

This report went further than previous ones by explicitly proposing the concept of "Sinification of Marxism." He said: "There is no abstract Marxism, only concrete Marxism. By concrete Marxism, we mean Marxism that has taken on a national form, Marxism that has been applied to the concrete struggles in the specific environment of China, and not abstractly applied. As members of the great Chinese nation, who are flesh and blood with this nation, communist members who speak of Marxism must do so in the context of China's characteristics; otherwise, it is just empty, abstract Marxism. Therefore, the Sinification of Marxism, making it reflect Chinese characteristics in every aspect, according to China's specific conditions, is something the whole Party urgently needs to understand and address. We must abolish the foreign stereotypes, sing fewer hollow and abstract tunes, and instead replace them with fresh, lively, Chinese-style, and Chinese-spirit work that the Chinese people love to see and hear."[40]

Thus, "Sinification of Marxism" has two meanings. First, it means combining the universal principles of Marxism with the concrete reality of the Chinese revolution. Second, it means a Marxism that has taken on a national form, i.e., a Marxism with a Chinese style and spirit, a concrete Marxism. He particularly emphasized: "The theories of Marx, Engels, Lenin, and Stalin are universally applicable. We must not view their theories as dogmas but as guides to action. We should learn not the literal meanings of Marxism-Leninism but their standpoints and methods of analyzing and solving problems."

Mao Zedong proposed to the entire Party: "Learning theory is a condition for victory. From the perspective of primary leadership responsibilities, if China had one hundred to two hundred comrades who systematically, rather than fragmentarily, practically rather than hollowly, learned Marxism, it would be equivalent to defeating Japanese imperialism."[41] This reveals Mao's sense of solitude in his theoretical pursuits, often feeling "few echo his sentiments."

From 1939, under Mao Zedong's directives, an organized learning movement was launched. The content of this movement, as proposed by Mao at the Sixth Plenary Session of the Sixth Central Committee, focused on learning Marxist theory, history, and current movements. The Central Cadre Education Department was established for this purpose, with Zhang Wentian as the minister and Li Weihan as the vice minister. In 1940, the Central Committee of the CPC issued over ten documents on learning, initially forming a system for cadre education.

During the learning movement, the disconnection between theory and practice became evident. Particularly in March 1940, Wang Ming (Chen Shaoyu) reprinted the third edition of his 1931 work *For a Bolshevized Communist Party of China*, a representative text of Wang Ming's "leftist" dogmatism. Many people, unaware of its context, also studied this book as an important theoretical work. This situation indicated that the task of correcting the ideological line and academic style could not be truly completed without thoroughly settling the political line errors of dogmatism. Thus, addressing the "leftist" adventurism political line from Wang Ming's period became an essential threshold to cross.

On December 4, 1940, at a meeting of the Political Bureau of the Central Committee, Mao Zedong formally proposed summarizing the policy errors in the Party's history, particularly during the latter period of the Soviet movement. He said as follows:

> Our Party has experienced three periods in history. At the end of the Great Revolution, Chen Duxiu advocated uniting with everyone and ordered the suppression of the workers' and peasants' movements. During the Soviet period, initially, the policy was to overthrow everything, which was corrected at the Sixth Congress. However, at the end of the Soviet period, it was again about overthrowing everything, estimating that it was a final showdown between the Soviet path and the colonial path. The policy to eliminate rich peasants and small landlords caused a stark red-white division. This "leftist" policy resulted in the loss of nine-tenths of our army and more than nine-tenths of the Soviet area, leaving only the Shaanxi-Gansu-Ningxia Border Region. The losses were even greater than those during the Li Lisan line.

He particularly emphasized: "The Zunyi Conference resolution only addressed military errors, not line errors. In reality, they were line errors, so the Zunyi Conference resolution needs some revision."[42]

However, at this meeting, some expressed disagreement with the notion that the errors in the latter period of the Soviet movement were line errors. Given the pressing situation with Chiang Kai-shek's deliberate instigation of the South Anhui Incident, there were many urgent matters requiring decisions. Mao Zedong did not push for an immediate consensus and agreed that past experiences and lessons needed special study.

On May 19, 1941, Mao Zedong delivered his report "Reform Our Study" at the Party School of the Central Committee of CPC. By this time, the second anti-Communist campaign by the KMT had been repelled, and the War of

Resistance situation was relatively stable. Drawing on the previous experience from the Political Bureau of the Central Committee meeting, he decided to once again use the issue of academic style as a breakthrough point.

The first sentence of this report highlighted its purpose: "I advocate reforming the study methods and system of our entire Party."

Regarding the three learning tasks proposed at the Sixth Plenary Session of the Sixth Central Committee, Mao expressed strong dissatisfaction with the current state of learning. On studying current issues, he noted, "There is a lack of a strong atmosphere for investigation and research into objective realities. 'Blindly catching sparrows,' 'blindly groping for fish,' superficiality, boasting, and being content with half-knowledge." On studying history, he remarked, "For many Party members, both modern and ancient Chinese history remains a dark void. Many Marxist-Leninist scholars are always citing Greece, but they are not loyal to their ancestors, forgetting them." On studying theory, he commented, "Although they have read, they cannot digest it. They can only cite individual phrases from Marx, Engels, Lenin, and Stalin but cannot apply their positions, viewpoints, and methods to concretely study China's present situation and history, analyze, and solve China's revolutionary problems."

Through the issue of academic style, Mao expounded on the famous concept of seeking truth from facts, stating: "'Facts' are all things that objectively exist. 'Truth' is the internal relations of these objective things, i.e., their laws. 'Seeking' means we study them. This attitude is a manifestation of Party spirit, the Marxist-Leninist style of unifying theory and practice. This is the basic attitude that every Communist Party member should have."

He sharply criticized the tendency to divorce theory from practice: "This anti-scientific, anti-Marxist-Leninist subjectivist approach is the great enemy of the Communist Party, the great enemy of the working class, the great enemy of the people, the great enemy of the nation, and a manifestation of impure Party spirit. Only by defeating subjectivism can the truth of Marxism-Leninism prevail, the Party spirit be strengthened, and the revolution be victorious."[43]

Hu Qiaomu recalled: "Chairman Mao's language was sharp, his satire profound, and his emotions intense, something many comrades had never experienced before."[44]

Following this report, the Central Committee issued the "Decision on Enhancing Party Spirit" on July 1, 1941, and the "Decision on Investigation and Research" on August 1, 1941. Before this, Mao Zedong wrote a preface and an afterword for his collection of rural investigation reports, *Rural Surveys*. In the preface, he sharply criticized those who despised practice and investigation, saying: "Many people, 'upon dismounting from their cars,' immediately start making comments and criticisms about everything, but nine out of ten such people will fail." In the afterword, he specifically pointed out that many policies during the latter part of the ten-year civil war were wrong.[45]

Following the preparations, from September 10 to October 22, 1941, the Political Bureau of the Central Committee held the Rectification Meeting (also known as the "September Meeting"). This intermittent meeting lasted over a month, focusing on reviewing the leadership line issues during the latter part of the ten-year civil war. Mao Zedong spoke multiple times, using extensive facts to illustrate the existence of an erroneous line characterized by dogmatism during the latter period of the Soviet movement. This meeting achieved a basic consensus on the leftist opportunist line errors committed by the Central leadership during the latter part of the ten-year civil war. The participants agreed that the "latter part of the ten-year civil war" referred to the period beginning in September 1931, under the interim Central leadership of the Communist Party. This effectively placed Wang Ming's leftist dogmatism in the Party's historical judgment seat. At the meeting, Zhang Wentian, Bo Gu (Qin Bangxian), Wang Jiaxiang, and others spoke and made self-criticisms. Only Wang Ming (Chen Shaoyu) did not make a self-criticism and shifted the blame to others.

Around this time, Mao Zedong oversaw the compilation of *Since the Sixth Congress* (also known as "the Party Book"), a collection of important historical documents within the Party. This was intended to help the senior leaders of the Party further understand the serious harm of dogmatism by studying and researching the Party's history. The compilation of this book played a crucial role in successfully holding the aforementioned Political Bureau of the Central Committee meeting. Mao Zedong said: "By May 1941, when I made the report 'Reform Our Study,' it had no impact. After June, we compiled the *Party Book*. Once it was published, many comrades were disarmed, making it possible to hold the September 1941 meeting, where everyone acknowledged the line errors of the Central leadership during the latter part of the ten-year civil war. The September 1941 meeting was pivotal; otherwise, I would not have dared to give a rectification report at the Party School, and my books like *Rural Surveys* could not have been published, nor could the rectification have been carried out."[46]

Hu Qiaomu recalled: "At that time, no one had mentioned that there was a 'leftist' line in the Central leadership after the Fourth Plenary Session. Now that these documents were compiled, it became evident that there was subjectivism and dogmatism among some Central leaders, leaving some people speechless. By comparing Chairman Mao's struggle against the 'leftist' line with the two types of leadership before and after, it became clear that Chairman Mao indeed represented the correct line, thus solidifying his leadership position within the Party. The compilation of *Since the Sixth Congress* was aimed at resolving the political line issue, and it became the basic weapon for the Party's rectification."[47]

After the September Meeting, the Rectification Movement gradually spread throughout the Party. It began in Yan'an and then extended to various resistance base areas, starting with senior leaders and eventually involving ordinary Party members and cadres. Particularly following *Reform Our Study*, Mao Zedong delivered the reports "Rectify the Style of Study, the Party, and Writing" at the opening ceremony of the Party School of the Central Committee of CPC on February 1, 1942, and "Oppose Stereotyped Party Writing" at the Central Publicity Department cadre meeting on February 8, 1942, further advancing the Rectification Movement.

Regarding the purpose of the Rectification Movement, he proposed: "Oppose subjectivism to rectify the style of study, oppose sectarianism to rectify the Party style, and oppose stereotyped Party writing to rectify the writing style. These are our tasks."

On the nature of theory, he pointed out: "There is only one genuine theory in the world, which is drawn from objective reality and has been proven in objective reality. Nothing else can be called the theory we speak of."

On what makes a theorist, he said: "Having read many Marxist-Leninist books, can we be considered theorists? No, we cannot. Because Marxism-Leninism is the theory created by Marx, Engels, Lenin, and Stalin based on reality, summarized from historical and revolutionary realities. If we merely read their works but do not further study China's historical and revolutionary realities based on their theories and do not attempt to theoretically reflect on China's revolutionary practice, we cannot claim to be Marxist theorists."[48]

The insights that seem like common knowledge today were hard-won truths for the CPC, painfully acquired through the cost of bloodshed due to dogmatism. Mao Zedong's elaborations during the Yan'an Rectification Campaign left a powerful and fresh impression on people.

On April 3, 1942, the Central Publicity Department issued a directive, revised and approved by Mao Zedong, titled "Decision on Studying and Discussing the Central Decisions and Mao Zedong's Reports on the Rectification of the Three Styles in Yan'an." This directive prescribed 18 documents for the rectification study.[49] Shortly after, on April 16, the Central Publicity Department issued another notice increasing the number of rectification documents from 18 to 22.[50]

On June 8, 1942, the Central Publicity Department issued the "Directive on Conducting the Rectification Study Movement Throughout the Party." This directive summarized the experiences from the Yan'an Rectification Campaign and promoted these experiences along with the "Plan for Studying 22 Documents in Four Months by the Central Direct System" throughout the Party. The second attachment of the directive, "Outline of the Yan'an Study Organization," stated: "The Central Committee has established a General Study Committee led by Comrade Mao Zedong, with Kang Sheng as his deputy, to lead all of Yan'an in the study." It also described the organization of rectification studies in Yan'an.

> Senior cadres from various agencies and schools in Yan'an formed central study groups (Group A), studying the documents themselves to lead other cadres in the study. There were also intermediate study groups (Group B) and regular study groups (Group C). Group A, although small in number, was the leadership core. Group B was the largest, consisting of intermediate cadres

who were the focus of the study movement, with members of Group A joining them accordingly. Group C, not large in number, included those with lower education levels who needed to study the documents. They mainly adopted a classroom approach. In total, 10,098 people participated in this rectification study in Yan'an.[51]

During and after the Rectification Movement, Mao Zedong engaged in extensive theoretical work based on China's reality, producing significant results that advanced the Sinification of Marxism and elevated the theoretical level of the entire Party. Some of these landmark works included "Preface to *The Communist*" (October 4, 1939), "Extensively Absorb Intellectuals" (December 1, 1939), "On New Democracy" (January 1940), "Prefaces and Postscripts to *Rural Surveys*" (March and April 1941), "Summary of the Second Anti-Communist Campaign" (May 8, 1941), "Reform Our Study" (May 19, 1941), "Rectify the Party's Style of Work" (February 1, 1942), "Talks at the Yan'an Forum on Literature and Art" (May 1942), "Economic and Financial Problems in the War of Resistance Period" (December 1942), and "Some Issues Concerning Methods of Leadership" (June 1, 1943). These works nurtured generations of Chinese Communists.

Through the Rectification Movement, Mao Zedong's prestige further increased, and the leadership collective centered around Mao Zedong was further consolidated. On March 20, 1943, the Political Bureau of the Central Committee passed the "Decision on Adjusting and Simplifying the Central Institutions," defining the authority of the Political Bureau of the Central Committee and the Central Secretariat. Regarding the Political Bureau of the Central Committee, it was stipulated: "Between the Central Committee plenums, the Political Bureau of the Central Committee is responsible for leading the entire Party and has the authority to decide all major issues. The Political Bureau of the Central Committee appoints Mao Zedong as Chairman. Major issues concerning ideology, politics, military, policy, and organization must be discussed and approved at Political Bureau meetings." Regarding the Central Secretariat, it was stipulated: "The Secretariat, composed of Mao Zedong, Liu Shaoqi, and Ren Bishi, with Mao Zedong as Chairman, is an executive body handling daily work according to the

Political Bureau's guidelines. The Secretariat must report its work to the Political Bureau."[52]

During the later stages of the Yan'an Rectification Movement, there was a prescribed task to review the cadres. This was a normal task to maintain the Party's organizational purity, previously conducted several times. Given the issues of forced confessions in past cadre reviews and anti-rebellion work, Mao Zedong emphasized: "We have painful lessons from past anti-rebellion efforts. This time, we must not engage in forced confessions. We must conduct investigations and gather evidence. If there is no physical evidence, there must be human testimony. Do not believe allegations based on mere statements. Analyze concretely and do not trust confessions easily. For those with issues, one should not be killed, and most should not be detained."[53]

Despite these precautions, the cadre review still went seriously awry, evolving into the so-called "Rescue the Fallen Movement," creating widespread panic and resulting in over 1,400 alleged spies being identified in the Yan'an area within days, leading to numerous wrongful convictions.

Mao Zedong took responsibility for these problems, often bowing and apologizing to those wrongfully harmed. He solemnly stated: "In the cadre review, the Party School committed many errors. Who is responsible? I am, because I am the head of the Party School. All of Yan'an committed many errors. Who is responsible? I am, because I was giving orders."[54]

The direct outcome of the Rectification Movement was the adoption of the "Resolution on Certain Historical Issues" at the Seventh Plenary Session of the Sixth Central Committee on April 20, 1945, after nearly a year of drafting and repeated revisions. This resolution concluded the Party's historical issues and fully affirmed the correct line represented by Mao Zedong, paving the way for the successful convening of the Seventh National Congress of the CPC.

From April 23 to June 11, 1945, the Seventh National Congress of the CPC was held in Yan'an. The congress officially named the theoretical achievements of the Sinification of Marxism as Mao Zedong Thought and enshrined it as the guiding principle for all the Party's work in the Party Constitution. The Party Constitution stipulated: "The CPC takes Marxism-Leninism and Mao Zedong Thought, the integration of Marxist-Leninist theory with the practice of the Chinese revolution, as its guiding principle, opposing all deviations of dogmatism and empiricism. The CPC, based on Marxist dialectical materialism and historical materialism, critically assimilates the historical heritage of both China and foreign countries, opposing all forms of idealism and mechanical materialism."[55]

In his report on amending the Party Constitution at the congress, Liu Shaoqi said: "Mao Zedong Thought is the continuation and development of Marxism in the colonial, semi-colonial, and semi-feudal countries' national democratic revolution of the current era. It is an outstanding example of the nationalization of Marxism." "Mao Zedong Thought, from his worldview to his work style, is the developing and perfecting Chinese Marxism. It is the complete revolutionary theory of the Chinese people for building a new nation. These theories and policies are entirely Marxist, and yet completely Chinese. This is the highest expression of Chinese national wisdom and the highest theoretical generalization."[56]

It was at this point, and only at this point, that the direction of the Sinification of Marxism represented by Mao Zedong was fully recognized and praised by the entire Party.

CHAPTER 9

Confrontation and Negotiation

We will certainly achieve victory one day. The reason is nothing else but the fact that the reactionaries represent backwardness, while we represent progress.

MAO ZEDONG,

Talk with American Journalist Anna Louise Strong (August 6, 1946)

On August 15, 1945, Japan publicly broadcast a recording of Emperor Hirohito reading the *Rescript on the Termination of the War*, thus announcing Japan's unconditional surrender. The news brought China into a state of joyous celebration.

For the Chinese people, this meant that the 14-year-long War of Resistance Against Japanese Aggression had finally ended in victory. This was unprecedented in China's modern history. However, as the Chinese people celebrated the victory over Japan, the shadow of civil war began to loom over the land.

Chiang Kai-shek had a firm bottom line: he would never agree to form a coalition government with the CPC, nor would he grant legitimacy to the CPC and its army. However, he was not yet ready to start a civil war immediately. He needed time. Harry S. Truman, President of the United States saw this clearly: "Chiang Kai-shek's authority was confined to the southwest corner, with the rest of South China and East China occupied by the Japanese. North China was controlled by the Communists and Manchuria by the Russians. There had been no roots of any kind of central Chinese government north of the Yangtze River." "In reality it would be only with the greatest difficulty that Chiang Kai-shek could even reoccupy South China. To get to North China he would need an agreement with the Communists, and he could never move into Manchuria without an agreement with the Communists and the Russians."[1]

Against this backdrop, on August 11, 1945, Chiang Kai-shek issued an order requiring the Eighteenth Group Army (i.e., the Eighth Route Army) to "remain in their current positions and await further orders." Simultaneously, on August 14, 20, and 23, he sent three telegrams inviting Mao Zedong to Chongqing to "discuss important national affairs."

Mao Zedong knew his old rival Chiang Kai-shek well. On August 13, in a speech titled "The Situation and Our Policy After the Victory in the War of Resistance Against Japanese Aggression," delivered at a cadre meeting in Yan'an, he pointed out as follows:

> What is the KMT like? Look at its past, and you will know its present; look at its past and present, and you will know its future. During the War of Resistance, we were behind enemy lines, and he went up the mountains. Now he wants to come down to seize the fruits of our victory. We must clearly see that the danger of civil war is very serious because Chiang Kai-shek has already decided on his policy. Chiang Kai-shek will seize every bit of power and profit from the people. What about us? Our policy is to confront him head-on and contest every inch of land. We will act according to Chiang Kai-shek's methods. Our policy must be based on our own strength, which we call self-reliance.

Thus, he established two principles for the upcoming struggle: confrontation and self-reliance.

Mao Zedong also outlined the theme of the future struggle: "Chiang Kai-shek talks about 'nation-building.' The future struggle will be about what kind of nation to build. Will it be a new democratic nation led by the proletariat and the masses, or will it be a semi-colonial, semi-feudal state ruled by the big landlords and big bourgeoisie? This will be a very complex struggle."[2]

After receiving Chiang Kai-shek's telegrams, Mao Zedong convened an enlarged meeting of the Political Bureau of the Central Committee on August 23 and decided to go to Chongqing for negotiations himself, while making the worst-case preparations by appointing Liu Shaoqi as Acting Chairman of the Central Committee. At that time, the Central Secretariat functioned similarly to the usual Standing Committee of the Political Bureau of the Central Committee. To strengthen the central leadership, the meeting added Chen Yun and Peng Zhen as alternate secretaries of the Central Secretariat, alongside the five secretaries Mao Zedong, Zhu De, Liu Shaoqi, Zhou Enlai, and Ren Bishi. The meeting also decided to appoint Mao Zedong as chairman of the Central Military Commission, with Zhu De, Liu Shaoqi, Zhou Enlai, and Peng Dehuai as vice chairmen.

Everyone was concerned about Mao Zedong's safety. On August 25, Mao told Liu Bocheng and Deng Xiaoping, who were returning to the Taihang Front by US military observation plane: "You go back to the front and fight freely. Don't worry about my safety in Chongqing. The better you fight, the safer I will be, and the better the negotiations will go. There's no other way."[3]

On August 26, Mao Zedong drafted a notification for the Central Committee regarding the peace negotiations with the KMT.

The notification expressed confidence in the Chongqing negotiations.

> Now that the Soviet Union, the United States, and the United Kingdom all oppose civil war in China, and our Party has put forward the three major slogans of peace, democracy, and unity, and sent Comrades Mao Zedong, Zhou Enlai, and Wang Ruofei to Chongqing to discuss national unity and nation-building with Chiang Kai-shek, the reactionaries' conspiracy for civil war may be thwarted. Under internal and external pressure, the KMT may conditionally recognize our Party's status, and our Party may conditionally recognize the KMT's status, creating a new stage of cooperation and peaceful development between the two parties (including the Democratic League, etc.)

The notification also prepared the whole Party for necessary concessions in the negotiations.

> In the negotiations, the KMT will undoubtedly demand that we significantly reduce the liberated areas and the number of liberation armies and prohibit the issuance of currency. We are also prepared to make necessary concessions that do not harm the fundamental interests of the people. Without such concessions, we cannot break the KMT's civil war conspiracy, gain political initiative, win the sympathy of international public opinion and domestic centrists, or achieve our Party's legal status and a peaceful situation. If, after we take these steps, the KMT still insists on launching a civil war, it will lose moral ground before the entire country and the world, giving our Party justifiable reasons to engage in self-defense and repel their attacks.[4]

After making thorough arrangements, at about 11 a.m. on August 28, Mao Zedong, Zhou Enlai, and Wang Ruofei, accompanied by Chiang Kai-shek's representative Zhang Zhizhong and US Ambassador to China Patrick Hurley, left Yan'an by plane. At about 3 p.m., they arrived at Chongqing's Jiulongpo Airport, where they were warmly welcomed by representatives from various sectors in Chongqing.

Before Mao Zedong arrived in Chongqing, meticulous arrangements were made for his residence, meeting, and office spaces. Zhang Zhizhong provided his official residence, the Gui Garden at Zengjiayan in the city, for Mao Zedong's use as a place for meetings and office work during his stay in Chongqing. For his nightly rest, Mao returned to the Eighteenth Group Army Office in Hongyan, located in the suburbs, which was also the site of the Southern Bureau of the CPC.

On the evening of his arrival in Chongqing, Mao Zedong went to Lin Garden, the official residence of Chiang Kai-shek, to attend a banquet hosted by Chiang to welcome Mao and his delegation. The banquet was a grand affair, attended by Zhang Zhizhong, Zhang Qun, Chen Cheng, Wu Guozhen, Shao Lizi, Wang Shijie, Zhou Zhirou, Chiang Ching-kuo, US Ambassador to China Patrick Hurley, and US Military Commander in China, General Albert

C. Wedemeyer. After the banquet, Chiang Kai-shek invited Mao Zedong to stay at Lin Garden.

This was the first meeting between the leaders of the KMT and the CPC since Chiang Kai-shek's "April 12 Massacre" in 1927. Many progressive members of the KMT, democratic parties, and socially prominent figures had high hopes for this meeting.

Chiang Kai-shek was not well-prepared for Mao Zedong's arrival in Chongqing for negotiations. In the preceding days, he had been urgently discussing strategies and principles with key officials of the KMT, government, and military. On August 26, Chiang wrote in his diary about the "Key Points and Strategies for Discussions with Mao," including "handling of Communist armies," "methods for the National Assembly," "methods for participating in government," and "methods for releasing Communist criminals."[5] On the day Mao arrived in Chongqing, August 28, Chiang noted in his diary: "Held a midday meeting to discuss the strategy for Mao Zedong's arrival. Decided to treat him with sincerity. All political and military issues should be resolved as a whole, showing extreme tolerance on political demands but strictly enforcing military unification without any concessions."[6] In other words, Chiang's approach was to make empty political promises to entice the Communists into military concessions.

The day after Mao Zedong arrived in Chongqing, on the afternoon of August 29, he had his first direct discussion with Chiang Kai-shek at Lin Garden. Chiang expressed willingness to hear the CPC's opinions on all issues and reiterated his claim that there was no civil war in China. Mao listed numerous facts from the ten-year civil war and the War of Resistance Against Japanese Aggression to refute Chiang's claim. Ultimately, Chiang proposed three principles for the negotiations: (1) All issues should be resolved comprehensively. (2) All resolutions must not violate the unity of administrative and military commands. (3) The reorganization of the government must not exceed the existing legal framework. That evening, Chiang once again invited Mao to stay at Lin Garden.[7]

On the same day, under the name of the KMT Government's Army Chief, He Yingqin, a secret order was issued to all war zones to distribute Chiang

Kai-shek's *Manual for Suppressing Bandits*, a document compiled during the campaigns against the Red Army. The hidden threats behind the negotiations were becoming apparent.

In the following days, the talks between the two sides remained general, with the KMT failing to present any substantial proposals or suggestions. During this period, Mao Zedong spent his time considering the CPC's suggestions, meeting with various figures in Chongqing, and continuing to direct work in Yan'an and the liberated areas.

On August 30, Mao Zedong sent a telegram to Liu Shaoqi and the Central Committee of the CPC outlining eleven points of opinion. On September 3, after slight modifications, Mao had Zhou Enlai and Wang Ruofei submit these eleven points to Chiang Kai-shek through Zhang Qun, Zhang Zhizhong, and Shao Lizi. The main points were as follows: (1) Achieve national unity on the basis of peace, democracy, and unity, and build a new China that is independent, free, and prosperous, thoroughly realizing the Three Principles of the People. (2) Support Mr. Chiang and recognize his leadership nationwide. (3) Recognize the equal legal status of the CPC, the KMT, and resistance against-Japanese parties, establishing a policy of long-term cooperation and peaceful nation-building. (4) Acknowledge the contributions and legal status of the military and local governments in the liberated areas during the War of Resistance. (5) Severely punish traitors and disband puppet armies. (6) Redefine the areas for accepting the surrender of Japanese forces, with the resistance army of the liberated areas participating. (7) Cease all armed conflicts and temporarily keep all units in their current positions. (8) Achieve political democratization, nationalization of the army, and equal legality for all parties, proposing necessary methods for political democratization, nationalization of the army, and party equality.[8]

On September 4, Chiang Kai-shek handed over his self-drafted "Key Points for Negotiations with the CPC" to Zhang Qun, Wang Shijie, Zhang Zhizhong, and Shao Lizi. The key points were fourfold: (1) The CPC's military forces should be limited to a maximum of twelve divisions. (2) Recognizing the liberated areas is absolutely out of the question. (3) The National Defense Supreme Council should be reorganized into a political council with representatives from all parties. (4) The previously elected representatives of the National Assembly should remain valid, with the possibility of increasing the number of seats. Chiang formally appointed these four as his negotiation representatives, asking them to draft a response to the CPC's proposal from September 3.[9]

From September 4 to October 5, CPC representatives Zhou Enlai and Wang Ruofei held twelve negotiation sessions with KMT Government representatives Zhang Qun, Zhang Zhizhong, and Shao Lizi.

The negotiations proceeded poorly, with the focus centered on the limit for the reorganization of the CPC's military forces and the legal status of the liberated areas. Since the KMT continually refused to accept the eleven points proposed by the CPC and failed to present alternative negotiation plans, the talks stalled from September 4 and resumed on September 8. By September 21, the representatives of both sides were still at an impasse on the issues of the military and the liberated areas. During this period, on September 12, Mao Zedong and Zhou Enlai discussed military reorganization with Chiang Kai-shek, Zhang Qun, Shao Lizi, and Zhang Lisheng. On September 17, Mao Zedong had another discussion with Chiang Kai-shek and Patrick Hurley, but no progress was made.

On September 13, the Central Secretariat of the CPC issued a communiqué on the status of the Chongqing negotiations.

> Our preliminary exchange of opinions with the KMT has concluded. The KMT has shown no sincerity, and there is a significant gap between the two sides' positions, causing a delay in the negotiations. ... Chiang outwardly treats Mao, Zhou, and Wang well, creating a facade of government efforts to promote unity. In reality, he does not relax his approach to weakening and eliminating us, leveraging the national fear and opposition to civil war, his legal status, and support from the US (which seeks to secure its advantageous position in the Far East against the Soviet Union), to exert strong pressure, hoping to force our submission. Thus, in his negotiations, he only demands that we recognize and acknowledge his legal and unified military and political orders while completely denying our proposals.[10]

On September 21, Hurley met with Mao Zedong, demanding the CPC surrender the liberated areas, stating it was a choice between acknowledgment or rupture. Mao remained unmoved and calmly replied: "We neither acknowledge nor rupture; the issue is complex and requires further discussion."[11]

On the same day, Zhou Enlai, exasperated by the stalemate, sternly pointed out: "Our discussions are based on an attitude of equality, yet the KMT's perspective is arrogant and does not treat the CPC equally. Both the KMT and its government have consistently viewed our Party as subordinate since the Xi'an Incident."[12]

Following this, the CPC representatives suspended negotiations with the KMT representatives and honestly communicated the reasons for the suspension to the public. Finally, the KMT could no longer remain passive and proposed resuming negotiations on September 27, showing a more restrained attitude than before.

Although the negotiations did not reach consensus on issues such as the military, liberated areas, the National Assembly, and the political council, the gap between the two sides was gradually narrowing. On October 5, Zhou Enlai submitted a draft "Minutes of the Meeting" to the KMT for discussion. This "Minutes of the Meeting" not only confirmed the content both parties had agreed upon but also detailed each side's views on unresolved issues. Regarding the local government in liberated areas, it outlined four solutions proposed by the CPC and the points of contention.

At this time, Chiang Kai-shek had no real intention of reaching an agreement with Mao Zedong. After reading the "Minutes of the Meeting," he was uneasy. In his diary on October 2, he wrote: "The Communist Party's main aim is subversion. Their arrival in Chongqing was less about making unreasonable demands militarily and politically, but more about overthrowing all the laws and organizations of the government without recognition, even wanting to completely overturn the date of constitutional implementation and the legally elected National Assembly, replacing them with Communist laws and organizations. Their ultimate goal is to have China completely under their control and become a purely Communist China, which I cannot accept."[13]

Despite this, Chiang Kai-shek was externally pressured by the United States and the Soviet Union and internally pressured by calls for peace and democracy. He did not want to bear the blame for obstructing the Chongqing negotiations. On September 27, Mao Zedong's statement was published in the *Xinhua Daily*, declaring that "under the conditions of achieving national peace, democracy, and unity, the CPC is prepared to make significant concessions, including reducing the army in the liberated areas."[14] Additionally, news of Yan Xishan's forces being defeated in the Shangdang region indicated that the KMT was not ready to start a civil war. These factors forced Chiang Kai-shek to reconsider signing the Chongqing negotiation minutes.

In his diary on October 6, Chiang Kai-shek wrote: "Regarding the Communist issue, I must consider carefully and dare not act rashly. Ultimately, I must follow the mandate of heaven to prevent any internal or external disruptions." At noon, while discussing the CPC draft of the "Minutes of the Meeting" and Mao Zedong's departure date from Chongqing, Chiang stated, "I agree to let them proceed quickly to avoid any doubts."[15]

Two days later, on the evening of October 8, Mao Zedong attended a farewell banquet hosted by Zhang Zhizhong at the KMT Military Commission Hall, attended by four to five hundred people from various parties and sectors. In his speech, Mao said: "Today, China has only one path, which is peace. Peace is the most valuable. All other plans are wrong."[16]

The 45-day Chongqing negotiations finally reached a hopeful conclusion. On the afternoon of October 10, representatives from both the CPC and the KMT—Zhou Enlai, Wang Ruofei, Wang Shijie, Zhang Qun, Zhang Zhizhong, and Shao Lizi—signed the "Minutes of the Talks Between the Government and the CPC Representatives" in the Gui Garden.

On the afternoon of October 11, at 1:30 p.m., Mao Zedong and Wang Ruofei safely returned to Yan'an, accompanied by Zhang Zhizhong. Mao immediately chaired a meeting of the Political Bureau of the Central Committee of the CPC, reporting on the Chongqing negotiations. The meeting unanimously agreed to the "Minutes of the Talks Between the Government and the CPC Representatives."

On October 17, at a cadre meeting in Yan'an, Mao Zedong delivered a report on the Chongqing negotiations. He stated: "As a result of the negotiations, the KMT acknowledged the policy of peace and unity. This is very good. If the KMT initiates a civil war again, they will lose moral ground before the entire country and the world, giving us more justification to engage in a self-defense war to crush their attacks."[17]

Although the Chongqing negotiations ended, Chiang Kai-shek did not abandon his preparations for a military solution to China's problems. On October 13, Chiang Kai-shek issued the "Youyuan Secret Order," instructing KMT forces: "In accordance with the model for bandit suppression established by Chiang Chung-cheng [Chiang Kai-shek], all units are to be urged to intensify their efforts in the suppression campaign, to complete their tasks swiftly. Those who render meritorious service to the nation will be duly rewarded, while those who delay or fail in their duties will be punished according to the law."[18] This secret order was captured by the Jin-Ji-Lu-Yu forces during the Handan Campaign and published by Xinhua News Agency on November 6, 1945, causing a great uproar.

Despite the KMT Army's entry into Northeast China, North China, and Shandong with the assistance of American ships and planes, they had not yet stabilized their positions or completed their preparations. They still needed to buy time through ceasefires and negotiations.

On January 10, 1946, the KMT and the CPC signed the "Order and Declaration on Ceasing Conflicts and Restoring Communications," stipulating a nationwide ceasefire, except in Northeast China, to take effect on January 13. On the same day, the Political Consultative Conference was held at the National Government Hall in Chongqing. According to the pre-arranged representation scheme, the KMT had eight representatives, the CPC had 7, the Young China Party had 5, the Democratic League had 9, and social dignitaries had 9, totaling 38 attendees. After intense debates, the conference reached varying degrees of agreement on issues such as government reorganization, policy guidelines, the military, the National Assembly, and the draft constitution, and concluded on January 31.

During this process, the CPC made as many concessions as possible. On the one hand, this was to demonstrate the CPC's sincerity in seeking domestic peace and avoiding civil war; on the other hand, it was to solidify and develop the cooperative relationships with democratic parties and social dignitaries that had been established since the latter part of the War of Resistance. Although these agreements were still on paper and the KMT authorities were not prepared to implement them earnestly, they established a political benchmark for distinguishing between civil war and peace.

By June 1946, the KMT Army had completed preparations for a full-scale attack on the liberated areas, with a total force of 1.6 million troops available for the offensive. On June 17, by signing the "Agreement Between the United States of America and the Republic of China for the Disposition of Lend-Lease Supplies," the KMT Government received $51.7 million worth of military supplies.[19] Especially in the Northeast, after the Soviet Union army began withdrawing from cities and railways according to an agreement in early March 1946, the KMT Army occupied Shenyang and launched multiple offensives against various bases in the Northeast. After losing over 10,000 troops, they captured the strategic city of Siping and, by late May, occupied Changchun, controlling most areas south of the Songhua River. In early May, the KMT Government announced its return to Nanjing, intensifying preparations for a comprehensive offensive.

Chiang Kai-shek chose the Central Plains as the breakthrough point for the first battle of the full-scale civil war. On June 26, the KMT Army launched a massive attack on the Central Plains Liberation Area, marking the outbreak of the full-scale civil war.

Mao Zedong anticipated the arrival of full-scale civil war. Three days before the breakout from the Central Plains, on June 23, he drafted a telegram for the Central Committee to the Central Plains Bureau, stating: "Agree to break through immediately, the sooner the better. Do not have any misgivings. Survival first, victory first." He also specifically instructed: "In future actions, you must decide everything for yourselves without requesting instructions to avoid delays and maintain confidentiality."[20]

At this time, the people's armed forces in the liberated areas were generally at a disadvantage. This disadvantage was not only in terms of equipment but also due to the fact that many veteran soldiers, weakened by years of war, had not yet recovered, and new recruits had not yet been adequately trained. Most units were unprepared for the sudden full-scale civil war and had not completed the transition from dispersed guerrilla warfare behind enemy lines to larger-scale mobile warfare. As early as August 11, 1945, in the instructions drafted by Mao Zedong for the Central Committee on "The Party's Tasks After Japan's Surrender," it was stated: "All localities should rapidly concentrate the majority of our troops, transitioning from dispersed guerrilla states to forming regiments, brigades, or divisions, becoming supra-regional regular forces."[21] However, achieving this transition required time.

Chiang Kai-shek completely underestimated the combat capabilities of the liberated areas under Mao Zedong and the CPC. He deployed 193 brigades (divisions) of the KMT Army, accounting for 80% of the regular army and totaling 1.6 million troops, to attack the liberated areas. He hoped to resolve the Communist forces in the interior within three to six months before turning to the Northeast. The specific deployments were as follows: using 220,000 troops centered in Zhengzhou to attack the Central Plains Liberation Area; 460,000 troops centered in Xuzhou to attack the East China Liberation Area; 250,000 troops centered in Zhengzhou and Xuzhou to attack the Shanxi-Hebei-Shandong-Henan Liberation Area; 260,000 troops centered in Beiping and Taiyuan to attack the Shanxi-Chahar-Hebei and Shanxi-Suiyuan Liberation Areas; and 155,000 troops centered in Xi'an to attack the Shaanxi-Gansu-Ningxia Liberation Area.[22]

Unlike Chiang Kai-shek, Mao Zedong always considered popular support as a crucial factor in the balance of power between the enemy and us. This was true during the War of Resistance Against Japanese Aggression and remained true in the face of the KMT Army's full-scale offensive. Mao observed that the comprehensive offensive, like a "dagger revealed at the end of a map," marked the beginning of Chiang Kai-shek's decline in political struggles since the "October 10 Agreement" and the "Political Consultative Conference Agreement." He believed that as long as there was confidence in fighting and winning, repelling the full-scale offensive could deliver a fatal blow to Chiang Kai-shek.

On July 20, 1946, Mao Zedong drafted an internal Party directive titled "Smash Chiang Kai-shek's Offensive Through Self-Defense War." While boosting morale, he outlined three strategies for defeating Chiang Kai-shek. The first was military: "The general combat method to defeat Chiang Kai-shek is mobile warfare. Therefore, the temporary abandonment of some places and cities is not only inevitable but necessary. Temporarily giving up certain places and cities is essential for final victory; otherwise, we cannot achieve final victory." The second was political: "To defeat Chiang Kai-shek's offensive, we must closely cooperate with the people and win over all possible allies. We should unite all middle forces and isolate the reactionaries. Within the KMT Army, we must win over all those who oppose civil war and isolate the warmongers." The third was economic: "To defeat Chiang Kai-shek's offensive, we must plan for a protracted war. We must use our human and material resources very sparingly and avoid waste."[23]

On August 6, Mao Zedong met with American journalist Anna Louise Strong in Yan'an. In the context of the full-scale self-defense war, he put forward the famous assertion that "all reactionaries are paper tigers." He also predicted: "Taking the situation in China as an example, we rely on millet and rifles, but history will prove that millet and rifles are stronger than Chiang Kai-shek's planes and tanks."[24]

In reality, Mao Zedong made the decision to oppose the full-scale offensive through self-defense warfare under tremendous pressure. Influenced by the increasingly tense international situation between the US and the Soviet Union, pessimism about an inevitable "US-Soviet Union War" and the outbreak of "World War III" pervaded the country. Some within the Party feared the United States and the prospect of triggering a new world war, thus showing hesitation and weakness in the face of the KMT Army's full-scale offensive. In response, Mao Zedong wrote "Some Estimates on the Current International Situation" in April 1946, before the full-scale offensive broke out.

Addressing the argument that "the US and the Soviet Union are bound to go to war," Mao pointed out: "The world's reactionary forces are indeed preparing for a third world war, and the danger of war exists. However, the democratic forces of the world's people surpass the reactionary forces and are advancing, so they must and will overcome the danger of war. Therefore, the relationship between the US, Britain, France, and the Soviet Union is not a matter of either compromise or rupture, but rather of earlier or later compromise." He added: "Such compromises will not be numerous in the short term. There is a possibility of expanding commercial and trade relations between the US, Britain, France, and the Soviet Union."

Addressing concerns that compromises between the US, Britain, France, and the Soviet Union might also require us to compromise, Mao Zedong stated: "Such compromises do not require the people of capitalist countries to follow suit domestically. The people of each country will continue to struggle according to their different situations."[25]

These internal documents and external communications accurately conveyed a clear message: the Chinese Communists could win this seemingly uneven war in terms of military power.

Over the next two months, this assessment proved accurate. In their offensives against the liberated areas, the KMT forces achieved some territorial gains but failed to inflict significant damage on the Communist forces. On the contrary, between July 13 and August 31, 1946, Su Yu and Tan Zhenlin commanded the Central China Field Army in the region of Taixing, Rugao, Hai'an, and Shaobo in southern Jiangsu. Concentrating superior forces, they achieved seven consecutive victories, annihilating six brigades and five traffic police battalions under Tang Enbo's command, totaling over 53,000 KMT troops, nearly half of their total forces. From September 3 to 8, Liu Bocheng and Deng Xiaoping led the Shanxi-Hebei-Shandong-Henan Field Army to victory in the Dingtao Campaign, destroying four brigades and over 17,000 KMT troops in the areas around Heze, Dingtao, and Caoxian in Shandong.

Mao Zedong summarized the successful experiences from these battles and, on September 16, drafted and issued a directive from the Central Military Commission titled "Concentrate Superior Forces to Annihilate the Enemy in Detail." He pointed out: "During the War of Resistance, our army primarily used dispersed forces for guerrilla warfare, supplementing it with concentrated forces for mobile warfare. In the current civil war period, the situation has changed, and our combat methods must change accordingly. Our army should now primarily use concentrated forces for mobile warfare, supplementing it with dispersed forces for guerrilla warfare. Given the increased firepower of Chiang's forces, we must particularly emphasize the method of concentrating superior forces to annihilate the enemy in detail."

Mao Zedong's decision to adopt this strategy was based on successful battlefield examples and his insight into the flaws in Chiang Kai-shek's overall offensive deployment, allowing him to concentrate attacks on the "soft spots." The flaws in Chiang's deployment were primarily a severe shortage of second-line troops and the difficulty of maintaining troop morale. Mao Zedong emphasized as follows:

> The effects of this strategy are first, it ensures complete annihilation of the enemy; second, it achieves quick victories. Complete annihilation most effectively strikes the enemy, reducing their forces unit by unit. For an enemy lacking second-line troops, this strategy is most effective. Complete annihilation also allows us to replenish ourselves most fully, as our primary source of weapons and ammunition and an important source of recruits. For the enemy, it demoralizes and disheartens their troops, while for us, it boosts morale and invigorates our forces. Quick victories allow us to annihilate enemy reinforcements in detail and avoid enemy reinforcements. Tactical and operational quick victories are necessary for strategic endurance.[26]

By February 1947, the KMT Army's full-scale offensive had ended. Chiang Kai-shek was forced to retract his forces, adjust deployments, and switch from a comprehensive offensive to focused attacks, selecting the Shandong and Shaanxi-Gansu-Ningxia liberated areas as his primary targets, committing 43% of his total offensive forces to these areas.[27] The development of subsequent battles proved that this deployment was a strategic blunder, exposing the Central Plains, which Mao Zedong and the People's Liberation Army (PLA) exploited, leading to the Liu-Deng Army advancing into the Dabie Mountains.

Starting March 13, 1947, the commander of the KMT Army's First Theater Command launched an attack on northern Shaanxi with 15 brigades, totaling over 140,000 troops, from Luochuan and Yichuan. At this time, the PLA's total forces in the northern Shaanxi battlefield were only about 30,000, creating a stark disparity in troop numbers. On March 19, Mao Zedong and the Central Committee, government, and military organs voluntarily evacuated Yan'an, beginning their strategic maneuvering in northern Shaanxi.

Mao Zedong had his reasons for abandoning Yan'an. First, it would burden the KMT forces, forcing them to garrison and defend it. Second, it would reveal Chiang Kai-shek's treachery to both domestic and international audiences. Third, it would foster arrogance in Chiang Kai-shek.[28] More profoundly, Mao aimed to exploit Chiang's eagerness to eliminate the CPC's central organs: "If we can draw the main enemy forces to Shaanxi-Gansu-Ningxia and destroy them, it will facilitate other liberated areas in striking and eliminating the enemy and recovering lost territory."[29]

As the supreme commander willing to disregard personal safety and use himself as a strategic pawn, Mao Zedong was unique in history.

On the night of March 29 to 30, Mao Zedong chaired a Central Committee meeting in Zaolin Gully, Qingjian County, northern Shaanxi. The meeting made an important decision: Mao Zedong, Zhou Enlai, and Ren Bishi would stay in northern Shaanxi with the Central organs and the PLA headquarters to oversee central work, while Liu Shaoqi, Zhu De, and Dong Biwu would form the Central Working Committee, with Liu Shaoqi as secretary, to proceed to northwest Shanxi or another appropriate location to carry out the Central Committee's entrusted tasks. From this point, Mao Zedong adopted the pseudonym "Li Desheng" (meaning triumph over an opponent).

In the following months, Mao Zedong, Zhou Enlai, and Ren Bishi led the Central Committee apparatus in a series of evasive maneuvers across northern Shaanxi, effectively evading the encirclement efforts of Hu Zongnan's KMT forces. Under the protection of the local populace, they moved frequently and unpredictably. Concurrently, Mao directed the main forces of Peng Dehuai's Northwest Field Army, which achieved a series of victories at Qinghuabian (March 25), Yangma River (April 14), and Panlong (May 2 to 4), at the cost of over 2,200 casualties, inflicting over 14,000 casualties on the KMT forces.[30] From August 18 to 20, in the Battle of Shajiadian, the main forces of the Northwest Field Army, at the cost of 1,800 casualties, annihilated the 36th Reorganized Division's headquarters and two brigades, totaling over 6,000 troops. This battle marked the turning point for the Northwest Field Army, shifting from a defensive to an offensive strategy, and thwarting Chiang Kai-shek's plans to annihilate the CPC Central Committee and the Northwest Field Army in Shaanxi or drive them east of the Yellow River.

Observing Hu Zongnan's deployments since the onset of his offensive against northern Shaanxi, particularly after the Battle of Panlong, Mao concluded that Hu aimed to drive the Northwest Field Army across the Yellow River. This further solidified his resolve to remain west of the river. On May 11, Mao drafted a telegram for the Central Military Commission to the commanders of East China, Shanxi-Hebei-Shandong-Henan, and Northwest Field Armies, as well as the Central Working Committee leaders. He stated: "Hu Zongnan's current offensive aims to drive us east of the river. On March 31, he occupied Qingjian but deliberately did not advance to Suide, leaving a route open for us. Nearly a month later, on April 26, he ordered Dong Zhao to lead eight and a half brigades northward, reaching Suide on May 2, thinking they could drive us across the river. On May 5, we captured Panlong, which shocked them, realizing we were near Yan'an, prompting Dong Zhao to quickly withdraw south without leaving a single soldier in Suide. This proves that Hu's goal was not to open the Xianyang–Yulin Highway but to drive us across the river." The telegram concluded: "Chiang will find his dream shattered."[31]

From the evacuation of Yan'an on March 19, 1947, Mao Zedong traveled through Qingjian, Zichang, Zizhou, Jingbian, Hengshan, Suide, Mizhi, Jiaxian, covering over 2,000 *li*, finally arriving at Yangjiagou in Jia County on November 22, where the Central Committee held its December Meeting. On March 21 of the following year, from here, he set off to cross the Yellow River and head to the Jin-Cha-Ji base area to command strategic decisive battles. During this period, Mao skillfully maneuvered against Hu Zongnan while simultaneously commanding the Northwest, Shandong, North China, Northeast, and Shanxi-Hebei-Shandong-Henan strategic areas, coordinating millions of troops across vast battlefields, demonstrating his superb military command skills.

The KMT Army's focus on the Shandong Liberation Area began in late March 1947. They amassed 450,000 troops, learning from their previous comprehensive offensive failures, and adopted a strategy of concentrated forces, close coordination, steady and gradual advances, and simultaneous frontal assaults, achieving their initial goal of occupying southern Shandong by early April, and then advanced toward central Shandong.

In this situation, Mao repeatedly instructed the East China Field Army to exercise great patience, hold the maximum strength at hand, allow the enemy to advance boldly, and seize the opportunity to annihilate them. In mid-May 1947, the East China Field Army encircled and isolated one of the KMT Army's five main forces, the 74th Reorganized Division, in Mengliangu and nearby areas. From May 15 to 16, they launched the Battle of Mengliangu, annihilating the 74th Reorganized Division and over 32,000 troops at the cost of over 12,000 casualties, killing division commander Lieutenant General Zhang Lingfu.

By June 1947, the overall situation changed significantly. The KMT Army's total strength dropped from 4.3 million to 3.73 million, with regular forces reduced from 2 million to 1.5 million. Their strategic objectives in both comprehensive and focused offensives had largely failed, and their weaknesses in troop deployment became more apparent. The proportion of forces used in attacking the liberated areas increased from 80% in June 1946 to 92%, but of the 248 brigades they could mobilize, 70 were concentrated in the North China and Northeast battlefields, and 157 in the Shandong, Shanxi-Hebei-Shandong-Henan, and Shaanxi battlefields, leaving only 21 brigades in southern China and the Northwest.

Mao Zedong keenly observed the fatal weaknesses in Chiang Kai-shek's deployments and noted his strategy of "continuing the war in the liberated areas, further destroying and depleting their manpower and resources, and preventing us from sustaining the fight."[32] Seizing this fleeting opportunity, Mao made the strategic decision in June 1947 to dispatch the main forces of the Shanxi-Hebei-Shandong-Henan Field Army, led by Liu Bocheng and Deng Xiaoping (known as the "Liu-Deng Army"), to advance a thousand *li* into the Dabie Mountains. This move aimed to shift from passive defense to active offense, bringing the war into the KMT-controlled areas, accelerating the progress of the liberation war, and transitioning from strategic defense to strategic offense.

From late June 1947, Liu-Deng Army crossed the Yellow River from northern Shandong, moving through southwestern Shandong into the border regions of Henan, Anhui, Jiangsu, and the Dabie Mountains. To support this advance, Mao Zedong ordered the Fourth Column of the Shanxi-Hebei-Shandong-Henan Field Army, led by Chen Geng and Xie Fuzhi (known as the "Chen-Xie Group"), to cease reinforcements to the Shaanxi battlefield and instead cross the Yellow River from southern Shanxi to support Liu-Deng Army in the border areas of Henan, Shaanxi, and Hubei. He also commanded Chen Yi and Su Yu to lead the East China Field Army's Western Corps (known as the "Chen-Su Army") to support the Liu-Deng Army in the Henan-Anhui-Jiangsu border region.

Under Mao Zedong's command, the Liu-Deng Army broke through multiple encirclements and entered the northern slopes of the Dabie Mountains on August 27, initiating strategic deployments in the border areas of Hubei, Henan, and Anhui, north of the Yangtze River. The Chen-Xie Group arrived in the border regions of Henan, Shaanxi, and Hubei by November, while the Chen-Su Army expanded the liberated areas in the Henan-Anhui-Jiangsu border region through a series of battles in October. These three armies formed a tripod, like a sharp blade pointed at the KMT-controlled Central Plains, causing Chiang Kai-shek significant unease and highlighting Mao Zedong's strategic prowess.

At this juncture, Mao Zedong glimpsed the dawn of victory. On October 10, 1947, the "Double Tenth Day," Mao drafted and publicly issued the "Proclamation of the Chinese PLA." Previously, he had cautiously referred to the ongoing conflict as a "self-defense war." Now, in the proclamation, he declared: "The objective of our military operations, repeatedly announced to both domestic and international audiences, is the liberation of the Chinese people and the Chinese nation. Today, it is to meet the urgent demands of the entire nation, to overthrow the chief instigator of the civil war, Chiang Kai-shek, and to organize a democratic coalition government, thereby achieving the overall goal of liberating the people and the nation."[33] This proclamation also outlined the CPC's eight-point program, including "overthrowing Chiang Kai-shek's dictatorial government and establishing a democratic coalition government." Additionally, the headquarters of the Chinese PLA issued an order to re-promulgate the "Three Main Rules of Discipline and Eight Points for Attention." These actions signaled the rapid approach of a new phase in the Chinese revolution.

Mao Zedong knew that the time had come to fully present the political, military, and economic programs for establishing a new China. From December 25 to 28, 1947, he presided over an expanded meeting of the Central

Committee in Yangjiagou, Mizhi County, northern Shaanxi, and submitted a written report titled "Current Situation and Tasks."

This report began with an air of triumphant anticipation.

> The Chinese people's revolutionary war has now reached a turning point. This is because the Chinese PLA has repelled the offensive of several million reactionary troops commanded by the American lackey Chiang Kai-shek and has turned to the offensive itself. This is the turning point from the development to the destruction of Chiang Kai-shek's 20-year counter-revolutionary rule. This is the turning point from the development to the destruction of over a century of imperialist domination in China. This is a great event. Its greatness lies in the fact that it is happening in a country with a population of 475 million people. Once this event occurs, it will inevitably lead to nationwide victory.

The report summarized the military victories of the liberation war and derived ten military principles, confidently stating: "Our strategy and tactics are based on people's war; no anti-people army can utilize our strategies and tactics." It clarified the policy of thoroughly implementing land reform: "Our policy is to rely on the poor peasants, firmly unite with the middle peasants, and eliminate the landlord class and the old-style rich farmers' feudal and semi-feudal exploitation system." It also elucidated the economic program for completing the Chinese revolution: "Confiscate the land of the feudal class and distribute it to the peasants, confiscate the monopolistic capital of Chiang Kai-shek, Soong Tse-ven, Kung Hsiang-hsi, and Chen Lifu, and place it under the ownership of the new democratic state, and protect national industry and commerce. These are the three major economic programs of the new democratic revolution." The report outlined the future economic structure of new China: "In summary, the economic structure of new China will be (1) state-owned economy, which is the leading component; (2) agricultural economy gradually moving from individual to collective ownership; and (3) economy of independent small business owners and small to medium private capital economy. These constitute the entire national economy of a new democracy. The guiding principle of the new democratic national economy must strictly follow the general goal of developing production, flourishing the economy, accommodating both public and private interests, and benefiting both labor and capital. Any policy, plan, or method that deviates from this general goal is wrong." It also elaborated on the basic political program: "Unite the oppressed classes of workers, peasants, soldiers, students, and merchants, all people's organizations, all democratic parties, all national minorities, overseas Chinese, and other patriotic elements to form a national united front, overthrow Chiang Kai-shek's dictatorial government, and establish a democratic coalition government." The report proposed and elucidated the task of Party rectification, stating: "Solving the problem of internal impurity, reorganizing the Party's ranks so that it can stand entirely with the broadest masses of workers and lead them forward, is a decisive link in solving the land problem and supporting a protracted war."[34]

Containing such a wide array of programs and policies in a single document was rare in Mao Zedong's writings. This indicated not only that Mao was at the peak of his theoretical and ideological creativity but also underscored the critical importance of these constructive programs and policies for the CPC at that moment. As Mao Zedong later profoundly remarked, "Only when the Party's policies and strategies are completely on the right track will the Chinese revolution have a chance of victory."[35]

Chapter 10

Carrying the Revolution to the End

Over Zhongshan swept a storm, headlong,

Our mighty army, a million strong, has crossed the Great River.

The city, a tiger crouching, a dragon curling, outshines its ancient glories,

In heroic triumph heaven and earth have been overturned.

With power and to spare we must pursue the tottering foe,

And not ape Xiang Yu the conqueror seeking idle fame.

Were Nature sentient, she too would pass from youth to age,

But Man's world is mutable, and seas become mulberry fields.

MAO ZEDONG,
"*Qi Lü* · The PLA Captures Nanjing" (April 1949)

As Chiang Kai-shek encountered difficulties on the military front, he also began to face unprecedented crises in the political arena. Ironically, these crises were largely of his own making, with a significant turning point being the convening of the National Assembly.

On October 11, 1946, after the KMT Army occupied Zhangjiakou, a key city in the North China Liberation Area, the illusion of victory in their comprehensive offensive reached its peak. That afternoon, Chiang Kai-shek announced the convening of the so-called National Assembly. In mid-November, this National Assembly convened in Nanjing, where it passed the so-called *Constitution of the Republic of China*. The CPC and the China Democratic League, among others, unanimously boycotted this National Assembly, which only the Youth Party and a few "social notables" attended. Liang Shuming, the Secretary-General of the China Democratic League, remarked pointedly upon hearing the news of Chiang Kai-shek's announcement: "We woke up to find that democracy is dead."[1]

Chiang Kai-shek's notable move during the ten-year civil war was to attract representatives from the national bourgeoisie and intellectuals. However, by this time, more and more were drifting away from the KMT. From sabotaging the Double Tenth Agreement and shutting down negotiations, to breaking the ceasefire agreement and launching a full-scale civil war, and then convening the National Assembly to tear up the Political Consultative Conference Agreement, Chiang Kai-shek repeatedly shattered his self-created visions of peace and democracy. Consequently, he not only lost the military battlefield supported by force but also the political battlefield supported by public sentiment. Especially after declaring the China Democratic League an "illegal organization" on October 27, 1947, he set himself on an irrevocable path to failure.

Mao Zedong was acutely aware of this. In May 1947, he pointed out in a commentary for Xinhua News Agency: "There are now two fronts in China. The first is the war between Chiang Kai-shek's invading army and the PLA. The second front is the sharp struggle between the great, just student movement and Chiang Kai-shek's reactionary government. The slogans of the student movement are for food, peace, and freedom—against hunger, civil war, and persecution." He continued, "The student movement is part of the broader people's movement. The rise of the student movement will inevitably promote the rise of the entire people's movement."[2] In a commentary titled "Chiang Kai-shek Dissolves the Democratic League" on November 3 for Xinhua News Agency, he predicted, "Declaring the Democratic League illegal does not harm the League but rather gives it a brighter path than before."[3]

As the KMT increasingly found itself politically isolated, more democratic figures abandoned the fantasy of a "third way" and sought new beginnings. At Mao Zedong's suggestion, the Central Committee of the CPC issued a call on April 30, 1948, for "all democratic parties, people's organizations, and social notables to quickly convene a Political Consultative Conference to discuss and realize the convening of a People's Representative Assembly and the formation of a democratic coalition government." This call was quickly met with enthusiastic responses from democratic parties, people's organizations, and independent democratic figures, who risked their lives to gather in the liberated areas.

In the face of impending victory, Mao Zedong remained particularly calm. His extensive political experience taught him that while the enemy was thoroughly isolated, this did not equate to victory. Mistakes in policy could still prevent victory and lead to failure. From crossing the Yellow River to the Jin-Cha-Ji liberated area, to briefly staying in Chengnanzhuang, and then moving to Xibaipo, Mao devoted significant effort to correcting various "leftist" errors in land reform, industrial and commercial policies, and united front policies. By the time of the Political Bureau of the Central Committee of the CPC meeting in Xibaipo from September 8 to 13, 1948, Mao believed that this work had achieved satisfactory results.

After meticulously planning the above strategies, Mao Zedong focused his main energy on leading and commanding the impending strategic decisive battles.

Where should the battleground for the strategic decisive battle be chosen? As the KMT forces bolstered their defenses in central China, leading to a stalemate, Mao once considered having Su Yu lead three corps south of the Yangtze River to engage the KMT forces, thereby drawing 20 to 30 KMT brigades back to the south and "bringing the war south of the Yangtze River, where the enemy could be defeated piece by piece in the Jianghuai and Han River regions."[4] On January 27, 1948, Mao drafted a telegram for the Central Military Commission to Su Yu, suggesting: "With 70,000 to 80,000 troops moving south, maneuvering between Hunan and Jiangxi for six months to a year, moving in leaps with more time spent resting than marching and fighting, ultimately reaching Fujian, Zhejiang, and Jiangxi. This would keep the enemy in a passive defensive position, unable to cope, and constantly fatigued."[5]

After receiving the Central Military Commission's telegram, Su Yu conducted thorough research and proposed to Mao and the Central Military

Commission that the main forces should temporarily remain in central China instead of moving south. Mao took this suggestion seriously and immediately decided to have Chen Yi and Su Yu come to the Central Committee as soon as possible. During the expanded meeting of the Central Committee's Secretariat from April 30 to May 7, 1948, Su Yu presented his report.

On May 5, Mao drafted a telegram from the Central Military Commission to Liu Bocheng, Deng Xiaoping, and the East China Bureau, deciding: "Currently, the mission of Su Yu's group (the 1st, 4th, and 6th Corps) is not to cross the river immediately but to open the way for crossing. In the next four to eight months, this group, along with three other corps, should aim to eliminate five to twelve regular brigades in the area north and south of the Kaifeng–Xuzhou line, preparing for the crossing." He also emphasized: "This plan was agreed upon with Chen (Yi), Su (Yu), Bo (Yibo), and (Li) Xiannian."[6]

The following months were crucial for Mao's decision to concentrate on annihilating the main KMT forces north of the Yangtze River. Not only did Su Yu's group achieve a significant victory in the Eastern Henan Campaign, liberating Kaifeng and annihilating over 90,000 enemy troops, but the Central Plains Field Army won the Xiangfan Campaign, and the Northwest Field Army recaptured Yan'an. Additionally, after reclaiming most of Shandong and northern Jiangsu, the East China Field Army captured Jinan on September 24, linking the North China and East China Liberated Areas and severing the KMT forces' connection between North China and the Central Plains. Meanwhile, the Northeast Field Army launched a winter offensive, compressing the KMT forces in the Northeast into isolated cities like Changchun, Shenyang, and Jinzhou. The overall situation in the north was fundamentally transformed.

In this context, on October 10, Mao issued the "Notice on the September Meeting from the Central Committee," which conveyed the spirit of the Political Bureau of the Central Committee's September Meeting, stating: "The KMT currently has 285 regular brigades, totaling 1.98 million troops. Of these, 249 brigades, or 1.742 million troops, are on the front lines (99 brigades, or 694,000 troops, in the north; 150 brigades, or 1.048 million troops, in the south). Only 36 brigades, or 238,000 troops, are in the rear, most of which are newly established and lack combat effectiveness. Therefore, the Central Committee has decided that the PLA will continue to fight entirely north of the Yangtze River and in North China and Northeast China for the third year."[7]

At this point, Chiang Kai-shek also realized the issues with dispersed frontline deployments and the severe lack of second-line troops, but it was too late. At the end of 1947, Chiang decided to establish the North China "Bandit Suppression" Headquarters, consolidating military and political power in Shanxi, Chahar, Hebei, Rehe, and Suiyuan under Fu Zuoyi as commander. From May to July 1948, the Northeast Liaison Office was abolished, expanding the authority of Wei Lihuang, Commander of the Northeast "Bandit Suppression" Headquarters. The Wuhan Liaison Office was also abolished, establishing the Xuzhou and Central China "Bandit Suppression" Headquarters, with Liu Zhi and Bai Chongxi appointed as commanders. Chiang even considered having the main KMT forces in the Northeast retreat to Jinzhou for potential redeployment to North or East China.[8] This deployment adjustment inadvertently created conditions for Mao to direct the PLA to annihilate these key KMT strategic groups north of the Yangtze River.

After carefully studying and considering all possibilities, Mao Zedong ultimately directed the strategic breakthrough toward the northeast, targeting Wei Lihuang's group.

At that time, Wei Lihuang's group had 100,000 troops defending Changchun, 300,000 in the Shenyang area, and 150,000 along the Yi County, Jinzhou, Jinxi, and Shanhaiguan lines. Mao's strategy was to create a "trap to catch a dog," sealing off the KMT forces in the northeast for piecemeal annihilation.[9] This required a bold move that the enemy would not expect: attacking Jinzhou first. On September 7, Mao telegraphed Lin Biao and Luo Ronghuan, saying: "To annihilate these enemies, you should prepare to use your main forces along this line, ignoring the enemies in Changchun and Shenyang, and be ready to destroy any enemy reinforcements from these locations when attacking Jinzhou." To achieve this, they needed to "(1) resolve to capture Jinzhou, Shanhaiguan, and Tangshan, and completely control this line; and (2) resolve to engage in a major annihilation battle unprecedented for you, daring to fight even if Wei Lihuang's entire army comes to aid."[10]

On September 12, the Liaoshen Campaign officially began. By October 1, the railway between Beining and Jinzhou was completely cut off, making Jinzhou an isolated city. This hit Chiang Kai-shek hard. On October 2, he hurriedly flew to Shenyang to consult with Fu Zuoyi and Wei Lihuang, directing North China "Bandit Suppression" forces and Yantai garrison troops to rapidly reinforce Huludao by sea, forming an eastern corps with forces from Jinxi and Huludao. The main forces in Shenyang were to form a western corps, commanded by the Ninth Corps Commander Liao Yaoxiang, to cooperate with Jinzhou's defenders in counter-surrounding the Northeast Field Army.

This situation caused Lin Biao to hesitate about attacking Jinzhou. On October 2 at 10 p.m., he telegraphed the Central Military Commission, proposing two plans: continue attacking Jinzhou or switch to attacking Changchun. After receiving Lin's telegram, Mao repeatedly telegraphed on the afternoon of October 3 at 5 p.m. and 7 p.m., and again on the morning of October 4, resolutely ordering the capture of Jinzhou, stating: "Once you take Jinzhou, you will gain the initiative in the campaign. Taking Changchun will not give you this advantage and will instead increase your difficulties in the next step. Consider this deeply."[11] This highlighted the significant differences between Mao's strategic vision and boldness as the supreme commander and Lin Biao's perspective as the field commander.

Following this, the Liaoshen Campaign proceeded very smoothly. Jinzhou was captured on October 15, Changchun was peacefully liberated on October 19, Liao Yaoxiang's corps was completely annihilated on October 28, and Shenyang and Yingkou were captured on November 2. The Northeast Field Army, with 700,000 main forces and 330,000 local troops, achieved a decisive victory, annihilating over 472,000 KMT troops and liberating the entire northeast. The Northeast Field Army then moved south, creating conditions for the victory in the Pingjin Campaign.

A key feature of Mao's military strategy was not giving the enemy any respite. Before the Liaoshen Campaign ended, he shifted his focus to the central China battlefield. On October 11, in a telegram to the leaders of the East China Field Army, copied to the East China Bureau and Central China Bureau, Mao outlined the Huaihai Campaign's operational strategy. It stated:

"The first phase of this campaign focuses on concentrating forces to annihilate Huang Baitao's corps, breaking through in the center, and occupying Xin'an Town, Yunhe Station, Caobaji, Yixian, Zaozhuang, Lincheng, Hanzhuang, Shuyang, Pixian, Tancheng, Tai'erzhuang, and Linyi."[12] The telegram also planned the subsequent phases of the Huaihai Campaign.

At that time, Mao envisioned the result of the Huaihai Campaign as "opening up the northern Jiangsu battlefield, linking Shandong and northern Jiangsu."[13] The actual result far exceeded Mao's expectations. The Huaihai Campaign evolved into a decisive strategic battle centered on Xuzhou, stretching from Haizhou in the east to Shangqiu in the west, from Lincheng (now Xuecheng) in the north to the Huai River in the south.

When initiating the Liaoshen Campaign, the Northeast Field Army had an absolute advantage over the KMT defenders. However, in the Huaihai Campaign, the forces were nearly evenly matched. The KMT forces, under the command of Xuzhou "Bandit Suppression" Commander-in-Chief Liu Zhi and Deputy Commander-in-Chief Du Yuming, included four corps and four pacification districts. With reinforcements from Huang Wei's corps in central China, the total strength was nearly 800,000 troops, including many of Chiang Kai-shek's elite units.[14] The PLA participated with 16 corps from the East China Field Army, seven corps from the Central Plains Field Army, and regional forces from the East China, Central China, and North China military districts, totaling over 600,000 troops.

In such a vast region, against such a powerful enemy, and with our two field armies participating in the battle, it is essential to strengthen unified command at the highest level. On November 16, as the Huaihai Campaign progressed, the Central Military Commission decided to form the General Front Committee, consisting of Liu Bocheng, Chen Yi, Deng Xiaoping, Su Yu, and Tan Zhenlin. This committee was empowered to hold five-person meetings to discuss important issues when possible, with Liu, Chen, and Deng serving as the regular standing members to handle everything on the spot. Deng Xiaoping was designated as the secretary of the General Front Committee.[15] The progress of the Huaihai Campaign demonstrated that this was a key decision ensuring victory.

After the fall of Jinan, Xuzhou became the first barrier protecting Nanjing and Shanghai. Xuzhou's surrounding area, with the Jinpu and Longhai Railway (Lanzhou–Lianyungang Railway) lines crisscrossing, offered convenient transportation and flat terrain suitable for large-scale mobile warfare. Along the Xuzhou-Bengbu line, the KMT forces deployed included the Seventh Corps (Huang Baitao), Second Corps (Qiu Qingquan), Thirteenth Corps (Li Mi), Sixteenth Corps (Sun Yuanliang), and Twelfth Corps (Huang Wei), along with four armies directly under the Xuzhou "Bandit Suppression" headquarters and two armies from the Third Pacification District (Feng Zhi'an). At the same time, preparations were made for the possible abandonment of Xuzhou.

On November 6, the KMT forces began to further shrink toward the sides of the Jinpu Railway between Xuzhou and Bengbu. Seizing this favorable opportunity, the main forces of the East China and Central Plains Field Armies launched the Huaihai Campaign. Mao Zedong instructed them to use the tactics applied in Jinan, surrounding Huang Baitao's Seventh Corps with half their forces while using the other half to block reinforcements. At the critical moment of encircling Huang Baitao's corps, underground Communist Party members He Jifeng and Zhang Kexia led 23,000 KMT troops to defect in the Tai'erzhuang area, enabling the PLA to swiftly cut off Huang Baitao's retreat. By November 11, Huang Baitao's corps, consisting of four armies, was surrounded in an area centered on Nianzhuang, covering less than 18 square kilometers.

Chiang Kai-shek, realizing the danger of Huang Baitao's encirclement and the potential fragmentation and annihilation of the Liu Zhi group in Xuzhou, hastily altered his plan to concentrate forces between Xuzhou and Bengbu, ordering the main forces of the Xuzhou "Bandit Suppression" headquarters to swiftly converge on Xuzhou and reinforce Huang Baitao's corps. In a letter to Huang Baitao dated November 10, Chiang wrote: "The Xuzhou-Huaihai battle is the most critical for the success or failure of our revolution and the survival of our nation."[16] This move was exactly what Mao Zedong had anticipated. On November 13, Mao Zedong sent a telegram to the East China Field Army, stating: "Now that Qiu Qingquan is advancing eastward to reinforce, please have Su (Yu), Chen (Shiju), and Zhang (Zhen) assess the situation of the destruction of Huang Baitao's forces. When Huang's forces are nearly completely annihilated, allow Qiu Qingquan's troops to advance further eastward to Daxujia and Caobaji, so that we can encircle Qiu's corps and prevent them from escaping, and then gradually plan their annihilation."[17] In a November 16 telegram, he added: "This victory will not only determine the situation north of the Yangtze River but also fundamentally resolve the national situation. Plan everything from this perspective."[18]

Meanwhile, in his commentary "The Major Changes in China's Military Situation," published by Xinhua News Agency on November 14, Mao publicly stated: "Originally, it was estimated that from July 1946, it would take about five years to fundamentally defeat the reactionary KMT Government. Now it seems that from now on, it will take only about one more year to fundamentally defeat the KMT reactionary government."[19]

On November 22, the East China Field Army completely annihilated Huang Baitao's corps, killing Huang Baitao himself. On November 15, the Central Plains Field Army captured the strategic hub of Su County, severing the connection between the enemies in Xuzhou and Bengbu. Subsequently, Mao adopted the General Front Committee's suggestion to encircle and annihilate Huang Wei's Twelfth Corps using all the Central Plains Field Army and part of the East China Field Army. By December 15, they had annihilated Huang Wei's corps, capturing Huang Wei himself.

Even while Huang Wei's Twelfth Corps was being encircled, Chiang Kai-shek urgently summoned the deputy commander of the Xuzhou "Bandit Suppression" headquarters and director of the forward command, Du Yuming, to Nanjing. Chiang decided to abandon Xuzhou and ordered the main forces to retreat south and rescue Huang Wei's corps. Du Yuming led the Second, Thirteenth, and Sixteenth Corps out of Xuzhou, taking with them a large number of KMT Government personnel and causing chaotic and crowded conditions. In desperation, Chiang airdropped a personal letter to Du, sternly ordering him to change his course and reinforce Huang Wei's corps. However, Du's forces were encircled by the East China Field Army during their rapid maneuver. Sun Yuanliang's Sixteenth Corps was completely annihilated during the breakout attempt, with Sun Yuanliang himself escaping in disguise.

After achieving the results of annihilating Huang Wei's Twelfth Corps and Sun Yuanliang's Sixteenth Corps and encircling Du Yuming's forces in the

Huaihai Campaign, Mao decisively hit the "pause button" to support the ongoing Pingjin Campaign, preventing Chiang from deciding to transport the Beiping defenders by sea to the south. On December 14, Mao issued an order in the name of the Central Military Commission, instructing all forces to "rest for several days in their current positions, adopting a defensive stance without offensive actions."[20] On December 16, he further ordered: "Launch continuous political offensives against Du Yuming, Qiu Qingquan, and Li Mi. In addition to what the troops are doing, draft broadcast speeches to be delivered every three to five days, adjusting the content based on the specific battlefield situation, and send them to us for approval and broadcast."[21]

In Mao Zedong's mind, the grand strategy was to annihilate the main forces of the KMT Army north of the Yangtze River. The three major campaigns, launched almost simultaneously, were closely coordinated, with a masterful balance of offensive and defensive maneuvers, demonstrating extraordinary command artistry.

Even before the Liaoshen Campaign concluded, Mao ordered Lin Biao and Luo Ronghuan to lead the main forces of the Northeast Field Army secretly into the region, thus commencing the Pingjin Campaign.

Mao Zedong was adept at identifying and resolving the key issues (main contradictions) driving the development of events. This skill was evident in his orchestration of the three major campaigns.

In the Liaoshen Campaign, the critical move was to capture Jinzhou and prevent the enemy in the Northeast from retreating into the interior. During the Huaihai Campaign, the KMT Army's heavy concentration of forces between Xuzhou and Bengbu necessitated a decisive mid-line breakthrough. Mao's strategic deployments capitalized on these key points, leaving Chiang Kai-shek struggling to respond and ultimately losing everything. Now, in the Pingjin Campaign, with Fu Zuoyi's forces already jittery and Chiang wavering between abandoning and defending the area, Mao recognized that the key was to prevent Chiang from quickly deciding to transport the Pingjin forces south by sea.[22] Mao's crucial moves opened the door to victory.

First, he ordered the Northeast Field Army to swiftly and secretly enter the region. On November 18, Mao instructed the main forces to take the fastest route to suddenly surround Tangshan, Tanggu, and Tianjin, preventing their escape.[23] He also directed the North China Military Region forces to attack enemy positions in Xuanhua and Zhangjiakou, cutting off Fu Zuoyi's westward retreat to Suiyuan.

Second, he established the attack sequence for the entire Pingjin Campaign. "The order of attack was approximately first, the Tanggu area; second, Xinbao'an; third, the Tangshan area; fourth, Tianjin and Zhangjiakou; and finally, Beiping." "Initially surround Tianjin, Tanggu, Lutai, and Tangshan," Mao wrote, "as long as Tanggu and Xinbao'an are captured, the whole situation will be unlocked."[24]

Third, during a specific time frame, he implemented a strategy of "encircling without attacking" or "isolating without encircling." "From now until two weeks later (December 11 to December 25), the basic principle is to encircle without attacking (for example, Zhangjiakou and Xinbao'an) and to isolate without encircling (i.e., only strategically encircling and cutting off enemy contacts without tactical encirclement, for example, Beiping, Tianjin, and Tongzhou), waiting for the completion of deployments before annihilating the enemy."[25]

These strategies proved effective. By around December 20, the main forces of the Northeast Field Army and the North China Military Region troops had encircled Fu Zuoyi's forces along the Pingjin and Pingzhang Railway (Beijing–Zhangjiakou Railway) lines, segmenting the enemy positions in Zhangjiakou, Xinbao'an, Beiping, Tianjin, and Tanggu. They then launched offensives following Mao's designated attack sequence: Xinbao'an fell on December 12, Zhangjiakou on December 24. Before attacking Tanggu, it was decided to alter the plan and concentrate forces on Tianjin from January 3, 1949. By January 15, Tianjin was liberated, and Tianjin Garrison Commander Chen Changjie was captured. Seeing the situation as hopeless, the Tanggu forces fled south by sea.

At this point, Beiping was an isolated city without any hope of reinforcement or defensible terrain. To preserve this historic city and ancient capital, Mao decided to strive for a peaceful resolution. After negotiations, the defending forces in Beiping, led by Fu Zuoyi, agreed to a peaceful reorganization. On January 31, 1949, the PLA entered Beiping, marking its peaceful liberation.

In the Pingjin Campaign, apart from the approximately 50,000 defenders who escaped by sea from Tanggu, over 520,000 KMT troops were either annihilated or reorganized. Inspired by the peaceful liberation of Beiping, the KMT forces in Suiyuan also announced their uprising and reorganization in September 1949.

Just as the Northeast Field Army was launching its offensive on Tianjin, eliminating the possibility of Fu Zuoyi's forces evacuating south by sea, Mao and the Central Military Commission ordered the final general offensive of the Huaihai Campaign.

At that moment, Du Yuming's two armies, totaling eight corps, were encircled in a narrow area centered on Chenguanzhuang, approximately ten kilometers long and five kilometers wide. Facing continuous rain and snow, suffering from cold and hunger, and with morale at rock bottom, over 14,000 soldiers had already defected before the final assault. On January 6, 1949, the general offensive of the Huaihai Campaign began. By January 10, the PLA had completely annihilated Du Yuming's forces; Du Yuming was captured, Qiu Qingquan was killed, and only Li Mi managed to escape by disguising himself. Thus, the massive Huaihai Campaign concluded with the destruction of 555,000 KMT troops.

Through the Liaoshen, Huaihai, and Pingjin campaigns, the main forces of the KMT Army were fundamentally annihilated, and the foundation of the KMT regime was fundamentally shaken. Consequently, Chiang Kai-shek had no choice but to announce his "retirement" on January 21, 1949, appointing Vice President Li Zongren as acting president. Before his retirement, on January 1, Chiang publicly stated, "As long as the Communist Party has a sincere intention for peace and can make a clear demonstration of it, the government will sincerely meet them and discuss concrete methods to stop the war and restore peace." In response, Mao Zedong issued a statement on the current situation on January 14, outlining eight conditions for peace talks.[26] On January 22, Li Jishen, Shen Junru, Ma Xulun, Guo Moruo, and 55 others jointly expressed their opinions on the situation, fully supporting the eight conditions proposed by the CPC.

While both sides were discussing the possibility of peace talks, from March 5 to 13, 1949, Mao Zedong presided over the Second Plenary Session of the Seventh Central Committee of the CPC in Xibaipo Village, Pingshan County, Hebei Province. The meeting was attended by 34 Central Committee members and 19 alternate Central Committee members. The plenary session summarized the War of Liberation and outlined the next steps, particularly in preparing for the establishment of a new China.

In his report, Mao emphasized that with nationwide victory in sight, the Party's focus must shift from rural areas to cities, with urban work centered on production and construction. He also outlined the development direction of transforming China from an agricultural country to an industrial one, and from a new democratic society to a socialist society.

At the end of his report, Mao warned the entire Party: "Winning nationwide victory is only the first step in a long march." He continued, "In a few decades, looking back at the victory of the Chinese people's democratic revolution, it will seem like just a short prologue to a long play. The play must start with a prologue, but the prologue is not the climax. China's revolution is great, but the journey after the revolution will be longer, the work greater and more arduous. This must be made clear within the Party now. We must ensure that comrades continue to maintain the style of modesty, prudence, and avoiding arrogance and impetuosity, and continue to uphold the style of hard work and struggle."

He also cautioned the Party to be wary of the "sugar-coated bullets" of the bourgeoisie: "Because of victory, the people will thank us, and the bourgeoisie will come out to praise us. The enemy's armed forces could not conquer us—this has been proven. But the bourgeoisie's flattery could conquer those among us who are weak-willed. There may be some Communists who were not conquered by the enemy's guns, who can rightfully be called heroes before those enemies, but who cannot withstand the sugar-coated bullets. We must prevent such a situation."[27]

The plenary session also formed six unwritten rules based on Mao's suggestions: (1) no celebrations for birthdays; (2) no giving of gifts; (3) fewer toasts; (4) fewer applause; (5) no naming places after people; and (6) do not equate Chinese comrades with Marx, Engels, Lenin, and Stalin.[28]

Shortly after the Second Plenary Session of the Seventh Central Committee, on March 23, Mao Zedong led the Central Committee and the Central

Military Commission from Xibaipo to Beiping. This move marked the formal commencement of preparations for the establishment of the new China and the shift of the CPC's focus from rural areas to cities after long-term armed struggle. As he left Xibaipo, Mao made a remark full of meaning: "We must never become like Li Zicheng."[29]

On March 25, Mao and the Central Committee, along with the Central Military Commission, moved into Beiping. At 5 p.m. that day, Mao, Zhu De, Liu Shaoqi, Zhou Enlai, Ren Bishi, Lin Boqu, and others met with more than 1,000 representatives and democratic figures from all walks of life at Xiyuan Airport in Beiping. They also reviewed the battle-hardened troops of the Chinese PLA. Afterward, they took up residence in the Shuangqing Villa in Xiangshan.

The next day, on March 26, the Central Committee of the CPC notified the KMT Government in Nanjing about the arrangements for peace talks: "(1) Start date of the negotiations: April 1. (2) Location of the negotiations: Beiping. (3) Representatives: Zhou Enlai, Lin Boqu, Lin Biao, Ye Jianying, and Li Weihan (Note: on April 1, it was decided to also appoint Nie Rongzhen as a representative), with Zhou Enlai as the chief representative, to negotiate with the Nanjing delegation based on Chairman Mao Zedong's statement on the current situation dated January 14 and the eight conditions he proposed as the foundation for the talks."[30]

On March 29, Mao Zedong, on behalf of the Central Military Commission, sent a telegram to Liu Bocheng, Chen Yi, Deng Xiaoping, and others, discussing the start date of the Yangtze River Crossing Campaign, stating: "We agree to postpone the crossing to April 15. We have set April 1 as the start date for negotiations with the KMT, and they should conclude around April 10. It will only be clear by then whether the negotiations will succeed or fail."[31]

On April 1, the KMT Government delegation from Nanjing, consisting of Zhang Zhizhong, Shao Lizi, Huang Shaohong, Zhang Shizhao, Li Zheng, and Liu Fei, arrived in Beiping and stayed at the Six Nations Hotel. Subsequently, the representatives from both sides began the peace talks. The negotiations extended beyond the scheduled time, with informal talks continuing until April 12 and the final revised version of the "Domestic Peace Agreement" being completed on April 15. The main reason for the delay was that Chiang Kai-shek was effectively controlling everything behind the scenes. He was unwilling to face the reality of his impending defeat and even more reluctant to accept what he saw as a humiliating agreement from Beiping.

To demonstrate the sincerity of the CPC, on April 8, Mao Zedong and Zhou Enlai met with Zhang Zhizhong at Shuangqing Villa in Xiangshan. Mao stated that, to reduce difficulties for the KMT delegation, they could refrain from listing the names of war criminals in the peace terms. He also expressed that it would be preferable if Li Zongren, He Yingqin, Yu Youren, Ju Zheng, and Tong Guanxian[32] could all participate in the signing.[33] On the same day, Mao responded to Li Zongren's telegram, outlining the standards for leniency toward war criminals: "The criterion is whether it benefits the advancement of the Chinese people's liberation cause and whether it facilitates the peaceful resolution of domestic issues. Based on this standard, we are prepared to adopt a lenient policy."[34]

At the same time, Mao Zedong did not abandon alternative preparations. On April 15, Mao sent a telegram to the General Front Committee, who were preparing for the Yangtze River Crossing Campaign, stating: "(1) The deadline for peace negotiations is set for April 20. Today, we will inform the Nanjing delegation that they must decide whether to sign the agreement by this date. After this date, our army will cross the Yangtze River. (2) The final revised draft of the peace agreement will be handed to the Nanjing delegation today. Tomorrow, they will send Huang Shaohong to Nanjing for instructions. It is still uncertain whether Nanjing will agree to sign. They might refuse. (3) Upon receiving this telegram, immediately prepare to attack and secure all positions on the northern shore and in the Yangtze River islands, except for Anqing and the two Pukou districts, by the twentieth. Do not delay."[35]

On April 20, the KMT Government in Nanjing refused to sign the "Domestic Peace Agreement (Final Revised Version)." That night, the Yangtze River Crossing Campaign began. On April 21, Chairman Mao Zedong of the Chinese People's Revolutionary Military Committee and Generalissimo Zhu De of the Chinese PLA issued the "Order to March on the Whole Nation," calling on the PLA to "advance courageously, decisively, thoroughly, and completely annihilate all KMT reactionaries who dare to resist, liberate the entire nation, and safeguard the independence and integrity of China's territorial sovereignty."[36]

From the night of April 20 to 21, the Second Field Army (formerly the Central Plains Field Army) and the Third Field Army (formerly the East China Field Army) launched the Yangtze River Crossing Campaign along a front extending over 500 kilometers in the middle and lower reaches of the Yangtze River, completely destroying the defensive line that the KMT Army had painstakingly established over three and a half months. On April 23, they captured Nanjing, signaling the collapse of KMT rule across the country.

Simultaneously, the North China forces led by Nie Rongzhen and Xu Xiangqian captured Taiyuan on April 24.

In the southeast coastal area, the Third Field Army led by Chen Yi, Su Yu, and Tan Zhenlin liberated Hangzhou on May 3, Nanchang on May 22, Shanghai on May 27, Fuzhou on August 17, and Xiamen on October 17.

In Central and South China, the Fourth Field Army (formerly the Northeast Field Army) led by Lin Biao and Luo Ronghuan liberated Wuchang, Hanyang, and Hankou on May 16–17. On August 4, the KMT Chairman of Hunan Province, Cheng Qian, and the Commander of the First Corps, Chen Mingren, announced their uprising, leading to the peaceful liberation of Hunan Province. Following this, they launched the Hengyang-Baoqing Campaign, annihilating the main forces of Bai Chongxi's KMT Army, and advanced into Guangdong and Guangxi. Guangzhou was liberated on October 14, Guilin on November 22, and Nanning on December 4.

In the northwest, the First Field Army (formerly the Northwest Field Army) led by Peng Dehuai and He Long liberated Xi'an on May 20, and together with the 19th and 20th Corps, captured Lanzhou on August 26, Xining on September 5, and Yinchuan on September 23, completely annihilating the KMT forces of Ma Bufang and Ma Hongkui. In late September, Tao Zhiyue, the KMT Commander of Xinjiang Province's garrison, and Bao Erhan, the provincial chairman, announced their uprising, leading to the peaceful liberation of Xinjiang.

In the southwest, the Second Field Army led by Liu Bocheng and Deng Xiaoping, along with the 18th Corps led by He Long and Li Jingquan and part of the First Field Army, liberated Guiyang on November 15 and Chongqing on November 30. On December 9, the KMT Chairman of Yunnan Province, Lu Han, and the Chairman of Xikang Province, Liu Wenhui, along with the deputy commanders of the Southwest Military and Political Headquarters, Deng Xihou and Pan Wenhua, announced their uprising, leading to the peaceful liberation of Yunnan and Xikang provinces. In late December, they launched the Chengdu Campaign, completely annihilating the KMT Army under Hu Zongnan, and liberated Chengdu on December 27.

By the end of December 1949, the PLA had completely annihilated the KMT forces on the Chinese mainland, liberating all of mainland China except for Xizang. Chiang Kai-shek was forced to flee from Chengdu to Taiwan on December 10 and never returned to the mainland.

On September 21, 1949, the long-awaited First Plenary Session of the Chinese People's Political Consultative Conference (CPPCC) officially opened. In his opening speech, Mao Zedong solemnly declared, "Fellow delegates, we all have a common feeling: our work will be recorded in the annals of human history, demonstrating that the Chinese people, who make up one-quarter of humanity, have now stood up."

"Our nation will henceforth join the family of peace-loving and freedom-loving nations of the world, working diligently and bravely to create its own civilization and happiness, while also promoting world peace and freedom. Our nation will no longer be one that is humiliated. We have stood up. Our revolution has won the sympathy and acclaim of the world's people, and we have friends all over the world."

"With the coming economic construction boom, an inevitable cultural construction boom will follow. The era when Chinese people were regarded as uncivilized is over. We will appear in the world as a nation with a high level of culture."

"Let the reactionaries at home and abroad tremble before us; let them say we are incapable of this or that. The unyielding efforts of the Chinese people will surely achieve their goal steadily."[37]

On September 30, 1949, following the closing of the First Plenary Session of the CPPCC, a foundation stone laying ceremony for the Monument to the People's Heroes was held at Tiananmen Square at 6 p.m. Mao Zedong and all the delegates of the CPPCC attended the ceremony. Zhou Enlai delivered a speech on behalf of the presidium. Mao Zedong read the inscription he personally wrote for the Monument to the People's Heroes.

> Eternal glory to the people's heroes who sacrificed their lives in the People's War of Liberation and the People's Revolution over the past three years!
>
> Eternal glory to the people's heroes who sacrificed their lives in the People's War of Liberation and the People's Revolution over the past thirty years!
>
> Eternal glory to the people's heroes who, since 1840, fought against internal and external enemies, fought for national independence and the freedom and happiness of the people, and who sacrificed their lives in the various struggles![38]

An era of heroes was coming to an end, and a new era of heroes was about to begin.

Chapter II

The World Has Changed

A rainstorm sweeps down on this northern land,
White breakers leap to the sky.
No fishing boats off Qinhuangdao
Are seen on the boundless ocean.
Where are they gone?
Nearly two thousand years ago
Wielding his whip, the Emperor Wu of Wei
Rode eastward to Jieshi; his poem survives.
Today the autumn wind still sighs,
But the world has changed!

MAO ZEDONG,
"*Langtaosha* · Beidaihe" (Summer 1954)

On October 1, 1949, an exhilarating day, Mao Zedong led the CPC and the Chinese people through the long, dark night to usher in a new chapter in Chinese history. At 3 p.m., atop Tiananmen Gate in Beijing, Mao, in his resonant Hunan accent, declared to the world, "The Central People's Government of the People's Republic of China is established today!"

However, Mao's feelings were far from relaxed. The newly born People's Republic of China inherited a ravaged land. The national treasury had been looted, the economy was in shambles, transportation was paralyzed, factories were damaged, the populace lived in hardship, the new government was not yet stable, and remnants of KMT troops and agents still roamed the mainland, menacing the public. Within the CPC, some members believed the great mission was accomplished and began indulging in pleasures. The national bourgeoisie and intellectuals remained hesitant, and Americans across the ocean awaited the "dust to settle." Whether the Communists could transition from war to governing the country was the immediate test they faced.

To consolidate the nascent regime, Mao first focused on stabilizing the economic front.

Amid the liberation celebrations, major cities like Shanghai experienced severe price fluctuations, and shops even began refusing to accept the new currency, the Renminbi (RMB). Some claimed, "The Communists scored a perfect 100 in military affairs, 80 in politics, but might get zero in economics." Stabilizing prices was crucial to stabilize public sentiment and the government. Mao entrusted this heavy responsibility to Chen Yun, who formed the Central Financial and Economic Commission and became its director.

On June 10, 1949, the Shanghai Municipal Military Control Commission shut down the Shanghai Securities Building, the hub of financial speculation, curbing the silver yuan speculation. However, speculative capital then shifted to the grain, cotton yarn, and coal markets. From late July to mid-October, the average price index in Shanghai rose by 1.5 times. To stabilize prices and combat speculative capital, the central government urgently allocated large quantities of grain, cotton yarn, and coal. On November 25, the peak day of price hikes, they opened the floodgates for sales, tightened monetary policy, and levied taxes, causing speculative capital to collapse. A prominent Shanghai capitalist later remarked, "In June, the silver yuan crisis was suppressed by political means. This time, the Communists suppressed it purely through economic means, something beyond the expectations of the Shanghai business community."[1]

Following Mao's decision, the Central Financial and Economic Commission adopted measures such as unifying financial and economic policies. By

March 1950, national prices had stabilized, hyperinflation was effectively curbed, and the RMB gained a solid foothold nationwide, laying the foundation for the rapid recovery of the national economy. The national bourgeoisie began to seriously accept the leadership of the CPC. Mao highly valued this economic victory, considering it as significant as the Huaihai Campaign.[2]

Next, Mao led the completion of the unfinished tasks of the democratic revolution, including promoting marriage freedom and women's liberation, completing land reform, implementing democratic reforms, and eradicating prostitution and drug abuse.

During the Great Revolution, Mao deeply criticized the feudal marriage system, noting, "In addition to the three aforementioned powers, women are also subject to the control of men (husband's authority). These four powers—political power, clan authority, divine authority, and husband's authority—represent the entire feudal patriarchal ideology and system, binding the Chinese people, especially peasants, with four great ropes."[3] After the establishment of the People's Republic of China, on May 1, 1950, the Central People's Government promulgated the *Marriage Law of the People's Republic of China*, the first law of the new China. It abolished arranged and forced marriages, male supremacy, and the neglect of children's interests, establishing a new marriage system based on freedom of marriage, monogamy, gender equality, and protection of the lawful interests of women and children. This law fundamentally changed the traditional male-dominated society in China, realizing true gender equality and marriage freedom for the first time in history, and significantly advancing the cause of women's liberation. Women across the country truly felt they had become masters of their own lives.

On June 30, 1950, the Central People's Government issued the *Land Reform Law of the People's Republic of China*, which aimed to "abolish the feudal exploitative land ownership system of the landlord class and implement the land ownership system of the peasants, thereby liberating productive forces in rural areas, developing agricultural production, and paving the way for the industrialization of new China."[4] By the winter of 1952, except for Taiwan Province and some minority areas, land reform was largely completed nationwide, distributing about 700 million *mu* (approximately 115 million acres) of land and other means of production to over 300 million landless or land-poor peasants. For the first time, these peasants experienced the profound sense of being masters of their own destiny.

Prostitution, gambling, and drug addiction were cancers of the old society. As early as the "Report on an Investigation of the Peasant Movement in Hunan," Mao Zedong praised the Communist-led peasant associations for establishing authority in the countryside, noting, "The peasants banned or restricted activities they disliked, especially gambling, opium, and prostitution."[5]

The campaign to abolish the system of prostitution began in Beijing. On the evening of November 21, 1949, at 5:30 p.m., a citywide operation shut down all 224 brothels in one night. Over 1,300 prostitutes received treatment for venereal diseases, learned cultural and labor skills, and were provided with jobs to support themselves, thus gaining a new lease on life.[6] Subsequently, cities like Shanghai also eradicated all brothels. Within a year, the system of prostitution was completely abolished.

The campaign against drug addiction was even more challenging. When the People's Republic of China was established, about 20 million people, or 4.4% of the national population, were drug addicts. On February 24, 1950, the Government Administration Council issued a directive prohibiting opium smoking and trafficking. In the latter half of 1952, a nationwide anti-drug campaign surged. Under intense social pressure, some drug traffickers voluntarily surrendered to the public security authorities. During the campaign, 82,056 serious drug offenders were arrested, and 880 of the most heinous and widely despised were sentenced to death.[7]

What concerned Mao even more was the situation within the Party. In November 1951, Mao read a report from the Northeast Bureau revealing instances of corruption, waste, and bureaucratism uncovered during the production and economy drive. In a November 20 directive for the Central Committee, he first called for a "determined struggle against corruption, waste, and bureaucratism."[8] Thus began the "Three-Antis Campaign" nationwide.

On November 29, the North China Bureau reported the serious corruption cases of Liu Qingshan and Zhang Zishan to the Central Committee. Both were veteran Party members who had joined during the Agrarian Revolutionary War, led revolutionary struggles, and shown steadfastness in KMT prisons. However, after the revolution's success, they became deeply corrupt while serving as secretaries of the Tianjin Prefectural Committee, engaging in embezzlement, collusion with private merchants, misappropriation of public funds, and illegal trade in steel.

Before their public trial and execution, some suggested sparing their lives. Mao responded, "Precisely because of their high positions, great merits, and significant influence, we must resolve to execute them. Only by doing so can we save 20, 200, 2,000, or 20,000 cadres."[9]

This event caused a great shock within the Party and deeply resonated with the public, reinforcing the perception that the new society was fundamentally different from the old, and that the current government was genuinely serving the people.

On December 6, 1949, Mao Zedong boarded a train heading west to visit the Soviet Union. This was his first trip abroad, carrying the mission to establish the new China's foreign relations.

On the eve of the new China's birth, Mao proposed three principles for its foreign policy: "start anew," "lean to one side," specifically toward socialism, and "clean the house before inviting guests." These principles became the foundation of the new China's foreign policy.[10]

In accordance with these principles, the new China did not recognize any unequal treaties signed by the old regime with other countries and sought to establish diplomatic relations with foreign governments based on the principles of equality, mutual benefit, and mutual respect for territorial sovereignty.[11] The Soviet Union was the first country to recognize and establish diplomatic relations with the People's Republic of China. However, before the two countries could forge a new relationship, there were historical issues to resolve, such as the 1945 Sino-Soviet Treaty of Friendship and Alliance signed with the KMT Government. Addressing these issues was a key objective of Mao's visit.

On December 16, upon his arrival in Moscow, Mao Zedong received a grand reception. He was also accommodated in Stalin's villa, "Sisters River" on the outskirts of Moscow, which had been used during the Soviet Great Patriotic War. That evening, Stalin met Mao for the first time at the Kremlin, where they held their first meeting.

According to Shi Zhe, who served as an interpreter, "At exactly 6 p.m., the hall doors opened. Stalin and the entire Political Bureau of the Communist Party of the Soviet Union (CPSU), along with Foreign Minister Andrey Vyshinsky, stood in line to welcome Chairman Mao. This was highly unusual, as Stalin typically did not greet foreign guests at the door. This special arrangement was made to show respect, trust, and exceptional courtesy toward the Chinese people and their leader."[12]

In a December 18 telegram to Liu Shaoqi, Mao described the meeting with four words: "情意恳切" (sincere and heartfelt). He wrote, "At 10 p.m., I met Marshal Stalin. The meeting was sincere and heartfelt, lasting for two hours. We discussed the possibility of peace, the treaty, loans, Taiwan, and the publication of Mao's Selected Works. I was the only one on our side. The Soviet side included Molotov, Malenkov, Bulganin, and Vyshinsky. Shi Zhe and Nikolai Fedorinko were the interpreters."[13]

Mao raised his first question to Stalin: "How and to what extent can we ensure international peace?" Stalin replied, "If we work together, we can ensure peace not just for five to ten years, but for twenty to twenty-five years, or even longer."[14]

Mao's concern for this issue stemmed from his considerations about domestic economic recovery and large-scale industrialization, which required an assessment of the risk of a new world war breaking out in the near term. Later, at the Political Bureau of the Central Committee's expanded meeting in February 1951, Mao proposed the concept of "three years of preparation and ten years of planned economic construction," which was directly related to this assessment. In his December 18 telegram to Liu Shaoqi, Mao noted, "Stalin said the Americans are very afraid of war; they incite others to fight, but others are also afraid. According to him, it is very unlikely that a war will break out, which matches our own assessment."[15]

The second, more sensitive issue Mao raised was the handling of the 1945 Sino-Soviet Treaty of Friendship and Alliance, signed with the KMT Government. Mao suggested replacing it with a new treaty, aligning with the spirit of "starting anew." Before this visit, on December 1, Mao had convened a discussion with 12 democratic figures, including Zhang Lan, Li Jishen, Guo

Moruo, Huang Yanpei, and Shen Junru, to hear their opinions on signing a treaty with the Soviet Union.[16]

According to records preserved in the Russian Presidential Archives, Stalin's response was that the treaty was concluded based on the Yalta Agreement, which outlined the treaty's main content. This meant that the treaty had essentially gained the consent of both the United States and the United Kingdom. Considering this, Stalin explained that they had already decided within their small circle not to make any modifications to the treaty for the time being. Any amendment to a single clause could legally give the United States and the United Kingdom a pretext to demand changes to clauses concerning the Kuril Islands, Southern Sakhalin, and other issues.[17]

In his telegram to Liu Shaoqi, Mao conveyed the Chinese perspective to Stalin, saying, "Respecting the legality of the Yalta Agreement is necessary. However, Chinese public opinion feels that since the original treaty was signed with the KMT and the KMT has now fallen, the original treaty seems to have lost its validity."

Stalin replied, "The original treaty will have to be modified eventually, probably in about two years."[18]

Thus, the discussion on the second issue concluded.

During the discussion of the second issue, Stalin mentioned the withdrawal of Soviet Union troops from Lüshun and the possibility of modifying the Sino-Soviet Treaty concerning the Chinese Eastern Railway based on Chinese wishes. Mao Zedong raised the question whether Zhou Enlai, who was also serving as the Foreign Minister, needed to come to Moscow.

In his telegram to Liu Shaoqi, Mao stated: "Regarding whether the Chinese Foreign Minister needs to come here, he (Stalin) said that it seems signing a declaration does not require the Foreign Minister. I said, let me consider whether we will sign agreements on loans, civil aviation, and trade at the same time. If we sign these agreements simultaneously, then it would be appropriate for the Foreign Minister to come here."[19]

Mao instructed Liu Shaoqi and Zhou Enlai to discuss this matter and hold a Political Bureau of the Central Committee meeting. On the 21st, Liu Shaoqi, Zhu De, and Zhou Enlai jointly replied: "Everyone agrees that if the Soviet Union is willing to sign agreements regarding Lüshun, loans, aviation, and trade now, Comrade Enlai should go to Moscow. However, if the Soviet side is not prepared to sign agreements on loans, aviation, and trade now, and only plans to issue a declaration on the stationing of troops in Lüshun and general political issues, then it is unnecessary for Comrade Enlai to go to Moscow."[20]

During the meeting, Mao raised the issue of China's lack of naval and air forces and expressed hope for Soviet Union assistance in liberating Taiwan. Stalin responded that providing assistance was not a problem, but the form of assistance needed to be considered carefully to avoid giving the United States a pretext for interference.[21] This once again highlighted to Mao the shortcomings of not having a strong industrial base.

On December 21, Mao attended the celebration of Stalin's 70th birthday at the Moscow Grand Theater. This was another significant purpose of Mao's first visit to the Soviet Union. That evening, he telegraphed the Central Committee of the CPC: "Today's (the 21st) celebration included speeches from representatives of the Soviet Union republics and thirteen countries. I was the first to speak on behalf of China among these thirteen countries. I received a grand welcome, with the audience rising to their feet and applauding for a long time three times."[22] This demonstrated the position of the new China led by the CPC in the socialist camp and the importance Stalin attached to Mao.

Influenced by the enthusiastic atmosphere, Mao arranged a conversation with Kovalev, who acted as an interpreter and liaison between the Chinese and Soviet parties, on December 22 at the Sisters River villa. Mao asked him to convey the conversation to Stalin. The conversation mentioned hopes for a scheduled meeting on December 23 or 22 to further discuss the following issues: the Sino-Soviet Treaty, loan agreements, trade agreements, and aviation agreements, and suggested that Zhou Enlai come to Moscow to complete the signing procedures.[23]

Stalin quickly arranged a second meeting with Mao on the evening of December 24. However, to Mao's disappointment, Stalin did not bring up the Sino-Soviet Treaty during the five-and-a-half-hour meeting. When discussing whether Zhou Enlai should come to Moscow, Stalin suggested that since the head of government was already there, having the Premier also come might have adverse effects on foreign perceptions, and it would be better if Zhou Enlai did not come.[24]

Despite this, Stalin continued to show warm and friendly gestures toward Mao. According to Mao's telegram to the Central Committee, "Comrade Stalin calls those hosting us daily to ask if I am comfortable, showing special concern."[25]

Nine days later, an unexpected development occurred. Stalin agreed to sign a new Sino-Soviet Treaty to replace the old one with the KMT Government and agreed to have Zhou Enlai come to Moscow to discuss the new treaty and other agreements. This news greatly pleased Mao, who had been anxiously waiting.

In his January 2, 1950, telegram to the Central Committee, Mao stated, "There has been an important development in the last two days. Comrade Stalin has agreed to have Comrade Zhou Enlai come to Moscow to sign a new Sino-Soviet Treaty of Friendship and Alliance, as well as agreements on loans, trade, and civil aviation."[26]

Mao also mentioned in the telegram that in his conversation with Molotov that afternoon, he proposed: "My telegram will reach Beijing on January 3. Zhou Enlai will prepare for five days, leave Beijing on January 9, travel by train for eleven days, arrive in Moscow on January 19, and from January 20 to the end of the month, spend about ten days negotiating and signing various agreements. Zhou and I will return to China together in early February." Mao also discussed sightseeing plans, such as visiting Lenin's Mausoleum, Leningrad, and Gorky, as well as visiting armament factories, the subway (suggested by Molotov and Mikoyan), and collective farms. He also mentioned talking to various Soviet officials (he had not yet visited any of them alone).[27]

Subsequent developments proceeded roughly as Mao anticipated.

On January 10, Zhou Enlai and his delegation left Beijing. They arrived in Moscow on January 20. On the evening of January 22, Mao Zedong and Zhou Enlai held a third meeting with Stalin to discuss the Sino-Soviet Treaty, the Chinese Eastern Railway, the return of Lüshun, and whether Dalian should be a free port.

The reason for Stalin's significant change within ten days was due to a false report by the British news agency claiming that Mao Zedong was under house arrest in Moscow. On January 2, 1950, TASS published an interview with Mao Zedong, in which he said, "The length of my stay in the Soviet

Union partly depends on the time required to resolve various issues related to the interests of the People's Republic of China." "Among these issues, the most important are the current Sino-Soviet Treaty of Friendship and Alliance, the Soviet loan to the People's Republic of China, trade and trade agreements between our two countries, and other issues."[28] These responses effectively dispelled the rumors. According to Mao, this interview was drafted by Stalin and approved by Mao.[29]

A more critical reason for this change was Stalin's reconsideration of the binding force of the Yalta Agreement. During their first conversation, Stalin explicitly stated that the Yalta Agreement's constraints could not be ignored. In Mao's December 18 telegram to Liu Shaoqi, he wrote: "Stalin said that because of the Yalta Agreement, it is not appropriate to change the legitimacy of the existing Sino-Soviet Treaty. If the existing treaty is changed and a new one is made, it will involve the issue of the Kuril Islands, and the Americans will have a reason to take the Kuril Islands."[30] However, in the January 22 evening conversation with Mao and Zhou Enlai, Stalin clearly stated that the existing treaties and agreements related to Sino-Soviet relations must be revised, despite the previous thought to keep them unchanged. These treaties and agreements had to be revised because they were based on the context of the War Against Japanese Aggression. Since the war had ended, Japan had been defeated, and the situation had changed, the treaty had become outdated.[31]

With Stalin's decision, the obstacles surrounding the signing of a new Sino-Soviet Treaty, the abolition of the old treaty with the KMT Government, and the agreements related to the Chinese Eastern Railway, Lüshun, and Dalian were resolved.

On February 14, 1950, Mao Zedong and Stalin attended the signing ceremony at the Kremlin. Zhou Enlai and Vyshinsky signed documents on behalf of the Chinese and Soviet governments, including the Sino-Soviet Treaty of Friendship, Alliance, and Mutual Assistance, the Sino-Soviet Agreement on the Chinese Eastern Railway, Lüshun, and Dalian, and the Sino-Soviet Loan Agreement to the People's Republic of China.

The Sino-Soviet Treaty of Friendship, Alliance, and Mutual Assistance was the first treaty new China signed with a foreign government on an equal basis, fundamentally changing the old China's submissive diplomatic stance and fulfilling the promise of "starting anew." It marked the beginning of the Chinese people standing independently in the international community.

The treaty emphasized that the alliance was to prevent the resurgence of Japanese militarism: "Both contracting parties guarantee to make every effort to take all necessary measures to prevent any country, whether directly or indirectly associated with Japan in acts of aggression, from committing further acts of aggression and disrupting peace."[32]

In the Sino-Soviet Agreement on the Chinese Eastern Railway, Lüshun, and Dalian, the new changes in the Far East after World War II were emphasized.

> The Central People's Government of the People's Republic of China and the Presidium of the Supreme Soviet of the Union of Soviet Socialist Republics confirm that since 1945, the situation in the Far East has fundamentally changed, namely: imperialist Japan has been defeated, the reactionary KMT Government has been overthrown, China has become a People's Democratic Republic, and a new people's government has been established; this new people's government has unified all of China, implemented a policy of friendly cooperation with the Soviet Union, and has proven its ability to uphold China's national independence and territorial integrity, national honor, and the dignity of its people. ... This new situation provides the possibility to readdress the issues related to the Chinese Eastern Railway, Lüshun, and Dalian.[33]

On August 14, 1945, while signing the Sino-Soviet Treaty of Friendship and Alliance, the Soviet government also signed agreements with the KMT Government on the Chinese Eastern Railway, Dalian, and Lüshun, with a term of 30 years. Over four years later, through negotiations for the Sino-Soviet Treaty of Friendship, Alliance, and Mutual Assistance, the new Chinese government reclaimed sovereignty that rightfully belonged to China.

The original agreement on the Chinese Eastern Railway stipulated: "After Japanese troops are driven out of Manchuria, the Chinese Eastern Railway and the South Manchuria Railway, from Manzhouli to Suifenhe and from Harbin to Dalian and Lüshun, will be merged into one railway, named the Chinese Eastern Railway, to be jointly owned and operated by the Republic of China and the Union of Soviet Socialist Republics."³⁴ In the new Sino-Soviet Agreement on the Chinese Eastern Railway, Lüshun, and Dalian (hereinafter referred to as the Package Agreement), it was stipulated: "Both contracting parties agree that the Soviet government will transfer all rights to jointly manage the Chinese Eastern Railway, along with all properties belonging to this railway, to the government of the People's Republic of China without compensation. This transfer will be implemented immediately after the conclusion of the peace treaty with Japan, but no later than the end of 1952."³⁵

The original agreement on Dalian stated: "To ensure the Soviet Union's interests in Dalian for the import and export of goods, the Republic of China agrees (1) to declare Dalian a free port, open to the trade and navigation of all nations; and (2) to lease designated docks and warehouses in this free port to the Soviet Union in accordance with a separate agreement."³⁶ The new Package Agreement specified: "Both contracting parties agree that the issue of Dalian Port must be addressed following the conclusion of the peace treaty with Japan." "As for the administration of Dalian, it shall be entirely under the jurisdiction of the government of the People's Republic of China." "All properties in Dalian currently under temporary Soviet administration or leased by the Soviet side shall be taken over by the government of the People's Republic of China."³⁷

The original agreement on Lüshun stated: "To strengthen the security of both China and the Soviet Union and prevent further Japanese aggression, the Republic of China agrees that the two contracting parties will jointly use Lüshun as a naval base." "The Soviet government has the right to station ground, naval, and air forces in the area described in Article 2 and to decide their locations."³⁸ In the January 24 meeting, Stalin admitted to Mao Zedong that the agreement on Lüshun was unequal.³⁹ The new Package Agreement stipulated: "Both contracting parties agree that following the conclusion of the peace treaty with Japan, but no later than the end of 1952, Soviet troops will withdraw from the jointly used naval base at Lüshun, and the equipment in the area will be handed over to the government of the People's Republic of China, which will reimburse the Soviet Union for the costs of restoration and construction of the equipment since 1945."⁴⁰

Securing these results in the negotiations was challenging. Particularly, the negotiations on returning the rights to the Chinese Eastern Railway involved significant contention, but the Chinese government's position ultimately prevailed. As Mao Zedong described, it was like taking meat from a tiger's mouth.[41]

On February 17, 1950, Mao Zedong and his delegation, bearing substantial achievements, left Moscow and returned to China.

Mao Zedong emphasized the significance of signing the Sino-Soviet Treaty of Friendship, Alliance, and Mutual Assistance, saying, "By solidifying the friendship between our two countries in the treaty, we can fully engage in economic construction. It is beneficial for both diplomacy and construction, as diplomacy also serves construction. As a newly established country, we face many difficulties. In case of trouble, having an ally reduces the possibility of war."[42]

New China was in a state of disrepair, but what concerned Mao Zedong the most was large-scale economic construction. He understood, "The reason for China's backwardness is primarily the lack of modern industry. The Japanese imperialists dared to bully China so severely because China did not have a strong industry. Therefore, eliminating this backwardness is the task of our entire nation."[43]

On the eve of the founding of the People's Republic of China, Mao Zedong estimated that it would take at least three years to restore the economy. To expedite the recovery and development of the national economy, he proposed the "Four Directions" economic policy: "Taking into account both public and private interests, ensuring benefits for both labor and capital, promoting mutual assistance between urban and rural areas, and facilitating domestic and international exchanges." He believed that implementing this policy would strengthen the alliance between the working class, the peasantry, the petty bourgeoisie, and the national bourgeoisie.

On November 29, 1949, in his speech at the second meeting of the First Standing Committee of the CPPCC, Mao put forward the idea of "three to five years for recovery, ten to eight years for development."

A little over a year later, in February 1951, at an expanded meeting of the Political Bureau of the Central Committee, he summarized this idea as "three years of preparation and ten years of planned economic construction."[44] The "three years of preparation" aimed to restore the national economy to its best level before Japan's full-scale invasion of China, laying the groundwork for large-scale industrialization. The "ten years of planned economic construction" was intended to establish a solid material foundation for transitioning to socialism through national industrialization.

In the early days of the new China, the country's financial foundation was extremely fragile, facing numerous dilemmas. It was necessary to stabilize prices while encouraging private industrial and commercial production; overcome stagnant sales while maintaining production; dismantle the old state machinery of the KMT Government while ensuring that former KMT military and political personnel continued to work and live normally. As Chen Yun put it at the time, "The government is carrying two baskets of eggs and must avoid breaking either end."[45]

These dilemmas seemed insurmountable to most people. However, for Mao, who excelled at managing complex contradictions, they were not insurmountable. At the fourth meeting of the Central People's Government Council on December 2, 1949, Mao summarized the national financial situation with three statements: "There are difficulties, there are solutions, and there is hope."[46]

After his first visit to the Soviet Union, Mao conducted thorough research and preparation. From June 6 to 9, 1950, he presided over the Third Plenary Session of the Seventh Central Committee of the CPC at Huairen Hall in Zhongnanhai, Beijing. The session was dedicated to studying the tasks during the period of national economic recovery. Mao presented a written report titled "Struggle for a Fundamental Improvement in the National Financial and Economic Situation."

The report first analyzed the international environment, stating: "The threat of war from the imperialist camp still exists, and the possibility of a third world war remains. However, the forces fighting to prevent the danger of war and to avoid the outbreak of a third world war are developing rapidly," concluding that "a new world war can be prevented." Even after the outbreak of the Korean War, Mao did not change this assessment.

The report outlined the task of achieving a fundamental improvement in the financial and economic situation within three years and analyzed three conditions necessary for this improvement: "(1) the completion of land reform, (2) the rational adjustment of existing industry and commerce, and (3) a significant reduction in the expenses required for state institutions."[47] It also outlined eight tasks, including the three mentioned above.

Mao consistently demonstrated his ability to navigate complex contradictions and work, always able to identify the main issues, articulate them clearly and concisely, and ensure that they were easily understood and implemented.

During the plenary session, Mao Zedong emphasized in his speech that the Party should avoid creating tensions in various relationships and refrain from making enemies everywhere. He advised against "attacking on all fronts" and stressed the importance of carefully and earnestly doing united front work, stating, "We must ensure that workers, peasants, and small handicraft producers support us, and that the vast majority of the national bourgeoisie and intellectuals do not oppose us."[48] This effectively curbed the impatience within the Party that was eager to eliminate private capital.

The recovery of the national economy proceeded smoothly. Soon, the unique situation of the Korean War arose, leading to a significant increase in national military expenditure, which posed some difficulties for economic recovery. However, Mao Zedong quickly proposed the policy of "fighting, stabilizing, and building simultaneously" and launched a widespread domestic campaign called "Resist US Aggression and Aid Korea; Defend the Homeland." This campaign boosted the enthusiasm of people from all walks of life to support the front lines and work hard in production, creating a situation where the people and the government worked together to overcome difficulties. As a result, the Korean War did not hinder the recovery of the national economy; instead, it became an effective driving force for recovery. This also reinforced Mao Zedong's belief in the necessity of mass movements for economic construction.

By the end of 1952, the national economy had achieved impressive results.

After three years of effort, the total output value of industry and agriculture in 1952 reached 81 billion yuan, an increase of 77.6% compared to 1949 and

23% higher than the best level before Japan's full-scale invasion of China in 1936. From 1950 to 1952, the total national fiscal revenue amounted to 36.107 billion yuan, while total fiscal expenditure in the same period was 36.219 billion yuan, fundamentally changing the situation of fiscal deficits. In fiscal expenditure, spending on economic construction was 12.57 billion yuan, accounting for 34.3% of total fiscal expenditure, with economic construction increasingly becoming the focus of the nation.

Agriculture, industry, and transportation were the key areas during the national economic recovery period. The total grain output increased from 113.184 million tons in 1949 to 163.931 million tons in 1952, a growth of 44.8%. Compared to 1936, it increased by 9.3%. This achievement, given the reliance on manual farming, was nothing short of miraculous and demonstrated the power of land reform, which had distributed land to the peasants. Key industrial products such as steel, pig iron, coal, crude oil, cement, and electricity also surpassed historical peak production levels.[49]

Railways have always been an obstacle to China's modern development. On the eve of the founding of new China, Mao Zedong once said, "In the past, China was a country dominated by imperialism. The construction of railways was mostly financed by loans from imperialist countries, and each railway built with such loans was in line with the invasion purposes of those imperialist countries. Railways became tools for imperialist oppression and exploitation of us." He envisioned, "Now that we are no longer under imperialist domination, we have the possibility and should restore and develop the railways well. Our country is so large, and currently, we only have more than 20,000 kilometers of railways, which is far too few. We need to have hundreds of thousands of kilometers of railways."[50]

After raising the slogan "Overthrow Chiang Kai-shek and Liberate All of China" during the War of Liberation, Mao Zedong proposed in a telegram to Lin Biao, Luo Ronghuan, and the Central Work Committee on January 8, 1948, "Please consider not destroying certain railways or only making tactical destructions without thorough destruction."[51] In January 1949, the Ministry of Railways was established, and following Mao's directive, "Wherever the PLA advances, the railways should be repaired." By the end of 1949, the total length of operational railways in China had reached 21,810 kilometers. By the end of 1952, an additional 1,320 kilometers of new railways had been built, and 1,170 kilometers had been restored. Among these, the most famous was the Chengdu–Chongqing Railway, which connected Chengdu and Chongqing. It was originally planned as part of the Sichuan–Hankou Railway during the late Qing dynasty and was proposed again by the KMT Government in 1936 but never commenced. Under the leadership of the new People's Government of China, the 505-kilometer Chengdu–Chongqing Railway began construction in June 1950 and officially opened on July 1, 1952.

While the national economy was rapidly recovering, the cause of unifying the mainland also made new progress. On May 23, 1951, the Agreement Between the Central People's Government and the Local Government of Xizang on Measures for the Peaceful Liberation of Xizang (hereinafter referred to as the Agreement on the Peaceful Liberation of Xizang) was signed in the Qinzheng Hall in Zhongnanhai, Beijing. On the evening of the 24th, Mao Zedong held a grand banquet to celebrate the signing of the agreement. In his speech, he pointed out, "For hundreds of years, the various ethnic groups in China have not been united, especially between the Han and Tibetan peoples, and there has been disunity within the Tibetan people as well. This was the result of the reactionary rule of the Qing dynasty and the Chiang Kai-shek government, as well as the machinations of imperialist powers. Now, the forces led by the Dalai Lama and the Panchen Erdeni, along with the Central People's Government, have all united. This unity has been achieved only after the Chinese people overthrew imperialist and domestic reactionary rule."[52] According to the agreement, on October 26, 1951, the PLA arrived in Lhasa. By July 1952, the PLA had reached the Shannan region, Ngari, and Yadong. From then on, the Five-Star Red Flag fluttered on the Tibetan Plateau. The long-cherished dream of the unity of all Chinese people became a reality.

The unification of mainland China also included addressing the Hong Kong issue, which was of great concern to the international community. Mao Zedong, however, approached the matter with a long-term perspective, creating more favorable conditions for breaking the Western blockade against the new China.

As early as December 9, 1946, in response to a question from a foreign journalist, Mao Zedong stated that China would not demand the immediate return of Hong Kong and that the issue could be resolved through negotiation in the future.[53]

When the three major campaigns concluded successfully, Stalin sent Soviet Politburo member Anastas Mikoyan to Xibaipo. Mao Zedong held multiple discussions with him starting from January 31, 1949. During these talks, the Hong Kong issue was brought up. Mao Zedong expressed that there was no need to rush the resolution of the Hong Kong and Macau issues, as maintaining their current status, especially that of Hong Kong, would be more beneficial for developing overseas relations and foreign trade. He emphasized that the final decision should be based on the evolving situation.[54]

Later, in a conversation with foreign guests on August 9, 1963, Mao Zedong reiterated as follows:

> As for Hong Kong, Britain does not have much military strength there. We could take control if we wanted to. However, there are treaty relations, with a small part being ceded and the larger part leased for ninety-nine years, with thirty-four years remaining. This is a special situation, and we do not plan to take action for the time being. ... Hong Kong is a vital trade route and taking control now would be detrimental to world trade and our trade relations with the world." He particularly emphasized, "Our decision not to take action now does not mean we will never take action. Britain is at ease now but will not be in the future.[55]

Subsequent history proved Mao Zedong's foresight. He never played a game of chess to a dead end. In his broad mind, he always considered both the present and the future of the Chinese nation.

CHAPTER 12

Resisting US Aggression and Aiding Korea to Protect the Homeland

> You all have your reasons, but when others are in a time of national crisis and we just stand by and watch, no matter how we justify it, it still feels uncomfortable in our hearts.
>
> Mao Zedong, Speech at the Expanded Meeting of the Political Bureau of the Central Committee of the CPC (October 4, 1950)

As Mao Zedong and the CPC were making efforts to restore the national economy, the Korean War broke out on June 25, 1950. On June 27, US President Harry S. Truman issued a statement announcing that American troops would enter Korea to support the South Korean army. He also dispatched the Seventh Fleet to the Taiwan Strait to prevent the PLA from liberating Taiwan. On July 7, the United Nations Security Council passed a resolution to form a "United Nations Command" under US leadership. On July 10, Truman appointed General Douglas MacArthur, Commander of the US Far East Command, as the Commander of the United Nations Command, which was headquartered within the US Far East Command's headquarters in Japan.

The successive moves by the United States in response to the Korean conflict indicated that it was considering the entire Far East region together and linking it to its global Cold War strategy against the Soviet Union.

Even before the US forces landed at Incheon on the western coast of the Korean Peninsula in mid-September, the US Air Force had been continuously invading Chinese airspace since August 27, conducting strafing and bombing along the China-Korea border. By September 30, US forces had reached the 38th parallel, a temporary military demarcation line established in 1945 for the surrender of Japanese troops to the Soviet Union and American forces.

In response, the Chinese government issued two warnings to the United States on September 30 and October 3, stating that if US forces crossed the 38th parallel, China would not sit idly by. Ignoring these warnings, the US forces launched a large-scale advance across the 38th parallel into North Korea on October 8. MacArthur, the Commander of the United Nations Command and US Far East Command, even proposed to end the war by Thanksgiving. If this were to happen, not only would the entire Korean Peninsula fall under US control, but the security of China's northeastern region and the Shandong Peninsula would also be threatened.

In Mao Zedong's view, the Korean War was both a war brought to China's doorstep by the United States and an unexpected yet unavoidable conflict.

From the day the United States announced its intervention in the Korean Civil War and its obstruction of the Chinese liberation of Taiwan on June 27, 1950, Mao Zedong closely monitored every move made by the United States and responded promptly. The difference was that while the United States was gradually escalating the situation, Mao Zedong hoped to contain the conflict within the Korean Peninsula.

On June 28, at the eighth meeting of the Central People's Government Committee held in the Qinzheng Hall of Zhongnanhai, Mao Zedong issued a stern warning to the US government: "The Chinese people have long declared that the affairs of every country in the world should be managed by the people of that country, and the affairs of Asia should be managed by the Asian people, not by the United States. US aggression in Asia will only provoke widespread and resolute resistance from the Asian people." He also responded to Truman's statement on the 27th: "Truman declared on January 5 this year that the United States would not interfere in Taiwan, and now he himself has proven that statement false, simultaneously tearing up all international agreements regarding non-interference in China's internal affairs."[1]

The content of Mao Zedong's speech was published in the *People's Daily* on the following day, June 29.

On June 28, Zhou Enlai, in his capacity as Foreign Minister, also issued a statement titled "On the Armed Invasion of Taiwan by the United States."

On July 7, following the United Nations Security Council's resolution to form a UN force to invade Korea, Mao Zedong immediately proposed the establishment of the Northeast Border Defense Army. He asked Zhou Enlai to convene two meetings of the Central Military Commission on July 7 and 10 to discuss national defense and the formation of the Northeast Border Defense Army. The plan at that time was to dispatch troops to support the Korean People's Army against the US forces if they crossed the 38th parallel.

After the July 7 Central Military Commission meeting, Acting Chief of General Staff Nie Rongzhen reported the meeting's decisions to Mao Zedong. Mao Zedong responded at midnight, "I agree with the decisions made at today's meeting. Please proceed accordingly. The original document is kept with me."[23]

This meeting decided on five key matters:

(1) Troop movement and deployment. Four armies and three artillery divisions were to be moved to Andong (now Dandong), Ji'an (now Jilin's Ji'an), and Benxi by the end of July.
(2) Command structure organization. Su Yu was appointed as Commander and Political Commissar of the Northeast Border Defense Army, with Xiao Hua as Deputy Political Commissar.
(3 Logistic preparations. Comprehensive logistic support plans were outlined.
(4) Recruitment and personnel reinforcement. The General Logistics Department was tasked with developing and implementing a plan to reinforce personnel, with a set deadline for completion.
(5) Political mobilization. Political mobilization under the slogan of national defense, with specific plans drafted by the General Political Department.

Originally, Su Yu, who had been primarily responsible for preparations to liberate Taiwan, was appointed as the Commander and Political Commissar of the Northeast Border Defense Army. Upon learning that Su Yu was unable to assume the post due to illness, Mao Zedong sent a personal telegram to Su Yu on July 10: "I have received your message. If you are ill, you should rest. You can delay coming, but I still hope you can come to Beijing in early August. If your health has improved by then, you can take up the post; if not, you should continue to rest." On the 17th, Mao Zedong, in the name of the Central Military Commission, sent a telegram to the East China Bureau and Su Yu: "Chairman Mao's previous telegram to Su asked him to come to Beijing in early August to either rest or take up work depending on his health. Su has now gone to Qingdao to rest, which is good. Please report on Su's health status in early August. If he is still seriously ill, he should continue to rest in Qingdao; if he has recovered, we hope he can come to Beijing."[4] Mao's concern for his trusted general was heartfelt and sincere.

On July 13, Mao Zedong received and approved a decision from Zhou Enlai regarding the defense of the Northeast border. This decision was based on comprehensive discussions from the Central Military Commission meetings on July 7 and 10. The decision involved redeploying the 38th, 39th, 40th, and 42nd Armies of the 13th Corps from Henan, Guangdong, Guangxi, Hunan, and Heilongjiang, as well as the 1st, 2nd, and 8th Artillery Divisions, an anti-aircraft artillery regiment, and an engineering regiment, totaling over 255,000 troops to form the Northeast Border Defense Army. The command structure included Su Yu as Commander and Political Commissar, Xiao Jinguang as Deputy Commander, Xiao Hua as Deputy Political Commissar, and Li Jukui as Logistics Commander. The 13th Corps headquarters was formed based on the 15th Corps headquarters, with Deng Hua as Commander, Lai Chuanzhu as Political Commissar, Xie Fang as Chief of Staff, and Du Ping as Director of the Political Department. Artillery, armored, engineering, and anti-aircraft units were under the command of Wan Yi. The Northeast Air Force Command was established with Duan Suquan as its commander. Detailed plans for troop transportation, assembly areas, logistic preparations, and personnel reinforcements were also made.[5]

The reason Mao Zedong and the Central Military Commission assigned Su Yu, initially in charge of preparing for the liberation of Taiwan, to the Northeast Border Defense Army, was due to the new circumstances following the outbreak of the Korean War. The Central Committee made the significant decision to "support the Korean people and postpone the liberation of Taiwan." However, since Su Yu was unable to assume the position due to illness, Mao Zedong drafted an order on August 5 in the name of the Central Military Commission, assigning Gao Gang, Commander and Political Commissar of the Northeast Military Region, to take primary responsibility.[6]

"Speed is of the essence in war." By early August, except for the anti-aircraft regiment, the Northeast Border Defense Army had reached its designated assembly positions.

With such a large-scale concentration of troops moving to the China-Korea border, the issue of air defense had to be considered. Without sufficient air defense capabilities of its own, Mao Zedong made a request to Stalin. Shortly thereafter, Stalin responded with a suggestion. On July 20, Mao Zedong replied to Stalin as follows:

> After studying the issue of providing air cover for our troops moving to the China-Korea border and the matter of transitioning our air force to jet aircraft while receiving all the equipment from two Soviet Union air divisions, we welcome your proposal and extend our special thanks to you and the Soviet Union government for your assistance. ... We plan to station the jet air division you are sending to cover our troops near Shenyang, with two regiments in Anshan and one regiment in Liaoyang. This deployment, in coordination with our air force's mixed brigade stationed near Andong, will resolve the issue of covering our troops and protecting the industrial areas of Shenyang, Andong, and Fushun.[7]

In early August, Mao Zedong also approved a report from Acting Chief of General Staff Nie Rongzhen, agreeing to send some anti-aircraft artillery units to the Korean side to ensure the safety of the Yalu River Bridge.

On August 4, Mao Zedong presided over a meeting of the Political Bureau of the Central Committee of the CPC to discuss the countermeasures China should adopt in response to the US armed invasion of Korea. In his speech, he stated: "If American imperialism wins, it will become arrogant and threaten our country. We cannot stand by and do nothing for Korea; we must help them in the form of volunteer forces, although the timing must be carefully chosen. We must be prepared. Taiwan must be recovered, but we cannot stand by regarding Korea and Vietnam."[8]

On August 5, Mao Zedong sent a telegram to Gao Gang, based on the changing situation in the Korean War, requiring the Northeast Border Defense Army to complete all preparations within the month and be ready for combat in early September. On the 18th, the deadline for completing all preparations was extended to before September 30.

The formation and early deployment of the Northeast Border Defense Army on the China-Korea border were crucial. Later, Peng Dehuai, who served as Commander and Political Commissar of the Chinese People's Volunteer Army, commented: "When the American imperialists launched their aggression, we immediately deployed five armies to the north bank of the Yalu River. When the enemy crossed the 38th parallel and approached our border, we surprised them with a heavy blow, achieving the first victory. This not only saved the then-retreating Korean People's Army but also gained the initiative in the war. Without this prior preparation, it would have been unimaginable to reverse the extremely unfavorable and severe situation at that time."[9]

By mid-August, the Korean War had reached a stalemate along the Nakdong River line. Mao Zedong decided to redeploy the 9th and 19th Corps as the second and third line units of the Northeast Border Defense Army. The 9th Corps entered the designated area along the Shandong section of the Jinpu Railway by late October, and the 19th Corps assembled along the Longhai Railway. These proactive measures provided a strategic advantage for the later decision to Resist US Aggression and Aid Korea.

After the Korean People's Army launched its fourth offensive on August 20, the war entered a stalemate. The US and South Korean forces were compressed into a small area of just over 10,000 square kilometers, where they tenaciously defended using their firepower and sea and air superiority.

The Korean People's Army, due to the extended front lines and significant losses of its main forces without timely reinforcements, saw its offensive weaken. Meanwhile, from August 27, US aircraft continuously attacked the Chinese side of the Yalu River border, including Ji'an, Linjiang, Dandong, and Kuandian.

Under these circumstances, Mao Zedong judged that the Korean War might become protracted. On September 5, at the ninth meeting of the Central People's Government Committee held in the Qinzheng Hall of Zhongnanhai, he clearly pointed out as follows:

> Given the current situation, the possibility of the Korean War becoming protracted is increasing. In the past, we considered both quick victory and prolonged conflict as possibilities. A quick victory meant the Korean People's Army would drive the remaining US and Rhee Syngman forces into the sea. Now that the US has increased its troops in Korea, the likelihood of a prolonged war has increased. The Korean people are likely to sustain this prolonged conflict. They have mobilized over a million people, and the Korean People's Army currently has hundreds of thousands of soldiers and can continue to be reinforced. The Korean people's struggle is very courageous. When US planes bomb bridges, the Korean people repair them. Initially, they bombed during the day and repaired at night. Later, they repaired the bridges immediately after the bombings. When planes came, the Korean people just took cover nearby and then resumed the repairs. At the beginning of the war, the American imperialists thought that the Korean people would be scared by airstrikes, but they hit a wall. ... Our wish is to avoid war, but if you insist on fighting, we will have to fight. You fight your way, and we fight ours. You use atomic bombs, we use hand grenades, exploiting your weaknesses and following you to the end, eventually defeating you. When the war breaks out, it won't be a small fight but a big one, not a short fight but a long one, not an ordinary fight but a fight with atomic bombs. We must be fully prepared. If you insist on doing it that way, we will follow suit.[10]

The new developments in the Korean War increased the likelihood of the Northeast Border Defense Army entering Korea under the guise of volunteer forces. On September 3, Mao Zedong sent a reply telegram to Gao Gang, instructing him to "educate the troops with a modern warfare perspective and to never underestimate the enemy." At the same time, Mao tasked Zhou Enlai with arranging for relevant personnel from the Northeast Border Defense Army to go to Korea under the guise of military attachés at the Chinese embassy to "conduct on-the-ground investigations of the combat situation" and use the findings to educate the troops.[11]

At this moment, a new situation arose. In late August, after extensive analysis, Mao Zedong concluded that there was a possibility of US forces landing at Incheon or other locations on the Korean Peninsula. He communicated this danger to both the Soviet Union and Korea, advising the Korean side to prepare for the worst-case scenario.[12]

The Korean People's Army, poised for action, launched its fifth offensive on August 31, breaking through enemy lines and temporarily approaching Daegu and Busan. After fierce seesaw battles, the Korean People's Army retreated to the western bank of the Nakdong River.

What had been anticipated finally happened. On September 15, US forces landed at Incheon, coordinating with US, British, and South Korean troops entrenched around Daegu and Busan, thus surrounding the main forces of the Korean People's Army. On September 28, US forces entered Seoul (the current capital of South Korea). The US forces advancing from the south and north met, and by September 29, they were pressing against the 38th parallel. At this time, the "United Nations Command" in the southern part of the Korean Peninsula had more than 330,000 troops. The main forces of the Korean People's Army were blocked south of the 38th parallel, leaving the vast area north of the 38th parallel poorly defended. The Korean War situation was on the brink of disaster.

On September 27, Kim Il Sung, Chairman of the Central Committee of the Workers' Party of Korea, Prime Minister of the Democratic People's Republic of Korea, and Supreme Commander of the Korean People's Army, stated in a speech: "At this stage, our party's strategic policy is to maximize delaying the enemy's advance, gain time to rescue the main forces of the People's Army, form new reserve units to build a strong counterattack force, and conduct a planned retreat."[13]

Mao Zedong expressed high concern and sympathy for the plight of the Korean People's Army. While urging the Northeast Border Defense Army to accelerate their preparations for going abroad to fight, he also provided as much advice and assistance as possible to Kim Il Sung and maintained constant communication with the Soviet Union.

On September 20, Mao Zedong reviewed and revised a telegram draft to Kim Il Sung regarding the Korean People's Army's combat strategy. The telegram was drafted by Zhou Enlai. At that time, US forces had not been at Incheon for long, and Seoul was still under the control of the Korean People's Army. The telegram stated: "It is estimated that the enemy may still increase its forces at Incheon, aiming to extend their occupation eastward, cut off north-south communications in Korea, and press toward the 38th parallel. The People's Army must strive to hold the area north of the 38th parallel and conduct a prolonged war to have a chance of success. Therefore, please consider how to preserve the main force to annihilate the enemy individually under the principle of self-reliance and long-term struggle."

It also reminded him of the danger: "If the enemy occupies Seoul, the People's Army's rear could be cut off." The telegram concluded: "The enemy seeks a quick victory and fears a protracted war, while our People's Army cannot achieve a quick victory but can only win through a prolonged war. The above is offered from the standpoint of a friend and comrade for your reference."[14] On the 21st, Kim Il Sung received this telegram through the Chinese Ambassador to Korea, Ni Zhiliang.

On September 27 and 30, Kim Il Sung twice summoned Chinese Ambassador Ni Zhiliang to report on the Korean War situation.

On the night of September 29, Zhou Enlai wrote to Mao Zedong, reporting: "The American imperialists have openly stated they will advance north of the 38th parallel. From Ni Zhiliang's telegram on the 27th, it seems there are no defending troops north of the 38th parallel. This situation is very serious, and the enemy may drive straight to Pyongyang."[15]

For China, this war, which it had tried hard to avoid, was now unavoidable.

At this time, the first anniversary of the founding of the People's Republic of China was approaching. On September 30, the National Committee of the

CPPCC held a celebration for the first anniversary. Zhou Enlai delivered a speech titled "Strive to Consolidate and Develop the People's Victory." Mao Zedong reviewed and revised this speech. Regarding the Korean War, he made a solemn statement: "The Chinese people love peace, but to defend peace, we are never afraid to resist aggressive wars. The Chinese people will never tolerate foreign aggression, nor will we stand by while imperialists invade our neighbors."[16]

October 1 was a day of significant changes in the Korean War. Mao Zedong ascended the Tiananmen Gatetower as usual, attending the first anniversary celebration of the founding of the People's Republic of China, reviewing the PLA troops and the parade. In the evening, he watched the fireworks display from the Tiananmen Gatetower.

On the same day, MacArthur issued an ultimatum to the Korean People's Army. Starting from September 30, South Korean troops began crossing the 38th parallel, and US forces were preparing to advance northward. On October 2, MacArthur issued the United Nations Command's Operation Order No. 2, ordering the US 8th Army to cross the 38th parallel and occupy Pyongyang.

Also on October 1, Stalin sent a telegram requesting that China immediately dispatch at least five or six divisions to the 38th parallel to help Korea organize the defense of the area north of the parallel.[17]

Likewise, on October 1, late at night, Kim Il Sung urgently summoned Ni Zhiliang, requesting Chinese military assistance. On October 3, Park Il-woo, a member of the Standing Committee of the Workers' Party of Korea, and Minister of the Interior, delivered a letter to Mao Zedong from Kim Il Sung and Pak Hon-yong, Vice Chairman of the Central Committee of the Workers' Party of Korea and Deputy Prime Minister and Foreign Minister of the Democratic People's Republic of Korea. The letter stated: "In the event of an enemy attack north of the 38th parallel, we urgently hope that the Chinese PLA will directly intervene to assist our military operations."[18]

In this context, at 1 a.m. on October 3, Zhou Enlai urgently met with Indian Ambassador to China, K. M. Panikkar, clearly stating: "First, if US forces attempt to cross the 38th parallel to expand the war, we must intervene. This serious situation is caused by the US government. Second, we advocate that the Korean issue should be resolved peacefully. Not only must the Korean War be stopped immediately, and the invading troops withdraw, but the relevant countries must also discuss peaceful solutions within the United Nations."[19] The US government quickly learned of this conversation but ignored Zhou Enlai's warning on behalf of the Chinese government.

At the same time, Mao Zedong was determined to first convene a meeting of the Central Secretariat to discuss whether to send troops to Resist US Aggression and Aid Korea.

At 2 a.m. on October 2, Mao Zedong, in the name of the Central Military Commission, sent a telegram to Gao Gang and Deng Hua: "(1) Comrade Gao Gang, upon receiving this telegram, please come to Beijing immediately for a meeting. (2) Comrade Deng Hua, please order the border defense troops to complete their preparations ahead of schedule and be ready to move out at any time, according to the original plan, to fight the new enemy. (3) Deng (Hua), please report the readiness status and whether the troops can move out immediately by telegram."[20] At that time, Deng Hua was the Commander and Political Commissar of the 13th Corps. Later, the headquarters of the Chinese People's Volunteer Army was established based on the leadership of the 13th Corps.

On October 2, before the Central Secretariat meeting, Mao Zedong drafted a reply to Stalin's telegram from October 1. He had initially planned to send it after the meeting, but it was temporarily shelved due to the majority of attendees opposing the troop deployment. However, this telegram provides insight into Mao Zedong's thoughts at the time.

> (1) We have decided to send some troops into Korea under the name of volunteer forces to fight against the US and its puppet Rhee Syngman's forces and to assist our Korean comrades. We believe this is necessary. If we allow the whole of Korea to be occupied by the Americans, the revolutionary forces in Korea will suffer a fundamental defeat, and the American aggressors will become more rampant, which will be unfavorable to the entire East. (2) Since we have decided to send Chinese troops into Korea to fight against the Americans, first, we must solve the problem effectively. That is, we must be prepared to annihilate and expel the US and other invading forces within Korea; second, since

Chinese troops will be fighting US troops within Korea (even though we are using the name of volunteer forces), we must be prepared for the possibility that the US will declare a state of war against China. We must be ready for the possibility that the US may use its air force to bomb many of China's major cities and industrial bases and its navy to attack coastal areas. (3) Among these two issues, the first question is whether Chinese troops can annihilate US forces within Korea and effectively resolve the Korean issue. As long as our troops can annihilate US forces within Korea, primarily defeating their 8th Army (a battle-hardened American unit), the seriousness of the second issue (the US declaring war on China) will still exist. However, by then, the situation will be more favorable for the revolutionary front and China. This means that if the Korean issue is resolved by defeating the US forces, it will be effectively concluded (though not formally, as the US may not recognize Korea's victory for a long time). Even if the US openly fights against China, the scale of the war may not be very large, and its duration may not be very long.[21]

The Korean War occurred under the severe confrontation of the Cold War between the US and the Soviet Union. At the time, both the Soviet Union and the United States believed that this war could potentially spark a new world war. However, Mao Zedong presented a new perspective in his analysis, considering it a controllable local war. He believed that as long as "the Korean issue is effectively resolved by defeating the US forces," "even if the US openly fights against China, the war may not be very large in scale or long in duration." The War to Resist US Aggression and Aid Korea validated Mao Zedong's judgment. In Mao's view, using war to eliminate war and to control war was the dialectical approach to the problem of war.

At this time, US forces had not yet crossed the 38th parallel, nor had Pyongyang rapidly fallen. Mao Zedong's idea of sending troops was still based on the judgment that the Korean War would be prolonged. Therefore, the unissued telegram suggested sending 12 divisions to appropriate locations in North Korea, "fighting only defensive battles in the first period, annihilating small enemy units, understanding all aspects of the situation, waiting for Soviet Union weapons to arrive, equipping our troops, and then cooperating with Korean comrades to launch a counteroffensive to annihilate US invaders."[22]

However, in the afternoon, at a meeting of the Central Secretariat held at Juxiang Studyroom in Zhongnanhai, although Mao Zedong believed that sending troops to Korea was extremely urgent, the majority of attendees opposed the deployment. Therefore, the meeting decided to convene another expanded meeting of the Political Bureau of the Central Committee to continue discussing the issue of sending troops to Korea.

After this meeting, Mao Zedong informed Stalin of the discussion results through the Soviet Union Ambassador to China, Nikolai Roshchin.

According to materials preserved in the Russian Presidential Archives, on October 3, Nikolai Roshchin conveyed Mao Zedong's initial opinion on China's temporary decision not to send troops to Stalin. Here is Roshchin's account of Mao Zedong's conversation.

> We originally planned to deploy several divisions of volunteer troops to North Korea to help our Korean comrades when the enemy attacked north of the 38th parallel. However, after careful consideration, we now believe that this move would have very serious consequences. First, it would be difficult to solve the Korean issue with just a few divisions (our troops are poorly equipped and have no assurance of victory against the US military), and the enemy would force us to retreat. Second, the most likely outcome is that this would lead to an open conflict between the United States and China, and the Soviet Union could be dragged into the war, making the situation extremely serious. Many comrades in the Central Committee believe that we must act cautiously in this regard. Therefore, it is best to restrain ourselves and not send troops for now, while preparing our forces. This approach will be more advantageous in seizing the opportunity to fight the enemy.[23]

It is worth noting that Roshchin's account included this remark: "No final decision has been made on this issue." "We will hold a Central Committee meeting, and major comrades from all departments will attend."[24]

On the afternoon of October 4, following the decision of the Central Secretariat meeting on October 2, Mao Zedong chaired an expanded meeting of the Political Bureau of the Central Committee at Yinian Hall in Zhongnanhai to discuss the Korean War situation and the issue of sending Chinese troops to aid Korea. The attendees included Mao Zedong, Zhu De, Liu Shaoqi, Zhou Enlai, Ren Bishi, Lin Boqu, Dong Biwu, Peng Zhen, Chen Yun, Zhang Wentian, Peng Dehuai (arriving midway), and Gao Gang. The following attended the meeting: Luo Ronghuan, Lin Biao, Deng Xiaoping, Rao Shushi, Bo Yibo, Deng Zihui, Li Fuchun, Hu Qiaomu, and Yang Shangkun.[25]

Mao Zedong first asked everyone to discuss the disadvantages of sending troops. The attendees expressed their views, with the majority either opposing or having various doubts about sending troops. Their opinion was that unless absolutely necessary, it would be best not to fight this war. Mao Zedong said, "You all have your reasons, but when others are in a time of national crisis and we just stand by and watch, no matter how we justify it, it still feels uncomfortable in our hearts."[26] He finally announced that the expanded meeting of the Political Bureau would continue the next day.

Mao Zedong never gave up the idea of sending troops to Resist US Aggression and Aid Korea and continuously urged comprehensive preparations. He knew that they would be facing a particularly formidable opponent, so the first battle must be approached with caution. On that day, while reviewing Zhou Enlai's reply to Ni Zhiliang regarding the arrangement for the military attaché observation group to Korea, he added a section, requiring one group to investigate the various conditions near Pyongyang and along the Pyongyang-Andong line and the Pyongyang-Ji'an line. Another group was to investigate the conditions along the Pyongyang-Wonsan line and the Wonsan-Chongjin line and the mountainous areas north of it. He also instructed that, if possible, they should briefly investigate the conditions between the Pyongyang-Wonsan line and the 38th parallel, but not go too deep.

The decision to send troops to Resist US Aggression and Aid Korea was the most difficult decision Mao Zedong had ever made. Its difficulty lay not only in its significance and the formidable opponent but also in the challenge of selecting the right commander.

Previously, when Mao Zedong formed the Northeast Border Defense Army, he had considered appointing Su Yu, but Su Yu was ill and unable to assume the post. He then considered Lin Biao, but Lin Biao also claimed to be in poor health. On September 3, Mao Zedong mentioned in a telegram to Gao Gang: "Lin (Biao) and Su (Yu) are both ill. The two Xiaos[27] have work here and cannot come for the time being, but it may be possible in a few months. We estimate there is time."[28]

Now, through the meetings on October 2 and 4, Mao Zedong had gained confidence, believing that he could ultimately convince everyone to support the deployment of troops. However, finding the right person to lead the campaign became an urgent problem. He placed his hopes on Peng Dehuai, known for his ability to fight tough battles.

Right after the Central Secretariat meeting on October 2, Mao Zedong instructed Zhou Enlai to dispatch a plane to Xi'an to bring Peng Dehuai to Beijing for the Political Bureau of the Central Committee meeting on the afternoon of October 4. When Peng Dehuai arrived, he was unfamiliar with the situation and did not speak.

On the afternoon of October 5, the expanded meeting of the Political Bureau of the Central Committee continued. That morning, Mao Zedong invited Peng Dehuai to Zhongnanhai to discuss the issue of sending troops to aid Korea. Mao Zedong directly asked: "Who do you think is suitable to lead the troops to aid Korea?" Peng Dehuai replied with a question: "Hasn't the Central Committee already decided to send Comrade Lin Biao?" After discussing Lin Biao's situation, Mao Zedong said: "Our opinion is that you must take on this responsibility." Peng Dehuai expressed: "I will obey the Central Committee's decision." Mao Zedong said: "Then I am relieved."[29]

In the afternoon meeting of the Political Bureau of the Central Committee, Peng Dehuai recalled: "After other comrades spoke, I said a few words: 'Sending troops to aid Korea is necessary. If we fail, it will only mean delaying the victory of the liberation war by a few years. If the US forces are stationed on the banks of the Yalu River and in Taiwan, they can always find an excuse to launch an invasion.' The Chairman decided I should go to Korea, and I did not refuse."[30] The meeting finally made the strategic decision to "Resist US Aggression and Aid Korea; Defend the Homeland." It was also decided that Peng Dehuai would lead the Volunteer Army into Korea and that Zhou Enlai and Lin Biao would go to the Soviet Union to discuss matters with Stalin.

A historic decision was thus made.

On October 8, when US forces made a large-scale advance north of the 38th parallel, Mao Zedong issued the order to form the Chinese People's

Volunteer Army, appointing Peng Dehuai as the Commander and Political Commissar. On the same day, Mao Zedong also informed Kim Il Sung of this decision with a definitive tone, asking him to send Pak Il-woo to Shenyang to discuss with Peng Dehuai and Gao Gang "various issues related to the Chinese People's Volunteer Army entering Korea."[31] That morning, Chinese Ambassador to Korea Ni Zhiliang handed this telegram to Kim Il Sung. On the 12th, Mao Zedong ordered Song Shilun, Commander and Political Commissar of the 9th Corps, to "move northward ahead of schedule, directly to the Northeast."

At this time, Mao Zedong felt a weight lifted off his shoulders, yet another weight pressed down. He knew that the upcoming conflict would be a modern war, vastly different from the War of Resistance Against Japanese Aggression and the War of Liberation. Once Peng Dehuai led the Chinese People's Volunteer Army into Korea, they would face the danger of lacking air superiority, which would mean many casualties. In Mao Zedong's military doctrine, the lives of soldiers were always paramount, with his famous saying, "The basic principle of war is to preserve oneself and destroy the enemy." He placed his hope for solving the air superiority issue on the Soviet Union.

On the same day Mao Zedong issued the order to form the Chinese People's Volunteer Army, Zhou Enlai and his delegation boarded a plane heading west. On October 11, they arrived in Crimea for talks with Stalin, who was recuperating there.

During the talks, Zhou Enlai proposed that as long as the Soviet Union agreed to deploy its air force to provide air cover, China could send troops to aid Korea. He also requested that the Soviet Union provide military equipment necessary for the War to Resist US Aggression and Aid Korea. Stalin expressed that the Soviet Union could fully meet China's requests for planes, tanks, artillery, and other equipment, but the Soviet Union air force was not yet ready and would need two to two and a half months before it could support the Volunteer Army.[32]

This was unexpected for Mao Zedong and was not anticipated by the earlier Political Bureau of the Central Committee meetings, meaning that the Chinese People's Volunteer Army would face greater difficulties and sacrifices in entering Korea. Mao Zedong decided to convene a Political Bureau meeting to discuss this matter and notified all parties to temporarily suspend the issued orders.

On October 13, Mao Zedong chaired a Political Bureau of the Central Committee meeting at Yinian Hall in Zhongnanhai to once again discuss the issue of sending Chinese troops to aid Korea. Since the previous meetings had thoroughly discussed whether to send troops, the opinions at this meeting were highly consistent. The participants unanimously agreed that even without Soviet Union air support, China should still send troops to aid Korea in the face of a large-scale advance by US forces north of the 38th parallel.

According to Peng Dehuai's conversation with his staff on February 8, 1955: "At this time (referring to the October 13 Political Bureau of the Central Committee meeting), Chairman Mao used the Soviet Union delay in providing air cover as a reason to ask me whether we could still fight and whether the Soviet Union was completely backing out. I said, 'This is a partial withdrawal (by the Soviet Union), but we can still fight.' In the end, Chairman Mao said, 'Even if we can't win, he still owes us a debt, and we can fight again whenever we want.'"[33]

That night at 10 p.m., Mao Zedong sent a telegram to Zhou Enlai, who had returned to Moscow from Crimea, stating: "We believe we should participate in the war and must participate. The benefits of participating are immense, and the harm of not participating is equally immense." He also suggested: "Please stay in Moscow for a few days and renegotiate the above issues with the Soviet Union comrades.[34] A prompt reply by telegram is eagerly awaited."[35] The final outcome of the discussions was that the Soviet Union side would only deploy their air force to the Chinese border for defense and would not be ready to enter Korea to fight within two to two and a half months.[36]

Given the Soviet Union's temporary inability to provide air cover, Mao Zedong needed to reconsider the specific deployment for entering Korea based on the new situation.

In a telegram to Zhou Enlai on October 14, he expressed agreement with Peng Dehuai's proposed combat plan for entering Korea.

Comrade Peng Dehuai, after studying the situation in Andong, believes that if our army can position one corps in the mountainous region around Tokchon, about 200 kilometers northeast of Pyongyang, and the remaining three corps and three artillery divisions north of Tokchon in the Huichon, Chonchon, and Kanggye areas, it might cause the US and puppet forces to hesitate and halt their advance. This could preserve at least the mountainous areas north of the Pyongyang-Wonsan line from enemy occupation. In doing so, our army could avoid engagement, gaining time for equipment and training. Second, if the enemies from Wonsan and Pyongyang advance north to the Tokchon mountainous area, our army could use the necessary forces to pin down the enemy in Pyongyang while concentrating the main forces to annihilate the puppet troops attacking from Wonsan. If we can eliminate one or two, or even two to three, complete divisions of the puppet army, the situation will greatly improve. Both Peng Dehuai and Gao Gang are confident in defeating the puppet forces, and like me, they believe participating in the war is necessary and beneficial.[37]

The PLA had no experience in foreign combat, much less in complex terrains surrounded by the sea and mountains and faced an enemy with strong air and sea superiority and extensive modern warfare experience. Under such circumstances, the possibility mentioned in the telegram that "our army could avoid engagement, gaining time for equipment and training" would undoubtedly increase the likelihood of a first victory for the Chinese People's Volunteer Army. Minimizing casualties and achieving victory in war is naturally the ideal goal for any military leader.

To gain a more comprehensive understanding of the situation in Korea, Mao Zedong decided to send Peng Dehuai ahead. At 1 a.m. on October 15, Mao Zedong drafted a telegram in Zhou Enlai's name to Kim Il Sung, "Please send a comrade familiar with the routes to Andong on October 16 to guide Comrade Peng Dehuai to meet with Comrade Kim Il Sung."[38] He simultaneously informed Zhou Enlai of this decision. In the telegram to Zhou Enlai, he specified that Peng Dehuai would meet with Kim Il Sung in Tokchon.

Based on the assessment at the time, "The US forces are still at the 38th parallel; advancing to Pyongyang will take time, and from Pyongyang to

Dechuan will take even more time. If the US forces in Pyongyang do not advance to Tokchon, the puppet forces in Wonsan will likely not be able to attack alone, giving our troops time to advance and build defenses."

Based on this judgment, Mao Zedong finally set the timeline for the Chinese People's Volunteer Army to enter Korea. "Our army will start moving on October 19. The lead troops will need seven days to march 200 kilometers to Tokchon. After resting for one or two days, they can begin constructing fortifications south of the Tokchon-Nyongwon line on October 28. It will take ten days for the entire 260,000-strong army to cross the Yalu River, completing the crossing by October 28." He also determined the strength of the volunteer forces to ensure a victory near Tokchon in November: "To prepare for a victory in November when the enemy attacks the Tokchon area, we have decided to deploy 260,000 troops (twelve infantry divisions and three artillery divisions). If the fortifications are completed and the enemy holds Pyongyang and Wonsan without daring to attack, we can send about half of the troops back to China for training and supply, and they can return when needed for major battles."[39]

Mao Zedong also made an important decision, approving his eldest son Mao Anying's request to join Peng Dehuai as a member of the Chinese People's Volunteer Army in the War to Resist US Aggression and Aid Korea. Fully understanding history, Mao Zedong used this extraordinary action to express his deep trust in Peng Dehuai and his confidence in the ultimate victory of the war. Later, when Mao Anying was tragically killed on the Korean battlefield, Mao Zedong bore his grief silently and instructed that Mao Anying's remains be buried in the Korean land he had defended. He also reminded Peng Dehuai to take care of his own safety. Mao Zedong kept Mao Anying's personal belongings in a suitcase by his side until his death.

On October 18, Zhou Enlai returned to Beijing from the Soviet Union. Mao Zedong immediately chaired a Political Bureau of the Central Committee meeting. Zhou Enlai reported on the discussions with Stalin, Molotov, and others regarding Soviet Union assistance for China's entry into the war, and Peng Dehuai reported on the preparations for the Volunteer Army's entry into Korea. The meeting decided that the Chinese People's Volunteer Army would cross the Yalu River and enter Korea on the 19th as planned.

At 9 p.m. on October 18, Mao Zedong formally issued the order for the Chinese People's Volunteer Army to enter Korea. He instructed: "To strictly maintain secrecy, the crossing troops should begin at dusk and stop by 4 a.m., ensuring they are fully concealed by 5 a.m. and thoroughly checked."[40]

October 19, 1950 is an unforgettable day in the history of new China. From this day forward, the Chinese People's Volunteer Army, "mighty and high-spirited, crossed the Yalu River," marking the beginning of the War to Resist US Aggression and Aid Korea.

At this time, significant changes were occurring in the northern Korean War situation. After crossing the 38th parallel, US forces rested for several days and then accelerated their northward advance. On October 17, MacArthur ordered a change in plans for the US 8th Army and the US 10th Corps to meet along the Pyongyang-Wonsan line, directing the 8th Army to command the western forces and the 10th Corps to command the eastern forces, both rapidly advancing toward the northern Korean border. On October 19, the same day the Chinese People's Volunteer Army began crossing the Yalu River, US and South Korean forces captured Pyongyang. They then split into multiple routes for a rapid advance, aiming to occupy all of Korea by Thanksgiving.

Thus, the original plan for Peng Dehuai to meet Kim Il Sung at Tokchon was no longer feasible. After crossing the Yalu River, Peng Dehuai immediately hurried to a small village called Taedong, located between Tongchang and Bukjin of Changseong County. On the morning of October 21, he met Kim Il Sung for the first time at Daedong. Later that day, at 4 p.m., he sent a telegram to Mao Zedong and others. The telegram stated: "This morning at 9 a.m., I met with Kim Il Sung at Taedong between Tongchang and Bukjin. The frontline situation is very chaotic; the units retreating from Pyongyang have not been in contact for three days, and the Korean side currently has only three divisions, all of which are new recruits. If the enemy continues to advance north, it will be difficult to stop them. At present, we should control the area south of the Myohyangsan and Hyangcheon-dong lines and construct fortifications. Please have Deng (Hua), Hong (Xuezhi), and Han (Xianchu) come to my location quickly to discuss the overall deployment."[41]

At this time, Mao Zedong had also learned about the situation on the northern Korean front through various channels and quickly made a judgment:

"As of now, neither the Americans nor the puppet forces have anticipated that our Volunteer Army will participate in the war, so they dare to advance boldly in two separate columns, east and west." "Now it is a matter of seizing the opportunity for battle, completing the deployment within a few days, and starting the battle a few days later, rather than first setting up a defensive period and then talking about attacking." He also sent a telegram to Deng Hua: "My idea is that the 13th Corps headquarters should immediately go to where Comrade Peng Dehuai is and reorganize as the headquarters of the Chinese People's Volunteer Army to facilitate combat deployment."

In another telegram, he advised: "Peng (Dehuai) and Deng (Hua) should stay together and not be dispersed."[42] This was an experience he had learned from long-term warfare.

In Mao Zedong's military philosophy, there was always an emphasis on the planning of operations as well as on their flexibility. Adapting to changing circumstances was a specialty of the People's Army, which had followed Mao through many battles. On October 24, Deng Hua led the 13th Corps headquarters to meet Peng Dehuai at Taeyu-dong in Changseong County. Peng Dehuai and others immediately readjusted the deployment and launched the first campaign shortly after entering Korea.

In the multi-pronged advance toward the border areas, the South Korean troops were in the front and the US forces were behind. On October 25, the Chinese People's Volunteer Army engaged the South Korean troops in the areas of Unsan and Onjong, marking the start of the War to Resist US Aggression and Aid Korea.

From this point on, under Mao Zedong's meticulous guidance, Peng Dehuai led the Chinese People's Volunteer Army in coordinated operations with the Korean People's Army. From October 25, 1950, to June 10, 1951, they launched five campaigns. Despite lacking naval and air superiority and modern logistics, they inflicted over 233,000 casualties on the enemy at the cost of more than 189,000 of their own, pushing the "United Nations forces" led by the US back from the Yalu River to south of the 38th parallel and even capturing Seoul (the current capital of South Korea) for a time. This was the first time in modern warfare history that the myth of the invincibility of the US military was shattered.

During the five campaigns, the fifth was the largest in scale, with both sides deploying a total of one million troops, and it inflicted the highest number of casualties on the enemy, totaling over 82,000. After this severe blow, General Albert C. Wedemeyer admitted in a hearing before the US Senate Armed Services and Foreign Relations Committees: "The Korean War is a bottomless pit, and there is no hope of victory for the United Nations forces."[43]

At this moment, Mao Zedong was also considering making significant adjustments to the strategy for the next phase.

Regarding military strategy, Mao Zedong decided to solve the Korean issue with a policy of protracted war, using the advantageous terrain near the 38th parallel to wear down the enemy through positional warfare. In his telegram to Stalin on June 3, 1951, he said: "Because our technical conditions are far inferior to the enemy's, we cannot quickly solve the Korean issue and have decided to resolve it through a protracted war strategy. This requires a phase of gradually weakening the enemy, followed by a final phase to solve the problem. During the phase of weakening the enemy, the locations and methods of fighting must be appropriate to the situation. The area near the 38th parallel has many mountains, favorable for defense, and is close to the rear, making supply relatively easy. These two conditions are much worse near and south of Seoul."[44]

In terms of negotiations, Mao Zedong proposed a strategy of fighting while negotiating and using fighting to promote talks. In early June of the same year, when he heard Yang Chengwu report on the 20th Corps' preparations for entering Korea, he said: "Now, the United States has shown some intention of negotiating, which is not an easy thing and indicates that we have fought well. The US authorities have realized that relying solely on military struggle cannot solve the problem." He stated: "Since the enemy is willing to sit down and negotiate with us, we certainly agree, but the enemy is also likely to use negotiations to achieve something. Our military comrades must stay clear-headed and not harbor any illusions of a quick victory. Our strategy is prolonged warfare, active defense, and simultaneous military and political struggle to strive for negotiations, using fighting to promote talks. This means preparing for a protracted war and positional warfare while striving for peace talks to end the war."[45]

In June 1951, Mao Zedong met with Kim Il Sung in Beijing and decided to adopt the strategy of fighting while negotiating based on changes in the Korean War situation, combining political and military struggles.[46] The Korean armistice negotiations began on July 10, 1951, and finally forced the United States to sign the Korean Armistice Agreement on July 27, 1953. The War to Resist US Aggression and Aid Korea, which lasted two years and nine months, finally ended with the victory of the Chinese people.

On September 12, 1953, in his speech at the 24th meeting of the Central People's Government Committee, Mao Zedong summarized the War to Resist US Aggression and Aid Korea. He said: "This time, we have understood the nature of the US military. If you don't engage with them, you will fear them. We fought with them for thirty-three months and got to know them well. American imperialism is not so terrible; it is just like that." He particularly emphasized: "Relying on the people, coupled with relatively correct leadership, we can use our inferior equipment to defeat a superiorly equipped enemy."[47]

Mao Zedong was convinced that just as this approach worked for war, it would also be effective for construction and development.

CHAPTER 13

Establishing a Socialist System

A group needs a constitution, and a country needs one too. The constitution is the fundamental law, the general charter. By using the constitution to solidify the principles of people's democracy and socialism, we provide the entire nation with a clear path, making the people feel there is a clear, definite, and correct road to follow, thus boosting their enthusiasm.

MAO ZEDONG,
"On the Draft *Constitution of the People's Republic of China*" (June 14, 1954)

By 1953, the situation across the country had fundamentally changed. The mainland was initially unified, the national economy had been restored, industrialization had begun, and victory in the Korean War was within sight. The prestige of the CPC and the people's government was at an all-time high.

In this context, Mao Zedong began to concretely consider the transition to socialism.

Sometimes, especially during periods of significant social change, the development of practice can often exceed initial expectations. This was the case with socialist transformation. The original plan was to first undertake three five-year plans for industrialization, and then, once a certain material foundation was established, to transition to socialism through nationalization.

This plan was based on the Soviet Union's experience with nationalization. However, actual circumstances exceeded these initial expectations.

First, through the confiscation of bureaucratic capital and the recovery and development of production, the leading position of the state-owned economy was already established. The high concentration of bureaucratic capital and the inherent weaknesses of national capital were significant characteristics of China's semi-colonial and semi-feudal economy. These conditions facilitated the relatively smooth establishment of the state-owned economy in the new China. After the restoration of the national economy in 1952, the proportion of state-owned industry in the total industrial output value increased from 34.2% in 1949 to 52.8% in 1952. The proportion of state-owned commerce in total social wholesale value grew even faster, from 23.2% in 1950 to 60.5% in 1952.[1]

Second, through policy adjustments that encouraged the recovery and development of national capital in industry and commerce, a series of forms of state capitalism, from low-level to high level, such as processing orders, consignment sales, unified purchase and sales, and public-private partnerships, had essentially taken shape.

Third, in the process of restoring agricultural production, 40% of farming households had already joined mutual aid teams, a low-level form of production cooperative organization.[2] Initially, it was estimated that China's rural areas were a vast sea of small producers and small private owners, and agricultural collectivization needed to follow a path of first mechanization, then collectivization. In reality, the old semi-colonial and semi-feudal society had already left a majority of self-sufficient farmers in a state of disintegration or semi-disintegration, making it difficult for them to carry out production independently. Therefore, after the land reform in new China, farmers who regained land had both individual production enthusiasm and a strong desire for mutual cooperation. After joining mutual aid cooperative organizations, their production and living conditions significantly improved, further enhancing their enthusiasm for mutual cooperation.

Through investigation and research, especially the survey on private industry and commerce entrusted to Li Weihan, Mao Zedong and the Central Committee of the CPC strongly felt these changes. Should they continue to adhere to the original plan, or adjust their thinking based on the new situation? Mao Zedong, who always valued investigation and research and insisted on seeking truth from facts, naturally chose the latter.

On June 15, 1953, Mao Zedong formally proposed the general line for the transition period at the Political Bureau of the Central Committee of the CPC. He stated, "From the founding of the People's Republic of China to the basic completion of socialist transformation, this is a transition period. The general line and general task of the Party during the transition period is to basically complete the country's industrialization and the socialist transformation of agriculture, handicrafts, and capitalist industry and commerce within ten to fifteen years or a bit longer." He particularly emphasized, "The Party's general line during the transition period is the beacon guiding all our work. Deviating from this general line will lead to either 'leftist' or rightist errors."[3]

At this moment, Mao Zedong was also guiding significant military and political struggles on the eve of the signing of the Korean Armistice Agreement. Simultaneously, a profound and unprecedented social transformation in China was unfolding under Mao Zedong's impetus.

The socialist transformation began with the agricultural mutual aid movement. By 1951, there were over 4.675 million mutual aid teams nationwide, involving 21 million farming households. This increase raised a practical issue: should these mutual aid teams be further developed into primary production cooperatives marked by land shareholding and profit distribution? On April 17, 1951, the Shanxi Provincial Committee of the CPC reported to the North China Bureau and the Central Committee, suggesting that the development of mutual aid teams in old revolutionary base areas had reached a turning point and needed to be elevated; otherwise, they would regress.[4] Liu Shaoqi and the North China Bureau did not agree with this viewpoint. On June 3, Liu Shaoqi, in a conversation with Bo Yibo, Liu Lantao, Tao Lujia, and others, pointed out: "In agricultural production, we cannot mobilize farmers to establish production cooperatives; we can only form mutual aid teams. The current rural class differentiation is the foundation for future socialism. In the future, we can rely on government orders to confiscate it. Agricultural collectivization must wait for machinery. Without machinery, it is impractical. Agricultural collectivization must be based on the industrialization of the state, allowing agriculture to use machinery and on the nationalization of land."[5] On July 3, in his critique of the Shanxi Provincial Committee's report, Liu Shaoqi wrote: "Some have suggested that we should gradually destabilize, weaken, and ultimately negate private ownership, elevating mutual aid organizations to agricultural production cooperatives as a new factor to 'overcome the spontaneous elements of farmers.' This is a mistaken, dangerous, and utopian idea of agricultural socialism."[6]

This matter alarmed Mao Zedong. Mao spoke with Liu Shaoqi, Bo Yibo, and Liu Lantao, who were in charge of the North China Bureau, and clearly expressed his opinions. According to Bo Yibo's recollection, "Chairman Mao criticized the view that mutual aid teams could not evolve into agricultural production cooperatives and the idea that private ownership could not be shaken at this stage. He said: Since Western capitalism, during its development, went through a stage of handicraft industry—where new productive forces were formed through division of labor without steam-powered machinery—Chinese cooperatives, by forming new productive forces through unified management, could also destabilize private ownership. His reasoning convinced us."[7]

Following Mao's vision of first achieving cooperation and then mechanization, China's agricultural socialist transformation broke away from the Soviet Union model of agricultural collectivization and embarked on a fast track suited to China's rural realities.

This fast track involved three main stages from low to high levels. First, mutual aid teams with simple mutual labor; second, primary agricultural production cooperatives with semi-socialist characteristics; and finally, advanced agricultural production cooperatives with fully socialist characteristics. Through this fast track, within less than four years after the nationwide land reform was completed in 1956, the socialist transformation of agriculture was basically accomplished, organizing the country's 110 million farming households into approximately one million variously sized advanced and primary agricultural production cooperatives.

The socialist transformation of capitalist industry and commerce was the most sensitive and crucial part of the "Three Major Transformations." If the breakthrough in the agricultural mutual aid movement was about overcoming the intellectual bottleneck of whether to mechanize before cooperation or vice versa, then finding transitional forms of state capitalism from low to high levels and encouraging national industrialists and commercialists to navigate socialism was key to ensuring the smooth transformation of capitalist industry and commerce.

The original plan envisaged, "When nationalizing the factories of capitalists, we might, in most cases, persuade the capitalists to donate their factories to the state, with the state retaining property for the capitalists' consumption and assigning work to those who can."[8]

In May 1953, based on Li Weihan's investigation into private industry and commerce, the report "Issues in Public-Private Relations in Capitalist Industry" described the development of various forms of state capitalism during the period of economic recovery. The report stated: "In the past three years, joint ventures have developed considerably, processing has greatly expanded, but the leasing form has not developed. However, several new forms have emerged, such as ordering, guaranteed sales, unified purchase and sales, monopolies, consignment, etc., forming a series of forms from low to high levels." The report concluded: "The process of state capitalization of these private factories, from low-level state capitalism to high-level state capitalism, is also the process of gradually transforming their production relations and gradually moving toward socialism."[9]

The insights presented in Li Weihan's report significantly inspired Mao Zedong. On the evening of June 29, Mao Zedong chaired an expanded meeting of the Political Bureau of the Central Committee of the CPC in the West Building conference room of Zhongnanhai to discuss the "Draft on Several Issues Concerning the Utilization, Restriction, and Transformation of Capitalist Industry and Commerce (Revised)." In his speech, he noted as follows:

> The Chinese bourgeoisie differs from those in the Soviet Union and the new democratic states of Eastern Europe due to their different historical backgrounds. Our bourgeoisie participated in the struggle against imperialism, so there is no reason to confiscate their enterprises. Our approach to the assets of imperialist countries in China also varies. For British, American, and French

assets, we adopt a requisition approach without transferring ownership. The current Chinese capitalism operates under the administration of the people's government, connected to, led by, and supervised by the socialist economy and the workers. This is state capitalism. State capitalism takes various forms. Before the "Five Antis" campaign, we didn't have time to implement it. After the "Five Antis," class relations have significantly changed, making it possible for us to gradually transform the capitalist economy into a socialist economy through state capitalism forms such as public-private partnerships, thereby eliminating capitalism.[10]

The fundamental question whether the national capital under the new China differs in nature from the national capital under the old China is the premise for determining the policy for the socialist transformation of capitalist industry and commerce. Getting this question wrong would lead to subsequent errors. Mao Zedong explicitly pointed out: "The current capitalism operates under the administration of the people's government, connected to, led by, and supervised by the socialist economy. Some comrades still view it as the same as under KMT rule, aiming to destroy it completely without adopting a positive attitude. We need to write a segment criticizing this mindset within the Party and the working class."[11]

Closely related to this issue is another question: whether it is still possible to utilize the economic laws of capitalism at this stage. Mao's stance was clear: "Under the governance of socialist economic laws, it is appropriate to utilize capitalist economic laws to a limited extent. Capitalist economic laws are restricted. The primary and fundamental socialist economic laws aim to develop production and ensure needs, playing a leading role. However, capitalist economic laws objectively exist. If something exists, its laws naturally exist and cannot be eliminated; if the entity is restricted, so are its laws. Failing to implement mutual benefits for both labor and capital, turning it into a single benefit, indicates a misunderstanding of these laws."[12]

The above two issues involve the judgment of the nature of private industry and commerce and the economic laws governing the transformation of capitalist industry and commerce. Resolving these issues naturally leads to solving the problem of implementing the policy of redemption for private industry and commerce.

After the socialist transformation entered a high tide, Mao Zedong expressed at a forum on October 29, 1955, addressing the issue of the socialist transformation of capitalist industry and commerce.

> Our current socialist transformation of capitalist industry and commerce is essentially the implementation of the redemption policy proposed by Marx, Engels, and Lenin. It is not about the state buying private property from capitalists with a lump sum of money or issuing government bonds (not living materials, but means of production, such as machinery and factories). It is also not a sudden method, but a gradual process, extending the transformation period, for example, to fifteen years. During this period, workers produce a portion of the profits for industrial and commercial entrepreneurs. ... Is it better to confiscate all capitalist industry and commerce as we did with bureaucratic capital in 1949, giving no compensation, or to take fifteen to eighteen years, during which the working class produces part of the profits for them, and gradually transform the entire class? There are two approaches: a harsh one and a benevolent one, and a forceful transformation and a peaceful one. The method we are currently adopting involves many transitional steps, extensive publicity, and education, and arranging positions for capitalists. This method should be considered relatively better. The main arrangements for capitalists include two aspects: work positions and political status, which should be properly organized.[13]

On March 4, 1954, Mao Zedong and the Central Committee of the CPC approved and issued the "Opinions on Gradually Transforming Capitalist Industry with Ten or More Workers into Public-Private Partnerships." After more than two years of effort, by the first half of 1956, the transformation of capitalist industry and commerce into public-private partnerships across the board was basically achieved.

Following this, public-private enterprises underwent asset clearing, stock determination, personnel arrangements, enterprise reforms, and economic restructuring. According to statistics from the end of 1956, in the stock determination and interest setting process, private shares in public-private enterprises nationwide totaled 2.4 billion yuan, involving 1.14 million private shareholders. After stock determination, the state issued each private shareholder an annual dividend of 5%, starting from January 2, 1956. This practice continued until it was abolished during the "Great Cultural Revolution."

Driven by the agricultural mutual aid movement and the socialist transformation of capitalist industry and commerce, the socialist transformation of handicrafts quickly began. In the semi-colonial and semi-feudal old China, traditional handicrafts had shown signs of decline. According to estimates of 18 types of handicraft products in key provinces and cities nationwide, about 47% of handicraftsmen went bankrupt from the War of Resistance Against Japanese Aggression to the liberation of the country in 1949. During the period of national economic recovery, handicrafts had recovered to 96.6% of their historical peak and began transitioning from consumer-oriented to production-oriented. By 1952, there were 7.364 million independent handicraftsmen nationwide, with over 12 million farmers also engaged in handicrafts.[14]

The basic characteristics of handicrafts at that time were scattered and backward. Therefore, the socialist transformation of handicrafts started with organizing handicraft production groups and establishing handicraft supply and marketing cooperatives or production cooperatives, gradually exploring the transition forms from handicraft production groups to handicraft supply and marketing cooperatives, and finally to handicraft production cooperatives. By the first half of 1956, over 90% of handicraftsmen were organized. Additionally, many individual peddlers joined cooperative groups or cooperative stores during the socialist transformation of handicrafts. By the end of 1956, there were 1.15 million small merchants and food service providers in cooperative groups, and 800,000 in cooperative stores. Another 540,000 individual peddlers remained unchanged due to their dispersion.[15]

By September 1956, Liu Shaoqi announced in his political report at the Eighth National Congress of the CPC: "The socialist transformation of our country's agriculture, handicrafts, and capitalist industry and commerce has now achieved decisive victory. The extremely complex and difficult historical task of transforming the private ownership of means of production into socialist public ownership has now been basically completed in our country."[16]

Under the leadership of Mao Zedong and the CPC, for the first time in China's long history, a society free from human exploitation was established, laying the material and institutional foundation for the people to be their own masters. This remarkable achievement is unprecedented in history. This profound social transformation in China's history was accomplished without causing major social upheaval. Instead of disrupting social productivity, it continued to advance.

By the end of 1956, the primary indicators set by the first national economic plan, which served as the material basis and productive force pillar for the socialist transformation, were mostly achieved ahead of schedule. In 1956, China produced its first Liberation brand heavy-duty truck, its first steam locomotive, and its first jet fighter. By 1957, the First Five-Year Plan was overfulfilled. Steel production reached 5.35 million tons, with an average annual growth of 32% over five years; grain production reached 195.05 million tons, with an annual growth of 3.7%. During these five years, the average wages of employees in state-owned enterprises increased by 42.8%, and farmers' incomes increased by 30%.[17]

Therefore, Mao Zedong was confident.

> The method we use for the socialist revolution is a peaceful one. There were many doubts both within and outside the Communist Party about this method. However, since the high tide of the corporatization movement in rural areas last summer (referring to 1955) and the recent months' high tide of socialist transformation in urban areas, these doubts have been largely resolved. Under our conditions, using peaceful methods, that is, methods of persuasion and education, not only can we transform individual ownership into socialist collective ownership, but we can also transform capitalist ownership into socialist ownership. The speed of socialist transformation over the past few months has greatly exceeded people's expectations. Some people were once afraid of the socialist hurdle, but now it seems that this hurdle is also easy to overcome.[18]

Such a grand social transformation could not be perfect. Mao Zedong quickly identified some issues.

On March 4, 1956, during a briefing on the handicrafts sector, he said, "I remind you not to eliminate many good things in handicrafts. The Wang Mazi and Zhang Xiaoqian knives and scissors should never be eliminated. All the good things from our national heritage that have been eliminated must be restored, and they should be made even better."[19]

On December 7 of the same year, during a discussion with the chairmen and Vice Chairmen of the All-China Federation of Industry and Commerce and the China National Democratic Construction Association in Beijing, Mao proposed an important idea: "We can eliminate capitalism while also developing capitalism, depending on the conditions. As long as there are raw materials and a market, it can be developed." From this perspective, he suggested: "The underground factories in Shanghai are also opposed to joint ventures. Since there is social demand, they have developed. We should legalize them, allowing them to employ workers. Currently, it takes three months to make clothes, and cooperative factory-made clothes have one leg longer than the other, with buttonholes missing and poor quality. It would be best to open private factories to compete with the cooperative ones. Even husband-and-wife shops can hire workers. This is called the new economic policy." He added, "Wang Mazi, Donglaishun, and Quanjude should be preserved forever. The content can be socialist, even if the names are from the feudal era."[20]

In 1956, with the establishment of the socialist system in China, Mao Zedong put forward many brilliant ideas. Following these ideas could have led to fewer detours, making China's socialism more distinctive and dynamic. However, history is history. The past is gone, leaving no room for what-ifs and hypotheticals.

By the end of 1953, as the nation embarked on the path toward socialism following the general line set by Mao Zedong for the transitional period, Mao led a capable team to Hangzhou, a place known as "Heaven on Earth," by the West Lake, to undertake another foundational task: drafting the first constitution of new China.

Mao Zedong always balanced his theoretical work with practical engagement, focusing his thoughts and vision ahead of the practice.

Drafting a constitution to replace the *Common Program*, which served as a provisional constitution, was a significant milestone in the history of new China.

As soon as the national economy began to recover and various tasks were getting on track, Mao Zedong promptly proposed the task of convening the National People's Congress and drafting the constitution on the basis of universal suffrage.

On December 24, 1952, at the 43rd meeting of the first Standing Committee of the CPPCC, Zhou Enlai, on behalf of the CPC, proposed that the CPPCC suggest to the Central People's Government Committee to convene the National People's Congress and local people's congresses at all levels in 1953, and to start preparing the drafting of the election law and the constitution. This proposal received unanimous approval.

On January 13, 1953, the 24th meeting of the Central People's Government Committee approved this suggestion and passed the "Resolution of the Central People's Government Committee on Convening the National People's Congress and Local People's Congresses at All Levels."

This resolution also decided to establish the Constitution Drafting Committee of the People's Republic of China, with Mao Zedong as the Chairman, and Zhu De, Soong Ching-ling, Li Jishen, Li Weihan, He Xiangning, Shen Junru, Shen Yanbing, Zhou Enlai, Lin Boqu, Lin Feng, Hu Qiaomu, Gao Gang, Ulanhu, Ma Yinchu, Ma Xulun, Chen Yun, Chen Shutong, Chen Jiageng, Chen Boda, Zhang Lan, Guo Moruo, Xi Zhongxun, Huang Yanpei, Peng Dehuai, Cheng Qian, Dong Biwu, Liu Shaoqi, Deng Xiaoping, Deng Zihui, Saifuddin Azizi, Bo Yibo, and Rao Shushi as members.[21]

Due to the formulation of the general line for the transitional period and the critical moment of the armistice negotiations in the Korean War, Mao Zedong was preoccupied, and the drafting of the constitution had not started. It wasn't until December 27, 1953, that Mao went to Hangzhou to begin drafting the *Constitution of the People's Republic of China*.

Half a month later, on January 15, 1954, Mao Zedong submitted a detailed plan for drafting the constitution to the central authorities. The plan also included a list of reference books on various national constitutions that Mao consulted during the drafting process. The full text of the plan is as follows:

To Comrade Shaoqi and all comrades of the Central Committee:

The work on drafting the constitution by the Constitution Group began on January 9. The plan is as follows:

(1) Strive to complete the first draft of the constitution by January 31[22] and submit this draft for review by all comrades of the Central Committee.

(2) Prepare to revise the draft in early February,[23] with Comrades Deng Xiaoping and Li Weihan participating, and then submit it to the Political Bureau (including Central Committee members in Beijing) for preliminary approval.

(3) Submit the draft to the Constitution Drafting Committee for discussion in early March,[24] complete the discussions within March, and preliminarily approve it.

(4) In April, the Constitution Group will review and amend the draft, then submit it to the Political Bureau for discussion, and then to the Constitution Drafting Committee for approval.

(5) On May 1, the Constitution Drafting Committee will publish the draft constitution,[25] and it will be open for public discussion for four months, so that in September, based on the people's opinions, necessary amendments can be made before submitting it to the National People's Congress for final approval.

To facilitate the Political Bureau's discussion in February, I urge all Political Bureau members and Central Committee members in Beijing to take time from now on to read the following major reference documents:

(1) The 1936 *Soviet Union Constitution* and Stalin's report (available in a separate booklet).

(2) The 1918 *Soviet Russian Constitution* (see the compilation of constitution and election law materials by the Government Office).

(3) Constitutions of Romania, Poland, Germany, and Czechoslovakia (see *Compilation of Constitutions of People's Democratic States*, published by the People's Publishing House; these constitutions are largely similar, with Romania and Poland's versions being more recent, and Germany and Czechoslovakia's versions being more detailed and having unique features. If time permits, additional readings are encouraged).

(4) The 1913 *Temple of Heaven Draft Constitution*, the 1923 *Cao Kun Constitution*, and the 1946 *Chiang Kai-shek Constitution* (see the compilation of constitution and election law materials, which represent three types: cabinet system, federal autonomy system, and presidential dictatorship system).

(5) The 1946 *French Constitution* (see the compilation of constitution and election law materials, representing a relatively progressive and complete bourgeois cabinet system constitution).

Please provide any feedback.[26]

From the wording of this book list, it is clear that Mao Zedong had already been seriously studying these constitutional texts and forming his own considerations when he drafted this list.

Mao Zedong later commented on many of the constitutions formed throughout history. On June 14, 1954, at the 30th meeting of the Central People's Government Committee, he explained the drafting process of the constitution. He stated as follows:

> This draft constitution summarizes historical experiences, especially the revolutionary and construction experiences of the past five years. It summarizes the experiences of the proletariat-led people's revolution against imperialism, feudalism, and bureaucratic capitalism, as well as the recent experiences in social reform, economic construction, cultural construction, and government work.

This draft constitution also summarizes the experiences regarding constitutional issues since the late Qing dynasty, from the "Nineteen Articles"[27] of the late Qing dynasty to the *Provisional Constitution of the Republic of China*[28] in the first year of the Republic, to several constitutions and draft constitutions of the Beiyang warlord government,[29] and to the *Provisional Constitution During the Tutelage Period*[30] and the pseudo-constitution of Chiang Kai-shek's reactionary government.[31] These contain both positive and negative aspects. For example, the *Provisional Constitution of the Republic of China* in the first year of the Republic was relatively good for that period. Of course, it was not perfect and had shortcomings; it was bourgeois in nature but had revolutionary and democratic elements. This provisional constitution was very simple, reportedly drafted and passed within a month. The other constitutions and draft constitutions were generally reactionary.

Our draft constitution mainly summarizes our revolutionary and construction experiences. At the same time, it is a combination of domestic and international experiences. Our constitution belongs to the socialist type. We mainly rely on our experiences while also drawing on good elements from the constitutions of the Soviet Union and various people's democratic countries.

Speaking of constitutions, the bourgeoisie was the pioneer. In Britain, France, and the United States, the bourgeoisie had revolutionary periods, and it was during these times that their constitutions were formulated. We cannot entirely dismiss bourgeois democracy and say their constitutions have no historical significance. However, the current bourgeois constitutions are entirely bad, particularly those of imperialist countries, which are especially deceitful and oppressive to the majority. Our constitution is of a new socialist type, different from the bourgeois type. Even compared to their revolutionary period constitutions, ours is much more advanced. We surpass them.[32]

We can also learn about Mao Zedong's evaluations of certain constitutions from the recollections of a few participants. According to Shi Jingtang, who was responsible for materials in the constitution drafting group, "Chairman Mao read the 1918 *Soviet Russian Constitution*, the 1936 *Soviet Union Constitution*, and the constitutions of Eastern European countries. The 1918 Soviet Russian Constitution placed Lenin's 'Declaration of the Rights of the

Working and Exploited People' at the forefront as its first section. Chairman Mao was inspired by this and decided to write a preamble at the beginning of the constitution's general principles."³³

During the drafting process, Mao Zedong and the drafting group members stayed in Building No. 1 of Liuzhuang by the West Lake and worked daily at No. 84 Beishan Road. Tan Qilong, the then Secretary of the Zhejiang Provincial Party Committee, recalled as follows:

> Chairman Mao lived in Building No. 1 of Liuzhuang. Every afternoon at three, he would lead the drafting group by car around Xishan Road, through Yuewang Temple, to the office at No. 84 Beishan Road. At that time, No. 30 of the courtyard at No. 84 Beishan Road consisted of both a main building and a bungalow. The main building was previously occupied by Tan Zhenlin's family. After Tan Zhenlin was transferred to Shanghai, my family moved in. After we vacated it, Chairman Mao used the bungalow as his office, and the constitution drafting group worked in the main building, often working through the night.³⁴

During the drafting process, there were differing opinions on how the constitution should be written. One opinion was that the constitution should only state facts. Another opinion was that it should, like Lenin's 1918 constitution, include both facts and guidelines. Mao Zedong supported the latter view. He later said, "Generally speaking, laws follow facts, but there are also guidelines before facts. The 1918 *Soviet Russian Constitution* had guidelines. Later, in 1936, Stalin said that the constitution could only recognize facts and should not include guidelines. When we were drafting the constitution, Qiaomu praised Stalin, but I did not agree. I agreed with Lenin. Our constitution has two parts: guidelines and facts. The sections on state institutions are factual, while some parts, like the Three Major Transformations, are about the future."³⁵ Thus, the writing style of the constitution was decided by Mao Zedong.

Before the constitution drafting group began its work on January 9, 1954, Chen Boda had drafted a version of the constitution between November and December 1953, but it was not adopted.

Starting from January 9, Mao Zedong led the constitution drafting group in an intense process of redrafting the constitution. After nearly 40 days of work, they completed the first draft around February 17. The drafting group then entered a phase of thorough review and revision. They completed the "second reading draft" by February 24, the "third reading draft" by February 25, and the "fourth reading draft" by March 9, marking the end of the drafting group's work on the initial draft of the constitution.

Mao Zedong was deeply involved in this high-intensity and highly creative work from beginning to end. According to a statement made by Chen Boda on March 23, 1954, at the first meeting of the Constitution Drafting Committee of the People's Republic of China, "The content of the draft constitution was written based on the instructions of the Central Committee of the CPC and Chairman Mao. The Central Committee appointed a constitution drafting group, which worked under the direct leadership and participation of Chairman Mao. Chairman Mao personally participated in the discussion of every chapter, every section, and every article of the draft constitution."[36]

Each draft, starting from the initial draft, was submitted to the meetings of the Political Bureau of the Central Committee for discussion and revision.

Upon completion of the initial draft on February 17, Mao Zedong sent a telegram to Liu Shaoqi and other comrades of the Central Committee.

> The initial draft of the constitution (five copies) is now being sent to you. Please print and distribute it to the Political Bureau members and Central Committee members in Beijing for review and discussion in meetings over the week following February 20. The revised opinions should be brought back by comrades Xiaoping and Weihan for further discussion and revision (approximately seven days). Then it will be submitted to the Central Committee for discussion and preliminary decision (still as a draft) before being submitted to the Constitution Drafting Committee for discussion. ... The person delivering the first draft will depart on the 18 and should arrive in Beijing by February 20.[37]

On February 24, after the "second reading draft" was completed, Mao Zedong wrote to Liu Shaoqi: "Here is the second reading draft of the initial draft of the constitution from the second chapter onwards, along with the report from the constitution drafting group. Please distribute it to all comrades for review."[38]

On February 25, the constitution drafting group produced the "third reading draft" of the "Initial Draft of the *Constitution of the People's Republic of China*." On February 28 and March 1, Liu Shaoqi chaired an expanded meeting of the Political Bureau of the Central Committee in Beijing to discuss and basically approve the "third reading draft" of the constitution. The meeting decided that Dong Biwu, Peng Zhen, and Zhang Jichun, led by Dong Biwu, would study and revise the "third reading draft" based on the opinions discussed at the expanded meeting. Legal advisers Zhou Gengsheng and Qian Duansheng, along with language advisers Ye Shengtao and Lü Shuxiang, were also appointed.

After the "fourth reading draft" was completed on March 9, Liu Shaoqi chaired an expanded meeting of the Political Bureau of the Central Committee on March 12, 13, and 15 to discuss the "fourth reading draft" of the "Initial Draft of the *Constitution of the People's Republic of China*." The meeting decided to form a constitution group, consisting of Chen Boda, Hu Qiaomu, Dong Biwu, Peng Zhen, Deng Xiaoping, Li Weihan, Zhang Jichun, and Tian Jiaying, responsible for the final revisions of the constitution draft. The Constitution Drafting Committee Office was established, with Li Weihan as the secretary-general.

At this point, a draft constitution was ready to be submitted to the Constitution Drafting Committee for discussion and revision.

In early March, Mao Zedong revised and approved the "Explanation of the Initial Draft of the Constitution." This explanation was intended for discussion by the Constitution Drafting Committee and addressed five main issues.

The first issue was that the draft constitution legally ensured the implementation of the general line for the transitional period. The draft constitution analyzed the existing forms of ownership of means of production in China and specified the state's relationship with each form. These provisions distinguished China's constitution from those of all capitalist countries and the various constitutions in China since the late Qing dynasty. Those constitutions did not dare to touch upon social systems, while the basic task of a constitution is to safeguard a certain social system.

The second issue was that the draft constitution legally ensured the development of the country's democratization.

> The socialist transformation of the state fundamentally guarantees the democratization of the state. At the same time, the socialist transformation of the state requires further democratization of the state. The draft constitution's provisions on state institutions and people's rights legally guarantee the development of state democratization. The National People's Congress elects the State Council as the executive body of the state and also elects its executive committee[39] as the daily working body of the state power organ. The State Council is responsible to and reports its work to the National People's Congress and, during the recess of the National People's Congress, to its executive committee. This thorough democratic system without mutual obstruction is something that no capitalist country has or can have. This system reflects the political unity of the broad masses of our people.

The third issue was that the draft constitution legally strengthened the unity of all ethnic groups. "The draft establishes in the preamble and general principles that our country is a unified multi-ethnic state where all ethnic groups enjoy equal status and form a family of mutual affection and assistance. It opposes both great Han chauvinism and local nationalism, prohibits discrimination and oppression among ethnic groups, and forbids actions that would divide ethnic unity. These are the fundamental principles of our country's ethnic relations."

The fourth issue was that the draft constitution was a development of the *Common Program*.

> The draft constitution fully utilized the *Common Program* during its drafting, so the preamble of the draft states that the constitution is based on the *Common Program* but has new developments in its content. The draft constitution retains various basic principles from the *Common Program* regarding our country's nature, people's democratic system, people's rights, and national

policies, and makes detailed provisions. Some principles of economic policy in the *Common Program* are still effective, while others are outdated. The draft constitution discards those outdated principles and makes new provisions, the most important of which are those regarding the implementation of the general line for the transitional period.

The fifth issue concerned the structure and wording characteristics of the draft constitution. The structure and wording of the draft constitution strive for simplicity. The draft is divided into only four chapters, and anything that can be provided for within these four chapters is not set out in a separate chapter. The preamble of the draft includes the general tasks of the constitution, the basic background of its creation, and the conditions for implementing the general tasks of the constitution. The draft constitution has less than one hundred articles, with the total number of words, including the preamble, being less than ten thousand. This makes it one of the shorter constitutions worldwide. This brevity is not only because the constitution is the fundamental law of the state and anything that can be provided for by ordinary laws generally does not need to be included in the constitution. "The constitution must be widely publicized and universally observed, so the articles must be as simple as possible, and the language must be as clear and accessible as possible. From this perspective, the draft constitution is written entirely in vernacular Chinese, avoiding difficult words wherever possible."[40]

On March 17, Mao Zedong returned to Beijing.

On March 23 at 3 p.m., the first meeting of the Constitution Drafting Committee of the People's Republic of China was held at the Qinzheng Hall in Zhongnanhai, chaired by Mao Zedong. At the meeting, Mao Zedong, on behalf of the CPC, formally presented the "Draft *Constitution of the People's Republic of China* (First Draft)." Subsequently, Chen Boda, entrusted by Mao Zedong, explained the drafting process of the initial draft.[41]

Over the next two months, the draft constitution was discussed by over 8,000 people, resulting in more than 5,900 suggestions for amendments. From May 27 to 31, Liu Shaoqi chaired four plenary meetings of the Constitution Drafting Committee to discuss the draft constitution chapter by chapter, resulting in a revised draft. On June 8, the sixth meeting of the Constitution Drafting Committee was held to discuss the revised draft.

On June 11, Mao Zedong chaired the seventh meeting of the Constitution Drafting Committee, deciding to submit the "Draft *Constitution of the People's Republic of China*" to the Central People's Government Committee for review and approval. In his speech, Mao Zedong reviewed the drafting process of the constitution.

> The drafting of the constitution took almost seven months. The first draft was written by Comrade Chen Boda alone in November and December of last year. The second draft was produced by a small group over two months at West Lake. The third draft was created in Beijing, proposed by the Central Committee of the CPC, and has since undergone many revisions. Each draft has gone through multiple revisions. The West Lake draft alone had seven or eight versions. In total, there were probably a dozen or twenty drafts. Many people have contributed a lot of effort. Over 8,000 people across the country discussed it, resulting in over 5,000 suggestions, of which we adopted about a hundred. Even today, we rely on the discussions and revisions by those present here. It has been a process of repeated research and detailed work. After it is published, we will seek opinions from the entire nation. This draft constitution has been created by seeking the opinions of the broad masses. It is generally suitable for the conditions of our country.[42]

After the 30th meeting of the Central People's Government Committee on June 14, the "Draft *Constitution of the People's Republic of China*" was published and submitted for nationwide discussion. This was the first time in China's history that such a process took place.

Over nearly three months, 150 million people participated in the discussion, accounting for a quarter of the total population at the time and proposed over 1.18 million suggestions for amendments.

September 15, 1954 is a date of great historical significance for the People's Republic of China. The much-anticipated first session of the First National People's Congress convened at the Huairen Hall in Zhongnanhai, Beijing. The

1,141 representatives, elected through universal suffrage, gathered to jointly exercise the historical mandate entrusted to them by the people.

At the plenary session on September 20, the *Constitution of the People's Republic of China* was unanimously adopted.

At the plenary session on September 27, Mao Zedong was elected as the first Chairman of the People's Republic of China, Zhu De as Vice Chairman, and Liu Shaoqi as the Chairman of the Standing Committee of the First National People's Congress. Upon Mao Zedong's nomination, Zhou Enlai was appointed Premier of the State Council.

From that moment, a new social system was born in China—a socialist system suitable for China's national conditions. From its inception, this system took root in the vast land of China, characterized by its distinct Chinese features. Its essence can be summed up in two guiding principles: people's democracy and socialism.

The first constitution of new China stipulates: "The People's Republic of China is a people's democratic state led by the working class and based on the alliance of workers and peasants." This defines the nature of the state. The term "people" has a much broader scope than in other countries, which is a notable feature of this state nature.

The constitution also stipulates: "All power in the People's Republic of China belongs to the people. The organs through which the people exercise their power are the National People's Congress and the local people's congresses at various levels." This establishes the fundamental political system of the republic. This system of congresses is characterized by the integration of legislative and executive functions, distinguishing it from the parliamentary systems of other countries.

Additionally, the constitution states: "The National People's Congress, local people's congresses at various levels, and other state organs all practice democratic centralism." This defines the political system of the republic. The widespread implementation of the principle of democratic centralism sets China's political system apart from those in Western Europe, the United States, and the Soviet Union and Eastern European countries.

Furthermore, the constitution formalizes the system of multi-party cooperation and political consultation under the leadership of the CPC, as well as the system of regional ethnic autonomy within a unitary state. In terms of the party system, this is distinct from the multi-party systems of Western countries and from one-party systems, offering the advantage of "long-term coexistence and mutual supervision." In addressing ethnic issues within a unitary state, it avoids both "federalism" and "national self-determination," instead implementing a system of regional ethnic autonomy where "all autonomous areas of various ethnic groups are inseparable parts of the People's Republic of China," ensuring the great unity of all ethnic groups in China.

These innovative systems have continued to this day, playing a foundational role in contemporary Chinese society and making the successors of the republic appreciate the ingenious ideas of the founding leaders.

CHAPTER 14

"Using the Soviet Union as a Reference"

Recently the Soviet Union has exposed some shortcomings and mistakes in the process of building socialism, and the detours they have taken. Do you still want to take those detours? In the past, we avoided some detours because we learned from their experience and lessons. Now, of course, we should be all the more vigilant.

MAO ZEDONG,
"On the Ten Major Relationships" (April 25, 1956)

Mao Zedong always pursued his own path. However, at the beginning of large-scale industrialization in new China, the country lacked technology, talent, and experience, and had no choice but to learn from the Soviet Union. Influenced by the Soviet Union, a highly centralized economic system was established in China. Over time, this system was seen as an inherent characteristic of socialism.

After the completion of the socialist transformation, Mao Zedong sought to explore a socialist path suitable for China's conditions, which required breaking blind faith in the Soviet Union model. He later reflected, "For the first eight years, we copied foreign experiences. But starting from 1956, when we proposed the ten major relationships, we began to find our own path suitable for China."[1]

As with every major work of Mao Zedong, the emergence of "On the Ten Major Relationships" began with investigation and research, and a systematic summary of experiences and lessons.

Mao Zedong later recalled as follows:

> In the eleven years since the founding of the People's Republic, I conducted two major investigations. One was on the issue of corporatization. I reviewed over a hundred documents, with several from each province, and compiled them into a book called *The Socialist Upsurge in China's Countryside*. I studied these materials several times to understand why some areas performed well. My investigation into corporatization relied on these materials. The second investigation was on the ten major relationships. I spent a month and a half discussing with the heads of thirty-four departments, listening to their reports and discussing with them. From these discussions, I concluded the ten major relationships, which was an investigation into the upper echelons and department heads.[2]

Before this investigation, Mao Zedong's main focus was on agricultural issues. In November 1955, he met with the Party secretaries of fourteen provinces and the Inner Mongolia Autonomous Region in Hangzhou and Tianjin, and together they agreed on the "Seventeen Articles on Agriculture." On December 21, he drafted a notice from the Central Committee, sending the "Seventeen Articles on Agriculture" to provincial, municipal, and autonomous region Party Committees for feedback. Subsequently, while traveling to Hangzhou, he held meetings with provincial, district, and county leaders in Baoding, Zhengzhou, Wuhan, Changsha, and Nanchang to gather opinions on the "Seventeen Articles on Agriculture." Upon arriving in Hangzhou, from January 1 to 9, 1956, he held consecutive meetings to revise the "Seventeen Articles on Agriculture" and formed the "Outline for the Development of Agriculture in China from 1956 to 1967 (Draft)" at a meeting of provincial and municipal Party secretaries at the Dahua Hotel in Hangzhou from January 5 to 9. He then wrote to Zhou Enlai, requesting that the draft be discussed at a Political Bureau of the Central Committee meeting and solicited opinions at the upcoming Central Committee meeting on intellectual issues.

Mao Zedong understood deeply that the fundamental issues in China were those of farmers, rural areas, and agriculture. Just as in carrying out democratic and socialist revolutions, industrialization had to start with agriculture. His effort to draft this outline was based on the idea that "the nationwide high tide of agricultural corporatization is triggering a high tide in agricultural production, which in turn promotes a new high tide in the entire national economy, science, culture, education, and healthcare."[3]

In reality, the process of drafting this outline was also a large-scale investigation and research into agricultural issues, laying the foundation for defining the development goals and strategies for agricultural modernization.

On the evening of January 12, Mao Zedong returned to Beijing. Bo Yibo recalled, "In early 1956, when Chairman Mao had just returned from Hangzhou, I went to report to him. During our conversation, I mentioned that Comrade Shaoqi was currently listening to reports from various ministries. Chairman Mao showed great interest and said to me, 'That's very good. I also want to listen. Can you organize some departments to report to me as well?' I was, of course, happy to take on this task. Not long after, the reports began."[4]

At that time, Liu Shaoqi was preparing for the Eighth National Congress of the CPC, which was the First National Congress of the CPC since the founding of new China. To prepare thoroughly for the congress, Liu Shaoqi invited the main leaders of 37 departments of the Central Committee and the State Council to report and discuss from December 7, 1955, to March 9, 1956. The reports covered various areas, including industry, agriculture, commerce, transportation, finance, culture, sports, health, and national economic planning.

Many historical inevitabilities find their pathways through coincidences, and Mao Zedong's investigation was no exception. The previous investigation focused on drafting the "Seventeen Articles on Agriculture," concentrating primarily on agriculture. This time, the investigation targeted economic sectors, following the sequence of heavy industry, light industry, transportation and telecommunications, agriculture and water conservancy, finance and trade, and national economic planning. These were precisely the areas where the Chinese Communists lacked experience and were most influenced by the Soviet Union. Therefore, Mao's reflections went beyond preparing for the Eighth National Congress of the CPC, essentially marking the beginning of independently exploring the path of socialist construction in China by using the Soviet Union as a reference.

Mao Zedong's investigation began on February 14, 1956 and concluded on April 24. Over these 43 days, he listened to work reports from 35 departments of the State Council[5] and received a report from the State Planning Commission on the Second Five-Year Plan.

The location for these briefings was fixed at Yinian Hall in Zhongnanhai. To accommodate the reporters' schedules, Mao changed his usual practice of working at night and began listening to reports as soon as he got up each day, with each session lasting four to five hours.

Mao Zedong's investigation had a unique style. He required departments to send written materials in advance and did not allow reporters to read their texts verbatim during the briefings. Instead, he adopted a method of questioning, interjecting, and commenting, creating a relaxed and lively atmosphere that encouraged the reporters to express their true thoughts and opinions.

Wu Lengxi, then head of Xinhua News Agency, recalled as follows:

> During the briefings I attended, I saw Chairman Mao listening very attentively, taking notes from time to time, and frequently asking questions for the reporters to answer or discuss with the comrades present. Many ministers were very nervous at the beginning of their reports, like they were undergoing an oral exam or defending a thesis. Although they had done a lot of preparation beforehand, they still encountered many questions they couldn't clarify or couldn't answer at all, making them sweat profusely. It was only as the discussions progressed, with the central comrades joking and expressing their views freely, that they relaxed and spoke openly.[6]

Mao Zedong raised many innovative ideas during his interjections and comments.

On the relationship between the central and local governments, Mao Zedong said as follows:

Last year, I went out and talked to comrades in the localities. They expressed dissatisfaction, always feeling that the central government was restraining them, that there were some contradictions between the central and local governments, and that certain matters were not being handed over to them. They are the blocks, while you are the stripes. You issue countless stripes downward, with inconsistent standards. They have several requests that you do not approve, thus restricting them. … The Soviet Union was very centralized for a period, which had its advantages, but the downside was that it reduced local initiative. We need to pay attention to this issue now. There are many local governments, and we should not make them feel they have nothing to do. … Is it that the central departments want to manage more? We should pay attention to promoting local initiatives. The main criterion for dividing central and local enterprises is the scope of supply and sales.

Regarding the relationship between coastal and inland areas, Mao Zedong said, "We should adopt a positive and reasonable development policy. Some industries can be relocated inland, but those that cannot be relocated should be actively and reasonably utilized, without imposing restrictions. Some comrades seem to think that war is imminent and are preparing for it by restricting the coastal areas. This is inappropriate. Seventy percent of light industry is located along the coast; if we don't actively utilize it, how can we increase production?" He also said that restricting development in the coastal areas is a mistake. "We should not restrict development but rather fully utilize or fully and reasonably utilize these areas. Enterprises in Shanghai and Tianjin should generally not be relocated inland; only those that meet certain conditions and are economically viable can be relocated."

On the relationship between infrastructure investment and improving people's livelihoods, he said: "Lowering profits might initially seem to reduce national fiscal revenue, but with more infrastructure development, production will also increase, ultimately resulting in greater profits. As infrastructure develops, more workers are employed, and the market for consumer and service goods expands."

On the relationship between solving systemic issues and ideological issues, Mao Zedong believed that solving systemic issues was more important and fundamental than solving ideological issues. He said: "It is necessary to write articles criticizing parochialism, but mere criticism and addressing issues from an ideological standpoint are not enough. We must also address systemic issues. People live within systems. The same people, under one system, may lack enthusiasm, but under another system, they become motivated. Solving issues related to production relations requires addressing various systemic issues, not just ownership. In agricultural production cooperatives, the implementation of a system where workers are paid according to their output has reportedly made even idlers enthusiastic, leaving no ideological issues. People respect systems, not individuals."

On developing maritime transport, Mao Zedong said: "Our country's maritime tonnage accounts for less than 0.3% of the world's total, which shows how poor we are. Our geographic terrain is relatively integrated, with the sea to the east and mountains to the west, making it difficult for imperialists to invade. Developing shipping is of great significance." He also said: "Transportation must align with industrial and agricultural development. We should build more highways. Developing local industries and building roads will enhance local initiative."

On Beijing's long-term planning, Wan Li asked: "Should Beijing's long-term plan include heavy industry? How much will the population grow?" Mao Zedong replied: "Currently, Beijing does not have heavy industry, but this is not permanent. According to natural development and economic growth, Beijing's population will reach ten million, as will Shanghai's. In the future, when there is no war and peace prevails, Beijing, Tianjin, and Baoding will be connected. Beijing is a good place and will host many factories in the future."

On learning from the Soviet Union, Mao Zedong said: "We should categorize our learning into two types. One type should be tailored to China, while the other should be learned rigorously and honestly. For example, we did not follow the Soviet Union model for land reform. In financial matters, Chen Yun did not adopt some of their suggestions. We also did not follow their policies toward capitalists. However, for technical issues, we can copy everything straightforwardly, especially the good ones or those we have no knowledge of."

On learning from Western countries, Zhou Enlai mentioned sending people to capitalist countries to learn technology. Mao Zedong added: "Regardless of whether it is the United States, France, Switzerland, or Norway, as long as they accept our students, we should send them." Zhou Enlai said: "We should learn from the experiences of all countries with this determination."[7]

Mao Zedong also discussed a vision that China's development speed could surpass that of the Soviet Union if the right path was found.

> Can our construction speed surpass that of the first few five-year plans of the Soviet Union? I believe it is possible. China's advantages are twofold. First, it is poor; second, it is a blank slate, with no burdens. When the United States was in the era of Washington, it was also a blank slate, which allowed for rapid development. We need to break the superstitions, whether they are Chinese or foreign. Our descendants must also break their superstitions about us. Our industrialization and construction should take fewer detours than the Soviet Union. We should not be constrained by the speed of the Soviet Union's first few five-year plans. We can surpass them for four reasons: international conditions are different; domestic conditions are different; the level of technology is different; and China has a large population and rapid agricultural development. Even in technological development, we can surpass the Soviet Union. With socialist enthusiasm, the mass line, and less bureaucracy, we can achieve more. We have a tradition of mass work and the mass line, which is our advantage.[8]

This extensive discussion highlighted the main purpose of Mao Zedong's large-scale investigation.

As Mao Zedong began his large-scale investigation of economic departments, the 20th Congress of the CPSU was held from February 14 to 25. At the end of the congress, during the night of February 24 to the early morning of February 25, Khrushchev delivered his four-and-a-half-hour speech, "On the Cult of Personality and Its Consequences" (commonly known as the "secret speech"), at an internal meeting attended only by CPSU representatives. After the meeting, the CPSU Central Committee informed the CPC delegation of the main content of Khrushchev's secret report. Subsequently, Mikoyan, a member of the CPSU Central Committee Presidium and First Deputy Chairman of the Council of Ministers, was sent to China to deliver the text of the secret report to the CPC Central Committee.[9]

On the evening of March 12, Mao Zedong chaired an expanded meeting of the Political Bureau of the Central Committee at Yinian Hall in Zhongnanhai. He used the method of "one divides into two" to analyze the impact of Khrushchev's secret report. He said: "It seems we can point out at least two things: first, it has lifted the lid; second, it has created a mess. By lifting the lid, I mean that his secret report shows that the Soviet Union, the CPSU, and Stalin are not infallible, which dispels the myth. By creating a mess, I mean that his secret report, in both content and method, has serious errors. Whether this is the case can be studied by everyone."[10]

On the evening of March 23, Mao Zedong chaired an expanded meeting of the CPC Secretariat at his residence by the Zhongnanhai swimming pool to discuss Khrushchev's secret report and the CPC's countermeasures. Mao Zedong expressed four opinions:

(1) The Communist movement. Starting from the publication of *The Communist Manifesto* by Marx and Engels, the communist movement has only been around for just over a hundred years. The history of the dictatorship of the proletariat, starting from the October Revolution, is less than forty years old. Achieving communism is an unprecedentedly great and arduous endeavor. Its greatness stems from its difficulty. In this arduous struggle, it is impossible not to make mistakes because we are walking a path that no one has walked before. I have always believed in the "inevitability of mistakes." It was inevitable for Stalin to make mistakes, and Khrushchev will also make mistakes. The Soviet Union will make mistakes, and we will make mistakes too. The issue is that the Communist Party can overcome its mistakes through criticism and self-criticism.

(2) Contradictions in socialist society. Socialist society still contains contradictions. Denying contradictions is to deny dialectical materialism. Stalin's mistakes prove this point. Contradictions exist everywhere and at all times. Where there are contradictions, there is struggle, but the nature and form of the struggle are different from those in class society.

(3) Stalin's errors and contributions. Stalin made serious mistakes but also had great achievements. In some aspects, he violated the principles of Marxism, but he was still a great Marxist. His works, although containing errors, are still worth studying, but with an analytical attitude.

(4) Khrushchev's actions. Khrushchev's actions have lifted the lid and created a mess. He dispelled the myth that everything about the Soviet Union, the CPSU, and Stalin was correct, which is beneficial for opposing dogmatism. We should no longer rigidly copy everything from the Soviet Union but use our own minds to think. We should combine the basic principles of Marxism-Leninism with the specific realities of China's socialist revolution and construction to explore the path of building socialism in our own country.

Finally, Mao Zedong proposed that the CPC should express its attitude toward Khrushchev's major criticism of Stalin at the 20th Congress of the CPSU. This could be done by publishing an article. The article should support the CPSU's stance against the cult of personality while addressing some of the errors in Khrushchev's secret report. It was decided that Chen Boda would draft the article, with assistance from the Publicity Department of the CPC Central Committee and Xinhua News Agency.

Mao Zedong's four points effectively set the tone for this article.

The first draft of this article was completed on March 29. After collective discussions by the Politburo and multiple revisions by Mao Zedong, the article was titled "On the Historical Experience of the Dictatorship of the Proletariat," with an added note under the title stating, "This article is based on discussions from the expanded meeting of the Political Bureau of the Central Committee of the CPC and written by the editorial department of the People's Daily."[11]

On April 4, at noon, Mao Zedong convened a meeting with Liu Shaoqi, Zhou Enlai, Peng Zhen, Deng Xiaoping, Chen Boda, Hu Qiaomu, Hu Sheng, Wu Lengxi, and Tian Jiaying for the final discussion and revision of "On the Historical Experience of the Dictatorship of the Proletariat." The article was published in the *People's Daily* on April 5, receiving positive international reactions.

During the April 4 meeting, Mao Zedong delivered a speech highlighting the purpose of publishing this article and the significance of the extensive reports from various economic departments of the State Council.

> This article is our preliminary summary of experiences and lessons. The most important lesson, I believe, is independence and self-reliance, investigation and research, understanding our national conditions, and combining the basic principles of Marxism-Leninism with the specific realities of our revolution and construction. During the democratic revolution period, we took a detour and suffered a great loss before successfully achieving this combination and winning the revolution. Now, in the socialist revolution and construction period, we need to make a second combination, finding the correct path for socialist revolution and construction in China. We now have our initial practices and the Soviet Union's experiences and lessons, so we should emphasize starting from China's conditions, thinking creatively, and making efforts to find a specific path for building socialism in China.[12]

From March 10, the briefings from the State Council departments were intermittently influenced by the study of Khrushchev's secret speech and the discussions and revisions of "On the Historical Experience of the Dictatorship of the Proletariat." Mao Zedong finished listening to the reports from 35 departments by April 11. From April 12 to 17, Mao Zedong spent six consecutive afternoons carefully viewing a mechanical industry exhibition at Yingtai in Zhongnanhai, gaining a better understanding of the mechanical industry.

From April 18 to 21, and on April 23 and 24, Mao Zedong listened to the reports from Li Fuchun, Vice Premier and Chairman of the State Planning Commission, about the Second Five-Year Plan every afternoon. During this time, Mao Zedong accumulated experiences from continuous briefings and systematic research, developed insights from studying Khrushchev's secret speech and discussing the article "On the Historical Experience of the Dictatorship of the Proletariat," and combined them with the macro-level issues covered in the State Planning Commission's reports. This process led to the formation of the ideas in "On the Ten Major Relationships."

From April 25 to 28, the expanded meeting of the Political Bureau of the Central Committee was held at Qinzheng Hall in Zhongnanhai. In addition to the Political Bureau members and alternate members, the first secretaries of provincial, municipal, and autonomous region Party Committees also attended the meeting, which was held every afternoon and chaired by Mao Zedong.

On the first day of the meeting, Mao Zedong delivered a speech titled "On the Ten Major Relationships." On May 2, at the 7th session of the Supreme State Council, he further elaborated on these ten relationships. The current version of the manuscript, "On the Ten Major Relationships," is a consolidated record of these two speeches, edited under Deng Xiaoping's direction in 1975. Deng Xiaoping submitted it to Mao Zedong on July 13 of the same year, and Mao Zedong approved it the same day.[13]

In "On the Ten Major Relationships," ten relationships were discussed: the relationship between heavy industry and light industry/agriculture; the relationship between coastal and inland industries; the relationship between economic construction and national defense construction; the relationship between the state, production units, and individual producers; the relationship between central and local authorities; the relationship between the Han majority and ethnic minorities; the relationship between the Party and non-Party individuals; the relationship between revolutionaries and counter-revolutionaries; the relationship between right and wrong; and the relationship between China and foreign countries. Among these, the first five pertain to economic construction, while the latter five concern political relations. Mao Zedong said: "Among the ten relationships, the relationships between industry and agriculture, coastal and inland areas, central and local authorities, the state, collectives and individuals, and national defense and economic construction are the main ones."[14]

A fundamental method used in "On the Ten Major Relationships" is the contradiction analysis method expounded in Mao Zedong's "On Contradiction," applying the law of the unity of opposites. The text lists ten relationships in the Party and state's economic and political life. Each pair of relationships forms a unity of opposites, a pair of contradictions. Properly handling each contradiction requires dialectical methods, emphasis on certain aspects, and careful balance. Mao Zedong said: "These ten relationships are all contradictions. The world is composed of contradictions. Without contradictions, there would be no world. Our task is to correctly handle these contradictions. Whether these contradictions can be entirely resolved in practice, we must prepare for both possibilities, and in the process of handling these contradictions, we will inevitably encounter new contradictions and new problems. However, as we often say, the road is tortuous, but the future is bright."[15]

Another fundamental method used in "On the Ten Major Relationships" is the comparative method between China and other countries. As Mao Zedong later stated: "The basic perspective of the ten relationships is a comparison with the Soviet Union. Besides the Soviet methods, can we find other faster and better approaches than those used in the Soviet Union and Eastern Europe?"[16] Using the Soviet Union as a reference is an application of the comparative method. Its practical significance lies in making fewer mistakes, avoiding detours, and finding and adhering to our path by learning from others' lessons. This speech's starting and ending point is precisely about using the Soviet Union as a reference to explore a socialist construction path suitable for China's conditions.

A guiding thought throughout "On the Ten Major Relationships" is mobilizing all positive factors. This idea later became the guiding thought of the Eighth National Congress of the CPC. Mao Zedong pointed out: "Raising these ten issues revolves around a basic policy of mobilizing all positive factors at home and abroad to serve the cause of socialism. We must strive to mobilize all positive factors inside and outside the Party, domestically and internationally, directly and indirectly, to build our country into a strong socialist state."

This thought is essentially the application of the united front strategy from the Revolutionary War period to socialist construction. As Mao Zedong said: "In the past, to overthrow the rule of imperialism, feudalism, and bureaucrat capitalism and achieve the victory of the people's democratic revolution, we implemented the policy of mobilizing all positive factors. Now, to carry out the socialist revolution and build a socialist state, we should implement the same policy."[17]

"On the Ten Major Relationships" embodies the dialectics of economic construction. For example, when discussing the relationship between "heavy industry and light industry, agriculture," Mao Zedong said: "This raises the question whether your desire to develop heavy industry is genuine or superficial, and to what extent. If your desire is superficial or weak, you will suppress agriculture and light industry, investing little in them. If your desire is genuine and strong, you will prioritize agriculture and light industry, ensuring more food and raw materials for light industry, which will lead to greater accumulation and eventually more investment in heavy industry."

Similarly, when addressing the relationship between "coastal and inland industries," Mao Zedong said: "Properly utilizing and developing the coastal industrial base will strengthen our ability to develop and support inland industry. If we take a passive approach, it will hinder the rapid development of inland industry. Thus, this is also a question whether you genuinely or falsely desire the development of inland industry. If you genuinely desire it, you must fully utilize and develop coastal industry, especially light industry."

Regarding the relationship between "economic and national defense construction," Mao Zedong stated: "In today's world, to avoid being bullied, we cannot do without this thing (referring to the atomic bomb). What should we do? The reliable approach is to reduce military and administrative expenses to an appropriate proportion and increase spending on economic construction. Only by accelerating economic development can we make significant progress in national defense construction."[18]

These discussions reflect a dialectical view of development, emphasizing long-term and sustainable perspectives.

"On the Ten Major Relationships" also embodies the spirit of "using the Soviet Union as a reference." For instance, when discussing the relationship between "heavy industry, light industry, and agriculture," Mao Zedong pointed out the following:

> In managing this relationship, we have avoided fundamental errors. We have performed better than the Soviet Union and some Eastern European countries. Issues like the Soviet Union's failure to reach pre-revolution grain production levels or the severe problems in some Eastern European countries

due to imbalanced industrial development do not exist here. They focused excessively on heavy industry, neglecting agriculture and light industry, leading to insufficient market goods and unstable currency. We, on the other hand, have paid relatively more attention to agriculture and light industry, ensuring the grain and raw materials needed for industrial development. Our daily consumer goods are relatively abundant, and prices and currency are stable.

Additionally, when discussing the relationship between "the state, production units, and individual producers," Mao Zedong said: "The Soviet Union method has been very harsh on the peasants. They have taken too much of the peasants' produce through so-called compulsory sales at very low prices. This method of accumulating funds has greatly damaged the peasants' enthusiasm for production. Expecting hens to lay more eggs without feeding them, or wanting horses to run well without giving them grass—how can there be such logic in the world?"

Furthermore, when addressing the relationship between "the central and local authorities," Mao Zedong stated: "Our country is so large, with such a large population and complex conditions. Having both central and local initiatives is much better than having only one. We cannot be like the Soviet Union, where everything is centralized, and local authorities are stifled with no flexibility."[19]

Just as he criticized dogmatism during the Yan'an Rectification Movement, Mao Zedong also sharply criticized dogmatism in construction issues. He pointed out: "In the past, some of our people did not understand and even learned from the shortcomings of others. By the time we thought we had learned something great, those places had already discarded it, and we ended up flipping over like Sun Wukong." "Some people do not analyze anything and follow the 'wind' completely. Today, if the north wind blows, they are part of the north wind faction. Tomorrow, if the west wind blows, they are part of the west wind faction. Later, if the north wind blows again, they return to being part of the north wind faction. They have no opinions of their own and often swing from one extreme to another."[20]

By this time, Mao Zedong had clearly recognized that learning from the advanced experiences of foreign countries was a long-term task in socialist construction. Therefore, he particularly emphasized: "Our policy is to learn from the strengths of all nations and peoples in politics, economics, science, technology, literature, and art. However, we must learn analytically and critically, not blindly or by mechanically copying everything. We should avoid learning from their shortcomings and weaknesses."[21]

From September 15 to 27, 1956, the Eighth National Congress of the CPC was grandly held at the National Committee of the CPPCC auditorium in Beijing. Mao Zedong delivered the opening address, Liu Shaoqi gave the political report, Zhou Enlai presented the recommendations for the Second Five-Year Plan for economic development, and Deng Xiaoping reported on the revision of the Party Constitution. The Congress unanimously adopted the resolution on the political report and elected the Eighth Central Committee.

On September 28, the First Plenary Session of the Eighth Central Committee of the CPC was held. The session elected Mao Zedong as chairman of the Central Committee and Liu Shaoqi, Zhou Enlai, Zhu De, and Chen Yun as vice chairmen, with Deng Xiaoping as general secretary. These six individuals formed the Standing Committee of the Political Bureau.

The Eighth National Congress of the CPC correctly analyzed the main contradictions in Chinese society after the completion of the socialist transformation and outlined the main tasks for the Party and the state. The Congress solemnly declared that the contradiction between the proletariat and the bourgeoisie in our country has been fundamentally resolved, and the history of class exploitation that lasted for thousands of years has essentially ended. The socialist social system has been largely established in our country. The main domestic contradiction now lies between the people's demand for the establishment of an advanced industrial nation and the reality of a backward agricultural country, as well as between the people's need for rapid economic and cultural development and the current state of development that cannot meet these needs. The current critical task for the Party and the people is to focus on resolving this contradiction and swiftly transforming our country from a backward agricultural nation into an advanced industrial one. The Congress called for the adoption of correct policies in economic, political, and cultural fields, unifying all forces that can be united at home and abroad and utilizing all favorable conditions to accomplish this great task.[22]

A brand-new social system, an unprecedented social transformation, and a grand construction blueprint were presented to the people nationwide through the Eighth National Congress of the CPC.

At the same time, various signs domestically and internationally indicated that a socialist society is not free from contradictions but is, in fact, full of contradictions. However, people were unclear about the nature of these contradictions and how to handle them, and they were unprepared to think about these issues.

Mao Zedong had a good reason to call 1956 an "eventful autumn."[23] Internationally, in June 1956, a bloody conflict occurred in Poznań, Poland. From late October to early November of the same year, large-scale demonstrations and riots erupted in Budapest and other areas in Hungary. From September 1956 to March 1957, there were approximately 10,000 workers' strikes and over 10,000 student protests in China. There were incidents of withdrawal from cooperatives and grain shortages in the countryside.[24] Some Party leaders treated these issues as contradictions between the enemy and us, which only intensified the contradictions.

Faced with various situations domestically and internationally, Mao Zedong fell into deep contemplation. He did not simplify or conceptualize these problems or see them as isolated incidents. Instead, he sought to understand the regularities of the specific historical conditions of major social changes. Mao Zedong's fundamental method remained the contradiction theory he proposed in his 1937 work "On Contradiction."

On November 15, 1956, in his speech at the Second Plenary Session of the Eighth Central Committee of the CPC, Mao Zedong pointed out: "The world is full of contradictions. The democratic revolution resolved the set of contradictions with imperialism, feudalism, and bureaucratic capitalism. Now, the contradictions with national capitalism and small production in terms of ownership have basically been resolved, and other contradictions have emerged. New contradictions have arisen."[25] He attributed the root cause of issues like workers' strikes and students' protests to bureaucratism rather than class enemy sabotage.

On December 4, in a letter to Huang Yanpei,[26] Mao Zedong further elaborated on the idea of two types of contradictions. He wrote: "Society is always full of contradictions. Even in socialist and communist societies, contradictions exist, but their nature differs from those in class societies. Where there are contradictions, there must be exposure and resolution. There are two methods for exposing and resolving them: one is the contradiction between us and the enemy (referring to spies and saboteurs), which requires suppression; the other is the contradiction within the people (including within and between parties), which requires persuasion, i.e., criticism."

Faced with the "eventful autumn," Mao Zedong did not feel overwhelmed but was instead full of confidence. At the end of the letter, he wrote: "There are many troublesome issues internationally, but there are always ways to solve them. I am an optimist, and I believe you are as well."[27]

After a period of deep thought and reflection, on the afternoon of February 27, 1957, at the 11th expanded meeting of the Supreme State Conference, Mao Zedong delivered a speech titled "On the Correct Handling of Contradictions Among the People."

This speech lasted nearly four hours, from 3 p.m. until almost 7 p.m. Mao Zedong attached great importance to this speech and prepared an outline in advance. Afterward, the speech was edited based on the original records, with repeated revisions and additions by Mao. It was officially published in the *People's Daily* on June 19, titled "On the Correct Handling of Contradictions Among the People."

This speech began by addressing "two types of contradictions" and pointed out that socialist society not only has contradictions but also two types of contradictions with different natures: contradictions between us and the enemy, and contradictions among the people. "Contradictions between us and the enemy are antagonistic contradictions. Contradictions among the people, among working people, are non-antagonistic; between the exploited class and the exploiting class, there are both antagonistic and non-antagonistic aspects."

The speech then addressed the nature of contradictions among the people. Mao Zedong stated: "Generally speaking, contradictions among the people are based on a fundamental unity of interests." He elaborated that, under the current conditions, these contradictions include those within the working class, the peasant class, intellectuals, between workers and peasants, between intellectuals, between the working class and other laboring people and the national bourgeoisie, within the national bourgeoisie, and so on. Additionally, there are contradictions between the people's government and the masses, which manifest as "contradictions between national, collective, and individual interests, between democracy and centralism, between leadership and those led, and between the bureaucratic practices of certain government officials and the masses."

Compared to Marxist theory, Mao Zedong's discussion on contradictions among the people not only broadens the concept of "the people" but also emphasizes that these contradictions are based on a fundamental unity of interests and are non-antagonistic. Notably, he includes the contradiction between the working class and the national bourgeoisie within the category of contradictions among the people. Mao pointed out: "The contradiction between the working class and the national bourgeoisie involves exploitation and being exploited, which is inherently antagonistic. However, under our specific conditions, this antagonistic contradiction can be transformed into a non-antagonistic one and resolved peacefully if handled properly."

Reflecting on the lessons from the Polish and Hungarian events, Mao Zedong noted: "Generally, contradictions among the people are non-antagonistic. However, if not handled properly or if vigilance is lost and complacency sets in, they can become antagonistic. In socialist countries, such situations are usually localized and temporary phenomena."

Therefore, he advocated using democratic methods to resolve contradictions among the people, stating: "Democratic centralism should be practiced among the people." "In the people's internal affairs, there should be both freedom and discipline, both democracy and centralism. The unity of democracy and centralism, freedom and discipline, is our democratic centralism. Under this system, the people enjoy extensive democracy and freedom while being bound by socialist discipline."

After addressing the nature of contradictions among the people and how to handle them, Mao Zedong proceeded to explain the basic contradictions in socialist society. He pointed out: "In a socialist society, the basic contradictions remain those between the relations of production and the productive forces, and between the superstructure and the economic base. However, these contradictions in socialist society differ fundamentally in nature and circumstances from those in the old society."

How do the basic contradictions in a socialist society differ from those in a capitalist society? Mao Zedong explained: "The basic contradictions in socialist society are non-antagonistic and can be resolved continuously through the socialist system itself." "The socialist relations of production have been established and are suited to the development of productive forces, but they remain imperfect. These imperfections are contradictory to the development of productive forces. Besides the contradictions between the relations of production and the development of productive forces, there are also contradictions between the superstructure and the economic base, which are both suited and contradictory to each other." He further stated: "Contradictions continuously arise and are continuously resolved, which is the dialectical law of development." These discussions provided the theoretical foundation for implementing socialist reforms.

In this speech, Mao Zedong implicitly criticized Stalin's metaphysical approach to contradictions in socialist society. He pointed out: "Marxist philosophy holds that the law of the unity of opposites is the fundamental law of the universe. This law is universally present in nature, human society, and people's thoughts." He continued: "Lenin explained this law very clearly. In our country, more people are gradually understanding this law. However, for many people, acknowledging this law is one thing, and applying it to observe and handle issues is another. Many people dare not openly admit that contradictions still exist among our people, and it is precisely these contradictions that propel our society forward."[28]

The speech also addressed various specific issues, such as the "problem of purging counter-revolutionaries," "problem of agricultural collectivization," "problem of industrial and commercial entrepreneurs," "problem of intellectuals," "problem of ethnic minorities," "coordinating overall planning with proper arrangements," "principle of letting a hundred flowers bloom and a hundred schools of thought contend," "problem of a few people causing trouble," "can bad things be turned into good things," "issue of thrift," and "path to China's industrialization." These issues largely represent specific manifestations of various contradictions in socialist society.

Among Mao Zedong's responses to these issues, two points stand out for their theoretical significance and far-reaching impact.

First, he established "coordinating overall planning with proper arrangements" as a fundamental principle of socialist construction.

> In the current transitional period of major social changes, there are still many difficulties. Development and difficulties coexist, which is a contradiction. Any contradiction should not only be solved but can also be solved. Our policy is to coordinate overall planning with proper arrangements. Whether it's the grain issue, disaster relief, employment, education, intellectuals, the united front of various patriotic forces, ethnic minorities, or other issues, all should be considered from the perspective of coordinating overall planning for the entire people. We must consult with people from all walks of life to make appropriate arrangements according to the actual conditions of the time and place. We must never push people away because there are too many people, people are backward, or things are troublesome and difficult to handle. Does this mean the government will take care of everything? Certainly not. Many issues and tasks can be handled by social organizations and directly by the masses, who can come up with many good ideas. This is also part of the policy of coordinating overall planning with proper arrangements.[29]

Second, he proposed "the path to China's industrialization," which further elaborated on the relationship between heavy industry, light industry, and agriculture, as discussed in "On the Ten Major Relationships." He first emphasized: "Our economic construction must be centered on heavy industry, and this must be affirmed." At the same time, he stressed: "China is a large agricultural country, with the rural population accounting for more than 80% of the total population. The development of industry must go hand in hand with the development of agriculture to provide raw materials and markets for industry and to accumulate more funds for establishing a strong heavy industry." He further explained: "During the Second and Third five-year plans, if our agriculture can achieve greater development and light industry correspondingly grows, it will benefit the entire national economy. With the development of agriculture and light industry, heavy industry will have markets and funds, enabling it to develop faster." With this strategic vision, Mao Zedong devoted significant energy to formulating the "National Agricultural Development Program from 1956 to 1967." His focus on agriculture in the present was ultimately for the long-term goal of the great development of heavy industry. From his painful experience of China's passive suffering in modern times, he deeply understood that without a modernized socialist strong nation, the People's Republic of China could not stand independently among the world's nations.

Mao Zedong soon made an important addition to China's industrialization path. On October 9, 1957, in his speech at the Third Plenary Session of the Eighth Central Committee of the CPC, he stated: "We must develop industry and agriculture simultaneously and gradually establish modernized industry and agriculture. In the past, we often talked about building China into an industrial country, which actually included the modernization of agriculture."[30]

In the arduous exploration of a socialist construction path suitable for China's conditions, "On the Correct Handling of Contradictions Among the People," along with "On the Ten Major Relationships," published on April 25, 1956, are two closely related sister articles. The former initially resolved the basic policies and principles of socialist construction, while the latter preliminarily answered what basic contradictions exist in socialist society and how to correctly handle contradictions among the people as a central theme of the Party and state's political life.

These two sister articles, together with the policy of the Eighth National Congress of the CPC, marked a good beginning in the exploration of China's socialist construction path.

CHAPTER 15

The Great Leap Forward

Perching as after flight, the mountain towers over the Yangtze,
I have overleapt four hundred twists to its green crest.
Cold-eyed I survey the world beyond the seas,
A hot wind spatters raindrops on the sky-brooded waters.
Clouds cluster over the nine streams, the yellow crane floating,
And billows roll on to the eastern coast, white foam flying.
Who knows whither Prefect Tao Yuanming is gone,
Now that he can till fields in the Land of Peach Blossoms?

MAO ZEDONG,
"*Qi Lü* · Ascent of Lushan" (July 1, 1959)

In 1957, Mao Zedong saw it as a year of comprehensive harvest.

That year, the First Five-Year Plan (1953 to 1957) was over-fulfilled.

A historic shift occurred as both industry and agriculture grew, with the total industrial output surpassing agriculture for the first time. In 1957, the total agricultural output reached 53.7 billion yuan, a 24.8% increase from 1952; the total industrial output reached 70.4 billion yuan, a 128.6% increase over the same period. The total output of industry and agriculture combined reached 124.1 billion yuan, with agriculture's share dropping from 56.9% in 1952 to 43.3%, and industry's share rising from 43.1% to 56.7%.[1]

Another significant change was the more rational regional layout. In old China, over 70% of heavy and light industries were concentrated in the eastern coastal areas, with only 30% of industrial facilities in the vast interior. Of the 156 key industrial construction projects established in the First Five-Year Plan,[2] 50 of the 106 civilian enterprises were located in the Northeast region, and 32 were in the central region; of the 44 defense enterprises, 35 were in the central and western regions, with 21 in Sichuan and Shaanxi. The construction of the power industry was mostly arranged in underdeveloped provinces and regions such as Hebei, Shandong, Shanxi, Inner Mongolia, Gansu, Henan, Hubei, Hunan, Sichuan, Yunnan, and Xinjiang.[3]

Another notable change was the significant increase in the output of major industrial and agricultural products, along with the remarkable enhancement of comprehensive national power, thanks to the commissioning of large key projects and the improvement of existing enterprises. In 1957, steel production reached 5.35 million tons, a 296% increase from 1952; electricity generation reached 19.3 billion kilowatt-hours, up 164%; metal cutting machine tools reached 28,000 units, a 104% increase; grain output reached 390.09 billion *jin* (195.05 million tons), a 19% increase; and cotton production reached 32.8 million *dan* (1.64 million tons), a 26% increase. Transportation conditions also improved significantly, with the railway mileage in operation reaching 26,700 kilometers, a 16.6% increase from 1952; highway mileage reaching 254,600 kilometers, doubling over the same period; inland waterway mileage exceeding 144,000 kilometers increasing by 51.6%; and postal routes totaling 2.22 million kilometers, with 70% of villages having telephone access.[4]

These changes, impossible in old China, showcased the advantages of the unified and independent new Chinese system.

Mao Zedong was well aware that the lifeline of agriculture lay in water conservancy. The prosperity of ancient Chinese agriculture relied on intensive cultivation and water conservancy projects.

On October 9, 1957, Mao Zedong read a report from the Dashan Agricultural Society of Lijiazhai, Junan County, Shandong Province, about their efforts to secure a good harvest. The report narrated an inspiring story: in the winter of 1955, the agricultural society organized farmers to transform fragmented plots into terraces and built 11 small reservoirs tailored to local conditions, planting trees on all barren hills. As a result, the average grain yield per *mu* in 1956 reached 558 *jin*, more than quadrupling the yield before the transformation. Mao Zedong immediately wrote a comment: "Like the Foolish Old Man who moved mountains, Lijiazhai serves as an exemplary model for transforming China."[5] He requested that this report and his comment be distributed to the ongoing Third Plenary Session of the Eighth Central Committee of the CPC.

With Mao Zedong's vigorous promotion, a nationwide surge in large-scale farmland and water conservancy construction began in the winter of 1957. By January 1958, nearly 100 million people across the country were engaged in leveling fields and building water conservancy projects. Through the construction of large, medium, and small reservoirs, irrigation channels, and other water conservancy projects, from October 1957 to April 1958, the country's irrigated area increased by 350 million *mu*, 80 million *mu* more than the total increase in irrigated area in the first eight years after the founding of the new China. Additionally, over 200 million *mu* of low-lying, flood-prone farmland was transformed, improving irrigation on 140 million *mu* and controlling soil erosion over 160,000 square kilometers; 290 million *mu* of trees were planted, equivalent to 1.5 times the total afforestation area in the first eight years after the founding of the new China.[6] Some localities' requests to form large communes arose from the need for farmland and water conservancy construction.

1957 also saw a major event, the first open Rectification Movement of the CPC. According to Mao Zedong's requirements, "opening" meant opening the doors to democratic parties, democrats, intellectuals, and the masses, allowing them to criticize the CPC and provide supervision to help improve the Party's organization and members.

This unprecedented event encountered unexpected situations. During the open rectification process, some people proposed that it was a "Party monopoly" and demanded "rotation of power," suggesting that the CPC withdraw from government offices, schools, and joint ventures, and advocating for the establishment of a "political design institute," a leading organization outside the CPC responsible for redressing grievances. They also sent anonymous letters to some democratic figures expressing support for the CPC, containing abusive and threatening language.

In response, Mao Zedong decided to launch a counterattack against rightist elements while continuing rectification. On June 8, the Central Committee of the CPC issued an internal directive to organize forces to counterattack the rightist elements, stating that without winning this battle, socialism could not be built, and there was a danger of incidents similar to those in Hungary. The rectification and anti-rightist struggle concluded completely by the summer of 1958, with over 550,000 people nationwide labeled as "rightists," most of whom were wrongly classified.[7]

The severe expansion of the anti-rightist struggle hindered the initial favorable exploration of the path of socialist construction in China by the CPC, causing setbacks in various undertakings and harming many intellectuals. However, these mistakes were not recognized at the time. Instead, it was generally believed that the rectification and anti-rightist struggle greatly stimulated the enthusiasm and creativity of the people for socialist construction, creating conditions for the ensuing Great Leap Forward, which was seen as the best rebuttal to rightist rhetoric.

On the morning of November 2, 1957, Mao Zedong boarded a special plane to Moscow, USSR, to attend the 40th-anniversary celebrations of the October Revolution and participate in the meetings of the Communist and Workers' Parties of Socialist Countries and the representatives of 64 Communist and Workers' Parties.[8]

On November 18, at a meeting of representatives from the Communist and Workers' Parties of 64 countries, Mao Zedong delivered a speech, making an optimistic assessment of the international situation, stating: "The current characteristic of the situation is that the east wind prevails over the west wind, meaning that the forces of socialism have overwhelming superiority over the forces of imperialism."[9]

Encouraged by this optimism, Mao proposed the goal of catching up with or surpassing Britain within 15 years.

> Comrade Khrushchev has told us that in fifteen years, the Soviet Union can surpass the United States. I can also say that in fifteen years we may catch up with or surpass Britain. I have talked with Comrades Pollitt and Gollan twice,[10] asking about their country's situation. They said that Britain currently produces 20 million tons of steel annually and might reach 30 million tons in fifteen years. As for China, we might produce 40 million tons in fifteen years; wouldn't that surpass Britain? So, in fifteen years, within our camp, the Soviet Union surpasses the United States, and China surpasses Britain.[11]

Mao's proposal was not impulsive. Before this, the State Planning Commission had made some calculations during the drafting of the Second Five-Year Plan. While listening to their report, Mao Zedong had a detailed understanding of the relevant situation. During this visit to Moscow, he met with British Communist Party leaders Pollitt and Gollan on November 8 and 9, inquiring in detail about Britain's situation in the meeting on the 9th. More importantly, he made a crucial judgment based on his observations over a period: a new world war would not break out anytime soon, allowing for 15 years or even longer of peaceful construction.

Thus, Mao Zedong stated at the meeting: "Ultimately, we must strive for fifteen years of peace. By then, we will be invincible in the world, no one will dare to challenge us, and the world can achieve lasting peace."[12]

On November 28, Mao Zedong returned to Beijing. On December 8, he convened a meeting at Yinian Hall in Zhongnanhai with leaders of various democratic parties and non-party figures, briefing them on the Moscow conference and discussing the idea of catching up with Britain in 15 years.

> Ultimately, it is about striving for fifteen years of peace. It is possible to catch up with or surpass Britain in steel and other key industrial products within fifteen years or a little more. Electricity: Britain currently produces over 90 billion kilowatt-hours, with a capacity of 24 million kilowatts; we have only 19 billion kilowatt-hours and over 4 million kilowatts. With an annual growth rate of 18.2%, we can catch up with Britain in fifteen years. We have abundant hydropower resources, while Britain has very few. Coal:

Britain produced 220 million tons in 1956, but their resources are nearly exhausted; we produced 120 million tons in 1956, with potential for growth. Our underground resources are rich. Steel: Britain reached 21 million tons in 1956; we produced 5.2 million tons in 1957, and the Second Five-Year Plan (by 1962) can reach 12 to 15 million tons, possibly exceeding 40 million tons by 1972, a level Britain cannot achieve. The crucial part is agriculture. Industry and agriculture are like the two legs of a person; missing one makes a cripple. In industrial production, 90 to 95% of machinery can be self-manufactured in the Second Five-Year Plan, and by the Third Five-Year Plan, we can manufacture all. In another ten to eight years, we can make satellites and rockets. The hardest to produce are cotton and grain; we must focus on agriculture. I hope the democratic parties and intellectuals will pay attention to this.

Here, Zhou Enlai interjected: We aim to surpass Britain's industry in fifteen years and surpass Japan's agricultural yield per unit area.

In the discussion, Mao Zedong also addressed the issue of handling rightists. He stated: This time, the rightists have staged a showdown with us. There are two types of showdowns, one incompatible and one coexisting peacefully. We should turn useless into useful, negative into positive. Criticize strictly but deal leniently, except for a few very bad ones, do not strip their voting rights, and give some positions. He particularly mentioned: "Among intellectuals, many are watching how we handle rightists. If we go too far, it will hurt their feelings and make them unhappy." He proposed hope for a 70–30 split; seven can be won over out of ten. Give them five to seven years; by then, their thoughts will be enlightened and reformed, and the rightist label can be removed.[13]

After this discussion, Mao Zedong traveled to Jinan and Nanjing to Hangzhou. From December 16 to 18, and on January 3 and 4, 1958, Mao Zedong chaired the meeting of the first secretaries of the Party Committees of the five provinces and one city in East China (known as the Hangzhou Conference), preparing for the launch of the Great Leap Forward.

At the Hangzhou Conference, Zhou Enlai faced direct criticism from Mao Zedong. Since June 1956, under Zhou Enlai's leadership, there had been an

Anti-rash Progress Campaign under the slogan "oppose both conservatism and rash progress," which brought the national budget and economic plans back to a normal track. Mao Zedong criticized at the Hangzhou Conference: "Last year's course correction caused significant losses. The editorial[14] in *People's Daily* last June did not position things correctly."[15]

On January 6, 1958, Mao Zedong arrived in Nanning, Guangxi. He was in high spirits and even enjoyed a swim in the Yong River.

From January 11 to 22, Mao Zedong chaired a meeting at Mingyuan in Nanning, attended by some Central Committee leaders and heads of some central ministries and localities (commonly known as the Nanning Conference). The main agenda was to discuss the national economic plan and budget for 1958.

In the first four days of the meeting, from January 11 to 16, except for January 13 when Vice Premier and Finance Minister Li Xiannian reported on the implementation of the 1957 national budget and the draft budget for 1958, Mao Zedong gave four speeches.

The subsequent sessions heard reports from some provincial and municipal Party Committee leaders attending the meeting and discussed the comprehensive development of the Yangtze River Basin, deciding that Zhou Enlai would oversee the work on managing the Yangtze River.

In his multiple speeches, Mao Zedong focused on several issues.

First, he opposed decentralism.

> I haven't read the State Council's report to the National People's Congress for two years. Providing only the final product without the raw materials is not acceptable. Financial departments don't report to the Political Bureau, and thus there is no common language. Centralization should be within the Party Committee, Political Bureau, Secretariat, and Standing Committee, with only one core. To oppose decentralism, I have formulated a mnemonic: "Centralize major powers, decentralize minor powers; Party Committees decide, various parties execute; execution should align with principles; and the Party Committee is responsible for work inspection." The Party Committee should primarily focus on industry, agriculture, and ideology.

Second, he criticized the Anti-rash Progress Campaign.

If we hadn't promoted the Anti-rash Progress Campaign back then, it wouldn't have become a trend that wiped out three things: the principle of "more, faster, better, and economical," the Forty Articles of the Outline, and the Promotion Committee. The rightist attacks pushed some comrades to the edge, almost aligning with the rightists, leaving only fifty meters. They panicked, saying things like "the present is not as good as the past" and "the losses from rash progress are greater than those from conservatism." We must be cautious; the greatest fear is that the 600 million people lose motivation, which would be terrible. We need a mass perspective, starting from the 600 million population, distinguishing between the main and the secondary, the essence and the phenomena. The Anti-rash Progress Campaign talked about balance but didn't realize it hurt many people's feelings; enthusiasm for water conservancy, collective farming, literacy campaigns, and the Four Pests campaign was lost. "Focusing on one point while neglecting the rest" has historically caused great losses; dogmatism has led to such situations before, losing big for the small.

Third, he emphasized the general line of socialist construction of "more, faster, better, and economical."

For eight years, I have fought for this working method (referring to more, faster, better, and economical).[16] On the evening of January 15, Mao Zedong spoke with Hu Qiaomu and Wu Lengxi, saying: "The New Year's editorial in *People's Daily* was well written, with a very striking title, 'Ride the Winds and Break the Waves.' During the Northern and Southern Dynasties, the Song man Zong Que said, 'I wish to ride the long winds and break the ten thousand-*li* waves.' We now need to ride the east wind to overpower the west wind and catch up with Britain in fifteen years. You in the press not only need to write good articles but also choose good titles to attract readers to your articles. News must also have striking headlines."[17]

At the Nanning Conference, Mao Zedong highly praised the report "Ride the Winds and Break the Waves, Accelerate the Construction of a

New Socialist Shanghai!" by Ke Qingshi, the First Secretary of the Shanghai Municipal Committee. Mao remarked: "This article surpasses us all." He then asked Zhou Enlai on the spot: "Can you write such an article?" Mao continued: "Zhou Enlai's report[18] is a Marxist article. The issue is how to discuss achievements and shortcomings."

On January 21, Mao Zedong delivered a concluding speech, focusing on the "Sixty Articles on Working Methods (Draft)." On January 22, the meeting concentrated on discussing Mao's concluding speech, marking the end of the Nanning Conference.

The Nanning Conference was an internal meeting of the Party's high-level leadership, where Mao's criticisms were direct and rather sharp. During the conference, he also had separate conversations with Liu Shaoqi, Zhou Enlai, Li Fuchun, Li Xiannian, and Bo Yibo, exchanging views.

The Hangzhou and Nanning Conferences cleared the ideological obstacles for the Great Leap Forward. However, Mao Zedong felt this was not enough. From March 9 to 26, another work conference was held in Chengdu, Sichuan, known as the "Land of Abundance," attended by central leaders, heads of relevant central departments, and first secretaries of most provincial, autonomous region, and municipal Party Committees (commonly known as the Chengdu Conference). The venue was the provincial reception house at Jinniuba.

Bo Yibo's recalled as follows:

Chair Mao made six important speeches at the Chengdu Conference in March, including two on his criticisms of the Anti-rash Progress Campaign. On March 9, Mao remarked: "The Anti-rash Progress Campaign was a policy mistake. The issue was raised at the Nanning Conference, and many comrades were tense, but now it's better. Clarifying the issue is to enable everyone to have a common language and do a good job, not to make it difficult for any comrade. I have no intention of making it difficult for anyone." On March 25, Chair Mao said again: "Regarding the Anti-rash Progress Campaign, I think there is no need to discuss it further. If we use it as an example of experience and methods, that is acceptable. The focus is not on responsibility but on using materialism and dialectics to deeply analyze the issue of the Anti-rash Progress Campaign. I believed that the Anti-rash Progress Campaign did not respect materialism or dialectics. It lacked a comprehensive view and did not grasp the essence and the main trends. The policy of anti-rash progress was made without consulting provincial Party secretaries in advance, and it was disconnected from most ministries within the State Council. The State Council had two opinions: only the financial and trade systems wanted to slow down, while the industrial departments wanted to speed up." Chair Mao also emphasized the need to break superstition and liberate thought, saying that the Anti-rash Progress Campaign was "searching and seeking, cold and cheerless, bleak and desolate," whereas rash progress was "vigorous and lively, happy and joyful." The Yangtze River flows incessantly, just as we need to oppose the slow route and embrace the fast one.[19]

Through the Hangzhou, Nanning, and Chengdu Conferences, the high-level leadership of the CPC unified their understanding. This paved the way for the Second Session of the Eighth National Congress of the CPC.

From May 5 to 23, 1958, the Second Session of the Eighth National Congress of the CPC was held in Beijing.

Liu Shaoqi, on behalf of the Central Committee, delivered a political report, interpreting the general line of "exert all efforts, strive for the best, and build socialism faster, better, and more economically," based on Mao Zedong's initiative.

The report summarized the main points of this general line, reflecting on the ideas and viewpoints Mao Zedong had proposed since his publication of "On the Ten Major Relationships" in 1956.

> The Central Committee believes that the basic point of the general line of exerting all efforts, striving for the best, and building socialism faster, better, and more economically is to mobilize all positive factors, correctly handle internal contradictions among the people; consolidate and develop the socialist system of public ownership and collective ownership, strengthen the dictatorship of the proletariat and international solidarity of the proletariat; while continuing to complete the socialist revolution on the economic, political, and ideological fronts, gradually achieve technological and cultural revolutions; under the

condition of giving priority to the development of heavy industry, promote both industry and agriculture; under the conditions of centralized leadership, comprehensive planning, and division of labor and cooperation, promote both central and local industries, and both large and medium-sized enterprises; through these, rapidly build our country into a great socialist nation with modern industry, modern agriculture, and modern science and culture.[20]

These viewpoints were theoretically sound and reflected the urgent desire of the CPC and the broad masses of the people to change the backward economic and cultural conditions. However, in guiding actual practice, neglecting the material conditions restricting subjective initiative and the laws of comprehensive balance in the national economy led to a serious deviation between subjective intentions and actual outcomes. Mao Zedong gradually recognized this issue a year later.

During the conference, there was a small episode. On the afternoon of May 21, before attending the Second Session of the Eighth National Congress of the CPC, Mao Zedong watched the first domestically produced "Dongfeng" (East Wind) car in the back garden of Huairen Hall in Zhongnanhai.

The origin of this domestic car is related to Mao Zedong. On February 13 of that year, Mao Zedong inspected the First Automobile Works of Changchun. He told the factory director, Rao Bin: "I am very pleased to see that the Chinese working class can manufacture automobiles." He then asked: "When can we ride in cars made by ourselves?" During Mao Zedong's second visit to the Soviet Union, the First Automobile Works of Changchun was already designing prototypes for domestic cars. Encouraged by Mao Zedong's assertion that "the east wind prevails over the west wind," the prototype was named "Dongfeng." At that time, Li Lanqing, the head of the planning department at the factory, specifically found Mao Zedong's handwritten "Dongfeng" for the prototype.

Mao Zedong happily circled the domestic car twice and then took Lin Boqu's hand and sat inside, having the driver circle the garden twice. After getting out of the car, he smiled and told the gathered conference representatives: "I have now ridden in a car made by ourselves!"

After the Second Session of the Eighth National Congress of the CPC, industry marked the Great Leap Forward with "taking steel as the key link, achieving a comprehensive leap forward," and agriculture marked it with "taking grain as the key link," establishing large-scale people's communes and launching high yield "satellites." The Great Leap Forward spread vigorously and enthusiastically across the country.

At that time, Mao Zedong and the Central Committee of the CPC enjoyed high prestige among the people, and there was a huge reservoir of socialist labor enthusiasm and creativity among the masses. For a time, it created a situation where one call received a unanimous response. This was unimaginable in the fragmented old China.

Starting in October 1958, Mao Zedong began to cool down. This "cooling" started from discovering problems in the fervor of the large-scale establishment of people's communes.

Before this, Mao's energy had been focused on promoting the People's Commune Movement, presiding over the Beidaihe Conference,[21] directing international struggles surrounding the shelling of Jinmen,[22] and dealing with Sino-Soviet frictions caused by issues such as "long-wave radio stations" and the "joint fleet." However, he also began to sense some incorrect sentiments growing from anonymous letters reflecting disasters in three townships in Lingbi County, Anhui, involving deaths from starvation and cadres beating people, as well as from Zhang Chunqiao's[23] article "Breaking the Bourgeois Legal Rights Ideology."

From October 13 to 17, Mao Zedong took a special train around the vicinity of Tianjin to understand some situations.

On October 16, he held a meeting at the Tianjin Cadre Club to discuss the issue of people's communes. Zhang Guozhong, the First Secretary of the Xushui County Committee, attended the meeting. Zhang talked about the pilot planning of happiness homes, kindergartens, and housing construction, where couples lived in one place, children in another, and the elderly in another. Mao immediately commented: "That's too monotonous. There should be a combination of large, medium, and small; how can the elderly not be combined with the able-bodied and children? Can it work if the elderly is always with the elderly? If communes build houses only for couples, not for the elderly and children, and they live separately, will the masses support it? I'm afraid it will alienate the elderly and children, displeasing both ends and the middle."

At the meeting the next day, Mao Zedong commented on the happiness homes in Xushui, saying: "I wouldn't want to enter your happiness home. Happiness needs analysis, and happiness with unhappiness is no good. The lonely, widowed, and solitary can enter happiness homes. But if the happiness home is a living unit, and one only sees the elderly all day without the able-bodied, is that good?" He also said: "In practice, we gradually recognize the objective world."[24]

After this meeting, to further ascertain the situation in Xushui, Mao instructed Liu Zihou, the governor of Hebei Province, to conduct a survey in Xushui. He also sent Chen Boda with a team to Chayashan Satellite Commune in Suiping County, Henan Province, for a field study of seven to ten days, instructing: "I will go to Zhengzhou next week; upon arrival, I will hear your report on the Satellite Commune's observations and discuss it at the First Secretaries Conference of the four provinces."[25] He later asked Chen Boda's research team to expand the survey scope to Suiping County and neighboring counties.

On October 26, Mao Zedong met with Wu Lengxi and Tian Jiaying, instructing them to lead a research team to the Xinxiang area in Henan. He designated two research points: one was Xiuwu County, known for its People's Commune, and the other was Qiliying Commune, which he had inspected before. He specifically instructed them not to make a fuss but to understand the real thoughts of various people.

On the evening of October 31, Mao Zedong departed by special train to attend the meeting in Zhengzhou. Along the way, he stopped to talk with local officials in Baoding, Shijiazhuang, Handan, and Xinxiang, gaining in-depth understanding of the situation. He also received reports from two research teams. By this time, he felt confident about how to conduct the Zhengzhou meeting.

From November 2 to 10, Mao Zedong presided over a central working conference in Zhengzhou with some Central Committee leaders, regional directors, and some provincial and municipal Party secretaries (commonly known as the First Zhengzhou Conference). The first four days of the meeting were held on Mao's special train. Starting from November 6, the meeting moved to the second guesthouse of the Henan Provincial Party Committee.

Mao Zedong was a person of sharp intellect and practical focus. Just as he was a poet of revolutionary romanticism, he was also a highly pragmatic revolutionary, statesman, and politician. Therefore, he possessed both a visionary perspective and the ability to sense emerging trends. He was the one who initiated the Great Leap Forward and the People's Commune Movement, and he was also the first to propose correcting "leftist" deviations.

At the First Zhengzhou Conference, Mao Zedong criticized some people for "conflating public ownership and collective ownership, which might be harmful. It seems that we are almost there, and communism has already arrived. This is too fast, much too fast! The struggle has been too easy!" He also stated: "Nowadays, people avoid this aspect; anyone who talks about commodity production and commodity exchange is probably not considered a communist."[26]

During the meeting, he introduced an important idea: "To greatly develop socialist commodity production in a planned way."

> Right now, some people are eager to eliminate commodity production. They long for communism and get anxious when talking about commodity production, thinking it's a capitalist thing. They fail to distinguish between socialist commodity production and capitalist commodity production, not understanding the importance of utilizing commodity production under socialist conditions. This shows a lack of recognition of objective laws and a failure to recognize the problem of the 500 million farmers. During the socialist period, we should use commodity production to unite the hundreds of millions of farmers. I believe that with the establishment of people's communes, commodity production and commodity exchange should be further developed. We need to greatly and systematically develop socialist commodity production.[27]

He also criticized the "exaggeration trend."

> Xushui County gathered the best pigs for people to see, which is not realistic. Some places exaggerated steel and iron production figures, which is also untruthful and needs to be corrected. We must oppose exaggeration, be realistic, and not report false numbers." He proposed: "Starting January 1 next year, farmers must sleep eight hours, eat and rest for four hours, and study for two hours each day. We need to establish a schedule for farmers; otherwise, it cannot be sustained. As for workers, working twelve hours a day is unsustainable.

He was also concerned about the "frightening targets for steel, machine tools, coal, and electricity." If these targets were announced and not met, what would happen?[28]

Through the First Zhengzhou Conference, Mao Zedong resolved to correct the "leftist" deviations. The results of this conference were concentrated in a letter from Mao Zedong on November 9 and the "Draft Resolution on Several Issues Concerning the People's Commune" from the Zhengzhou Conference.

Mao Zedong's letter was addressed to members of the Party Committees at the central, provincial, municipal, autonomous region, prefecture, and county levels. In his letter, he suggested everyone read two books: *Economic Problems of Socialism in the USSR* by Stalin and *Marx, Engels, Lenin, and Stalin on Communist Society*. He also recommended that, when time permits, they read the Soviet Union's *Textbook of Political Economy*.[29]

From November 21 to 27, Mao Zedong chaired an expanded meeting of the Political Bureau of the Central Committee at the Hongshan Hotel in Wuchang. This meeting continued and deepened the discussions from the First Zhengzhou Conference, focusing on the issues of people's communes and the 1959 national economic plan, preparing for the upcoming Sixth Plenary Session of the Eighth Central Committee of the CPC.

In his speech on the last day, Mao Zedong specifically addressed the 1959 steel production target issue.

What should the steel production target for 1959 be? The Beidaihe Conference suggested a target of 27 million tons, aiming for 30 million tons, but that was just a recommendation. This time we need to decide whether it is achievable or not and provide the basis for it. Should we consider lowering the target? Previously, others criticized my "rash progress," and now I criticize theirs. This year, the actual high-quality steel production is 8.5 million tons out of a target of 11 million tons. For next year's so-called target of 18 million tons, we need to ensure it is high-quality steel. If we can't achieve 18 million tons, I think we should reduce it further, perhaps to 15 million tons. Similarly, all departments should correspondingly lower their targets.[30]

Through this meeting and the First Zhengzhou Conference, the main issues of the Great Leap Forward" and the People's Commune Movement were exposed, cooling the previously escalating enthusiasm for transitioning to communism and high targets. This unified the understanding among the Party's high-level leadership, paving the way for the Sixth Plenary Session of the Eighth Central Committee of the CPC.

From November 28 to December 10, the Sixth Plenary Session of the Eighth Central Committee of the CPC was held in Wuchang, still at the Hongshan Hotel. The session focused on discussing the "Draft Resolution on Several Issues Concerning the People's Commune" and the "Draft Resolution on the 1959 National Economic Plan." Following Mao Zedong's proposal, a decision was also made to agree with Mao's suggestion that he would not be a candidate for the next Chairman of the People's Republic of China.

The "Draft Resolution on Several Issues Concerning the People's Commune" was drafted under Mao Zedong's guidance, revised based on discussions from the First Zhengzhou Conference and the expanded meeting of the Political Bureau of the Central Committee in Wuchang, reflecting the Central Committee's initial efforts to correct the "leftist" errors in the People's Commune Movement.

The "Draft Resolution on the 1959 National Economic Plan" was formulated according to Mao Zedong's spirit of "compressing the air," aiming to reduce high targets. However, due to the limited understanding at the time, apart from the reduction in investment in capital construction and steel production, other targets were not reduced. Chen Yun had reservations about these targets and suggested to Hu Qiaomu, who was responsible for drafting the document, that they should not be published in the conference communiqué, but this opinion did not reach Mao Zedong.

By early 1959, the consequences of the Great Leap Forward and the People's Commune Movement further revealed themselves, leading to severe imbalances in the national economy. The nationwide steel Production Campaign not only intensified the strain on raw material production and transportation but also caused shortages in light industrial products and agricultural products. Additionally, the exaggerated grain production reports led to excessive grain procurement by the state in 1958, resulting in incidents of commune members hiding production and privately distributing it.

Mao Zedong gradually realized that the First Zhengzhou Conference and the two meetings in Wuchang had only exposed some problems, but the issues were far from resolved. Under these circumstances, Mao Zedong convened an expanded meeting of the Political Bureau of the Central Committee on his special train from February 27 to March 5, 1959 (commonly known as the Second Zhengzhou Conference).

The Second Zhengzhou Conference focused on resolving the "Communist Wind" issues in the People's Commune Movement. In his speech, Mao Zedong pinpointed the crux of the issue: "Currently, there is a rather tense relationship between us and the peasants on some issues. A prominent phenomenon is that after the bumper harvest in 1958, the procurement of grain, cotton, oil, and other agricultural products has not yet been completed. Furthermore, there has been widespread hiding of production and private distribution across the country, except in a few disaster-stricken areas, resulting in large-scale unrest over the 'insufficiency' of grain, oil, pork, and vegetables. This situation is even more severe than the grain crises of 1953 and 1955."

He further analyzed the manifestations of the "Communist Wind": "After the establishment of communes in the autumn of 1958, a 'Communist Wind' emerged. The main content includes three aspects: leveling the rich and poor, excessive accumulation, and too much compulsory labor." "Equalization, adjustment, and collection have caused great panic among the peasants. This is the most fundamental issue in our current relationship with the peasants."

He also reflected on this issue.

> The resolution of the Sixth Plenary Session clearly stated that the transition from collective ownership to public ownership and from socialism to communism must go through stages of development. However, it did not specify that the collective ownership of communes also needs a development process, which is a shortcoming. At that time, we did not recognize this issue. As a result, comrades at lower levels blurred the distinctions between the three levels of ownership within the communes (commune, production brigade, and production team), effectively denying the still highly significant ownership of the production teams (or production brigades, roughly equivalent to the former advanced cooperatives), leading to inevitable and strong resistance from the peasants.[31]

The Second Zhengzhou Conference was difficult, as many people initially could not accept Mao Zedong's speech. However, through discussion, they eventually unified their thoughts.

The conference concluded with the formation of the "Zhengzhou Conference Summary," distributed as an internal Party document. The most important outcome was the creation of 14 principles for rectifying and building people's communes: "Unified leadership, with the team as the basis; hierarchical management, with decentralized power; three-tier accounting, with each level responsible for its own profits and losses; distribution plans determined by the commune; appropriate accumulation, with reasonable adjustments; equivalent exchange of materials and labor; distribution according to work, recognizing differences."[32] These 14 principles, drafted by Mao Zedong and extensively consulted, were easy to remember and understand but contained profound insights, playing a crucial role in correcting the "leftist" tendencies.

The "Communist Wind" issue in the People's Commune Movement was initially resolved. Mao Zedong then began to focus on solving another problem—the "high targets" in the massive steel Production Campaign.

During the Sixth Plenary Session of the Eighth Central Committee of the CPC, on December 1, 1957, Mao Zedong wrote an article titled "On the Question Whether Imperialism and All Reactionaries Are Real Tigers," which was circulated within the Party. In this article, he criticized some people for being "overheated." He wrote: "In our country, at present, some people are a bit too hot-headed. They do not want their minds to have a period of cooling down. They are unwilling to analyze, and they only love the heat. Comrades, this attitude is not conducive to leadership work, and they may stumble. These people should be reminded to cool down their minds. Some people prefer the cold and not the heat. They do not understand some things and cannot keep up.[33] These people should be gradually warmed up."[34]

However, the persistently high targets remained unchanged until the Seventh Plenary Session of the Eighth Central Committee of the CPC.

From April 2 to 5, 1959, Mao Zedong presided over the Seventh Plenary Session of the Eighth Central Committee of the CPC in Shanghai. During the discussion of the 1959 National Economic Plan draft, the target for steel production in 1959 was set at 18 million tons (including 16.5 million tons of high-quality steel). Based on the adjustments to the steel and coal targets, the targets for other major industrial products were also modified. This target was two million tons less than the one set at the Sixth Plenary Session of the Eighth Central Committee. However, subsequent events revealed that even this target contained a considerable amount of "water" (inflated figures).

Mao Zedong was still uneasy about the target of 18 million tons of steel and entrusted Chen Yun to conduct further research. After thorough research and verification, Chen Yun and the Central Financial and Economic Leading Group concluded: "It is possible to produce 9 million tons of steel and 13 million tons of steel billets this year, but it will require a great deal of effort."[35]

On the afternoon of June 13, Mao Zedong held a meeting at Yinian Hall in Zhongnanhai to discuss industrial, agricultural, and market issues. The meeting decided to lower the 1959 steel production target to 13 million tons,[36] and the number of capital construction projects was also significantly reduced.

At the meeting, Mao Zedong reviewed the process of lowering the steel production target.

> Whether it's industry or agriculture, we agreed on the targets, such as the 20 million tons of steel set at the Wuchang Conference last December. By this

January, some comrades, represented by Comrade Chen Yun, suggested that 20 million tons would be difficult to achieve. But at that time, it was hard to change because it was still January, and people were eager to work hard. At that time, we could have shifted, but it would have been more proactive. However, it was impossible to change to the 16.5 million tons target set at the Shanghai meeting or the current 13 million tons. People in the world do not change course without hitting a wall and gaining experience. ... Such high targets, we blew them up and now we don't want them. We set up a deity ourselves and then blindly worshipped this deity. We need to break superstition; 20 million tons of steel or tens of thousands of bales of cotton, we don't care. At one point, we lost our heads.[37]

Thus, under Mao Zedong's leadership and relentless efforts, by June and July 1959, significant progress was made in correcting the "leftist" deviations in the industrial and agricultural sectors.

In a relaxed and joyful mood after a period of tension, Mao Zedong visited his long-lost hometown of Shaoshan, Xiangtan, from June 25 to 27. He saw his familiar yet somewhat estranged childhood home, reunited with his long-separated teachers, childhood friends, relatives, and neighbors, and paid respects at his parents' graves.

At his residence in Shaoshan, Mao Zedong wrote the poem "*Qi Lü · Shaoshan Revisited*," expressing his longing for his hometown.

> Like a dim dream recalled, I curse the long-fled past,
> My native soil two and thirty years gone by.
> The red flag roused the serf, halberd in hand,
> While the despot's black talons held his whip aloft.
> Bitter sacrifice strengthens bold resolve,
> Which dares to make sun and moon shine in new skies.
> Happy, I see wave upon wave of paddy and beans,
> And all around heroes home-bound in the evening mist.

Before this poem, he wrote a short preface: "On June 25, 1959, I arrived in Shaoshan. It has been 32 years since I left this place."

Afterward, Mao traveled to Wuchang, then took the "Jiangxia" ship and landed in Jiujiang, Jiangxi. On July 1, he stayed at Villa 180 on Mount Lushan (Meilu).

On the same day, Mao wrote another poem, "*Qi Lü* · Ascent of Lushan."

Perching as after flight, the mountain towers over the Yangtze,
I have overleapt four hundred twists to its green crest.
Cold-eyed I survey the world beyond the seas,
A hot wind spatters raindrops on the sky-brooded waters.
Clouds cluster over the nine streams, the yellow crane floating,
And billows roll on to the eastern coast, white foam flying.
Who knows whither Prefect Tao Yuanming is gone,
Now that he can till fields in the Land of Peach Blossoms?

Writing two poems in a few days reflects his good mood and high spirits at the time.

From July 2 to August 1, Mao Zedong chaired an expanded meeting of the Political Bureau of the Central Committee in Lushan, Jiangxi.[38]

During the July 2 meeting and his conversation with the regional director on the ship to Jiujiang on June 29, Mao raised 18 issues to be discussed at the meeting. He shared his thoughts on each issue.

Discussing comprehensive balance, Mao said: "One of the important lessons of the Great Leap Forward is the lack of balance. We talked about walking on two legs, but in practice, we did not balance them. In the overall economy, balance is fundamental. With comprehensive balance, we can follow the mass line." He summarized: "There are three kinds of balance: balance within agriculture (farming, forestry, animal husbandry, side occupations, and fisheries); balance within industry (different sectors and links); and balance between industry and agriculture. The proportional relationship of the entire national economy is based on these comprehensive balances."

He emphasized: Among these 18 issues, "the basic problems are (1) comprehensive balance, (2) the mass line, (3) unified leadership, and (4) attention to quality. Among these four issues, the most fundamental are comprehensive balance and the mass line. We must pay attention to quality, even if it means producing less, but it must be better and more comprehensive."

It seems that the serious shortages and tensions caused by the "one horse leading, ten thousand horses galloping" approach of the Great Leap Forward left a deep impression on him.

Regarding the current situation, Mao Zedong stated: "Overall, as a comrade from Hunan Province said, it can be summed up in two sentences: 'There are great achievements and rich experiences.' 'Rich experiences' is cleverly put, but it actually means there are great achievements but also many problems. The future is bright."[39] He hoped to unify the attendees' understanding based on this tone.

Since the First Zhengzhou Conference, the understanding of major issues among the attendees had gradually converged. Mao Zedong led the discussion of problems, encouraging everyone to fully discuss the shortcomings and issues, creating a relatively relaxed atmosphere for the meeting. Chen Boda, Hu Qiaomu, Tian Jiaying, and Wu Lengxi, the "scholars," had begun drafting the "Lushan Conference Agreement Summary" according to Mao's requirements, setting the tone for the meeting.

At this moment, Peng Dehuai[40] wrote a long letter to Mao Zedong on July 13. On July 16, Mao Zedong instructed: "Distribute to all comrades for reference." He also titled Peng's letter as "Comrade Peng Dehuai's Opinion Letter." On July 17, the letter was distributed at the meeting, sparking a heated discussion and forming two sharply opposing views.

In his letter, Peng Dehuai first acknowledged the achievements of 1958 but also pointed out the serious problems of the Great Leap Forward. He wrote: "The prominent contradiction we face in our construction work now is the tension caused by imbalance." This contradiction "has developed to the point where it affects the relationships between workers and peasants, different urban sectors, and different rural sectors, making it a political issue."

Peng objectively analyzed the causes of these problems, noting that the reasons were multifaceted. "Objectively, we are unfamiliar with socialist construction and lack complete experience." Simultaneously, "in our thinking methods and work styles, many problems have emerged." First, "exaggeration has become quite common." Second, "petty-bourgeois fanaticism has made us prone to leftist errors." "Some leftist tendencies have developed significantly, with the idea of leaping into communism ahead of time taking precedence, sidelining the mass line and the practical approach that the Party has long adhered to."[41]

Peng Dehuai's letter was objective, calm, and factual. However, in the atmosphere of the time, it sparked differing opinions during group discussions. Many, including Huang Kecheng, Zhang Wentian, and Zhou Xiaozhou,[42] agreed with Peng's basic viewpoints. Others felt the letter underestimated achievements and exaggerated mistakes, expressing frustration and discouragement.

On the morning of July 23, at 8 a.m., Mao Zedong convened a full meeting at the Lushan People's Theater, sharply criticizing Peng Dehuai in his speech and refuting Peng's letter point by point.

> We need to analyze the "Communist Wind." It involves petty-bourgeois fanaticism. Who are these people? The "Communist Wind" mainly arises at the county and commune levels, especially among some commune cadres, affecting production teams and small production units. This is not good; the masses do not welcome it. We spent more than a month in March and April to suppress this trend. We rectified accounts between the communes and the teams. This education and accounting were beneficial, making them understand quickly that egalitarianism does not work, and "equalization, adjustment, and collection" are not feasible. ... If people do not offend me, I will not offend them; if people offend me, I will certainly offend them; if people first offend me, I will later offend them. I still do not abandon this principle. ...
>
> I advise some comrades not to waver in such an urgent situation. From my observation, some comrades are wavering. They also say that the Great Leap Forward, the general line, and the People's Commune are correct, but it depends on their thinking and direction and which side they are speaking to. These people are the second type, "basically correct, but partially incorrect," but they are wavering. Some people waver at critical moments, showing instability during historical upheavals. ... They are not rightists, but they put themselves on the edge of being rightists, within 30 kilometers of them, as rightists welcome such arguments. These comrades adopt a marginal policy,

which is quite dangerous. If you don't believe it, you will see in the future. I am speaking publicly, and some words may hurt people. Not speaking now is disadvantageous to these comrades.[43]

Mao's speech disrupted the initially relaxed and lively atmosphere of the Lushan Conference, shifting the theme from continuing to correct "leftist" tendencies to starting to combat rightist tendencies.

Following Mao's proposal, the Eighth Plenary Session of the Eighth Central Committee was held at Lushan from August 2 to 16. In an unusual atmosphere, the plenary session passed documents such as the "Resolution on the Errors of the Anti-Party Group Headed by Comrade Peng Dehuai" and the "Struggle to Defend the Party's General Line and Oppose Right-eaning Opportunism."

Mao Zedong delivered several speeches at the meeting. In his speech on August 2, he stated: "We have been correcting 'leftist' tendencies for nine months. Now, the primary issue is no longer this. The Lushan Conference is not about correcting 'leftist' tendencies but about combating rightist ones. Rightist opportunism is launching a frenzied attack against the Party, against the Party's leadership organs, against the people's cause, and against the vigorous socialist cause of the 600 million people." In his speech on August 11, he introduced the concept of "allies within the Party." He said: "They joined the Communist Party as bourgeois democrats. During the bourgeois democratic revolution, they participated actively, but they often made mistakes in their methods. They are actually allies within the Party, allies of Marxism, Marxists' allies during the bourgeois democratic revolution stage. They are not mentally prepared for the proletarian revolution."[44]

The introduction of "allies within the Party" and the erroneous handling of Peng Dehuai and others severely damaged the democratic life within the Party, from the central to the grassroots levels. It disrupted democratic centralism to varying degrees, making it difficult for the CPC to effectively prevent and resist the further development of "leftist" erroneous guiding thoughts.

These judgments contributed to extending social class struggles into the Party, having adverse effects.

After the Eighth Plenary Session of the Eighth Central Committee, a widespread "anti-rightist" struggle was launched, which not only interrupted the process of correcting "leftist" tendencies but also led to the resurgence of "high targets" and the "Communist Wind," resulting in the severe difficulties from 1960 to 1962.

CHAPTER 16

Reflections After Calming Down

Now that we have entered the socialist era, a series of new problems have emerged. Having just "On Practice" and "On Contradiction" is not enough to meet these new needs. New works must be written, and new theories formed to adapt to the current circumstances.

MAO ZEDONG,
"Talks on Reading the Soviet *Political Economy Textbook*"
(December 1959–February 1960)

While correcting the "Left" errors during the Great Leap Forward and the People's Commune Movement, Mao Zedong repeatedly urged the entire Party to study, especially Stalin's *Economic Problems of Socialism in the USSR* and the Soviet *Political Economy Textbook*. After the Lushan Conference, he spent two months, from December 10, 1959, to February 9, 1960, concentrating on reading the socialist section of the Soviet *Political Economy Textbook* in places such as Hangzhou and Guangzhou.

The purpose of Mao's reading, much like his large-scale industrial construction research in 1956, was to "use the Soviet Union as a reference" and explore the path of socialist construction in China.

He made this clear in his letter on reading suggestions written during the First Zhengzhou Conference on November 9, 1958. He wrote: "We should read these two books in connection with the socialist economic revolution and economic construction in China to gain a clear head, benefiting the guidance of our great economic work. Many people now have a lot of confused thoughts, which may be clarified by reading these two books. In recent months, some comrades who claim to be Marxist economists have shown such tendencies. When they read Marxist political economy, they are Marxists, but their Marxism is discounted when faced with specific problems in current economic practice. Now there is a need for reading and debate, which will benefit all comrades."

He also mentioned, "During the Great Leap Forward and the period of the People's Communes, there was great interest in reading such books." In his speeches during this period, he often talked about this feeling.

Regarding reading methods, he wrote in the letter: "Everyone should carefully read each book three times, thinking and analyzing as they go, discerning which parts are correct (I believe this is the majority); which parts are incorrect, somewhat incorrect, or vaguely explained—the author himself may not be very clear on some points. During reading, groups of three to five people should discuss each chapter and section. Within two to three months, it is possible to thoroughly understand the content."[1] This was exactly how Mao approached it.

The Soviet *Political Economy Textbook* Mao read was compiled by the Soviet Academy of Sciences Institute of Economics and was divided into two volumes. The first volume covered capitalism, and the second was socialism. Since its first edition in 1954, the textbook saw an augmented second edition in 1955 and a revised third edition in 1958. Mao read the revised third edition of the second volume.

Before this reading, Mao had also frequently read Stalin's *Economic Problems of Socialism in the USSR* before and after the First Zhengzhou Conference in 1958. During two sessions of the First Zhengzhou Conference, he discussed his views on Stalin's book in relation to China's construction practices.

Practical errors are often the external manifestations of theoretical confusion. During the Great Leap Forward and the People's Commune Movement, the emergence of the "Communist Wind" and "Leap Forward Wind" had its roots in theoretical issues such as whether socialist society should have commodity production, economic laws, the law of value, and whether there should be developmental stages. Stalin's book, written between February and September 1952, summarized the historical experience of Soviet socialist construction and clarified some misconceptions, including the erroneous idea of abolishing commodity production. Therefore, Mao's rereading of this work resonated deeply with him. He read it three times in succession, each time making annotations.

At the First Zhengzhou Conference on November 9, 1958, he said: "Stalin's book *Economic Problems of Socialism in the USSR* should be read again. Provincial and district Party Committee members should study it. Everyone should study the first, second, and third chapters. Previously, we weren't interested; now it's different. There are many noteworthy points in these three chapters, some of which are poorly written, and some that even Stalin himself did not fully understand."[2]

He then discussed his views on these three chapters one by one.

Mao said: "In the first chapter, Stalin contrasts a planned economy with an anarchic economy. He asserts that a planned economy is an objective law that should be distinguished from things determined by people's will. This is worth studying." He argues that subjective planning should strive to conform to objective laws. He raised the issue but did not elaborate. "They did not pay attention to light industry and agriculture, which cost them; they couldn't combine immediate and long-term interests. Up to now, their commodities are fewer than ours. This is like walking with one leg. Our current approach is to develop both industry and agriculture simultaneously under the condition of prioritizing the production of means of production (heavy industry), walking on two legs. He did not emphasize politics or mass line, only technology, which is also walking on one leg." The first chapter raised the issue for us to consider and study, but he did not develop it, only stating it needed study and mastery.

Regarding the second and third chapters, he said as follows:

> The second chapter discusses commodities, and the third chapter discusses the law of value. I agree with many points here; it's essential to clarify these issues. In the Soviet Union, Stalin believed that the means of production were not commodities; in our country, they were different. Some means of production are commodities. For example, we sell agricultural machinery to cooperatives. Stalin insisted on not selling agricultural machinery to collective farms but keeping it in state hands. Overall, he did not find a way to transition from collective to public ownership. He criticized Yaroshenko for wanting to eliminate production relations, leaving only productive forces and making production relations a part of productive forces. This criticism is correct. However, Stalin hardly discusses the relationship between the superstructure and the economic base in his entire article. He barely mentions how the superstructure should adapt to the economic base of the socialist era. The benefit of his book is that it raised some issues in socialist economics that no one had previously addressed or only slightly touched upon. Only Lenin had mentioned some, such as the new economic policy of doing business under socialism. Lenin also proposed the slogan of an all-out attack, which I think was too fast.[3]

On November 10th, Mao Zedong changed his approach to discussing Stalin's *Economic Problems of Socialism in the USSR*. Instead of speaking chapter by chapter as he did the previous day, he targeted specific viewpoints for discussion.

Regarding the proposal to eliminate commodity production, Mao Zedong said as follows:

> Engels once said, "With the seizing of the means of production by society, production of commodities is done away with, and, simultaneously, the mastery of the product over the producer."[4] In the old society, products had a controlling influence over people. Stalin's analysis of Engels' formula is correct. Stalin said, "Engels, in his formula, was referring not to the nationalization of part of the means of production, but to the nationalization of all means of

production, meaning not only the means of production in industry but also the means of production in agriculture should be transferred to the ownership of the whole people. Engels considered that in such a state, simultaneously with the nationalization of all means of production, commodity production should also be abolished."[5] Currently, our state ownership is only a small part, accounting for only a small portion of the means of production and social products. Only when all means of production are owned can commerce be abolished. It seems that our economists have not understood this point.

Addressing the issue of confiscating farmers' property during the "Communist Wind," Mao Zedong said:

> Stalin mentioned that some "poor Marxists" believe that rural small and medium producers should be expropriated.[6] We have such people in our country too. Some comrades are eager to declare people's communes as wholly state-owned, abolish commerce, and implement product allocation, which essentially expropriates farmers, only pleasing Taiwan. ... Now, the farmers' labor, like the land and other means of production (seeds, tools, irrigation works, trees, fertilizers, etc.), is their own, so they own the products. For some reason, our philosophers and economists seem to have forgotten these issues. Forgetting this, we risk alienating the farmers.[7]

On the eve of the expanded meeting of the Political Bureau of the Central Committee of the CPC in Wuhan on November 20, 1958, Mao Zedong saw an internal document from the Publicity Department of the CPC Central Committee titled "The Major Revisions and Additions in the Third Edition of the Soviet Political Economy Textbook." He immediately instructed that it be distributed to the participants of the expanded meeting of the Political Bureau of the Central Committee of CPC.[8]

On November 21, during his speech at the expanded meeting of the Political Bureau of the Central Committee of CPC in Wuhan, Mao Zedong addressed the sixth issue, "Commodity Economy Issue," and urged everyone to read the book.

There is news now that the Soviet Union has released the third edition of the *Political Economy Textbook*, expanding the scope of commodities to include not only consumer goods but also means of production. This issue needs to be studied. For a while, it seemed like the fewer commodities, the better, and that they should be abolished within two to three years. Now I think that commodities need to exist for a longer period, if not a hundred years, then at least twenty or thirty years. If commodities hinder economic development, then they should be abolished. The third edition of the Soviet *Political Economy Textbook* hasn't undergone significant changes, retaining many of Stalin's views. Stalin's work cannot be entirely discarded because it is scientific; only parts of it should be rejected because it has flaws and errors. We, including myself, did not care about the laws of socialist economics in the past. Now that we are actually working on it, and the whole nation is debating it, we need to look at Stalin's *Economic Problems of Socialism in the USSR* and the Soviet *Political Economy Textbook*. Comrade Shangkun, distribute the textbook to everyone, and let's read the socialist section. We need to be pragmatic; this is a theoretical issue of political economy.[9]

Mao Zedong's wish to delve deeper into the Soviet *Political Economy Textbook* was interrupted by the need to rectify "Left" deviations, reduce steel production targets, and the Lushan Conference. It wasn't until the expanded meeting of the Political Bureau of the Central Committee of the CPC[10] from November 30 to December 4, 1959, that he could return to his original intention.

For this reading session, Mao Zedong appointed Chen Boda, Hu Sheng, Deng Liqun, and Tian Jiaying to study with him. The reading took place at Liuzhuang Dingjia Mountain or the Nanping Swimming Pool in Hangzhou, where they read for half a day every afternoon. Mao set the reading schedule, and they discussed and analyzed each chapter and section of the second volume of the Soviet *Political Economy Textbook*, which consists of 17 chapters[11] and a conclusion. The study group read through the entire book, and Mao made some annotations during the reading.

Simultaneously, Liu Shaoqi, Zhou Enlai, and others organized their own study groups to read the book thoroughly. Under Mao's leadership, this effort effectively marked a renewed understanding and exploration of the path of China's socialist construction since 1956. The difference was that this time, it was enriched by new experiences from the Great Leap Forward and the People's Commune Movement.

Mao Zedong's secretary, Lin Ke, recalled as follows:

According to my diary, the study group led by Mao Zedong included Chen Boda, Hu Sheng, Tian Jiaying, and Deng Liqun. I also participated in this study session from beginning to end. The study started in Hangzhou on December 10, 1959, and concluded in Guangzhou on February 9, 1960, with a total of 24 sessions. Each session averaged reading about a dozen pages over two to three hours, taking a chapter by chapter, section-by-section approach, discussing as we read. ... In Hangzhou, the study took place in the lounge by the Nanping Swimming Pool and in a pavilion on Dingjia Mountain, where Mao Zedong often strolled. Due to Mao's need to attend an expanded meeting of the Political Bureau in Shanghai, the study was paused for a while. After arriving in Guangzhou on February 4, 1960, the study resumed and concluded on February 9 with the completion of the socialist section of the *Political Economy Textbook*.[12]

Deng Liqun, who was the deputy editor-in-chief of *Red Flag* magazine at the time, recalled as follows:

Mao Zedong personally arranged the study sessions, scheduling reading every afternoon and instructing Hu Sheng, Tian Jiaying, and me to take turns reading aloud, with discussions following each section. The three of us then coordinated, deciding that they would take turns reading aloud while I took notes. The study began on December 10, and as we read and discussed, we listened to Chairman Mao's comments, occasionally adding a few of our own. Initially, Chairman Mao did not notice our arrangement and asked me, "Why aren't you reading?" I replied, "My pronunciation is not standard." Chairman Mao looked at me, saw that I was taking notes, and said nothing further.[13]

During his stay in Hangzhou, Mao Zedong read chapters 20 to 32 of the second volume of the Soviet *Political Economy Textbook*, and part of chapter 33. Deng Liqun left behind some fragmented memories of this reading period, excerpts of which are as follows.

December 26, 1959 was a special day. According to Deng Liqun: "It was Chairman Mao's 66th birthday, but the reading session was not interrupted. Chairman Mao invited a few of us from the study group to have dinner with him. The only guests were Jiang Hua, who was working in Zhejiang at the time, and his wife Wu Zhonglian. Jiang Hua was an old comrade from the Jinggang period. After dinner, Chairman Mao presented each of us with a thread-bound volume of the *Collected Poems of Mao Zedong*[14] and two of his newly written poems as a souvenir."

On December 30, it rained by the West Lake. Mao Zedong was highly enthusiastic about reading. According to Deng Liqun: "Our reading location was a bungalow on Dingjia Mountain by the West Lake, which could only be reached on foot. On the 30th, despite the rain, Chairman Mao climbed Dingjia Mountain with his cane to read. From 6 p.m. to 10 p.m., we read 20 pages, the most in a single day."

On January 5, 1960, Mao Zedong set off for Shanghai to preside over the expanded meeting of the Political Bureau of the Central Committee of the CPC.

Before leaving Hangzhou, Deng Liqun organized the notes of Mao Zedong's comments during the reading sessions, preparing to take them to Shanghai to show the members of the Standing Committee of the Political Bureau. He recalled: "During this period in Hangzhou, we finished chapter 32 and started chapter 33. I took notes daily and, with the help of Comrade Mei Xing, organized them each day. Before leaving Hangzhou, I compiled the notes into a volume titled *Notes on Reading the Political Economy Textbook (Socialist Section)*. After Hu Sheng and Tian Jiaying reviewed it and made minor textual changes, it was finalized."

Chapter 33 was completed on Mao Zedong's special train. Deng Liqun recalled: "On the afternoon of the 5th, on the train stopped at Shanghai Station, we finished reading chapter 33. I immediately handed over the organized notes to the General Office of the Central Committee for printing and distribution to the Standing Committee of the Political Bureau."

During the expanded meeting of the Political Bureau of the Central Committee of the CPC from January 7 to 17, 1960, Mao Zedong's discussions on the Soviet *Political Economy Textbook* (socialist section) were conveyed.

Deng Liqun recalled: "During the group discussions at the expanded meeting of the Political Bureau of the Central Committee of the CPC, each group requested those of us who participated in Chairman Mao's study group to relay his comments. I was assigned to the group with Zhu De and Deng Xiaoping. I asked, 'Chairman Mao did not instruct us to relay this. Can we do it?' Comrade Deng Xiaoping said: 'Yes, you can relay it.' So, I detailed the notes I had organized. Chen Boda, Hu Sheng, and Tian Jiaying also relayed Chairman Mao's comments in other groups."

Deng Liqun also recalled: "At the Shanghai meeting, after listening to the relay, Comrade Hu Qiaomu took the notes and the book I was reading to examine. Afterward, he told me: 'Your book has places where Chairman Mao made marks and simple annotations, which are not reflected in the organized notes. From what I see, the notes predominantly criticize the textbook, with fewer affirmations, whereas the annotations mostly affirm the textbook, with fewer criticisms. Only by combining these two parts can we fully and accurately reflect Chairman Mao's views on the reading.' Hu Qiaomu's opinion was correct."[15]

After the meeting, Mao Zedong stayed in Hangzhou for a few more days before heading to Guangzhou to celebrate the Spring Festival.

Starting from February 4, Mao Zedong continued reading the second volume of the Soviet *Political Economy Textbook* every afternoon at the Jijingkeng Guesthouse of the Guangzhou Military Region, joined by Chen Boda, Hu Sheng, Deng Liqun, and Tian Jiaying, with the addition of Tao Zhu and Hu Qiaomu. During this period, they completed the last three chapters and the conclusion of the book.

Mao Zedong's discussions on the second volume of the Soviet *Political Economy Textbook* were incredibly rich in content. After being organized by Deng Liqun and others, the record of these discussions amounted to nearly

100,000 words. Essentially, it serves as an encyclopedia for exploring the path of socialist construction in China. Due to historical limitations, not all of the ideas reflected in these discussions could be entirely correct, but they undoubtedly provide a treasure trove of thoughts for future generations to continue exploring China's own development path.

In these discussions, Mao Zedong reflected on the overstepping errors during the Great Leap Forward and the People's Commune Movement, proposing: "The socialist phase might be divided into two stages. The first stage is underdeveloped socialism, and the second stage is relatively developed socialism. The latter stage may require more time than the former."[16]

In leading the Great Leap Forward and the People's Commune Movement, Mao Zedong's urgency primarily manifested in his desire to build a socialist, modernized, strong nation. This urgency was shared by those who had experienced the impoverished and weak old China and the era where backwardness led to being bullied. However, what is modernization? Mao Zedong had been exploring and contemplating this question. In these discussions, he finally provided a more comprehensive answer: "Building socialism initially required industrial modernization, agricultural modernization, and scientific and cultural modernization. Now, we must add national defense modernization. In a country like ours, completing socialist construction is a formidable task. We should not talk about achieving socialism too early."[17] Later, in his speech at the expanded Central Work Conference in January 1962, he further stated: "Capitalist economies took more than three hundred years to become powerful. In our country, it would be good to build a strong socialist economy within fifty to a hundred years."[18]

The severe lessons of the Great Leap Forward and the People's Commune Movement included disrupting the national economy's proportional relationships and comprehensive balance. Mao Zedong was deeply distressed by this. A considerable part of his discussions while reading the second volume of the Soviet *Political Economy Textbook* focused on the issue of comprehensive balance. He said: "During the development of the socialist economy, disproportionate and unbalanced situations often arise, requiring us to achieve proportional and comprehensive balance." "Without basing plans on laws, the effect of planned proportional development cannot be realized." He recognized that while planning according to proportion, there is another aspect of the socialist economy. He said: "One cannot assume that there is no spontaneity or self-flow in a socialist society. Our understanding of laws is not perfect from the start. Practical work tells us that, within a certain period, there can be various plans; plans by different people. We cannot say that all these plans entirely conform to laws. In reality, some plans conform to laws, or basically conform, while others do not, or basically do not." These insights were gained from painful lessons.

Mao Zedong was a master at navigating complex contradictions, and the storms of the past two years had deepened his understanding of the contradictions within socialist society. However, he never wavered in his optimistic approach to these contradictions. In his discussions, he remarked: "In the socialist era, contradictions remain the driving force of social development. Because of differences, there is a task of unity, and a need to struggle for unity." "The contradictions and imbalances between the productive forces and the relations of production, as well as between the relations of production and the superstructure, are absolute. The adaptation of the superstructure to the relations of production, and the relations of production to the productive forces, or their balance, is always relative." Thus, he proposed a bold thesis: "We should take the balance and imbalance between the productive forces and the relations of production, and between the relations of production and the superstructure, as the key to studying economic issues in a socialist society." This essentially touched upon the starting point and purpose of reform.

At this moment, Mao Zedong strongly felt the theoretical inadequacies in socialist construction. Having experienced many events, encountered numerous situations, and paid significant costs, he found himself struggling to explain and summarize these experiences theoretically. Through reading the first work on the political economy of socialist construction, he came to a realization: "It is impossible to write good economics without the mind of a philosopher. Marx could write *Capital*, and Lenin could write *Imperialism, the Highest Stage of Capitalism*, because they were also philosophers, with the minds of philosophers and the weapon of dialectics."[19]

From the depths of his heart, Mao Zedong issued this call: "Now that we have entered the socialist era, a series of new problems have emerged. Relying solely on "On Practice" and "On Contradiction" is no longer sufficient to meet these new needs. New works must be written, and new theories must be developed to adapt to the current circumstances."[20]

Chapter 17

The Struggle with Khrushchev

Winter clouds snow-laden, cotton fluff flying,
None or few the unfallen flowers.
Chill waves sweep through steep skies,
Yet earth's gentle breath grows warm.
Only heroes can quell tigers and leopards,
And wild bears never daunt the brave.
Plum blossoms welcome the whirling snow,
Small wonder flies freeze and perish.

MAO ZEDONG,
"*Qi Lü* · Winter Clouds" (December 26, 1962)

This is the only poem Mao Zedong wrote on his birthday. It uses metaphors to vividly depict his struggle with Nikita Khrushchev. Mao's conflict with Khrushchev directly led to the Sino-Soviet Polemics, which were not an isolated or accidental event.

In January 1964, Mao Zedong delivered a lengthy speech that encapsulated his views on the origins and development of the Sino-Soviet differences.

After the 20th Congress of the CPSU, we already sensed that something was wrong with Khrushchev. However, from then until the first half of 1958, we took a stance of helping him, considering that it was not easy for the Soviet people to change their leader.

Later, in 1958, the issue of the naval base arose.[1] That year, Khrushchev visited Beijing. Why did he come? The Soviet Ambassador to China had disagreed with us over the naval base issue, so Khrushchev had to come and resolve it himself. I told him, "You can have the entire Chinese coastline." He asked, "Then what will you do?" I replied, "I'll go to the mountains and fight guerrilla warfare." He said, "Guerrilla warfare is useless." I responded, "You've blocked my nose; what else can I do but fight guerrilla warfare?"

Then there was the Sino-Indian Border Incident in 1959.[2] Before his visit to the US, Khrushchev issued a statement through TASS, declaring "neutrality" on the Sino-Indian border issue. After his US visit, he came to Beijing. He brought up the Taiwan question, suggesting we handle Taiwan as the Soviet Union had handled the Far Eastern Republic.[3] I told him, "The Far Eastern Republic was established by you, but the Chiang Kai-shek regime was not created by us." Additionally, he wanted us to release four or five American prisoners held in our jails. Neither issue was resolved. He said, "Eisenhower told me at Camp David that my visit to Beijing would be futile."

From the 20th Congress of the CPSU until July of last year (1963), we were relatively passive. Now we have moved to the offensive, with the momentum of "creating havoc in heaven," breaking their old rules. We cannot fully comply with their old rules!

They accuse us of dogmatism, Trotskyism, empty talk, false revolution, and nationalism. Yet, they fear our "empty talk." They say it's empty talk, but they treat it like a plague, blocking it so vigorously that they even use the same stations previously used to jam Voice of America broadcasts to jam our broadcasts.

Now they demand an end to public debate, they are quite tense. In March of last year, I told the Soviet ambassador, "You call us dogmatists, Trotskyists, people who talk empty words, fake revolutionaries, and nationalists. If we are truly such, you should criticize us freely." He said it couldn't go on like this. I replied, "What's so bad about a war of words? First, the sky won't fall; second, the grass and trees on the mountain will still grow; third, women will still give birth; fourth, fish will still swim in the river. If you don't believe me, go to the river and see for yourself." Their recent letters even quoted this remark of mine.

Stopping the debate cannot be decided by one side alone; a fair agreement must be acceptable to both sides. The parties involved are not just two, but the parties of dozens of countries. Therefore, it is very difficult to stop the debate.[4]

From February 1956, at the 20th Congress of the CPSU, the main disagreements between the CPC and the CPSU were threefold: the assessment of Stalin, relations between socialist countries, and the peaceful transition of capitalist countries to socialism. Among these, the assessment of Stalin was the most prominent.

As Mao Zedong said, "In 1956 when Stalin was criticized, we were both pleased and concerned. It was necessary to lift the lid, dispel the superstition, remove the pressure, and liberate the mind. But we did not agree with total repudiation. While they stopped displaying Stalin's portraits, we continued to hang them."[5]

Under Mao's leadership, two articles were drafted: "On the Historical Experience of the Proletarian Dictatorship" and "More on the Historical Experience of the Proletarian Dictatorship," published on April 5 and December 29, 1956, respectively, in the People's Daily. These were the first public, albeit unnamed, expressions of the CPC's dissent with the CPSU Central Committee's views after Stalin's death.

The issue of inequality has always been the crux of the relationship between the Soviet Union and other socialist countries, and China was no exception. This problem began during Stalin's era, and although it improved somewhat under Khrushchev, it never fundamentally changed. The Polish events in the second half year of 1956 were an eruption of these contradictions.

In June 1956, the Poznań protests broke out in Poland, revealing the bureaucratic mishandling by the Polish government of a workers' strike. At the Seventh Plenum of the Polish United Workers' Party in July, the lessons from the Poznań Incident were summarized, and several reform measures were proposed. It was then decided to convene the Eighth Plenum ahead of schedule in October, with plans to reorganize the Politburo and elect Gomułka as the First Secretary. These independent actions offended the CPSU, which always regarded itself as the "elder brother" among socialist parties. From October 17, Khrushchev, the First Secretary of the CPSU, ordered Soviet troops stationed in and near Poland to move toward Warsaw and other regions. At the same time, he led a four-member Soviet delegation to forcibly attend the Eighth Plenum of the Polish United Workers' Party. This immediately heightened tensions between the Soviet Union and Poland.

On October 19, 1956, the Soviet Ambassador to China, Yudin, handed Mao Zedong a letter from the Central Committee of the CPSU, indicating their intention to use force in Poland and inviting a Chinese delegation to Moscow to discuss the Polish issue at a meeting of socialist countries.

In a meeting with Yudin in the early hours of October 22, Mao Zedong stated that if the Soviet Union refrained from using force and did not convene an international conference to condemn Poland but agreed to resolve the Soviet-Polish differences peacefully, China would agree to send a delegation to Moscow to discuss solutions. On the same day, Mao Zedong met with the Polish Ambassador to China, Kiryluk, and communicated this response to Polish leaders.

From October 23 to 31, Liu Shaoqi led a Chinese delegation to Moscow to discuss the Polish issue with Soviet Union leaders. During the talks on October 29, Liu Shaoqi conveyed Mao Zedong's suggestions regarding Soviet relations with Eastern European countries: Allow them to handle their political and economic affairs independently, consult them on military matters, and ask whether they wanted to maintain the Warsaw Pact, have Soviet troops stationed, or prefer the Warsaw Pact without Soviet troops, with Soviet intervention only if there was an enemy attack. After prolonged discussions, Khrushchev agreed with Mao's views. On October 30, the Soviet Union government issued a declaration on "Developing and Strengthening Friendship and Cooperation Between the Soviet Union and Other Socialist Countries," acknowledging past mistakes and expressing a desire to improve mutual relations. On November 1, the Chinese government issued a statement supporting the Soviet Union government's declaration.

After the resolution of the Polish events, Mao Zedong met with Polish Ambassador Kiryluk on October 31, advocating against great-power chauvinism. He said, "Stalin practiced social chauvinism. Although he did many good things, he made mistakes of great-power chauvinism in inter-ethnic relations within the Soviet Union and in international relations."[6]

At that time, Mao Zedong hoped that the Soviet Union leaders would abandon great-power chauvinism, treat other socialist countries as equals, and respect their sovereignty and strategic interests. However, this hope ultimately proved to be in vain.

The possibility of a peaceful transition from capitalism to socialism was first introduced in the report of the 20th Congress of the CPSU. The Chinese delegation took a cautious stance, avoiding a direct response.

In October 1957, while drafting the declaration for the Communist and Workers' Parties of the Socialist Countries Conference in Moscow (known as the Moscow Declaration), the CPSU included content regarding the peaceful transition of capitalist countries to socialism. The Soviet side sought feedback on the draft from the CPC. After deliberation, Mao Zedong met with Soviet Ambassador Yudin on October 29, 1957, to express his views on the matter.

> Generally speaking, there are two possibilities in capitalist countries. The first is the possibility of a peaceful transition. By acknowledging this possibility, we are making it clear that we do not advocate war or the use of violence to overthrow governments. The second possibility arises if the bourgeoisie resorts to violence to suppress the proletariat, launching a civil war against them. In that case, the proletariat will be compelled to respond with civil war. Thus, the proletariat must pursue a peaceful transition with one hand while preparing to counter bourgeois violence with the other, ensuring that the revolution is not delayed due to a lack of preparedness. It is difficult to imagine many bourgeois regimes allowing the proletariat to transition peacefully. Therefore, both possibilities must be presented simultaneously.[7]

During Mao Zedong's second visit to the Soviet Union, the biggest disagreement between the Chinese and Soviet Union delegations while drafting the Moscow Declaration was about the transition from capitalism to socialism. Considering the Soviet side's repeated insistence on aligning with the propositions of the 20th Congress of the CPSU, the Chinese delegation made some concessions and submitted a memorandum titled "Outline of Opinions on the Issue of Peaceful Transition" to the Central Committee of the CPSU on November 10.

The Moscow Declaration stated that in some capitalist countries, "the working class, relying on the majority of the people and resolutely striking against the opportunistic elements unwilling to abandon the compromise policy toward the capitalists and landlords, may defeat the reactionary, anti-people forces, secure a stable majority in parliament, transform parliament from an instrument serving the class interests of the bourgeoisie into an instrument serving the working people, and simultaneously carry out extensive mass struggles outside parliament, destroy the resistance of the reactionary forces, and prepare the necessary conditions for the peaceful realization of the socialist revolution."[8]

The Chinese delegation's "Outline of Opinions on the Issue of Peaceful Transition" stated: "Considering the current state of the international communist movement, from a tactical viewpoint, it is beneficial to express the desire for peaceful transition, but it is not advisable to overemphasize its possibility." They elaborated on seven points, with the most important being three. First, it might weaken revolutionary resolve and disarm oneself ideologically; second, "this possibility currently lacks practical significance in any country"; and third, "for socialist parties, it cannot make them more revolutionary."[9]

Had the disagreements ended there, the relations between the two parties and countries might have remained at a normal level. However, the events following 1958 made this relationship increasingly irreparable.

In April of that year, Soviet Defense Minister Malinovsky proposed a joint construction of a 1,000-kilowatt long-wave radio station and a special long-distance communication reception center, with an investment of 110 million rubles, 70 million from the Soviet Union and 40 million from China, to be located in China.[10] At the Central Military Commission meeting on May 10, it was decided that the Navy and the General Staff's Communication Department should study this proposal and give their opinions.

On May 23, Peng Dehuai chaired a Central Military Commission meeting to discuss this proposal again. He explicitly stated that this large radio station should not be jointly managed and should be handled by China alone. He also said: "It is not good for foreigners to establish military bases in China."[11]

Subsequently, the Soviet side insisted on the original plan for joint investment and proposed sending experts to China in early June to conduct site selection, surveys, and design work. On June 5, Peng Dehuai wrote a report to Mao Zedong, suggesting that they could initially agree to the Soviet experts coming to China for technical work while postponing discussions on investment and usage issues.

On June 7, Mao Zedong approved Peng Dehuai's suggestion, emphasizing, "The money should be decided by China, not by the Soviet side. Usage should be joint. This matter should be agreed upon by the governments of both countries." He also said, "If the Soviet side applies pressure, we should not respond and delay for a while."[12]

This was the origin of the long-wave radio station issue.

The matter of the joint nuclear submarine fleet arose on June 28 when, based on the advice of Soviet advisers, the Chinese side requested Soviet technical assistance for developing Chinese naval nuclear submarines. On July 21, Soviet Ambassador to China Yudin met with Mao Zedong, conveying Khrushchev and the Presidium of the Central Committee of the CPSU's suggestion of establishing a joint nuclear submarine fleet between the Soviet Union and China, and hoped that Zhou Enlai and Peng Dehuai could come to Moscow for discussions. Mao Zedong replied, "First, the policy must be clear: Is it us managing with your assistance, or must it be jointly managed, and without joint management, you will not provide assistance, thereby forcing us into joint management?"[13]

The next day, on July 22, Mao Zedong met with Yudin again, clarifying China's stance.

> It seems that the navy's request for nuclear submarines can be withdrawn. I had no impression of this issue in my mind, but after asking, I found out that there were some enthusiasts in the Navy Headquarters, particularly the Soviet advisers, who said that the Soviet Union already had nuclear submarines and

could provide them with a mere telegram. Now we have decided not to pursue nuclear submarines and withdraw our request. Otherwise, we would hand over the entire coastline to you, expanding the former Lüshun and Dalian bases. But we should not mix our operations; you do your part, and we do ours. We must have our fleet. It is difficult to manage with two hands on the same project. ... My words may sound unpleasant, and you might say I am a nationalist, another Tito. If you say so, I could say you are extending Russian nationalism to China's coastline. Your suggestion of a naval "cooperative" raises the question of ownership. You proposed that each side holds 50% ownership. Your words upset me so much yesterday that I couldn't sleep all night.

At this point, Peng Dehuai brought up the issue of the long-wave radio station again. He said, "This year, Soviet Defense Minister Malinovsky sent me a telegram requesting the construction of a long-wave radar observation station on the Chinese coast to command the submarine fleet in the Pacific. The required funds amount to 110 million rubles, with the Soviet Union bearing 70 million and China 40 million." Mao Zedong reiterated, "This issue, like the naval 'cooperative,' cannot be explained to the people or to foreign countries and is politically disadvantageous."

Mao Zedong firmly declared, "When it comes to political conditions, not even half a finger's worth will do. You can tell Comrade Khrushchev that if there are conditions, we don't need to discuss it at all. If he agrees, he can come; if not, then he shouldn't come—there's nothing to talk about. Even a small condition is unacceptable. On this matter, we can go without assistance for ten thousand years."[14]

Upon hearing this, Khrushchev rushed to Beijing on the afternoon of July 31. From 5 p.m. to 9 p.m. that day, he had his first meeting with Mao Zedong at Huairen Hall in Zhongnanhai.

From July 31 to August 3, Mao Zedong and Khrushchev held four meetings. After the fourth meeting on the afternoon of August 3, a communiqué was issued, and Mao Zedong personally saw Khrushchev off at Nanyuan Airport.

In the first meeting, Khrushchev explained the issues regarding the joint nuclear submarine fleet and the long-wave radio station, blaming Yudin and Malinovsky and assuring that "such issues would never be raised again."[15]

In the subsequent three meetings, the atmosphere eased. Mao Zedong and Khrushchev discussed the international situation, work methods, and the relations between the two parties.

This episode of distrust and displeasure, sparked by the long-wave radio station and the joint nuclear submarine fleet, thus came to an end. However, the damage caused to Sino-Soviet relations by the Soviet style of elder-brother party behavior and great-power chauvinism was irreparable.

On the surface, this seemed like normal military cooperation, with the Soviet Union appearing to assist China generously. However, hidden behind it was a significant political and strategic issue: whether China would accept the Soviet nuclear protection, similar to Western Europe's relationship with the United States at that time, and whether China would allow foreign military forces to be stationed on its territory and establish military bases, even under the guise of "joint management" and "joint use."

In fact, since the first visit to the Soviet Union, Mao Zedong and the CPC have been striving to establish an equal alliance with the Soviet Union, not a subordinate strategic relationship. In this context, the Soviet leaders' proposal to establish a long-wave radio station and a joint nuclear submarine fleet in China, from their strategic needs, naturally provoked strong dissatisfaction among Chinese leaders. To Mao Zedong, this confirmed his judgment: In the minds of Soviet leaders, who were accustomed to acting as the "elder brother" and exhibiting great-power chauvinism, China had not attained equal status, and its sovereignty and strategic position were not respected. The Soviet Union did not genuinely support China's efforts to develop its nuclear weapons.

Therefore, during this period, Mao Zedong repeatedly emphasized the need for self-reliance in developing advanced national defense technology. On May 17, at the Second Session of the Eighth Congress of the CPC, he proposed, "The Soviet Union has launched satellites; should we consider making one or two satellites? We also need to develop some satellites."[16] On

June 21, at an Expanded Meeting of the Central Military Commission, he stated, "Developing atomic bombs, hydrogen bombs, and intercontinental missiles is entirely possible within ten years."[17]

Just as one wave subsided, another arose. From August to September 1958, strategic mistrust between China and the Soviet Union increased further due to China's shelling of Jinmen.

The Jinmen Artillery Battle was triggered by the United States' plot to create "two Chinas." To shake the US's stubborn stance on the Taiwan question, demonstrate to the world the Chinese people's determination to liberate Taiwan, and counter Chiang Kai-shek's aggressive stance of "counterattacking the mainland," Mao Zedong and the CPC Central Committee decided to initiate the Jinmen Artillery Battle. This was essentially a political and diplomatic battle. Before the battle began, Mao Zedong, in a note to Peng Dehuai on August 18, proposed the strategy of "preparing to attack Jinmen, directly targeting Chiang, and indirectly targeting the US."

Due to the recent disputes over the long-wave radio station and the joint nuclear submarine fleet and China's promise not to drag the Soviet Union into the fray, Khrushchev and other Soviet leaders maintained a restrained and cautious approach during the Jinmen Artillery Battle. On September 6, Soviet Foreign Minister Gromyko met with Zhou Enlai in Beijing and expressed support for China's position and actions. On September 7, Khrushchev wrote to US President Eisenhower, urging the US government to adopt a wise stance on the Taiwan question, withdraw the US fleet from the Taiwan Strait, and recognize the legitimate rights and interests of the People's Republic of China. This indeed put some pressure on the United States.

However, in Khrushchev's view, this was an act of "adventurism," akin to a "combative rooster."

In early 1959, the 21st Congress of the CPSU further clarified a strategy of easing tensions with the United States, centered on peaceful coexistence, peaceful competition, and peaceful transition. Khrushchev also urged President Eisenhower to hold a US-Soviet summit to seek compromises on nuclear disarmament and the Berlin issue.

To achieve this strategic goal, Khrushchev took several steps toward China.

On June 20, 1959, the CPSU Central Committee sent a letter to the CPC Central Committee, refusing to provide atomic bomb teaching models and technical materials. In 1957, Soviet leaders voluntarily offered to help China develop an atomic bomb. On October 15 of the same year, the two governments signed an agreement on new defense technology, which stipulated that the Soviet Union would provide China with teaching models and blueprints for the atomic bomb. However, the Soviet Union continuously delayed the fulfillment of this agreement. In the letter dated June 20, 1959, they cited their ongoing negotiations with the United States and other Western countries on a nuclear test ban agreement and Khrushchev's upcoming meeting with Eisenhower as reasons to postpone assistance, suggesting a reassessment in two years based on the situation. Additionally, Soviet experts left for a vacation back home, never to return.

The CPC Central Committee studied the June 20 letter from the CPSU Central Committee and decided to "start from scratch and prepare to develop an atomic bomb within eight years."[18] In July, Zhou Enlai conveyed this decision to Song Renqiong and others responsible for this project. Mao Zedong and other Chinese leaders learned a profound lesson from this: In terms of strategic and core technologies, China could only rely on its own efforts, perseverance, and self-reliance.

Since March 1959, the Sino-Indian border dispute has gradually escalated. While the governments of China and India were negotiating, and Zhou Enlai had just responded to Indian Prime Minister Nehru's White Paper on Sino-Indian relations on September 8, the Soviet government issued a TASS statement on the Sino-Indian Border Incident on September 9. This statement, despite the alliance between China and the Soviet Union, expressed the Soviet government's "neutral stance," effectively encouraging India's territorial claims.

From September 25 to 27, 1959, Khrushchev held informal talks with Eisenhower at Camp David in the United States. This was the first meeting between the heads of the Soviet Union and the United States since Khrushchev took power. Although the talks covered a wide range of international issues and achieved no substantial results, Khrushchev heavily promoted the "Spirit of Camp David" and prepared for a four-power summit in Paris involving the Soviet Union, the United States, the United Kingdom, and France.

China was Khrushchev's first stop after his Camp David meeting. From September 30 to October 4, 1959, Khrushchev visited China and held multiple meetings with Mao Zedong and other Chinese leaders. The discussions were very unpleasant.

At a National Day reception hosted by the Chinese government, Khrushchev even warned China not to "test the stability of the capitalist system by force." On his way back, he made several remarks criticizing Chinese leaders.

To Mao Zedong, Khrushchev's actions indicated the Soviet leader's willingness to sacrifice Sino-Soviet relations to appease the United States and other Western countries, which he saw as a "capitulationism." This led to China's publication of three articles, including "Long Live Leninism," in April 1960, marking the beginning of the Sino-Soviet Polemics.

Although the Soviet Union made some progress in easing tensions with the United States and other Western countries, their haste proved counterproductive. The incident involving the American U-2 spy plane's invasion of Soviet airspace in May 1960 and the subsequent failure of the Paris summit highlighted this.

After 1960, the relationship between the CPC and the CPSU began to move toward an inevitable rupture.

On April 22, 1960, marking the 90th anniversary of Lenin's birth, three articles—"Long Live Leninism," "Advance Along the Great Road of Lenin," and "Unite Under Lenin's Revolutionary Banner"—were published on April 16 and 22 based on Mao Zedong's suggestions. These articles emphasized the basic Marxist-Leninist viewpoints on imperialism, war and peace, proletarian revolution, and the dictatorship of the proletariat, effectively critiquing the international line and theories of the CPSU since its 20th Congress.

From June 24 to 26, a meeting of the representatives of the communist and workers' parties of various countries was held in Bucharest, the capital of Romania. Before the meeting, Mao Zedong proposed that they should prepare for two scenarios: one where they might face criticism and another where they might be pulled into an alliance.[19] As expected, Khrushchev organized an attack on the CPC delegation and even prematurely distributed a letter from the CPSU to the CPC.

On July 16, the Soviet government informed the Chinese government that they had unilaterally decided to recall all Soviet experts working in China. Between July 25 and September 1, a total of 1,390 Soviet experts were recalled, and the assignments of 900 more who were supposed to come to China were canceled.[20] This showed Khrushchev's attempt to pressure the CPC into compliance. However, he underestimated his opponent and misjudged the situation.

At this time, Mao Zedong was presiding over a central work meeting in Beidaihe. In the plenary session on July 18, he stated, "From 1917 to 1945, the Soviet Union was self-reliant, building socialism in one country. This is the Leninist path. We must also follow this path. We must remember that during the past ten years of our construction, the Soviet people gave us assistance. We must resolve to develop advanced technologies."[21]

In the plenary session on July 31, he further stated, "Next year, we aim to repay the 2.3 billion rubles. Is this possible? If we can muster the resources to meet their needs, it will be beneficial. It will give hope to our Party, our people, and our country." On July 20, in an expanded meeting of the Standing Committee of the Political Bureau, he also said, "They have their socialism, and we have ours."[22]

After this, Khrushchev, taking advantage of China's severe economic difficulties and the continuous provocations by the Indian army on the Sino-Indian border, adopted an aggressive stance, pressuring and attacking China on various occasions. Mao Zedong and the CPC Central Committee, however, established a general policy toward the Soviet Union: "Adhere to principles, maintain unity, persist in the struggle, and leave room for maneuver."[23]

In 1962, two significant events in Sino-Soviet relations caused a sudden rise in tension. The first was the Ili Incident in Xinjiang from April to May, where tens of thousands of Chinese citizens fled to the Soviet Union. The Soviet consulate in Ili was deeply involved, ultimately leading to the severance of consular relations between the two countries. The second event was in August when the Soviet government notified the Chinese government that the Soviet Union would reach an agreement with the United States to prevent nuclear proliferation. At this time, China had made a breakthrough in its atomic bomb development and was only two years away from a successful test.

That year, the correspondence between the two parties began to take the form of open letters, evolving from exchanging opinions to public debates. As a result, Sino-Soviet relations rapidly deteriorated, making the Sino-Soviet Polemics.

On February 21, 1963, the CPSU sent a letter to the CPC, proposing to cease public debates and convene an international conference. They also suggested that the CPC and the CPSU hold talks first to prepare for the international meeting. On February 23, Mao Zedong met with Soviet Ambassador Chervonenko and welcomed the CPSU's proposal. The CPC formally responded to the CPSU on March 9.

Subsequently, on June 14, the CPC replied to the CPSU's letter of March 30, presenting suggestions on the general line of the international communist movement. Mao Zedong was personally involved in drafting this reply.

Following this, from July 5 to 20, Sino-Soviet Party Talks were held in Moscow. Mao Zedong personally appointed Deng Xiaoping, then General Secretary of the CPC, to lead the delegation throughout the talks. The discussions yielded no results, as expected. On July 22, both parties issued a communiqué stating that further talks would be held in the future.

In truth, Khrushchev did not expect any substantive results from these talks; he merely wanted to make a gesture.

During the talks, on July 14, the CPSU published an "Open Letter from the CPSU Central Committee to Party Organizations and All Party Members," directly attacking the CPC, which intensified the already tense atmosphere of the talks.

Shortly after the conclusion of the talks, on July 25, the Soviet government signed the Treaty Banning Nuclear Weapon Tests in the Atmosphere, in Outer Space, and Under Water with representatives from the United States and the United Kingdom in Moscow. On July 31, the Chinese government issued a statement proposing a summit of world leaders to discuss the comprehensive prohibition and complete destruction of nuclear weapons. Unexpectedly, this proposal was rejected by the Soviet Union government.[24]

In response, Mao Zedong decided to publish a series of commentaries under the names of the editorial departments of the People's Daily and Red Flag magazine, systematically criticizing the July 14 "Open Letter from the CPSU Central Committee to Party Organizations and All Party Members." Beginning with "The Origin and Development of the Differences Between the CPSU Leadership and Ours" on September 6, 1963 and culminating with "On Khrushchev's Phony Communism and Its Historical Lessons for the World" (Ninth Commentaries) on July 14, 1964, a total of nine articles were published.[25] At the same time, Khrushchev mobilized resources to rebut the CPC's articles, leading to what became known as the "Sino-Soviet Polemics."

History often has coincidences that lend it a sense of mystery. Shortly after the publication of the "Ninth Commentaries," on October 16, 1964, China successfully tested its first atomic bomb through self-reliance. On the same day, the CPSU Central Committee and the Presidium of the Supreme Soviet of the USSR announced in a communiqué that Khrushchev had been relieved of all his leadership positions.

On November 21, *Red Flag* magazine published an editorial titled "How Khrushchev Was Ousted," marking the end of the Sino-Soviet Split.

Through the struggle for control and counter-control during the Sino-Soviet Polemics, China effectively broke away from the Soviet-led socialist camp and embarked on an independent development path. This was another historic contribution by Mao Zedong to the Chinese nation.

However, in the later stages of the Sino-Soviet Polemics, particularly in the "Ninth Commentaries," Mao Zedong mistakenly applied the theory of opposing and preventing revisionism and the guiding principle of "class struggle as the key link" to domestic political life, which ultimately led to the outbreak of the "Great Cultural Revolution."

CHAPTER 18

Launching the "Great Cultural Revolution"

When Heaven's in trouble,
I come to the South to see its bloom.
The tall pine soars skyward,
Fallen leaves float away with the green stream.
Suddenly a storm shakes the world,
And flags of all colors parade through the street.
I lean on the railing and listen to the pitter-patter of rain,
The people of the old country are full of thoughts.

MAO ZEDONG,
"*Qi Lü* · Thoughts" (June 1966)

On June 1, 1966, Peking University posted what Mao Zedong hailed as "the first Marxist-Leninist big-character poster in the nation," which was broadcast nationwide. On June 4, the Central Committee of the CPC announced its decision to reorganize the Beijing Municipal Party Committee. Soon, the sight of "flags of all colors parade through the street"[1] became common in Beijing and other places.

Around this time, on the afternoon of June 17, 1966, Mao Zedong traveled by car to his hometown of Shaoshan, staying in Dripping Water Cave for ten days. On the morning of June 28, he moved from there to Changsha and then to Wuhan.

He did not engage in many activities during his stay in Dripping Water Cave. However, on June 26, when meeting with leaders from the Hunan Provincial Party Committee, Xiangtan Prefectural Party Committee, and the County Party Committee, he made a significant, double-meaning statement: "Previously, I led you on the Long March; now, I will lead you on another 'Long March.'"[2]

Shortly after arriving in Wuhan on July 8, Mao Zedong penned a long letter to Jiang Qing. He wrote: "The current task is to essentially (though not entirely) overthrow the rightists in the Party and nationwide. Furthermore, in seven or eight years, there will need to be another campaign to thoroughly sweep away the ghosts and monsters, and subsequently, several more purges will be necessary."[3]

Before this, at Mao Zedong's suggestion, the Political Bureau of the Central Committee held an enlarged meeting in Beijing from May 4 to 26, which resulted in the issuance of the "Notification from the Central Committee of the CPC" (commonly known as the May 16 Notification). Before the meeting, while revising this notification, Mao Zedong added two specific paragraphs.

One paragraph concerned the assessment of the Party's situation. "The representatives of the bourgeoisie who have infiltrated the Party, the government, the military, and various cultural circles are a group of counter-revolutionary revisionists. Once the time is right, they will seize power, transforming the dictatorship of the proletariat into a dictatorship of the bourgeoisie. Some of these individuals have been exposed, some have not, and some are trusted by us and are being groomed as our successors, such as characters like Khrushchev. They are currently lying beside us. Every level of the Party Committee must pay full attention to this."

The other paragraph addressed the purpose of launching the "Great Cultural Revolution." "Raise high the great banner of the proletarian cultural revolution, thoroughly expose the bourgeois reactionary stance of those so-called 'academic authorities' who oppose the Party and socialism, and thoroughly criticize the bourgeois reactionary thoughts in academic, educational, journalistic, literary, artistic, and publishing fields. To achieve this, it is necessary to simultaneously criticize and purge the bourgeois representatives who have infiltrated the Party, the government, the military, and the cultural circles. Some need to be transferred from their positions."[4]

These two paragraphs reflect Mao Zedong's initial intentions for launching the "Great Cultural Revolution," as he mentioned in his letter to Jiang Qing, to conduct a nationwide exercise in anti-revisionism and defense against revisionism.

On June 10, in Hangzhou, Mao Zedong presided over an expanded meeting of the Standing Committee of the Political Bureau of the Central Committee. At that time, work teams were dispatched to some universities. Mao Zedong stated as follows:

> Let go, don't fear chaos, and let the masses be fully mobilized. Expose all the ghosts and monsters. There is no need to send work teams. Right-wing disruptions are not to be feared. The big-character poster at Peking University has ignited the fire of the cultural revolution, a storm that no one can suppress. This movement is characterized by its ferocity, with leftists particularly active and rightists resisting and sabotaging but generally not dominating. The scope of the crackdown is broad but not to be feared; it will be classified and eliminated later. Establish a core of leftist leaders during the movement so that they take control. Qualifications, ranks, and reputations should not matter; otherwise, we will not be able to seize this cultural front. In past struggles, many activists emerged, and in this movement, more will emerge. Rely on these people to carry the cultural revolution to the end.[5]

Following Mao Zedong's views, the Central Committee decided on July 26 to withdraw the work teams.

From August 1 to 12, Mao Zedong presided over the Eleventh Plenary Session of the Eighth Central Committee of the CPC, which passed the "Decision of the Central Committee of the CPC on the Great Proletarian Cultural Revolution."

On August 5, Mao Zedong wrote "Bombard the Headquarters—My First Big-Character Poster," which was distributed as a plenary document and later as an internal Party document. In it, he implicitly mentioned a "bourgeois headquarters" within the Party, clearly referring to Liu Shaoqi and other central leaders who were managing the central work at the time.

Based on Mao Zedong's suggestions, this plenary session reorganized the central leadership structure, increasing the number of members of the Standing Committee of the Political Bureau from 7 to 11[6] and adjusting their ranks. Lin Biao was placed second, while Liu Shaoqi was demoted from second to eighth.

Mao Zedong's launch of the "Great Cultural Revolution" was not a sudden impulse.

As early as the latter half of 1957, based on the experience of the Anti-Rightist Campaign, he proposed: "This is a great socialist revolution on the political and ideological fronts. Having only the 1956 socialist revolution on the economic front (in the ownership of the means of production) is insufficient and unstable. The Hungarian incident is proof of this. There must also be a thorough socialist revolution on the political and ideological fronts."[7] This is why Mao Zedong referred to the political movement he launched in 1966 as the "Great Cultural Revolution."

The severe expansion of the Anti-Rightist Campaign also had another consequence: Mao Zedong changed the correct judgment on the primary contradiction in society made by the Eighth National Congress of the CPC, believing that "the contradiction between the proletariat and the bourgeoisie, the contradiction between the socialist road and the capitalist road, is undoubtedly the main contradiction in our society today," which was formally confirmed at the Second Plenary Session of the Eighth National Congress of the CPC in May 1958. However, because the entire Party's attention was focused on the Great Leap Forward and the People's Commune Movement, its negative impact did not immediately become apparent.

In the declaration issued at the meeting of Communist and Workers' Parties of Socialist Countries in November 1957, there was a crucial statement: "The existence of bourgeois influence is the domestic root of revisionism. Succumbing to the pressure of imperialism is the foreign root of revisionism."[8] This statement, insisted upon by the Chinese delegation, greatly influenced Mao Zedong's view of intra-Party struggles in later years.

From July 25 to August 24, 1962, Mao Zedong chaired a Central Work Conference in Beidaihe. On August 6, during this conference, he delivered a speech on class, situation, and contradictions, shifting the focus of the Beidaihe Conference to class struggle, preparing for the Tenth Plenary Session of the Eighth Central Committee of the CPC, held from September 24 to 27.

In multiple speeches at the Beidaihe Conference and the Tenth Plenary Session, Mao Zedong, starting from the viewpoint that the main contradiction in current society was the class struggle between the proletariat and the bourgeoisie, regarded normal intra-party disagreements as reflections of societal class struggles within the Party. He linked this perspective to Khrushchev's criticisms of the Great Leap Forward and the People's Commune Movement, thus blurring the lines between intra-party contradictions and class contradictions, as well as between differing intra-party views and revisionism. From this perspective, he concluded that preventing the restoration of capitalism and combating revisionism should be prioritized from then on.

From 1963 to 1965, a nationwide socialist education movement was carried out in both urban and rural areas. During this movement, the overall situation was judged too harshly, with claims that one-third of grassroots units nationwide were not under the Party's leadership. To correct the "leftist" deviations in the movement, Mao Zedong oversaw the formulation of "Some Current Problems Raised in the Rural Socialist Education Movement" (commonly known as the "Twenty-Three Articles") in late 1964 to early 1965. However, this document also included Mao Zedong's opinion that "the focus of this movement is to rectify those within the Party who are in power and taking the capitalist road."[9] Simultaneously, erroneous political criticisms were carried out in the ideological field against the cultural and academic sectors.

Particularly, during the concluding phase of the Sino-Soviet Polemics, the "Ninth Commentaries" published on July 14, 1964, systematically summarized Mao Zedong's theories and policies on preventing the restoration of capitalism, forming 15 key points.

The second key point stated: "The socialist society is a long historical stage. In a socialist society, there still exist classes and class struggle, the struggle between the socialist and capitalist paths. A socialist revolution in the economic field (the ownership of means of production) alone is insufficient and unstable. There must also be thorough socialist revolutions in the political and ideological fields. In the political and ideological realms, the struggle between socialism and capitalism for dominance will take a very long time to resolve. It cannot be solved within decades and will require a century or even several centuries to succeed."

The fourth key point proposed: "The mass movements of big debates, big disclosures, and big discussions, created by our people during the long revolutionary struggle, are an important form of revolutionary struggle, relying on the masses to resolve internal and enemy contradictions."[10]

Before the launch of the "Great Cultural Revolution," these "leftist" erroneous guiding thoughts had not yet fully dominated the overall situation, and their impact was somewhat constrained. However, during the "Great Cultural Revolution," after evolving into the "theory of continuing the revolution under the dictatorship of the proletariat," their consequences became increasingly apparent.

After the Eleventh Plenary Session of the Eighth Central Committee of the CPC, schools across the country formed Red Guard organizations, taking to the streets and society. Under slogans like "seize power from those in authority taking the capitalist road," "overthrow reactionary bourgeois academic authorities," and "sweep away all ghosts and monsters," they severely disrupted normal social order.

On August 18, 1966, Mao Zedong ascended Tiananmen to attend a mass rally of a million people in the capital, celebrating the "Great Cultural Revolution," and met with representatives of the Red Guards. In early September, the Central Committee of the CPC and the State Council issued a notice about organizing students and teachers from other regions to visit Beijing to observe the "Great Cultural Revolution," initiating a nationwide mass "exchange tour."

From August 18 to late November, Mao Zedong met with the Red Guards from various regions six times, totaling 11 million attendees.

These actions significantly accelerated the rapid rise of mass movements represented by the Red Guards nationwide.

Mao Zedong's primary motivation for launching the "Great Cultural Revolution" was to prevent the Party and the country from changing color, essentially to "prevent the restoration of capitalism," as he described it. He believed he had found a new way to effectively and from the bottom up expose the dark sides of the Party and the state. This method was the mass movement of big democracy.

On February 3, 1967, in the Great Hall of the People, he met with Kapo, a member of the Politburo and Secretary of the Central Committee of the Albanian Labor Party, and Baluku, a member of the Politburo, Deputy Prime Minister, and Minister of Defense of Albania. Mao said to them: "In the past five years, we have only addressed individual issues and individuals, conducted struggles in the cultural field, in rural areas, and in factories, such as the socialist education movement. These efforts did not solve the problems; we had not found a form or method to expose our dark sides openly and comprehensively from the bottom up." He added, "The only way to solve such problems is to mobilize the masses. Without the masses, we have no way."[11]

Mao Zedong believed in the power of the masses throughout his life. In July 1945, he told Huang Yanpei, who was visiting Yan'an: "We have found a new path to escape the cyclical pattern. This new path is democracy. Only by letting the people supervise the government will the government not slacken. Only when everyone takes responsibility will the regime not collapse."[12]

However, if mass movements are well-guided, they can have a significant positive impact. If not, especially if leadership is completely abandoned, they can have substantial negative effects. The chaotic situation at the beginning of the "Great Cultural Revolution" is a prime example. Red Guard organizations, under slogans like "rebellion is justified" and "destroy the four olds,"[13] destroyed historical relics, persecuted so-called "black gangs," "capitalist roaders," "monsters and demons," and "landlords, rich peasants, counter-revolutionaries, bad elements, and rightists," creating a serious state of anarchy.

Under the impact of the Red Guards and mass movements, the National People's Congress and its Standing Committee could not function normally, the CPPCC and its local committees ceased activities, democratic parties stopped operating, public security, procuratorial and judicial organs were attacked, and socialist legality was trampled upon. The "big debates, big disclosures, big-character posters, and big discussions" of big democracy lost their legal constraints, and without proper guidance, the mass movements became like runaway horses, easily exploited by a few ambitious and conspiratorial individuals for personal vendettas.

By January 1967, Mao Zedong clearly supported the power seizure struggle by the rebels in Shanghai, describing it as "a class overthrowing another class, a great revolution." He sent a congratulatory telegram to the revolutionary rebel groups in Shanghai in the name of the Central Committee of the CPC, the State Council, the Central Military Commission, and the Central Cultural Revolution Group. From then on, the power seizure trend intensified, and various rebel organizations began to split and even engage in armed conflicts. Nationwide, under the banner of "criticizing the bourgeois reactionary line," the trend of "doubting everything," "overthrowing everything," and "total civil war" quickly spread.

To control the situation, with Mao Zedong's approval, the Central Committee of the CPC and the Central Military Commission issued the "Decision on Resolutely Supporting the Revolutionary Leftist Masses by the PLA" on January 23, 1967. The military sent personnel to participate in the "three supports" and "two militaries" initiatives.[14] Particularly, military control played a crucial role in maintaining stability in key areas. On January 11, 1967, the Central Committee of the CPC decided to place all local radio stations under military control. Subsequently, public security organs, civil aviation, railways, coal mines, and transportation departments were also placed under military control.

On March 19, 1967, Mao Zedong approved a notice submitted by Zhou Enlai, canceling the previously planned mass exchange tours scheduled for spring.

To stabilize the national situation and further understand the actual progress of the "Great Cultural Revolution," Mao Zedong embarked on an inspection tour of North China, Central-South China, and East China on July 14, 1967. This was his first trip outside Beijing since returning on July 18, 1966, and it lasted until September 23, 1967.

In his talks during this inspection, he repeatedly emphasized the need for revolutionary mass organizations to achieve great revolutionary unity. He stated: "Within the working class, no fundamental conflicts of interest exist. Under the dictatorship of the proletariat, there is even less reason for the working class to split into two antagonistic factions." "Revolutionary Red Guards and revolutionary student organizations must achieve great revolutionary unity. As long as both factions are revolutionary mass organizations, they must achieve great revolutionary unity under revolutionary principles."

When discussing who should be the core of revolutionary unity, Mao Zedong said: "The issue of 'taking me as the core' must be resolved. The masses recognize the core in struggle and practice, not self-proclaimed. It is foolish to claim oneself as the core."

Mao Zedong also specifically pointed out: "Red Guards need to be educated and their studies strengthened. Tell the revolutionary rebel leaders and young Red Guards that now is the time they will most likely make mistakes." This indicates that he was beginning to worry about the deviations in the mass movement, particularly the Red Guard movement.

Due to Mao Zedong's high prestige among the masses, his call for revolutionary unity and triple combination played a significant role in stabilizing the situation quickly.

In addition to calling for revolutionary unity among mass organizations, cadre issues were also a key focus of Mao Zedong's inspection tour.

He pointed out: "Properly handling cadres is key to implementing the revolutionary triple combination, consolidating revolutionary unity, and achieving success in the struggle, criticism, and transformation within each unit. This issue must be resolved well."

> The vast majority of cadres are good; only a very small number are not. We need to rectify those within the Party who are taking the capitalist road, but they are a small handful. Among our cadres, aside from those who have surrendered to the enemy, defected, or betrayed us, the vast majority have done some good deeds over the past few decades! We must unite the majority of cadres. Cadres who have made mistakes, including serious ones, as long as they are not stubborn and repeatedly refuse to change, should be united

and educated. We should broaden the scope of education and narrow the scope of attack, using the formula of "unity—criticism and self-criticism—unity" to resolve our internal contradictions. During criticism and struggle, we should engage in ideological struggle, not physical struggle or disguised forms of physical struggle. Some comrades who have made mistakes may not understand immediately; they should be given time to reflect. They must be allowed to have moments of vacillation; once they understand, they might have doubts again when faced with certain issues. We must allow cadres to make mistakes and correct them. We should not overthrow them just because they make a mistake. ... We need to liberate a group of cadres and let them come forward.

He further explained as follows:

Why have the masses criticized and struggled against some cadres? One reason is that they have implemented the bourgeois reactionary line, which angers the masses. Another reason is that they have become officials, earning high salaries, thinking highly of themselves, and putting on airs. They do not consult the masses, do not treat people equally, are undemocratic, and like to scold and reprimand others, thus severely alienating themselves from the masses. This results in grievances among the masses. Normally, there is no opportunity to speak out, but during the Great Proletarian Cultural Revolution, these grievances explode, creating significant trouble for these cadres. In the future, we must learn from this and solve the issue of the relationship between superiors and subordinates, as well as the relationship between cadres and the masses. In the future, cadres should go down to the grassroots level, see the situation for themselves, consult with the masses more often, and become students of the masses.[15]

A year after launching the "Great Cultural Revolution," Mao Zedong emphasized the liberation of cadres and stated that the vast majority of cadres were good for a reason. He understood that since the start of the "Great Cultural Revolution," the cadres who struggled to keep up with the changing situation and resisted the mass movement were often the leaders. However, the leadership cadres were also the ones most severely impacted by the "Great Cultural Revolution." Yet, the future restoration of normal order would still depend on these leadership cadres.

The question whether to completely overthrow these leadership cadres or continue to use them through criticism and education distinguished Mao Zedong from ambitious conspirators like Lin Biao and Jiang Qing.

Not long after the start of the "Great Cultural Revolution," at the Central Work Conference held from October 7 to 28, 1966, Mao Zedong said as follows:

> Aren't the students very aggressive now? Unexpected things have come up. Since they have come up, let's deal with them. The impact, in my view, is beneficial. Over the years, we have not considered many issues; now, we must think about them. It's merely making some mistakes; what's the big deal? If there's a mistake in the line, it can be corrected. Who wants to overthrow you? I do not want to overthrow you, and I believe the Red Guards do not necessarily want to overthrow you either. I have read almost all the briefings from this meeting. I am worried that you cannot pass the test.[16]

In February 1967, at a central meeting presided over by Zhou Enlai, senior leaders such as Tan Zhenlin, Chen Yi, Ye Jianying, Li Fuchun, Li Xiannian, Xu Xiangqian, and Nie Rongzhen openly opposed members of the Central Cultural Revolution Group like Jiang Qing, Chen Boda, Kang Sheng, and Zhang Chunqiao. This confrontation was later stigmatized as the "February Adverse Current." However, Mao Zedong did not agree to completely overthrow these leaders. When Wang Li, Guan Feng, and Qi Benyu subsequently proposed "attacking a small handful within the military," Mao Zedong immediately stopped them. Later, Wang Li, Guan Feng, and Qi Benyu were put under investigation, curbing the extreme leftist forces.

By September 1968, revolutionary committees had been established in various provinces, cities, and autonomous regions. From October 13 to 31, the Expanded Twelfth Plenary Session of the Eighth Central Committee of the CPC was held in Beijing. Under highly abnormal political circumstances, the session passed a resolution to "expel Liu Shaoqi from the Party forever and remove him from all his positions inside and outside the Party," resulting in the largest wrongful case in the history of the People's Republic of China. It was not redressed until after the Third Plenary Session of the Eleventh Central Committee of the CPC.

The Ninth National Congress of the CPC was held in Beijing from April 1 to 24, 1969. Lin Biao delivered the political report on behalf of the Central Committee. The Party Constitution adopted by the congress stated that Lin Biao was "the closest comrade-in-arms and successor of Comrade Mao Zedong." Key figures and trusted followers of the Lin Biao and Jiang Qing factions entered the Central Committee.

After the Ninth National Congress, Mao Zedong hoped to bring the "Great Cultural Revolution" to a relatively satisfactory conclusion.

According to Mao Zedong's vision for the "Great Cultural Revolution," after the Ninth National Congress had essentially resolved the Party's reconstruction issues, the Fourth National People's Congress needed to be convened as soon as possible to address government reconstruction issues. On March 7, 1970, Mao Zedong proposed convening the Fourth National People's Congress and amending the constitution, suggesting the abolition of the position of State Chairman. Lin Biao, however, persistently advocated for the establishment of the State Chairman position.

From August 23 to September 6, 1970, the Second Plenary Session of the Ninth Central Committee of the CPC was held at the Lushan People's Theater.

On the eve of the plenary session, August 22, Mao Zedong presided over a meeting of the Standing Committee of the Political Bureau of the Central Committee of the CPC to discuss the agenda of the plenary session and other matters. Lin Biao, Zhou Enlai, Chen Boda, and Kang Sheng attended.

During the meeting, when discussing the constitutional amendment and whether to establish the position of State Chairman, everyone except Mao Zedong favored establishing the position to unify the roles of Party Chairman and State Chairman. Mao Zedong insisted on not establishing the State Chairman, saying: "Establishing the State Chairman is merely a formality. My proposal to amend the constitution is precisely to consider not having a State Chairman. We have received many foreign guests, but it's okay not to meet them; some have not been met. Being State Chairman or head of state and not meeting foreign guests seems somewhat inappropriate. However, the main point is still the Party's leadership and the State Council's administrative responsibility." "If you want the State Chairman, go ahead; I won't do it."

Sensing something, he specifically emphasized: "We must make this plenary session a united and victorious one, not a divisive and failed one."[17]

On the afternoon of August 23, the Second Plenary Session of the Ninth Central Committee of the CPC opened. Lin Biao continued the discussion on amending the constitution and spoke about the issue of establishing the position of State Chairman. He said: "This time, I have studied this constitution, and it reflects a distinctive feature: it formally enshrines Chairman Mao as the great leader, head of state, and supreme commander, and Mao Zedong Thought as the guiding ideology of the entire nation in legal form. This is excellent! Very good! It can be said to be the soul of the constitution." He added: "We say Chairman Mao is a genius, and I still hold this view."[18]

During the group discussions, a peculiar phenomenon emerged, unprecedented in previous central meetings. Chen Boda and several key members of the Lin Biao faction, including Wu Faxian, Ye Qun, Li Zuopeng, and Qiu Huizuo, disrupted the meeting agenda by making speeches in their respective groups. Their speeches defended the establishment of the State Chairman and the "genius theory," aligning with Lin Biao's speech and a selected compilation of quotes on "genius." Under their instigation, many attendees, unaware of the underlying agenda, mistakenly believed, as Chen Boda claimed, that "some people are exploiting Chairman Mao's modesty to undermine Mao Zedong Thought," and thus, many spoke in favor of establishing the position of State Chairman. The atmosphere of the meeting grew increasingly tense, shifting the central theme of this plenary session.

With his rich political experience, Mao Zedong sensed the subtle signs from the briefings containing the speeches of Chen Boda and others, as well as the abnormal situations during the group discussions.

On August 25, Mao Zedong held separate talks with Lin Biao, Zhou Enlai, Chen Boda, and Kang Sheng, the members of the Standing Committee of the Political Bureau of the Central Committee. He then convened an expanded meeting of the Standing Committee of the Political Bureau of the Central Committee with the group leaders.

Mao Zedong announced to those present: "Just now, after consulting with several Standing Committee members, we believe that the issues currently being discussed in each group do not align with the original three items on the plenary session agenda. The issue of establishing the position of State Chairman should not be raised again. Whoever insists on it can take the position themselves, but I won't! I advise you, Lin Biao, not to become State Chairman either!"

Mao Zedong continued: "Originally, our meeting was intended to be a good, united, and victorious meeting. It has now turned into a meeting of division and failure. We should strive to have a united meeting and achieve greater victory. It is not a big deal if this can't be done and division persists. Our Party has endured setbacks and has been tempered through numerous trials. If things go poorly, I will retreat to the mountains, and you can continue the meeting. Once it's over, I'll come back down. If necessary, I'll resign as Chairman of the Central Committee."[19]

This meeting decided to immediately cease discussion on Lin Biao's speech, retract the briefings containing Chen Boda's speech, and order Chen Boda and others to make self-criticisms.

On August 31, Mao Zedong wrote a lengthy comment in response to the compilation "Selected Quotes from Engels, Lenin, and Chairman Mao on the Concept of Genius," edited by Chen Boda. The next day, Mao Zedong added the title "My Opinion" to his comment and included the term "Comrade" before Chen Boda's name, distributing it to the entire plenary session. The full text read as follows:

> Comrade Chen Boda compiled this material and has misled many comrades. First, there is no quotation from Marx here. Second, only one quote from Engels is included, and *The Eighteenth Brumaire of Louis Bonaparte* is not one of Marx's primary works. Third, there are five quotes from Lenin. The fifth quote states that leaders must be tested, trained, educated for a long time, and be able to cooperate well with each other, listing four conditions. Among the comrades of our Central Committee, not many meet these conditions. For example, in my cooperation with Comrade Chen Boda, the so-called genius theorist, we have never coordinated well on major issues over the past thirty

years, let alone very well. Just to cite the three Lushan meetings as examples: He sided with Peng Dehuai at the first meeting. During the discussion on the Seventy Articles on Industry at the second meeting, he said he went down the mountain after a few days without any clear reason. After descending, he disappeared somewhere. This time, however, he coordinated very well by launching a surprise attack, stirring up trouble, and hoping for chaos everywhere, as if trying to flatten Lushan and stop the earth from turning. My words merely illustrate the broad intentions of our so-called genius theorist—whether these stem from a clear conscience rather than ambition, I do not know. As for whether the proletarian world will be thrown into chaos, Lushan flattened, or the earth stopped, I think not. An ancient person who climbed Lushan once said: "The people of Qi do not worry about the collapse of the sky." We should not emulate that person. Finally, regarding my own words, they will not help him much. I said that talent is not primarily due to innate genius but to social practice. Comrade Chen Boda has quoted Comrade Lin Biao seven times, as if he found a treasure. Lin Biao and I have discussed this issue and agree on the historical and philosophical debate over whether it is heroes or the masses who create history, whether human knowledge (and talent falls within this category) is innate or acquired—whether it is the idealist theory of pre-existence or the materialist theory of reflection. We can only stand on the Marxist-Leninist position and must not be confused with Chen Boda's rumors and sophistry. We also believe that this Marxist epistemological issue still requires further study and is far from being settled. We hope comrades adopt this attitude, unite, and strive for greater victories without being misled by those who claim to understand Marx but do not.[20]

The final sentence, "Comrade Chen Boda has quoted Comrade Lin Biao seven times, as if he found a treasure," was deleted by Mao Zedong before it was distributed to the plenary session. He even sent the revised version to Lin Biao, demonstrating his protective and salvaging attitude toward him.

Mao Zedong waited a long time for Lin Biao to change his mind. However, Lin Biao chose a path of no return, refusing to reflect, continuing to engage in factional activities, and ultimately plotting an armed coup.

Mao Zedong gradually became aware of Lin Biao's underhanded activities. From August 15, he left Beijing for an inspection tour, passing through Wuhan, Changsha, Nanchang, Hangzhou, and Shanghai, and returned to Beijing on September 12.

At each stop, Mao Zedong met with local Party, government, and military leaders to address the issue of Lin Biao. He warned them: "You must uphold Marxism-Leninism and reject revisionism; you must maintain unity and avoid division, factionalism, and parochialism; you must act with integrity and avoid conspiracy and intrigue." He also made it clear: "Some people see that I am getting old and think that I'm about to pass away, so they are eager to become Chairman, to split the Party, and to seize power. This Lushan Conference is a struggle between two headquarters." With great confidence, he declared: "I don't believe our army will rebel. Even within the military, there are divisions, regiments, and command, political, and logistic departments. They cannot mobilize the military to do harm."[21]

Mao Zedong's warnings along the way played a significant role in unifying thoughts and preventing potential disasters. However, some of Lin Biao's loyalists secretly reported Mao's conversations to Lin Biao.

On September 13, 1971, the Trident aircraft No. 256 carrying Lin Biao and others crashed in Öndörkhaan, Mongolia.

The Lin Biao Incident objectively marked the bankruptcy of the "Great Cultural Revolution" theory and practice. This plunged Mao Zedong into great mental anguish and self-blame. However, he quickly regained his composure and, with extraordinary political courage, tried to rectify the perceived errors. He actively supported Zhou Enlai in managing the central daily affairs, bringing a turn for the better in various aspects of work.

On the evening of November 14, 1971, Mao Zedong met with the leaders of the Chengdu Military Region and the Sichuan Provincial Party and government who had come to Beijing to attend a symposium on the Chengdu region. After the discussion began, Ye Jianying joined the meeting. Mao Zedong publicly stated as follows:

> You should stop talking about the so-called "February Adverse Current." What was the nature of the "February Adverse Current"? It was their oppo-

sition to Lin Biao, Chen Boda, Wang Li, Guan Feng, and Qi Benyu. Wang, Guan, and Qi wanted to overthrow everyone, including the Premier and the veteran marshals. Naturally, the veteran marshals were angry and vented some frustrations. They acted openly at a Party meeting, causing an uproar at the Huairen Hall! They had some shortcomings, but it was acceptable for them to express their grievances. They could have come to me to discuss the matter. At that time, we were not fully clear on the situation. Wang, Guan, and Qi had not yet exposed themselves. Some issues take many years to fully understand."[22]

On the evening of November 20, Mao Zedong met with the leaders of the Wuhan Military Region and the Hubei Provincial Party and government who had come to Beijing to attend a symposium on the Wuhan region. Mao said: "A Marxist-Leninist party should not pursue actions or use terminology that are detrimental to the people. Has the term 'four greats' been revised? (Zhou Enlai replied: 'Only one is still in use.')[23] As for 'three loyalties,' I don't understand it. You should meet to discuss this and abolish inappropriate terms or adjectives. Stop using them."[24]

At noon on January 6, 1972, Mao Zedong met with Zhou Enlai and Ye Jianying to discuss foreign affairs. After the discussion, Mao said: "The 'February Adverse Current' has been tested by time and has proven to be non-existent. In the future, do not mention the 'February Adverse Current.' Please convey this to Comrade Chen Yi." Ye Jianying immediately went to the hospital to relay Mao's message to the critically ill Chen Yi.

On the same day, Marshal Chen Yi passed away due to illness. On January 10, a memorial service was held for Chen Yi at the Babaoshan Revolutionary Cemetery in Beijing. Mao Zedong personally attended to bid farewell to his old comrade-in-arms who had fought alongside him since Jinggang Mountain.

Before the memorial service began, Mao Zedong emotionally told Chen Yi's wife, Zhang Qian: "Comrade Chen Yi was a good person, a good comrade. He contributed to the Chinese revolution and the world revolution, and he achieved great merits, which has already been concluded. He was different from Xiang Ying. Comrade Chen Yi followed the Central Committee's line.

Comrade Chen Yi could unite people. Lin Biao opposed me, but Chen Yi supported me. If Lin Biao's conspiracy had succeeded, they would have eliminated all our old comrades. He also stated that Deng Xiaoping's issue was an internal contradiction among the people."[25]

Mao Zedong's series of speeches not only reversed the distortions but also involved a series of policy adjustments and significant personnel changes. Mao hoped that the Fourth National People's Congress could be successfully convened through these adjustments, thereby creating the conditions to end the "Great Cultural Revolution."

Mao Zedong naturally relied on his capable comrade, Zhou Enlai, to turn these plans into reality.

During his tenure in charge of the daily work of the Central Committee, Zhou Enlai raised the issue of concentrating on criticizing the extreme leftist ideology. This made it possible to end the "Great Cultural Revolution."

However, it was precisely on this issue that Mao Zedong and Zhou Enlai held different views. Mao believed that the primary task was still to oppose the "extreme right." On December 17, 1972, Mao Zedong pointed out in a conversation: "Should we criticize the extreme left or the extreme right? Criticize the extreme left ideology, but only a little. The essence of the Lin Biao line is extreme right, revisionist, divisive, conspiratorial, and traitorous to the Party and the country."[26] The subsequent Criticize Lin and Criticize Confucius Campaign thwarted efforts to end the "Great Cultural Revolution" once again.

Starting from the second half of 1974, preparations for the Fourth National People's Congress resumed. Jiang Qing and her faction saw this as a prime opportunity to sideline Zhou Enlai and expand their power.

At this critical moment in the preparations for the Fourth National People's Congress, on October 4, Mao Zedong proposed appointing Deng Xiaoping as the First Vice Premier of the State Council. Since 1972, Mao repeatedly suggested reinstating Deng Xiaoping. In March 1973, the Central Committee decided to restore Deng Xiaoping's Party organization life and his position as Vice Premier of the State Council. In December of the same year, another decision was made to appoint Deng as a member of the Political Bureau of the Central Committee and the Central Military Commission, involving him in central and military leadership work. As Zhou Enlai's health deteriorated, Mao increasingly relied on Deng Xiaoping.

In the notice issued by the Central Committee on October 11 regarding the preparations for the Fourth National People's Congress, Mao's opinion was conveyed: "The Great Proletarian Cultural Revolution has been going on for eight years. Now, stability is good. The whole Party and the military must unite."[27]

Fearing changes, Jiang Qing and her faction sent Wang Hongwen, Vice Chairman of the Central Committee, to Changsha on October 13 to report on Zhou Enlai and Deng Xiaoping to Mao. After listening, Mao criticized Wang, saying: "If you have opinions, discuss them face to face. This approach is not good! You must unite with Comrade Xiaoping." He also advised him: "When you return, talk more with the Premier and Comrade Jianying, and avoid aligning with Jiang Qing. Be cautious of her."[28]

On November 12, in Changsha, Mao met with President Rubai of the Presidential Council of South Yemen, accompanied by Deng Xiaoping. After the meeting, Mao had a private conversation with Deng, expressing support for Deng's struggle against Jiang Qing in the Political Bureau of the Central Committee and his displeasure with Jiang Qing: "I am also unhappy with imposing things on others." When discussing Deng's heavy responsibilities, he said: "First Vice Premier and Chief of the General Staff. The Chief of the General Staff has no tasks now, but if danger arises, there will be tasks."[29]

On the same day, Mao Zedong read a letter from Jiang Qing that included a self-criticism, and he made the following remarks: "Don't appear in public too often, don't criticize documents, and don't take charge of forming a cabinet (acting as the power behind the scenes). You have accumulated a lot of resentment; you need to unite with the majority. This is my earnest advice." He added, "It is valuable for a person to have self-awareness."[30] Between the lines, one can sense a complex mix of love and resentment.

Mao Zedong always clearly distinguished between personal and state affairs, never letting personal feelings interfere with state matters.

On December 23, 24, 25, and 27, in Changsha, Mao Zedong listened to reports from Zhou Enlai and Wang Hongwen on the preparations for the Fourth National People's Congress. During these discussions, Mao, in Wang

Hongwen's presence, referred to Jiang Qing, Zhang Chunqiao, Wang Hongwen, and Yao Wenyuan as the "Gang of Four" for the first time, stating: "The 'Gang of Four' should not continue their actions. The Central Committee has limited members and must unite. Avoid factionalism; those who engage in factions will stumble. If you fall, it is good to get back up. Jiang Qing has ambitions. Do you think she does? I think she does. I am working on Jiang Qing, advising her on "three nos": do not arbitrarily criticize, do not seek the limelight, and do not participate in organizing the government (cabinet formation). Also, regarding Jiang Qing, we must take a dialectical view; she was correct in criticizing Liu Shaoqi and Lin Biao but claiming that the Premier's mistakes were the eleventh-line errors is incorrect."

Discussing Party and state personnel arrangements, Mao said: "Comrade Xiaoping is politically strong and a rare talent. At the Second Plenary Session, he should be added as a Standing Committee member and Vice Chairman, and appointed as Vice Chairman of the Military Commission, First Vice Premier of the State Council, and Chief of the General Staff." He also told Zhou Enlai: "You are still our Premier. After the Fourth National People's Congress, you should focus on recuperating, and Comrade Xiaoping will take over the State Council's work."

Regarding personnel arrangements for the National People's Congress, Mao specifically mentioned several individuals. He agreed to nominate Zhu De as chairman of the Standing Committee, with Dong Biwu and Soong Ching-ling as the top two vice chairmen. He also proposed listing the full names of all vice chairmen. He inquired: "What about Zhang Naiqi and Liang Shuming? Are they not delegates?" Zhou Enlai replied: "Liang Shuming is a member of the CPPCC, and Zhang Naiqi still carries the rightist label." Mao immediately stated: "Remove the rightist label from him."[31] He also asked Zhou Enlai to convey his regards to Guo Moruo.[32]

At 3 a.m. on December 27, Mao had a private meeting with Zhou Enlai to discuss personnel arrangements and other issues. During this conversation, Mao stated: "We need stability and unity, and we must boost the national economy."[33]

Thus, the attempt by Jiang Qing and her faction to gain more power through the Fourth National People's Congress fell through.

In January 1975, at the Second Plenary Session of the Tenth Central Committee, Deng Xiaoping was elected Vice Chairman and Standing Committee member of the Central Committee. At the subsequent First Session of the Fourth National People's Congress, based on the Central Committee's recommendation, Deng Xiaoping was appointed Vice Premier of the State Council. With Mao Zedong's support, Deng began to oversee the central daily work.

At the beginning of 1975, Deng Xiaoping began a comprehensive rectification of various sectors. The rectification program was based on Mao Zedong's "Three Directives." First, to study theory and oppose revisionism; second, to maintain stability and unity; and third, to boost the national economy. He stated: "These three directives are interconnected and form a whole. We cannot discard any of them. They are the guiding principles for our work during this period."[34]

This rectification came suddenly but was well-planned, theoretical, methodical, and strategic. With Mao Zedong's support, Deng Xiaoping convened a series of meetings starting on February 9, 1975, including the National Industrial Secretary Conference, the Steel Industry Symposium, the National Agricultural Learn from Dazhai Conference, the Expanded Meeting of the Central Military Commission, the National Defense Industry Key Enterprises Meeting, and the Rural Work Symposium. He also received reports from the Chinese Academy of Sciences, initiating a comprehensive rectification that quickly yielded results and garnered widespread support.

After several months of rectification, there was a significant improvement in the national industrial and agricultural production and transportation sectors. Intellectuals, long suppressed by extreme leftist ideology, began to feel a renewed sense of pride. More importantly, with Mao Zedong's support, Deng Xiaoping engaged in a direct struggle against Jiang Qing's faction, which forced Jiang Qing to submit a written self-criticism to Mao Zedong and the Political Bureau of the Central Committee on June 28.[35] This rare event greatly weakened the influence of the extreme leftist ideology.

However, Deng Xiaoping's rectification efforts, targeting the various factional issues created by the "Great Cultural Revolution," inevitably clashed with the vested interests of the "Gang of Four." They were biding their time, waiting for an opportunity to strike back.

On October 19, after meeting with foreign guests, Mao Zedong discussed with Li Xiannian and Wang Dongxing the letter from Liu Bing and others at Tsinghua University accusing Chi Qun and Xie Jingyi. Mao said, "I find the motives of the letter questionable." He added, "I am in Beijing; why did they write the letter to Xiaoping instead of directly to me? Tell Xiaoping to be cautious and not be deceived. Xiaoping is biased toward Liu Bing."[36]

On November 2, Mao Zedong told Mao Yuanxin, "There are two attitudes: one is dissatisfaction with the 'Great Cultural Revolution,' and the other is to settle accounts, to settle the accounts of the 'Great Cultural Revolution.' The targets of Liu Bing and others in their letter are aimed at me." He also said, "The issues at Tsinghua are not isolated; they reflect the current struggle between two lines."[37]

At the end of the year, Mao Zedong approved the launch of the Criticize Deng, Counter the Right-Deviationist Reversal-of-Verdicts Trend Campaign. With the agitation of the "Gang of Four," the country once again plunged into chaos.

However, what Jiang Qing and her allies could not have imagined was that on April 7, 1976, even while Mao Zedong mistakenly labeled the "Tiananmen Incident"[38] as a "counter-revolutionary incident," he proposed Hua Guofeng as the First Vice Chairman of the Central Committee and Premier of the State Council. When Jiang Qing suggested expelling Deng Xiaoping from the Party, Mao proposed, "Retain his Party membership and observe his future actions."

"The just lasts forever, while the selfish lasts for a short time."[39] As Mao Zedong approached the end of his life, his critical decisions for the CPC and the People's Republic of China can be seen as pivotal to the fate of the nation.

CHAPTER 19

Opening the Door to Normalizing China-US Relations

I also mentioned during the Geneva Conference that we could have some contact with the United States. In fact, the United States may not necessarily want to make contact. Having a deadlock with the United States for twenty years has been advantageous to us. We must ensure that when the United States finally comes to us, dressed up and ready, they find themselves surprised by China's strength and resilience. If you don't acknowledge us now, there will come a day when you have to.

MAO ZEDONG,
Speech on the International Situation (June 16, 1958)

On July 16, 1971 (Beijing Time), a joint announcement by China and the United States shocked the world.

The announcement read as follows:

Premier Zhou Enlai and Dr. Henry Kissinger, Assistant to the President of the United States for National Security Affairs, held talks in Beijing from July 9 to 11, 1971.

President Nixon had expressed his desire to visit the People's Republic of China. Premier Zhou Enlai, on behalf of the Chinese government, invited

President Nixon to visit China before May 1972. President Nixon happily accepted this invitation.

The meeting between the leaders of China and the United States aimed to seek the normalization of relations between the two countries and to exchange views on issues of mutual concern.[1]

No one had anticipated that these two nations, adversaries for over twenty years and combatants on the Korean battlefield, would so swiftly come to the negotiating table for normalizing relations.

In fact, this dramatic shift was the result of a series of changes in the international Cold War landscape from the late 1960s to the early 1970s.

On August 20, 1968, the Soviet Union invaded Czechoslovakia, brutally interfering in the internal affairs of a sovereign state, and subsequently put forward the Brezhnev Doctrine, known for its "Socialist Family" and "Limited Sovereignty" concepts. This event had significant implications for both US-Soviet and Sino-Soviet relations. It demonstrated that, amid the US-Soviet standoff, the Soviet Union had moved from a period of policy adjustment to a more aggressive stance. It also indicated that the Soviet Union, with a million troops on the Sino-Soviet and Soviet-Mongolian borders, posed a threat of armed invasion to China.

To Mao Zedong, the Soviet invasion of Czechoslovakia showed that the Soviet Union had transformed into a "social-imperialist" state—socialist in name but imperialist in reality—thus more aggressive and adventurous than the United States. This confirmed his mid-1960s judgment that the greatest threat to China's national security might come from the north.

From that point on, Mao repeatedly discussed with foreign guests the possibility of a new world war. On October 5, 1968, Mao told Albania's Defense Minister Beqir Balluku: "It seems the world is still in turmoil because there are contradictions and struggles. How it will be chaotic is hard to say now. A world war? That's one way of chaos. No world war, but local wars, that's another way of chaos."[2] He also expressed, "We do not wish to fight, but if they want to fight, we will have to fight."

On November 28, 1968, Mao further raised the danger of world war with Chairman Ted Hill of the Communist Party of Australia (Marxist-

Leninist). He believed that the current state of neither war nor revolution would not last long. He said, "If a war breaks out, the United States and the Soviet Union, the two major powers, can fight, followed by Japan, West Germany, and Italy, the former defeated countries. As for Britain and France, they are less inclined to fight." He noted, "The situation after World War II seems somewhat different from after World War I. The defeated countries have not been able to break away from the victorious countries, not only in financial and investment aspects but also in international politics and military matters." He observed, "The two major powers in the world not only have conventional weapons but also atomic bombs. This thing is not easy to handle; they themselves know it. Khrushchev's theory is that a nuclear war would destroy the earth, with no victor. The United States says the same thing."[3]

At this moment, Mao Zedong was more acutely aware than ever of the severe threat that a combined assault by the US and the Soviet Union from the south and north could pose to China. He began seriously reflecting on the "leftist" errors in his diplomatic guiding ideology.

On March 22, 1969, during a conversation with members of the Central Cultural Revolution Group and officials including Chen Yi, Li Fuchun, Li Xiannian, Xu Xiangqian, Nie Rongzhen, and Ye Jianying, Mao candidly expressed his concerns: "It would be better to ease up a bit. We are now isolated; no one is dealing with us."[4]

On July 13, 1970, while meeting with a French government delegation, he remarked: "On some issues, countries like ours are caught between two major powers." He added, "The world is not very peaceful now. Loving independence is one thing, but others will always interfere with you."[5]

Mao also keenly observed the irreconcilable contradictions between the US and the Soviet Union over spheres of influence and identified the fatal weakness in America's global strategy—its overly dispersed military forces. On November 17, 1968, in a meeting with Vietnamese Prime Minister Pham Van Dong, Mao said, "The United States is repeating its past mistakes by spreading its forces too thinly. This is not only our observation; even Nixon says so. They are spreading their forces too thinly not just in the Americas and Europe but also in Asia."[6]

From this strategic weakness of the US, Mao saw an opportunity for a breakthrough in Chinese diplomacy. On July 24, 1972, in a discussion on international issues with Zhou Enlai and others, Mao said, "Now, the US, Britain, France, and West Germany all want to push the Soviet Union eastward, to push the Soviets toward China, so that the West remains conflict-free." He continued, "The Soviet Union is making a show of attacking China but is actually focusing on Europe and the Mediterranean." Mao concluded, "We can exploit the contradictions between the two superpowers, which is our policy. We should try to win over one of the two superpowers rather than fight on two fronts."[7] This indicated that Mao was contemplating how to establish a new framework for Chinese diplomacy.

After the Zhenbao Island Incident, Mao's first major strategic adjustment was to make preventing a large-scale armed invasion by the Soviet Union the central task of strategic defense, thus shifting the focus of military preparations from the south to the north.

On March 15, 1969, while receiving reports from Zhou Enlai and others on the Zhenbao Island self-defense counterattack, Mao discussed how to deal with a potential invasion war initiated by the Soviet Union. He said, "The Northeast, North China, and Northwest must prepare for a Soviet invasion, while the southern provinces must prepare for the Americans. If they don't come, we are prepared; if they do come, we won't suffer a loss. Without preparation, we would suffer."[8]

At the same time, on May 24, 1969, the Chinese government issued a statement on the Sino-Soviet border issue, reiterating its consistent position that boundary disputes should be resolved through diplomatic negotiations and maintaining the status quo at the border to avoid conflict until a resolution is reached.

On September 11, Premier Zhou Enlai met with Soviet Premier Alexei Kosygin. On October 20, the Sino-Soviet border negotiations formally began, marking the longest border negotiation in history. Both governments paid significant attention to these talks. The head of the Soviet delegation was Deputy Foreign Minister Kuznetsov, while the head of the Chinese delegation was Deputy Foreign Minister Qiao Guanhua.

Simultaneously, based on the agreement reached by the two premiers at the airport, ambassadors were exchanged, and annual trade negotiations were resumed. These efforts played a positive role in easing the tense relations between China and the Soviet Union. However, the situation of enormous military pressure exerted by the Soviet Union on the Sino-Soviet border did not fundamentally change.

Mao clearly understood that alleviating the Soviet threat to China's national security required efforts in another strategic direction. Opening the door to normalizing China-US relations was another crucial strategic adjustment Mao made based on national security interests. Efforts in this area had actually begun before the Zhenbao Island Incident.

The first step Mao took to open the door to normalizing China-US relations was to entrust Chen Yi, Xu Xiangqian, Nie Rongzhen, and Ye Jianying with studying international issues and China-US relations.

On February 19, 1969, Mao Zedong convened a meeting with members of the Central Cultural Revolution Group and officials including Chen Yi, Li Fuchun, Li Xiannian, Xu Xiangqian, Nie Rongzhen, and Ye Jianying. He proposed, "You senior leaders should study international issues, with Chen Yi leading, and Xu Xiangqian, Nie Rongzhen, and Ye Jianying participating. Some international issues are peculiar. American and British newspapers often talk about potential problems in the Soviet Union, Soviet exercises in the Far East without much publicity. We never bother with the issue of recognition. Recently, Italy and Canada want to recognize us, making Chiang Kai-shek a bit nervous, and Japan uneasy. The Japanese people are not happy with their government following the US. We should pay attention to some countries we haven't focused on before."[9]

The study conducted by the four marshals began in March and concluded in October. They concluded that Sino-Soviet contradictions were greater than Sino-American contradictions, and that US-Soviet contradictions were greater than Sino-Soviet contradictions. They assessed that a major anti-China war was unlikely to occur.[10] Strategically, China should utilize US-Soviet contradictions and consider opening relations with the US, necessitating corresponding strategies. When the Warsaw talks resumed, they suggested proactively proposing high-level talks to resolve fundamental issues between China and the US.[11] This provided a scientific basis for the Central Committee of the CPC and Mao Zedong to decisively open the door to China-US relations.

At this time, the Nixon administration in the United States further showed signs of easing China-US relations. On July 21, 1969, the US government announced the removal of certain trade restrictions with China and eased travel restrictions to China.

In December of the same year, the US ambassador to Poland, under Nixon's orders, proposed resuming ambassadorial-level talks between China and the US. Mao Zedong immediately approved the resumption of the Warsaw talks. On January 20, 1970, China-US ambassadorial-level talks, which had been suspended for more than two years, resumed.

In early March 1969, President Richard Nixon had conveyed to French President Charles de Gaulle his decision to dialogue with China, hoping de Gaulle would relay his desire to improve relations with China to the Chinese leaders.

On October 25, 1970, Nixon met with Pakistani President Yahya Khan, who was in Washington to attend the 25th anniversary celebrations of the United Nations. Nixon asked him to convey to the Chinese leaders during his visit to China the need to reopen negotiations with China. He assured that the US would not conspire with the Soviet Union against China and was willing to send a high-level envoy to China.[12] He also passed the same message to Romanian President Nicolae Ceaușescu.

On November 10, during Yahya Khan's visit to China, he had a private meeting with Zhou Enlai, where he conveyed Nixon's message. On November 14, in their fifth private meeting, Zhou Enlai verbally responded that if the US genuinely wished to resolve the Taiwan question, the Chinese government would welcome the US President's special envoy to Beijing for discussions, with the timing to be agreed upon through President Yahya Khan.[13]

On November 21, Zhou Enlai met with the visiting Vice Premier of the Romanian Council of Ministers, Ion Gheorghe Maurer. Maurer, on behalf of Ceaușescu, reiterated Nixon's message. Zhou Enlai gave a similar verbal response.

After receiving Zhou Enlai's verbal response, Henry Kissinger, on December 16, through the Pakistani channel, conveyed a reply to Premier Zhou Enlai. The reply stated, "The US government believes it would be beneficial to begin discussions in Beijing to facilitate higher-level talks. These talks in Beijing should not be limited to the Taiwan question but should include other steps aimed at improving relations between our two countries and easing tensions. However, regarding the US military presence in Taiwan, you should understand that the US government's policy is to gradually reduce its military presence in the Far East and Pacific regions as the tension in these areas eases."[14]

Thus, one major obstacle in China-US relations—the Taiwan question—had, for the first time, the possibility of being discussed at a high level between the two countries.

Meanwhile, China also sent positive signals.

On July 10, 1970, the Chinese government announced the release of the American prisoner Bishop James E. Walsh, who had been sentenced to 20 years in prison in 1960 for espionage.

On October 1, 1969, Mao Zedong invited American writer Edgar Snow and his wife to attend the National Day celebration of the People's Republic of China at Tiananmen Square.

During a conversation with Edgar Snow on December 18, 1970, Mao Zedong explicitly stated that to resolve China-US relations, it was necessary to talk with the US leadership. He said, "He (referring to Nixon) has been writing letters everywhere saying he wants to send representatives here, but we haven't published them to keep it a secret! He isn't interested in the Warsaw talks; he wants to come and talk in person. So, I say if Nixon wants to come, I am willing to talk with him. Whether the talks succeed or not, whether we argue or not, whether he comes as a traveler or as the President, it all works for me."[15] This open and accommodating attitude effectively opened the door to the US. According to Nixon, "We learned of Mao's statement within a few days after he made it."[16]

On January 11, 1971, the Romanian Ambassador to the US handed over a letter from Zhou Enlai to Henry Kissinger. The letter welcomed an American special envoy to Beijing and noted that "this letter has been reviewed by

Chairman Mao and Vice Chairman Lin Biao." In a supplementary note, Zhou Enlai for the first time expressed welcome for President Nixon to visit China.[17]

After this, secret contacts between China and the US were briefly stalled due to the continued expansion of the war in Vietnam by the US.

In April 1971, Mao Zedong approved an invitation for the American table tennis team to visit China and personally orchestrated a "Ping-Pong diplomacy" to use "small balls" to move the "big ball."

From March 28 to April 7, 1971, the 31st World Table Tennis Championships were held in Nagoya, Japan. As this was the first time a Chinese sports delegation had gone abroad to participate in an international event since the beginning of the "Great Cultural Revolution," it drew significant attention. On March 15, Mao Zedong approved Zhou Enlai's request report about sending the Chinese table tennis team to participate in the 31st World Championships in Nagoya. He even specifically instructed, "Our team should go and be prepared to lose some lives. It's better if no one dies. Be unafraid of hardship and death."[18] The request report also proposed the slogan "Friendship First, Competition Second."

On March 21, the Chinese table tennis delegation arrived in Nagoya, Japan. At that time, Mao Zedong was leading a struggle against the Lin Biao faction but still instructed his staff to relay daily reports from foreign news agencies about the reactions to the Chinese table tennis delegation. This showed the importance of China-US relations in his mind.

During the 31st World Table Tennis Championships, a dramatic scene unfolded. On the morning of April 4, an American table tennis player, Glenn Cowan, passed by the Chinese team's bus. A Chinese player waved for him to get on the bus and ride to the venue together. On the bus, the Chinese athletes talked with Cowan, and Zhuang Zedong even gave him a silk embroidery depicting Chinese scenery. At the stadium, they took a group photo together. The next morning, Cowan presented a gift to Zhuang Zedong in return. This symbolic event, reported by news agencies such as Kyodo News, the Associated Press, and Agence France-Presse, became explosive news of the championship.

During this period, the American table tennis team requested to visit China.[19] On April 3, the Ministry of Foreign Affairs and the National Sports

Commission wrote a report to Zhou Enlai on whether to invite the American table tennis team to visit China, suggesting that the time was not yet ripe. On April 4, Zhou Enlai agreed with this opinion and forwarded it to Mao Zedong.

This matter caused Mao Zedong to hesitate. On April 6, he initially approved the report. On the morning of April 7, he instructed his staff to call the Ministry of Foreign Affairs and notify them to invite the American table tennis team participating in the 31st World Table Tennis Championships in Nagoya to visit China.[20] Later, on June 3, he told the visiting Nicolae Ceaușescu, "We recently played a game of Ping-Pong."[21]

This news spread to Nagoya, overshadowing the reports of the 31st World Table Tennis Championships with the excitement of this world-shaking event.

In his memoirs, Nixon wrote as follows:

On March 15, the State Department announced the termination of all restrictions on the use of American passports for travel to mainland China. On April 6, a breakthrough occurred in a totally unexpected way: We received from the American Embassy in Tokyo that an American table tennis team competing in the world championships in Japan had been invited to visit the PRC in order to play several exhibition matches.

I was surprised as I was pleased by this news. I had never expected that the China initiative would come to fruition in the form of a Ping-Pong team. We immediately approved the acceptance of the invitation, and the Chinese responded by granting visas to several Western newsmen to cover the team's visit.

On April 14, I announced the termination of the twenty-year-old embargo between us. I also ordered a series of new steps taken for easing currency and shipping controls applying to the PRC. The same day Zhou Enlai personally welcomed our table tennis players in Beijing.[22]

On April 14, Zhou Enlai met with the invited table tennis delegations from the US, Canada, Colombia, England, and Nigeria in China. During his conversation with the American team, Zhou Enlai stated, "Your visit has opened the door for friendly exchanges between the peoples of our two countries."[23]

Following this, preparations for high-level Sino-American contacts entered a substantive phase.

On April 21, Zhou Enlai, through the Chinese Embassy in Pakistan, conveyed a message to President Nixon via the Pakistani side. The message stated: "To fundamentally restore relations between China and the United States, all US armed forces must withdraw from Taiwan and the Taiwan Strait area. This critical issue can only be resolved through direct talks between senior leaders. Therefore, the Chinese government reiterates its willingness to publicly receive a special envoy from the US, such as Dr. Kissinger, the US Secretary of State, or even the President himself in Beijing for direct discussions."[24] On April 24, President Yahya Khan of Pakistan relayed this message to Nixon.

On April 29, upon receiving this message, President Nixon immediately verbally agreed. On May 17, he instructed the US Ambassador to Pakistan to convey the following opinion: "To resolve the differences between our two countries and due to the importance placed on the normalization of relations, he is prepared to hold serious talks with the leaders of the People's Republic of China in Beijing, allowing both sides to freely raise their main concerns." He also suggested, "Dr. Kissinger should hold a secret preliminary meeting with Premier Zhou or another appropriate senior Chinese leader." He proposed the timing: "Kissinger will visit China after June 15."[25]

Five days later, on May 22, Nixon sent a supplementary message to avoid any misunderstanding: the agreement announced by the US President on May 20 regarding the US and Soviet governments' consent to draft a treaty limiting the deployment of anti-ballistic missile systems within the year would not affect the US President's policy, which is not to sign agreements targeting the People's Republic of China.[26]

Thus, the secret negotiations between China and the US advanced another step, not only broadly defining the main content of the talks but also determining the level, steps, and approximate time for "secret preliminary talks." Under these circumstances, China needed to develop a preliminary plan for China-US talks.

On May 23, following Mao Zedong's instructions, Zhou Enlai chaired a meeting of the Political Bureau of the Central Committee of the CPC to discuss China-US relations and establish the principles for talks with Nixon. After the meeting, Zhou Enlai drafted the "Report of the Political Bureau of the Central Committee of the CPC on China-US Talks," which was reviewed and approved by Mao Zedong.

The report reviewed the evolution of China-US relations since World War II, assessed the various scenarios that might arise from the preliminary talks with Kissinger and Nixon's visit to China, and proposed corresponding strategies. The report also addressed specific concerns and doubts about the China-US talks.

The report proposed eight guidelines for China-US talks, with the main points as follows:

(1) All US armed forces and military installations should be withdrawn from Taiwan and the Taiwan Strait region within a specified timeframe. This is the key issue for restoring China-US relations. If this point cannot be agreed upon in principle beforehand, Nixon's visit may be postponed.
(2) Taiwan is Chinese territory, and its liberation is China's internal affair, which foreign powers should not interfere with. Vigilance against Japanese militaristic activities in Taiwan is essential.
(3) China will strive for the peaceful liberation of Taiwan and must diligently carry out work related to Taiwan.
(4) Firm opposition to the creation of "two Chinas" or "one China, one Taiwan." If the United States wishes to establish diplomatic relations with the People's Republic of China, it must recognize the PRC as the sole legitimate government representing China.
(5) If the first, second, and fourth points are not achieved, and formal diplomatic relations cannot be established, liaison offices may be set up in each other's capitals.
(6) China will not proactively raise the issue of the United Nations. If the US brings it up, China will make it clear that it will not accept the arrangement of "two Chinas" or "one China, one Taiwan."
(7) China will not proactively raise the issue of Sino-American trade. If the US mentions it, negotiations can proceed after the principle of US military withdrawal from Taiwan is confirmed.

(8) The Chinese government advocates that the US armed forces should withdraw from the three countries of Indochina, Korea, Japan, and related countries in Southeast Asia to ensure peace in the Far East.[27]

While China was formulating its plan for the talks, Nixon and Kissinger experienced two anxious weeks. Nixon recalled, "For almost two weeks we waited, wondering what kind of decision-making process was underway in Beijing."[28]

On May 31, the Chinese government asked President Yahya Khan of Pakistan to relay a formal response to President Nixon. The message stated that Premier Zhou Enlai had carefully studied Nixon's messages from April 29, May 17, and May 22, 1971, and reported to Chairman Mao Zedong that Nixon was prepared to accept his suggestion to visit Beijing for direct talks with Chinese leaders. Chairman Mao expressed his welcome to Nixon's visit, and Premier Zhou Enlai welcomed Dr. Kissinger to China for a secret preliminary meeting to prepare for Nixon's visit and make necessary arrangements, with the timing set between June 15 and 20.[29]

Two nights later, Nixon received this letter, sealed by the Pakistani government in a diplomatic pouch. Nixon recalled, "'This is the most important communication that has come to an American President since the end of World War II,' Kissinger said when I had finished reading." "For nearly an hour, we talked about the China initiative—what it might mean to America and how delicately it must be handled lest we lose it. It was close to midnight before we noticed the time, and Kissinger rose to go." Only then did they think to toast this historic moment.[30]

On June 4, Nixon replied, saying, "President Nixon looks forward to the opportunity to exchange views personally with the leaders of the People's Republic of China." Regarding the timing of Kissinger's visit to China, the reply suggested, "Due to tight scheduling and the need to find a suitable pretext for this trip, Dr. Kissinger now finds it impossible to leave Washington before the first week of July. Therefore, President Nixon proposes that Dr. Kissinger visit China on July 9 and leave on July 11, flying directly to and from the designated Chinese airport on a Pakistani Boeing aircraft." The reply also stated, "Dr. Kissinger will be authorized to discuss a possible joint communiqué to be issued upon his return to the United States."[31]

As Kissinger's secret visit to China approached, Zhou Enlai drafted "Several Key Issues in China-US Preliminary Talks" in early July. On July 4, he submitted this report along with drafts of two announcements to Mao Zedong. Mao quickly approved them. The report outlined several key issues for Sino-American preliminary talks:

(1) The status of the People's Republic of China and the Chiang Kai-shek regime. China must expose the conspiracy of the "undetermined status of Taiwan."
(2) The agreement on US withdrawal from Taiwan and the Taiwan Strait and the liberation of Taiwan.
(3) The restoration of China's legitimate rights in the United Nations and the issue of the Chiang Kai-shek regime's representation. As long as the Chiang Kai-shek regime represents China or even just Taiwan in the UN, China will not enter.
(4) The issue of a five-nuclear-power conference. China does not support the Soviet proposal for a five-nuclear-power conference.
(5) The issue of US troop withdrawal from Indochina, South Korea, Japan, and Southeast Asia.
(6) The establishment of US liaison offices.
(7) Nixon's visit to China and the preliminary announcement issue.[32]

On July 9, at 12:15 p.m. Beijing time, Kissinger's plane landed at Nanyuan Airport in Beijing.[33] From that afternoon until July 11, Zhou Enlai and Kissinger held six meetings, focusing on the Taiwan question and the timing of President Nixon's visit to China. They also jointly drafted an announcement. Both sides agreed to release the announcement simultaneously at 10:30 a.m. Beijing time on July 16. They further agreed that future contacts would take place in Paris and that the China-US ambassadorial-level talks in Warsaw would not resume.[34]

The China-US announcement, once published, shocked the world.

From October 20 to 26, Kissinger visited China again. This visit differed in that he arrived openly on the presidential aircraft Air Force One, partly to test the route. On October 20, he arrived in Beijing via Shanghai.

Starting on October 21, the two sides held talks in separate groups. Zhou Enlai and Kissinger discussed substantive issues privately, while Zhou's assistant, Xiong Xianghui, discussed general relations with State Department representative John H. Holdridge, and Deputy Minister of Public Security Yu Sang handled security and communications issues with the US side.

Zhou Enlai and Kissinger held ten meetings. The first five focused on situational policies and the latter five on the draft joint communiqué for Nixon's visit to China. The two sides agreed that Nixon's visit would begin on February 21, 1972. They also exchanged views on issues such as Indochina, Taiwan, Korea, Japan, and the South Asian subcontinent. Starting on October 24, they discussed the draft joint communiqué. Zhou Enlai rejected the US draft of October 22, suggesting that differences be clearly stated alongside common points. Mao Zedong agreed with the "each stating their own" approach. By October 26, they had reached a basic agreement on the draft joint communiqué, but the Taiwan question remained unresolved, to be further discussed during Nixon's visit.[35]

At this time, an unexpected event occurred. As Kissinger was boarding his plane to leave Beijing, the 26th United Nations General Assembly in New York passed a resolution on October 25, with a vote of 76 in favor, 35 against, and 17 abstentions, restoring the People's Republic of China's legitimate seat at the UN.

On November 20 of the previous year, during the 25th United Nations General Assembly, the vote to restore China's legitimate seat had for the first time seen more votes in favor than against. Although it did not pass because it failed to achieve a two-thirds majority, China's growing influence in the world was undeniable.

The result of the vote at the 26th United Nations General Assembly expressed the widespread desire of Third World countries and the hope of a significant portion of developed countries for China to join the international community. Mao Zedong poignantly remarked, "Let's not forget, it was our 'poor friends' who carried us into the United Nations."

From January 3 to 10, 1972, US Deputy National Security Adviser Alexander Haig led an advance team to China to make technical arrangements for Nixon's visit.

In the early morning of January 4, Zhou Enlai met with Haig. Haig brought a message from Nixon and Kissinger: "The Soviet government has decided to rapidly and significantly change its policy toward the subcontinent. They are attempting to establish enemies or agents of enemies around the People's Republic of China." The US believed that China's "survival capability" was threatened, and the US wanted to "maintain" China's "independence and survival capability." He also said that Nixon hoped his visit to China would "strengthen the President's image as a world leader, which would be beneficial to both of us."[36]

After the meeting, Zhou Enlai immediately instructed Xiong Xianghui to draft a "Response to the US Message" and personally reported to Mao Zedong.

Two days later, at noon on January 6, Mao Zedong met with Zhou Enlai and Ye Jianying. Zhou Enlai presented the draft "Response to the US Message" to Mao for review. Mao said, "Good, I think you can tell him. After all, it's just boasting. He hasn't come for 22 years; he can wait another hundred years! If you don't push him a bit, he won't feel comfortable. In short, it's just boasting. I think he will come within a few years."

Zhou Enlai asked, "Except for the Taiwan question, the Americans didn't mention anything else in the draft joint communiqué. Should we leave it unchanged?" Mao replied, "Leave it unchanged. If we change it, we'll only change a little, like replacing 'people want progress' with 'people want revolution.' They are afraid of revolution; the more they fear it, the more we should emphasize it. Actually, this communiqué does not address the fundamental issue. The fundamental issue is that neither the US nor China can fight on two fronts. Verbally, we can say we can fight on two, three, four, or five fronts, but in reality, we cannot fight on two fronts. Of course, it wouldn't be good to write that down!"[37]

At 11:30 p.m. on the same night, Zhou Enlai held a second meeting with Haig, providing a response based on the "Reply to the US Message." The main points of the Chinese reply were as follows:

(1) As the Sino-American leaders' meeting approaches, some hostile forces are intensifying their sabotage efforts, and China is prepared for this.

(2) Following the announcement of Nixon's visit to China, the Soviet Union's actions in Europe and Asia have further exposed its expansionist nature, and the subcontinent will become increasingly turbulent.

(3) There are fundamental differences between China and the US on the Vietnam issue, and the current US policy toward Vietnam presents unfavorable factors for the President's visit to China.

(4) The US expresses doubts about China's "survival capability" and claims it wants to "maintain" China's "independence and survival capability." This is surprising. China believes that no country can rely on external forces to maintain its independence and survival; otherwise, it can only become a protectorate or colony. The new socialist China was born and has grown in the struggle against foreign aggression and oppression, and it will continue to exist and develop.

(5) Although China-US relations have not normalized, China will receive President Nixon with proper etiquette and will make efforts to ensure positive results from the high-level talks.

(6) Regarding the Taiwan question, China has tried to consider the US difficulties in the communiqué draft. On this question, the Chinese people have very strong feelings. If the US genuinely wishes to improve China-US relations, it should take a positive attitude toward solving this key issue.[38]

During the meeting with Haig, Zhou Enlai also stated, "We have long said that we are prepared for enemies to attack from all sides. We are willing to bear the greatest national sacrifice and fight to the end, contributing to the cause of human progress. Facts have proven and will continue to prove that all attempts to isolate, encircle, contain, and subvert China will end in shameful failure." Regarding the hope that Nixon's visit would "enhance the President's image as a world leader," Zhou Enlai remarked, "A person's image depends on his actions, not any other factors. We never believe in self-proclaimed world leaders." He also told Haig, "We have our self-respect, and you have yours. Mutual respect is essential for equality."[39]

This candid exchange laid the foundation for Nixon's successful visit to China, based on mutual respect and equality.

From February 21 to 28, 1972, President Nixon visited China despite the lack of formal diplomatic relations between the two countries. This visit marked the beginning of the end of the long-standing US policy of isolating and containing China since the founding of the People's Republic.

At 11:30 a.m. on February 21, President Nixon's plane arrived at Capital Airport. Nixon descended the aircraft steps and extended his hand to Zhou Enlai, who was there to greet him. Nixon later recalled, "When our hands met, one era ended, and another began."[40]

Unfortunately, an important intermediary did not live to see this moment. Six days earlier, on February 15, Edgar Snow passed away in Switzerland due to illness. During his serious illness, Mao Zedong had sent a Chinese medical team to assist in his care. After Snow's death, Mao sent a condolence message on February 16, stating, "Mr. Snow was a friend of the Chinese people. Throughout his life, he made significant contributions to enhancing mutual understanding and friendship between the peoples of China and the United States."[41]

That afternoon, from 2:40 p.m. to 3:50 p.m., Mao Zedong met with Nixon at his residence by the swimming pool in Zhongnanhai, with Zhou Enlai and Kissinger present. This was the first meeting between the highest leaders of China and the United States since the founding of the People's Republic of China.

Just nine days earlier, on February 12, Mao Zedong had suddenly gone into shock but revived after emergency treatment. At this time, his health had not yet fully recovered. The originally scheduled meeting time of 15 minutes was extended to 1 hour and 10 minutes.

According to Nixon's recollection, "Although Mao spoke with some difficulty, it was clear that his mind was moving like lightning." He wrote in his diary, "We were escorted into a room that was not elaborate, filled with books and papers. Several of the books were open to various pages on the coffee table next to where he was sitting. His girl secretary helped him to his feet. When I shook his hands, he said, 'I can't talk very well.'"

"The transcript of the conversation may not have caught probably the most moving moment when he reached out his hand, and I reached out mine, and he held it for about a minute."[42]

This historic meeting began as follows:

Mao Zedong (hereafter referred to as Mao): Yesterday on the airplane, you put forward a very difficult problem for us. You said that what is required to talk about are philosophical problems. (Laughter)

Richard Nixon (hereafter referred to as Nixon): I said that because I have read the Chairman's poems and speeches, and I know he was a professional philosopher.

Mao: (looking at Dr. Kissinger) He is a doctor of philosophy?

Nixon: He is a doctor of brains.

Mao (pointing to Kissinger): What about asking him to be the main speaker today?

Nixon: He is an expert in philosophy.

Henry Kissinger: I used to assign the Chairman's collective writings to my classes at Harvard.

Mao: Those writings of mine aren't anything. There is nothing instructive in what I wrote.

Nixon: The Chairman's writings moved a nation and have changed the world.

Mao: I haven't been able to change it. I've only been able to change a few places in the vicinity of Beijing.

Mao then moved on to the Taiwan question.

Mao: Our common old friend, Generalissimo Chiang Kai-shek, doesn't approve of this. He calls us communist bandits. He recently issued a speech. Have you seen it?

Zhou Enlai (hereafter referred to as Zhou): Yes, it was at their recent "Congress."

Nixon: Chiang Kai-shek calls the Chairman a bandit. What does the Chairman call Chiang Kai-shek?

Zhou: Generally speaking, we call them Chiang Kai-shek's clique. In the newspapers, sometimes we call him a bandit.

Mao: Isn't he a bandit? We are also called bandits in turn. Anyway, we abuse each other. Actually, the history of our friendship with him is much longer than the history of your friendship with him.

Zhou: Since 1924.

Later, the conversation turns to the US presidential elections.

Mao: But let us speak the truth. As for the Democratic Party, if they come into office again, we cannot avoid contacting them. I voted for you during your election.

Nixon: When the Chairman says he voted for me, he voted for the lesser of two evils.

Mao: I like rightists. People say you are rightists, that the Republican Party is to the right, that Prime Minister Heath is also to the right. They also say the Christian Democratic Party of West Germany is also to the right. I am comparatively happy when these people on the right come into power.

The discussion also covered the normalization of China-US relations. Mao Zedong expressed in the conversation as follows:

At the present time, the question of aggression from the United States or aggression from China is relatively small; that is, it could be said that this is not a major issue, because the present situation is one in which a state of war does not exist between our two countries. You want to withdraw some of your troops back on your soil; ours do not go abroad. Therefore, the situation between our two countries is strange because during the past 22 years our ideas have never met in talks. Now the time is less than ten months since we began playing table tennis; if one counts the time since you put forward your suggestion at Warsaw it is less than two years. Our side also is bureaucratic in dealing with matters. For example, you wanted some exchange of persons of a personal level, things like that; also trade. But rather than deciding that we stuck with our stand that without settling major issues there is nothing to do with smaller issues. I myself persisted in that position. Later on, I saw you were right, and we played table tennis.

The conversation returned to the initial topic of philosophy.

Nixon: Mr. Chairman, I am aware of the fact that over a period of years, my position with regard to the People's Republic was one that the Chairman and Prime Minister totally disagreed with. What brings us together is a recognition of a new situation in the world and a recognition on our part that what is important is not a nation's internal political philosophy. What is important is its policy toward the rest of the world and toward us.

Mao: Exactly.

Nixon: Looking at the two great powers, the United States and China—we know China doesn't threaten the territory of the United States.

Mao: Neither do we threaten Japan or South Korea.

Zhou: Nor any other country.

Nixon: Nor any country. Nor do we. I think you know the United States has no territorial designs on China. We know China doesn't want to dominate the United States. We believe you too realize the United States doesn't want to dominate China. Also—maybe you don't believe this, but I do—neither China nor the United States, both great nations, want to dominate the world. Because our attitudes are the same on these two issues, we don't threaten each others's territories. Therefore, we can find common ground, despite our differences, to build a world structure in which both can be safe to develop in our own way on our own roads. That cannot be said about some other nations in the world.

Mao, seemingly uninterested in this lengthy declaration, asked, "Do you have other plans for the afternoon? What time is it now?" Zhou: "The plenary meeting is at 4:30 p.m. It is now 3:45 p.m." Mao: "Do you think we have covered enough today?"[43]

At the end of the conversation, Mao praised Nixon's book *The Six Crises* as well written.

Mao insisted on seeing his guests off to the door. Nixon recalled, "Mao walked us to the door. His walk was a slow shuffle, and he said he had not been feeling well. 'But you look very good,' I replied. He said with a slight shrug, 'Appearances are deceiving.'"[44]

With mutual efforts, Nixon's first visit to the People's Republic of China was a success.

On February 28, the China-US Joint Communiqué was issued in Shanghai. Both governments solemnly declared to the world: "The two countries have fundamental differences in their social systems and foreign policies. However, both sides agree that countries, regardless of their social systems, should conduct their relations based on the principles of respect for sovereignty and territorial integrity, non-aggression, non-interference in each other's internal affairs, equality and mutual benefit, and peaceful coexistence. International disputes should be resolved on this basis, without resorting to force or the threat of force."

As time passes, many promises have faded from memory. However, the following statement remains recorded in history: "The US side declares: The United States acknowledges that all Chinese on both sides of the Taiwan Strait maintain that there is one China and that Taiwan is a part of China. The United States government does not challenge this position. It reaffirms its interest in a peaceful settlement of the Taiwan question by the Chinese themselves. With this prospect in mind, it affirms the ultimate objective of the withdrawal of all US armed forces and military installations from Taiwan."[45]

Even more unforgettable is Mao Zedong's final remark to Nixon: "Appearances are deceiving." Changing history requires courage. Creating history requires wisdom.

CHAPTER 20

Unfulfilled Aspirations

As long as Chiang Kai-shek and his son can resist the United States, we can cooperate with him. We support Chiang Kai-shek's policy of holding onto Jinmen and Mazu. If Chiang Kai-shek retreats from Jinmen and Mazu, the situation will be lost, morale will waver, and there is a high likelihood of collapse. As long as he does not collaborate with the United States, Taiwan, Penghu, Jinmen, and Mazu can be under Chiang's control for as many years as necessary, but there must be open navigation, and he must not send spies to the mainland. Ultimately, Taiwan, Penghu, Jinmen, and Mazu must all return to the mainland.

MAO ZEDONG,
Conversation with Cao Juren and others (October 13, 1958)

Mao Zedong's aspiration was to see Taiwan return to the embrace of the motherland. From the founding of the People's Republic of China, he devoted considerable effort to this cause.

The Taiwan question is a remnant of China's civil war. After the liberation of mainland China, Mao Zedong led the PLA in preparing for the liberation of Taiwan. However, the outbreak of the Korean War in June 1950 provided the United States with an opportunity to intervene. On June 27, 1950, the US announced the deployment of the Seventh Fleet to the Taiwan Strait, preventing the PLA from liberating Taiwan, thus complicating the Taiwan question. The US established naval and air force bases in Taiwan and sent military advisers to train the KMT forces stationed there.

In July 1953, the Korean Armistice Agreement was signed. Taiwan's strategic importance in the US policy of containment against China became more pronounced. The US sought to control Taiwan through a "one China, one Taiwan" or "two Chinas" policy.

In September of the same year, the US and the KMT authorities in Taiwan signed the Mutual Defense Assistance Agreement, stipulating that the US would oversee the reorganization, training, supervision, and equipping of KMT forces. In the event of war, the movement and command of these forces required US approval. The defense area specified in the agreement included Taiwan, Penghu, Jinmen, Mazu, and Dachen Islands, with a "Coordination and Liaison Staff" established in Taipei under US direction.

Mao Zedong took note of this development and, in December 1953, proposed building a navy to liberate Taiwan. In a speech at an expanded meeting of the Political Bureau of the Central Committee of the CPC on December 4, he emphasized: "To eliminate the harassment of coastal pirates, ensure the safety of maritime transportation, prepare forces to recover Taiwan at an appropriate time, achieve the final reunification of all territories, and prepare against imperialist invasions from the sea, we must, over a considerable period, gradually build a powerful navy according to the development of our industry and financial capabilities."[1]

At that time, there were also plans to attack Jinmen. However, due to the nascent stage of large-scale industrialization and tight state finances, this plan had to be abandoned. On December 22, Mao Zedong reviewed a budget estimate for the attack on Jinmen, instructing: "Comrade Chen Yi's opinion is that not attacking Jinmen at present is beneficial; otherwise, we would be in a very passive position and not have full confidence in success. I agree with this opinion. The required expenditure is nearly five trillion yuan, which we cannot afford; at least in 1954, we should not use such a large sum."[2]

On April 26, 1954, an international conference to address the Korean and Indochina issues was convened in Geneva. Before and after the Geneva Conference, the US organized a Southeast Asia Defense Group against China and began reconsidering a new defense treaty with the Taiwan authorities. Starting in May and June 1954, US presidential envoys frequently visited Taiwan to discuss the so-called Mutual Defense Treaty. This trend drew Mao Zedong's keen attention.

On July 7, 1954, Mao Zedong chaired an expanded meeting of the Political Bureau of the Central Committee of the CPC, hearing Zhou Enlai's report on attending the Geneva Conference and visits to India, Burma, and talks with Vietnam. In his speech, Mao Zedong stated: A significant issue in our relations with the United States now is the Taiwan question, which will be a long-term problem. We must thwart the possibility of the US signing a treaty with Taiwan.[3]

The following afternoon, at the 57th expanded meeting of the National Committee of the CPPCC, Mao Zedong proposed establishing a peaceful zone in Southeast Asia, developing cooperation, and signing mutual assistance or collective peace agreements, striving to build an international peace united front. He also stated that without the development of the diplomatic front, protecting construction and industrialization would be impossible.[4]

Afterward, Mao Zedong led the fight to defend sovereignty over territorial waters and airspace and initiated domestic publicity against the US-organized Southeast Asia Defense Group.

On July 27, following Mao Zedong's instructions, Deng Xiaoping drafted a telegram from the Central Committee of the CPC to Zhou Enlai, who was visiting Poland at the time. The telegram stated as follows:

> In recent times, the United States and Chiang Kai-shek have been discussing the signing of a US-Chiang Mutual Defense Treaty, and the US has been continuously increasing its military aid to Chiang's forces in Taiwan. This is something we must pay close attention to. According to public reports, the US seems to have reservations about the treaty and has not made a final decision. If the US and Chiang sign such a treaty, our relations with the US will remain tense for a long time, making it harder to seek relaxation and maneuvering space. Therefore, breaking the US-Chiang Mutual Defense Treaty and the Southeast Asia Defense Treaty is our current central task in the struggle against the US.

The telegram suggested that it was timely to raise the task of liberating Taiwan.

We believe that after the victorious conclusion of the civil war on the mainland and the successful armistice in the Korean War, there remains a war before us, namely the war against Chiang Kai-shek's forces in Taiwan. There also remains the task of liberating Taiwan. After the armistice in Korea, we did not timely (about six months late) present this task to the entire nation, nor did we take necessary measures and effective actions in military, diplomatic, and publicity aspects based on this task. This is inappropriate. If we still do not present this task and do not carry out a series of actions, we will make a serious political mistake. Raising this task not only aims to break the US-Taiwan military treaty but, more importantly, to raise the political awareness and vigilance of the entire nation, thereby stimulating the enthusiasm of the people to complete national construction tasks. Additionally, we can use this struggle to strengthen our national defense capabilities and learn the skills of maritime combat.

The telegram proposed future political and military measures.

(1) Politically, domestically, we have begun publicity on the necessity of recovering Taiwan and exposing the US-Chiang collusion. After your return to Beijing, we plan to have the Foreign Minister make a public statement on the Taiwan question,[5] followed by a joint statement from various parties.[6] Based on these two statements, we will conduct extensive and in-depth long-term publicity and education among the people. We are also organizing specialized broadcasts targeting Taiwan. ... (2) Militarily, the Military Commission has issued specific instructions to strengthen naval and air combat against Chiang Kai-shek's forces, strictly limiting our naval and air targets to Chiang's military aircraft and ships. Our forces are not to proactively attack US aircraft and ships unless they attack us. ... (3) Given that our struggle with the US and Chiang along the coast is a long-term issue and our forces lack capability and experience in maritime combat, strengthening naval and air force construction becomes a long-term task in our military development. Our navy plans to

adopt a 'boats first, then ships' construction policy, and our air force must learn maritime combat skills. To meet the urgent needs of the current struggle, we plan to increase orders for naval and air force equipment from the Soviet Union over the next three years, with a proposed order of about 500 million rubles. While there are no financial budget difficulties, more foreign exchange solutions need to be sought. This matter will be further considered after your return.[7]

This marked an important policy shift on Taiwan, focusing on preventing the internationalization of the Taiwan question and stopping Taiwan from becoming a forward military base for the US against China.

At this time, the US frequently tested the waters, attempting to challenge the Chinese government's bottom line on the Taiwan question. On August 17, US President Eisenhower announced the deployment of the Seventh Fleet to intervene in China. On August 19, the US Pacific Fleet Commander led six warships into the waters near the Dachen Islands.

On September 3 and 22, the PLA conducted two punitive shellings of Jinmen to demonstrate the Chinese people's determination to oppose foreign interference and to liberate Taiwan.

On December 2, despite opposition from the Chinese government and people, the US government signed the Mutual Defense Treaty with the Taiwan authorities.[8] The treaty stipulated that the US would help Taiwan maintain and develop armed forces; in the event of "armed attack" on Taiwan, "the US will take action" to deal with "common danger"; the US had the right to deploy land, sea, and air forces in and around Taiwan and Penghu, and extend to other territories recognized by both parties. The treaty came into effect on March 3, 1955.

In this context, Mao Zedong officially approved the coordinated operation of the army, navy, and air force to liberate Yijiangshan Island and then the Dachen Islands.

According to the original operational plan, the action to liberate the southeastern coastal islands involved first recovering Jinmen and Mazu, then the coastal islands of eastern Zhejiang, and finally liberating Taiwan. In December 1953, Zhang Zhen, Director of the Operations Department of the

Military Commission, twice suggested first attacking the Dachen Islands and then Jinmen, which received Mao Zedong's high attention.[9] Following Mao's directive spirit, the East China Military Region proposed a joint army, navy, and air force operation to attack the Dachen Islands in January 1954. Subsequently, specific plans were formulated to first capture Yijiangshan Island, then the Dachen Islands, and opportunistically capture other islands.

Dachen Island was the command center of the KMT forces in the coastal islands of eastern Zhejiang, housing the "Dachen Defense Zone Command" with a total force of about 20,000 troops. Yijiangshan Island, serving as the gateway to Dachen Island, featured steep terrain and a strong defensive system, making it easy to defend and hard to attack. The PLA chose to launch their first assault here, a strategy akin to pulling a tooth from a tiger's mouth.

On November 1, 1954, the young naval and air force units of the PLA initiated the first phase of the operation to liberate Dachen Island. After more than two months of fighting, they had gained basic control over the air and sea in the battle area.

On January 18, 1955, the PLA launched a joint amphibious assault on Yijiangshan Island. After ten hours of fierce combat, they captured Yijiangshan Island.

Starting January 19, the US government dispatched six aircraft carrier groups to the waters east of Dachen Island to apply military pressure. On January 19, US President Eisenhower called on the United Nations to mediate "to stop the fighting along the Chinese coast."[10] On January 24, Eisenhower submitted a special message to Congress, requesting authorization for the President to use US military forces to ensure the safety of Taiwan and the Penghu Islands. The US House of Representatives and Senate passed emergency resolutions on January 25 and 28, respectively, approving Eisenhower's request.

On the same day as Eisenhower's address to Congress, January 24, Zhou Enlai issued a statement on "The US Government's Interference in the Liberation of Taiwan by the Chinese People."

From the end of January to early February, a diplomatic struggle unfolded in the United Nations Security Council regarding the tense situation in the

Taiwan Strait. Under Mao Zedong's guidance, Zhou Enlai clarified the Chinese government's principled stance through various channels, emphasizing that the root cause of the tension lay with the US and that the Chinese government would not agree to Chiang Kai-shek's participation in the proposed international conference.

Meanwhile, the operation to liberate Dachen Island continued. On January 30, orders were issued to the troops for the attack on Dachen Island. On February 5, the Taiwan authorities decided to withdraw from Dachen Island and other coastal islands of eastern Zhejiang. By February 25, under the cover of the US Navy and Air Force, the KMT forces had completely retreated to Taiwan, and all the coastal islands of eastern Zhejiang were liberated.

Through this military and diplomatic struggle, Mao Zedong grasped the essence of the US-Taiwan Mutual Defense Treaty and clearly and unequivocally demonstrated the Chinese government's stance: the resolution of the Taiwan question, including the timing and manner, is purely a domestic affair of China, and no foreign interference will be tolerated.

At the same time, this diplomatic struggle brought international attention to the situation in Taiwan, creating a glimmer of opportunity. On April 23, 1955, at the Bandung Conference, Zhou Enlai, on behalf of the Chinese government, announced: "The Chinese people are friendly with the American people and do not want to fight with the United States. The Chinese government is willing to sit down and negotiate with the US government to discuss the issue of easing tensions in the Far East, particularly in the Taiwan region."[11] This statement had a strong international impact, prompting countries like India and the United Kingdom to engage in diplomatic mediation to facilitate China-US talks.

On August 1, the first China-US ambassadorial-level talks were held in Geneva. A total of 73 meetings were held until December 12, 1957. The talks were eventually interrupted due to the US side's unilateral attempt to downgrade the level of the discussions.

During this period, the KMT authorities under Chiang Kai-shek first took advantage of the Korean War and the US intervention in China's internal affairs regarding the liberation of Taiwan to establish a foothold in Taiwan.

After the Korean War ended, the KMT's security was ensured through the signing of the Military Assistance Agreement and the Mutual Defense Treaty with the US government. However, as the US gradually increased its military and political control over Taiwan, fissures began to develop between Chiang Kai-shek and the Americans. These tensions were particularly heightened following the Wu Guozhen Incident and the Sun Liren Incident, which amplified Chiang Kai-shek's wariness toward the US.

After the 1955 Bandung Conference, the Chinese government made significant efforts to ease tensions in the Taiwan Strait. On September 15, 1956, Liu Shaoqi reiterated in his political report at the Eighth National Congress of the CPC: "We are willing to use peaceful negotiations to bring Taiwan back into the embrace of the motherland and avoid the use of force. If force has to be used, it will only be after all possibilities for peaceful negotiations have been exhausted or if peaceful negotiations fail." On April 16, 1957, during a banquet to welcome the Chairman of the Presidium of the Supreme Soviet of the USSR, Kliment Voroshilov, Mao Zedong explicitly stated: "We are still prepared for a third cooperation between the KMT and the CPC."[12]

"The tree desires calm, but the wind will not subside." Following the signing of the Mutual Defense Treaty between the US and Taiwan, US military involvement in Taiwan deepened.

In January 1956, the US and Taiwan signed the US-Taiwan Military Agreement, through which the US appointed a "Commander of the Defense of Taiwan," expanded military bases, and increased the number of air and naval forces stationed in Taiwan. In May 1957, the US deployed "Matador" missile units, capable of carrying nuclear warheads, to Taiwan. In March 1958, the US consolidated various military institutions in Taiwan to establish the "US Taiwan Defense Command." The US also provided Taiwan with $150–200 million worth of military equipment annually, including a total of 1,117 aircraft by 1958. With US support, Taiwan's defense forces on Jinmen were strengthened, with 85,000 troops stationed there by 1958, accounting for one-third of its total military strength.[13]

In this context, on December 18, 1957, Mao Zedong issued a directive to "consider having our air force enter Fujian in 1958,"[14] marking the beginning of preparations for a new round of military struggles along the southeast coast. On April 27, 1958, Han Xianchu, Commander of the Fuzhou Military Region, and Ye Fei, Political Commissar, submitted a plan for large-scale artillery bombardment and blockade of Jinmen at an appropriate time.[15]

Before the military struggle against Taiwan commenced, Mao Zedong first led a diplomatic struggle. On June 30, 1958, the Chinese government issued a statement on the China-US ambassadorial-level talks, stating: "The Chinese government demands that the US government send ambassadorial representatives to resume talks within fifteen days from today. Otherwise, the Chinese government will have no choice but to consider that the US has decided to break off the ambassadorial talks."[16]

The US government did not take this solemn statement seriously, thereby missing an opportunity to ease tensions.

On the night of July 17, the Central Military Commission issued orders to prepare for the Jinmen Artillery Battle. On the night of July 18, Mao Zedong convened a meeting with the Central Military Commission, General Staff, and heads of the air force, navy, and artillery. He stated: "The Jinmen Artillery Battle is intended to deter the US. Jinmen and Mazu are Chinese territories. Attacking Jinmen and Mazu and punishing the KMT forces is an internal affair of China, for which the enemy will find no pretext, but it will have a restraining effect on US imperialism."[17]

On August 20, three days before the Jinmen Artillery Battle, Mao Zedong decided to concentrate forces immediately to strike the KMT forces in Jinmen and block them off. He further noted that after a period of time, the opposition might withdraw from Jinmen and Mazu or face great difficulties and continue to struggle. At that point, whether to consider an island landing operation would depend on the situation.[18]

The Jinmen Artillery Battle began on August 23, at 5:30 p.m. The first bombardment lasted more than two hours, with nearly 30,000 shells fired. The shelling continued until September 3. Mao Zedong decided to cease fire for three days starting September 4 to observe the situation.

On September 4, the Chinese government issued a declaration on the 12-nautical-mile territorial sea rights and warned the United States that all foreign aircraft and military ships must not enter China's territorial waters and airspace without permission from the Chinese government. Any violation would be met with immediate artillery fire.

Ignoring the Chinese government's warning, the US began escorting KMT ships with its navy starting September 7.

On September 7, Mao Zedong received a report from Ye Fei through Wang Shangrong, head of the Operations Department of the General Staff: US and KMT forces formed a large maritime convoy, with US warships positioned on the left and right sides for escort, while KMT ships and transport vessels were sandwiched in the middle, sailing from Taiwan to Jinmen. Ye Fei asked for instructions: Since the US military is involved, should we attack the US-KMT combined naval convoy? Mao Zedong replied: Proceed as planned. Ye Fei further asked: Should we attack the US ships as well? Mao Zedong answered: Only attack KMT ships, not US ships. Mao also instructed Ye Fei to wait until the combined convoy reached the port of Liaoluo Bay in Jinmen before attacking and to report the convoy's position, formation, and navigation status every hour. When they reached Liaoluo Bay, they were to wait for the order to open fire. Ye Fei asked: If we are not to attack the US ships, but they open fire on us, should we return fire? Mao replied: Do not return fire without orders.[19]

At noon on September 8, the US and KMT naval convoy arrived at Liaoluo Bay in Jinmen, and the transport vessels began unloading supplies at the port docks. Ye Fei immediately reported this to Beijing. Mao Zedong then ordered to open fire. Ye Fei quickly commanded all artillery units to fire according to the pre-arranged battle plan, launching a sudden and intense attack on KMT warships and transport vessels. As soon as the PLA opened fire, the US escort ships abandoned the KMT ships and transport vessels, promptly retreating to the open sea.

The continuous artillery battle presented a dilemma for the US government and the Taiwan authorities: whether to continue holding Jinmen and Mazu or to withdraw their troops. It also taught the Taiwan authorities a lesson about the reliability of the Mutual Defense Treaty.

The US government decided to return to the negotiating table. On September 15, after a nine-month hiatus, the China-US ambassadorial-level talks resumed in Warsaw, the capital of Poland. During these talks, the US side did not propose a plan, while the Chinese side presented five suggestions.[20]

The US misunderstood these suggestions, mistakenly believing that the Chinese government was eager to liberate Jinmen and Mazu, and thus refused to accept them. On September 18, the US representative formally proposed a "ceasefire plan." On the same day, US Secretary of State John Foster Dulles, speaking at the United Nations General Assembly, also called for China to "ceasefire" as soon as possible. In response, Chinese Foreign Minister Chen Yi issued a statement on September 20, asserting that China was not at war with the US in Jinmen and Mazu, and therefore the concept of a "ceasefire" did not apply. He emphasized that China's punitive actions against Chiang Kai-shek's forces in Jinmen and Mazu were internal affairs, and foreign interference would not be tolerated.[21]

Through the talks, the United States realized that China would not extend the shelling of Jinmen to Taiwan, but neither could China be forced to renounce the right to use force. Recently, to quell popular revolutions in Iraq and Lebanon, the US deployed Marine Corps units in Lebanon on July 15. At this moment, many US warships were stuck in the Taiwan Strait, which was bound to negatively affect America's global strategy. Consequently, Dulles began to shift from his high-pressure "brinkmanship" policy to a "ceasefire" and "disengagement" policy.

On September 30, Dulles stated at a press conference that if a reliable "ceasefire" was achieved in the Taiwan region, it would be foolish, unwise, and imprudent to maintain a significant number of troops in Jinmen and Mazu. On October 1, President Eisenhower also expressed, "I do not think it is a good idea to have all those troops stationed there." He added that Jinmen and Mazu were not extremely important to Taiwan.[22]

At this point, Chiang Kai-shek immediately voiced his opposition. On October 2, Chiang told an Associated Press reporter that Dulles' remarks were merely a unilateral statement by the United States and that Taiwan had no obligation to comply. He also stated his refusal to withdraw KMT troops from Jinmen and Mazu. The contradictions between the Taiwan authorities and the US government began to surface.

The initiative began to shift toward Mao Zedong.

On the evening of October 3, Mao Zedong chaired an expanded meeting of the Standing Committee of the Political Bureau of the Central Committee of the CPC at Yinian Hall in Zhongnanhai, primarily to analyze and discuss Dulles' September 30 remarks.

Zhou Enlai said: "Dulles' policy, in a nutshell, is to exchange Jinmen and Mazu for Taiwan and Penghu. This aligns with what we recently detected as the US bottom line in the China-US ambassadorial-level talks in Warsaw."

Mao Zedong said: "The reconnaissance task is complete, but the question is what the next move should be. Regarding Dulles' policy, we have common ground with Chiang Kai-shek—both oppose the concept of two Chinas. Chiang Kai-shek is reluctant to withdraw from Jinmen and Mazu, and we do not necessarily have to land on these islands. One can imagine the benefits of letting Chiang Kai-shek keep Jinmen and Mazu. These islands are very close to the mainland, allowing us to maintain contact with the KMT. We can shell them whenever needed, tighten the noose when we need more tension, and loosen it when we need less tension. This strategy keeps them neither alive nor dead, serving as a means to deal with the Americans. Every time we shell, Chiang Kai-shek will ask the Americans for help, making the Americans nervous and worried that Chiang Kai-shek will cause trouble for them."

After the discussion, Mao Zedong concluded: "The policy is set. We will continue to shell but not land, cut off but not kill, leaving Chiang's troops in Jinmen and Mazu. However, the shelling will not be daily or involve tens of thousands of shells each time; it can be intermittent."[23]

On October 5, Zhou Enlai met with the Soviet chargé d'affaires in China, Antonov, to inform him of the Chinese government's latest decision on the Taiwan question. He said: "We originally planned to proceed in two steps: first, recover the coastal islands, and second, liberate Taiwan." "Now, after discussion within the Central Committee, we still believe it is best to keep Chiang Kai-shek on the coastal islands of Jinmen and Mazu." He added: "We aim to eventually reclaim these coastal islands, the Penghu Islands, and Taiwan."[24]

Thus, the strategy of Mao Zedong and the Central Committee of the CPC on the Taiwan question evolved from a "two-step" approach to a "comprehensive" resolution.

On October 6, a letter from Peng Dehuai, Minister of National Defense of the People's Republic of China, drafted by Mao Zedong, was published. The full text is as follows:

To the military and civilian compatriots of Taiwan,
Penghu, Jinmen, and Mazu:

We are all Chinese. Of the thirty-six strategies, harmony is the best policy. The battle at Jinmen is punitive in nature. Your leaders have been too rampant for a long time, ordering planes to intrude into the mainland, reaching as far as Yunnan, Guizhou, Sichuan, Xikang,[25] and Qinghai, dropping leaflets, planting spies, bombing Fuzhou, and harassing Jiangsu and Zhejiang. How can we tolerate this any longer? Therefore, we fired some artillery to get your attention. Taiwan, Penghu, Jinmen, and Mazu are Chinese territories; you agree on this point, as evidenced by your leaders' announcements. They are definitely not American territories. Taiwan, Penghu, Jinmen, and Mazu are part of China, not another country. There is only one China in the world, not two. You agree with this too, as seen in your leaders' announcements. Your leaders' military agreements with the Americans are unilateral and we do not recognize them; they should be abolished. The Americans will undoubtedly abandon you one day. Do you not believe this? History will prove it. The signs were already there in Dulles' speech on September 30. Standing in your position, can you not feel disheartened? Ultimately, American imperialism is our common enemy.

The 130,000 soldiers and civilians in Jinmen are suffering from shortages of supplies and are in dire straits. Out of humanitarian concern, I have ordered the frontline in Fujian to cease shelling for seven days starting October 6, allowing you to freely transport supplies, but only on the condition that there is no American escort. If there is an escort, this does not apply. The war between us has lasted thirty years and remains unresolved, which is undesirable. I suggest holding talks to achieve a peaceful resolution. Premier Zhou

Enlai already conveyed this to you several years ago. This is an internal matter between us Chinese and is not a matter between China and the US. The US occupation of Taiwan, Penghu, and the Taiwan Strait is a matter between China and the US and should be resolved through bilateral negotiations, which are currently taking place in Warsaw. The Americans will eventually leave; they must. It is in their interest to leave sooner, as they can take the initiative. Delaying their departure is disadvantageous, as it keeps them on the defensive. Why should a country from the Eastern Pacific come to the Western Pacific? The Western Pacific belongs to the people of the Western Pacific, just as the Eastern Pacific belongs to the people of the Eastern Pacific. This is common sense that Americans should understand.

There is no war between the People's Republic of China and the United States, so there is no need for a ceasefire. Talking about a ceasefire without a war is a joke. Friends in Taiwan, there is a war between us, which should be stopped and extinguished. This requires negotiations. Of course, fighting for another thirty years is not a big deal, but an early peaceful resolution is more appropriate. The choice is yours.[26]

Within this letter are a few key phrases that set the tone for future cross-Straits relations. First, "We are all Chinese," emphasizing that any issue between the two sides is an internal affair of China, not subject to foreign interference. Second, "Of the thirty-six strategies, harmony is the best policy," indicating that the Taiwan question should ultimately be resolved through peaceful negotiations. Third, "There is only one China in the world, not two. You agree with this too, as seen in your leaders' announcements," highlighting the political common ground between Mao Zedong and Chiang Kai-shek. Fourth, "I suggest holding talks to achieve a peaceful resolution," presenting peaceful negotiations as the righteous path out of the Taiwan dilemma.

This announcement declared a seven-day suspension of shelling starting from October 6. On October 13, another order from the Ministry of National Defense, also drafted by Mao Zedong, was issued, stating: "The shelling of Jinmen will be suspended for another two weeks starting today."[27]

The US made another misjudgment, thinking that China's repeated announcements of ceasing shelling were a result of their "tough" policies and mistaking this for the "ceasefire" they had called for. On October 18, the US announced that Dulles would visit Taiwan on the 21. On the 19, they dispatched four warships to escort KMT forces in the Jinmen area. Upon hearing this, Mao Zedong immediately decided to take punitive action.

On October 20, the day before Dulles arrived in Taiwan, at 4 p.m., the PLA launched the fifth large-scale shelling of Jinmen. On October 22, *The Scotsman* published a commentary stating, "They (the Chinese leaders) will probably stop and start their attacks. For them, keeping Jinmen as a means to cause trouble between Chiang (Kai-shek) and the Americans and to keep the Taiwan question hot is more valuable than having Jinmen fall into their hands."[28]

On October 21–22, Chiang Kai-shek and Dulles held talks. Chiang Kai-shek refused to withdraw troops from Jinmen and Mazu, but under US pressure, he agreed to declare that he would not use force against the mainland. The talks ended with Dulles failing to achieve his goals, further deepening the contradictions between the US and Chiang Kai-shek.

In this context, on October 25, Mao Zedong, in the name of Defense Minister Peng Dehuai, wrote a second letter to the Taiwan compatriots, which was publicly released on October 26.

The key point of this second letter to Taiwan compatriots was to counter the US scheme of "two Chinas" or "one China, one Taiwan." It stated, "We fully understand that the vast majority of you are patriotic, and only a very few are willing to be slaves of the Americans. Compatriots, Chinese affairs can only be resolved by Chinese people ourselves. If it cannot be resolved immediately, we can take our time to discuss it."

The letter also said, "American political broker Dulles loves to meddle in others' affairs, trying to insert himself into the historical disputes between the KMT and the CPC, ordering Chinese people to do this and that, harming Chinese interests to suit American interests. In other words, the first step is to isolate Taiwan; the second step is to place Taiwan under trusteeship. If these steps do not succeed, they can resort to the most ruthless means." "I advise you not to rely too much on others, letting them take all the power."

The letter sternly warned Chiang Kai-shek: "This communiqué from the Chiang-Dulles talks is just a statement, with no legal effect. It is easy to break away from it if you have the determination. There is only one China in the world, not two. On this point, we are united. The Chinese people, including you and the overseas Chinese, will never allow the American scheme of creating two Chinas to succeed. This era is full of hope, and all patriots have a way out. Do not fear the imperialists."[29]

The phrase "good medicine tastes bitter" comes to mind. Reading these words today, one cannot help but be moved by Mao Zedong's deep understanding of Chiang Kai-shek.

During this period, on the morning of October 13, Mao Zedong met with Cao Juren, a writer for the *Nanyang Siang Pau* from Singapore, who resided in Hong Kong, at Yinian Hall in Zhongnanhai. Zhou Enlai, Li Jishen, Cheng Qian, Zhang Zhizhong, Zhang Shizhao, and Tong Xiaopeng were also present.

Mao Zedong told Cao Juren that as long as Chiang Kai-shek and his son can resist the United States, we can cooperate with him. We support Chiang Kai-shek's policy of holding onto Jinmen and Mazu. If Chiang Kai-shek retreats from Jinmen and Mazu, the situation will be lost, morale will waver, and there is a high likelihood of collapse. As long as he does not collaborate with the United States, Taiwan, Penghu, Jinmen, and Mazu can be under Chiang's control for as many years as necessary, but there must be open navigation, and he must not send spies to the mainland. Ultimately, Taiwan, Penghu, Jinmen, and Mazu must all return to the mainland. The troops on Jinmen and Mazu should not rebel. If they run out of food, we won't shell them, allowing them to stock up on supplies. But there might still be some minor shelling in the future, just not enough to cause significant losses. If we don't shell them at all, Chiang Kai-shek will also find it hard to manage. "In heaven, we wish to be two birds flying wing to wing; on earth, we wish to be two branches growing together." Taiwan's small branch is connected to America's large branch, and it will inevitably be broken off. In the future, Taiwan will either become a colony or be placed under trusteeship.

When Cao Juren mentioned that people in Taiwan were concerned about their way of life, Mao Zedong replied: "Let them live according to their own way. Fish have their regional habitats; fish from Maoergai cannot survive elsewhere. But if the US no longer supports him, Chiang can come to the mainland, and that would be a great contribution, marking the US's failure."

Mao Zedong also said: "Tell Taiwan that in Warsaw, we fundamentally do not discuss the Taiwan question. The US representative has no credentials for Taiwan nor any letter of introduction. He said: Why does Chiang Kai-shek not run for president again? We are all "supporters of Chiang"; the problem is that the US wants to suppress him. We will not negotiate with the US about Taiwan and Penghu; we only demand that the US leave. Chiang should not fear that we will conspire with the Americans against him."

Mao Zedong expressed: "The mainland is so vast; Taiwan, Penghu, Jinmen, and Mazu are just a few small points. Let them continue with their Three Principles of the People and the Five-Power Constitution, propagandizing against communism every day. We will counter with our own publicity about reunification. If they dissolve their connection with the US and reconnect with the mainland, the roots will still be theirs, and they can maintain their system. No rectification movements, no anti-rightist campaigns—just not collaborating with the US would be a great victory."

When Zhang Shizhao mentioned that such a scenario would lead to the US cutting off aid to Taiwan, Mao Zedong said: We will supply everything they need, which will cost only a small amount. Their army can be maintained without reducing troops, and administrative simplification will not be needed. Let them continue with their Three Principles of the People. Only when the US abandons them will they be able to join us. Open negotiations are currently unfavorable; we can only scare the Americans, saying, "You can negotiate, but I won't." For now, the US cannot completely control Taiwan. In a few years, the climate will change, and the situation will not be favorable to them. The US is now more isolated than ever on both Middle Eastern and Far Eastern issues. Taiwan has already done three things against the US: removing Sun Liren, attacking the US embassy, and opposing the *Free China* magazine. Chiang fears that we will undermine his troops' morale, but we will not. First, we can satisfy Jinmen and Mazu's material needs; second, we will not negotiate with the US about Taiwan, Penghu, Jinmen, and Mazu. We should be more relaxed toward Taiwan; if we press too hard, the US will pressure them. Prepare for ten or twenty years. The US wants to exchange Jinmen and Matzu for Taiwan and Penghu, but we refuse, allowing Chairman Chiang to hold on for a few more years.

When Cao Juren mentioned that Taiwan was considering organizing a delegation to visit the mainland, Mao Zedong said, "If they come, we welcome them."[30]

Mao Zedong's talk during this meeting outlined the fundamental principles and basic policies for peacefully resolving the Taiwan question.

In January 1963, Zhou Enlai summarized Mao Zedong's principles into "One Guideline, Four Objectives" and conveyed them to the Taiwan authorities through a letter from Zhang Zhizhong to Chen Cheng on January 4. This letter was circulated among the members of the Standing Committee of the Political Bureau of the Central Committee of the CPC before it was sent.[31]

The main content of the "One Guideline" is that as long as Taiwan returns to the motherland, all other issues will be handled appropriately, respecting the opinions of Taiwan's leaders; and the "Four Objectives" include the following: (1) After Taiwan returns to the motherland, aside from diplomatic affairs, which must be unified under the central government, Taiwan's leaders will fully manage all military, political, and personnel arrangements. (2) The central government will cover all military and administrative expenses and construction costs that fall short. (3) Social reforms in Taiwan can proceed slowly, waiting for conditions to mature and respecting the opinions of Taiwan's leaders through consultation and decision-making. (4) Both sides agree not to send people to disrupt each other's unity.[32]

"Without conflict, there can be no understanding." Through the complex struggle that combined military, political, and diplomatic efforts during the 1958 shelling of Jinmen, Mao Zedong and Chiang Kai-shek, in a unique way, reached a consensus on maintaining one China and opposing "two Chinas" or "one China, one Taiwan." Although Chiang Kai-shek never responded to the "One Guideline, Four Objectives," his actions suggested an implicit understanding with Mao's vision.

On October 5, 1959, during a meeting with delegations from 17 Latin American Communist parties, Mao Zedong emphasized an important principle regarding the Taiwan question, stating, "The international issue of Taiwan should not be confused with the domestic issue." He elaborated: "The Taiwan question is complex, involving both domestic and international aspects. For the US, it is an international issue, which should be resolved through peaceful means and not by force. For Chiang Kai-shek, Taiwan is a domestic issue. It does not necessarily have to be resolved by force; we are ready to negotiate with Chiang Kai-shek, but he is unwilling. We have no choice; it might lead to conflict someday. Domestic issues have two solutions: peaceful resolution or armed conflict." He further stated: "We oppose 'two Chinas,' and so does Chiang Kai-shek. We share common ground."[33]

More than ten years later, on February 21, 1972, during his meeting with US President Nixon, Mao Zedong still referred to Chiang Kai-shek as "our common old friend" in a double entendre.[34]

It is particularly noteworthy that an event deserves attention during the period when Mao Zedong was planning the "Ping-Pong diplomacy" with the US.

In mid-April 1971, Zhou Enlai, known for his meticulousness, submitted a report to Mao Zedong. The report stated that there had been significant global reactions within ten days since the decision to invite the US table tennis team to visit China. The immediate issue to address was when the US table tennis team visits, emphasize the renewed friendship between the Chinese and American people; our stance of supporting revolutionary struggles of peoples worldwide remains unchanged; and express willingness to openly negotiate with the US government, either immediately or at a later date, but not to miss the opportunity.

The report specifically suggested that Taiwan's authorities be informed, acknowledging Taiwan's firm stance against "two Chinas" or "one China, one Taiwan," which is commendable and aligns with our position. Mao Zedong approved the plan, writing, "Agree to this deployment."[35]

On April 5, 1975, Mao Zedong's old rival, Chiang Kai-shek, passed away in Taipei at the age of 87. Mao Zedong received the news calmly.

During meetings with foreign guests in the following months, Mao Zedong frequently mentioned Chiang Kai-shek, as naturally as he had when he discussed him with Nixon. These conversations also revealed Mao's concern for resolving the Taiwan question.[36]

On September 9, 1976, Mao Zedong passed away in Beijing at the age of 83.

Forty-nine years earlier, on the same day, Mao Zedong had raised the banner of armed resistance against the KMT reactionaries, eventually driving Chiang Kai-shek to retreat to a few islands.[37] Yet, "recovering those islands" remained his unfulfilled aspiration.

Notes

Chapter 1   "A Startling Emergence"
1. Edgar Snow, *Red Star over China (Chinese Edition)* (Beijing: JDX Joint Publishing Company, 1979), 110.
2. Ibid., 110–111.
3. Ibid., 111–112.
4. Ibid., 117.
5. Ibid., 120.
6. Ibid.
7. Ibid.
8. Ibid.
9. Great Teacher, Great Leader, Great Supreme Commander, and Great Helmsman.
10. Pang Xianzhi and Feng Hui, eds., *Chronicle of Mao Zedong (1949–1976)*, vol. 6 (Beijing: Central Literature Publishing House, 2013), 358.
11. Edgar Snow, *Red Star over China (Chinese Edition)* (Beijing: JDX Joint Publishing Company, 1979), 121.
12. Ibid., 121–122.
13. Zeng Guofan (styled Disheng) was a Chinese statesman, military general, and Confucian scholar of the Qing dynasty, known for his role in suppressing the Taiping Heavenly Kingdom Movement and his efforts in Self-Strengthening Movement.—Trans.
14. Liang Qichao (styled Ren Gong) was a late Qing dynasty reformist, journalist, and intellectual who significantly influenced modern China's political and cultural landscape.—Trans.
15. Yang Changji, *Diary of Dahuazhai* (Changsha: Hunan People's Publishing House, 1978), 163.
16. A *jiazi* is a 60-year cycle in the traditional Chinese calendar, symbolizing a full life cycle and implying great experience and wisdom.—Trans.
17. Mao Zedong, *Collected Works of Mao Zedong*, vol. 1 (Beijing: People's Publishing House, 1993), 477.

18. Edgar Snow, *Red Star over China (Chinese Edition)* (Beijing: JDX Joint Publishing Company, 1979), 125.
19. *Xinmin Institute Materials* (Beijing: People's Publishing House, 1980), 3.
20. Edgar Snow, *Red Star over China (Chinese Edition)* (Beijing: JDX Joint Publishing Company, 1979), 126.
21. Ibid., 125.
22. *Xinmin Institute Materials* (Beijing: People's Publishing House, 1980), 43–44.
23. Edgar Snow, *Red Star over China (Chinese Edition)* (Beijing: JDX Joint Publishing Company, 1979), 126–127.
24. Ibid., 127.
25. Ibid., 126.
26. Ibid., 127–128.
27. Ibid., 127.
28. Ibid., 128.
29. Ibid., 129.
30. *Mao Zedong's Early Manuscripts*, vol. 1 (Changsha: Hunan People's Publishing House, 2013), 270–271.
31. *Mao Zedong's Early Manuscripts*, vol. 1 (Changsha: Hunan People's Publishing House, 1990), 312, 356, and 359.

Chapter 2 Initial Show of Strength

1. Pang Xianzhi, ed., *Chronicle of Mao Zedong (1893–1949) (Revised Edition)*, vol. 1 (Beijing: Central Literature Publishing House, 2013), 50.
2. Mao Zedong, "On the People's Democratic Dictatorship" (June 30, 1949), in *Selected Works of Mao Zedong*, vol. 4 (Beijing: People's Publishing House, 1991), 1470.
3. *Xinmin Institute Materials* (Beijing: People's Publishing House, 1980), 59 and 61–62.
4. Ibid., 63–65.
5. Pang Xianzhi, ed., *Chronicle of Mao Zedong (1893–1949) (Revised Edition)*, vol. 1 (Beijing: Central Literature Publishing House, 2013), 57.
6. Ibid., 57–58.
7. Ibid., 53 n. 1, 54, and n. 1.
8. Ibid., 49 and n. 1.
9. *Mao Zedong's Early Manuscripts*, vol. 1 (Changsha: Hunan People's Publishing House, 2013), 493.
10. Ibid., 498.
11. *Selected Letters of Mao Zedong* (Beijing: Central Literature Publishing House, 2003), 4 and 6–8.
12. Edgar Snow, *Red Star over China (Chinese Edition)* (Beijing: JDX Joint Publishing Company, 1979), 131.
13. *Xinmin Institute Materials* (Beijing: People's Publishing House, 1980), 23.
14. *Selected Letters of Mao Zedong* (Beijing: Central Literature Publishing House, 2003), 11.
15. Edgar Snow, *Red Star over China (Chinese Edition)* (Beijing: SDX Joint Publishing Company, 1979), 135.
16. Ibid., 135–136.

17. *Collected Works of Mao Zedong*, vol. 1 (Beijing: People's Publishing House, 1993), 37 and 41.
18. Ibid., 16–17.
19. Edgar Snow, *Red Star over China (Chinese Edition)* (Beijing: SDX Joint Publishing Company, 1979), 136.
20. Pang Xianzhi, ed., *Chronicle of Mao Zedong (1893–1949) (Revised Edition)*, vol. 1 (Beijing: Central Literature Publishing House, 2013), 182 n. 1.
21. *Selected Letters of Mao Zedong* (Beijing: Central Literature Publishing House, 2003), 14.
22. *Collected Works of Mao Zedong*, vol. 7 (Beijing: People's Publishing House, 1999), 460.
23. Party History Research Office of the CPC Central Committee, *History of the Communist Party of China*, vol. 1 (1921–1949), pt. 1 (Beijing: Party History Publishing House, 2011), 220.
24. Ibid., 232.

Chapter 3   Pioneering a New Path

1. Mao Zedong, *Collected Works of Mao Zedong*, vol. 1 (Beijing: People's Publishing House, 1993), 47.
2. *Early Manuscripts of Mao Zedong* (Changsha: Hunan Publishing House, 1990), 554.
3. Pang Xianzhi, ed., *Chronicle of Mao Zedong (1893–1949) (Revised Edition)*, vol. 1 (Beijing: Central Literature Publishing House, 2013), 209.
4. Mao Zedong, *Collected Works of Mao Zedong*, vol. 1 (Beijing: People's Publishing House, 1993), 47.
5. Pang Xianzhi, ed., *Chronicle of Mao Zedong (1893–1949) (Revised Edition)*, vol. 1 (Beijing: Central Literature Publishing House, 2013), 206–207.
6. Mao Zedong, *Collected Works of Mao Zedong*, vol. 7 (Beijing: People's Publishing House, 1999), 105.
7. Mao Zedong, *Selected Works of Mao Zedong*, vol. 1 (Beijing: People's Publishing House, 1991), 62.
8. The "Sixteen-Character Formula" refers to a set of guerrilla warfare tactics developed by Mao Zedong and Zhu De during the Chinese Communist Revolution. Each of the four phrases contains four Chinese characters, making up the sixteen characters in total. These tactics emphasize strategic retreat, harassment, and opportunistic attacks, essential for the Red Army's survival and success against a more powerful adversary.
9. Mao Zedong, *Selected Works of Mao Zedong*, vol. 1 (Beijing: People's Publishing House, 1991), 204.
10. *Selected Central Documents Since the Founding of the Party*, vol. 6 (Beijing: Central Literature Publishing House, 2011), 453.
11. Mao Zedong, *Collected Works of Mao Zedong*, vol. 1 (Beijing: People's Publishing House, 1993), 54–56 and 61–62.
12. Ibid., 64.
13. Ibid., 65.
14. Jin Chongji, ed., *Biography of Zhu De*, rev. ed., vol. 1 (Beijing: Central Literature Publishing House, 2016), 212.
15. Mao Zedong, *Collected Works of Mao Zedong*, vol. 1 (Beijing: People's Publishing House, 1993), 75.

16. *Selected Important Documents Since the Founding of the Party*, vol. 6 (Beijing: Central Literature Publishing House, 2011), 512.
17. Ibid.

Chapter 4 Difficult Days

1. Tu Zhennong, "Report on the Inspection Work of the First Army Corps and the Western Jiangxi and Western Fujian Areas" (September–October 1930), quoted in Jin Chongji, ed., *Biography of Mao Zedong (1893–1949)* (Beijing: Central Literature Publishing House, 2004), 215–216.
2. *Collected Works of Mao Zedong*, vol. 3 (Beijing: People's Publishing House, 1996), 127.
3. *Manuscripts of Mao Zedong Since the Founding of the People's Republic of China*, vol. 11 (Beijing: Central Literature Publishing House, 1996), 85.
4. Guo Huaruo, *Memoirs of Guo Huaruo* (Beijing: Military Science Press, 1995), 48.
5. *Selected Works of Mao Zedong*, vol. 1 (Beijing: People's Publishing House, 1991), 217.
6. *Huainanzi · Chapter on Astronomy*.
7. Pang Xianzhi, ed., *Chronicle of Mao Zedong (1893–1949) (Revised Edition)*, vol. 1 (Beijing: Central Literature Publishing House, 2013), 323.
8. Mao Zedong used the ancient meaning of "*yuan*" (元), which refers to a person's head.
9. *Selected Works of Mao Zedong*, vol. 1 (Beijing: People's Publishing House, 1991), 218.
10. Ibid., 220–221.
11. Ibid., 219.
12. Ibid., 204–205.
13. "Brief Report on the Process of the Ningdu Conference of the Central Bureau of the Soviet Area" (October 21, 1932), quoted in Jin Chongji, ed., *Biography of Mao Zedong (1893–1949)* (Beijing: Central Literature Publishing House, 2004), 307.
14. Quoted in Pang Xianzhi, ed., *Chronicle of Mao Zedong (1893–1949) (Revised Edition)*, vol. 1 (Beijing: Central Literature Publishing House, 2013), 388–389.
15. Quoted in Jin Chongji, ed., *Biography of Mao Zedong (1893–1949)* (Beijing: Central Literature Publishing House, 2004), 333–334.
16. *Autobiography of Peng Dehuai* (Beijing: People's Publishing House, 1981), 183.
17. Quoted in Jin Chongji, ed., *Biography of Mao Zedong (1893–1949)* (Beijing: Central Literature Publishing House, 2004), 334.

Chapter 5 "The Red Army Fears No Difficult Expedition"

1. Mao Zedong, *Collected Works of Mao Zedong*, vol. 7 (Beijing: People's Publishing House, 1999), 460.
2. *Selected Important Documents Since the Founding of the Party*, vol. 11 (Beijing: Central Literature Publishing House, 2011), 656.
3. Chen Yun, *Selected Works of Chen Yun*, vol. 1 (Beijing: People's Publishing House, 1995), 36.
4. Ibid., 37.
5. Chen Yun, *Collected Works of Chen Yun*, vol. 1 (Beijing: Central Literature Publishing House, 2005), 8–9 and 34.
6. Mao Zedong, *Selected Works of Mao Zedong*, vol. 1 (Beijing: People's Publishing House, 1991), 205.
7. Ibid., 182.

8. Liu Bocheng, *Memoirs of Liu Bocheng* (Shanghai: Shanghai Literature and Art Publishing House, 1981), 7–8.
9. Wu Jiqing, *In the Days by Chairman Mao's Side* (Nanchang: Jiangxi People's Publishing House, 1983), 217–219.
10. Pang Xianzhi, ed., *Chronicle of Mao Zedong (1893–1949) (Revised Edition)*, vol. 1 (Beijing: Central Literature Publishing House, 2013), 459.
11. Peng Dehuai, *Memoirs of Peng Dehuai* (Beijing: People's Publishing House, 1981), 201.
12. Ibid.
13. "Letter from the Central Committee to Comrades on the Implementation the Northward Policy" (September 10, 1935), in *Selected Important Documents Since the Founding of the Party*, vol. 12 (Beijing: Central Literature Publishing House, 2011), 305.
14. Mao Zedong, *Selected Works of Mao Zedong*, vol. 1 (Beijing: People's Publishing House, 1991), 213.
15. Ibid., 149–150.
16. Pang Xianzhi, ed., *Chronicle of Mao Zedong (1893–1949) (Revised Edition)*, vol. 1 (Beijing: Central Literature Publishing House, 2012), 531.
17. Jin Chongji, ed., *Biography of Zhou Enlai (1898–1949)* (Beijing: People's Publishing House, 1989), 309.
18. Pang Xianzhi, ed., *Chronicle of Mao Zedong (1893–1949) (Revised Edition)*, vol. 1 (Beijing: Central Literature Publishing House, 2012), 533.
19. Ibid., 532.
20. Ibid., 534.
21. Ibid., 622.
22. Jin Chongji, ed., *Biography of Mao Zedong (1893–1949)* (Beijing: Central Literature Publishing House, 2004), 428.
23. Pang Xianzhi, ed., *Chronicle of Mao Zedong (1893–1949) (Revised Edition)*, vol. 1 (Beijing: Central Literature Publishing House, 2012), 623.
24. Liping and Fang Ming, eds., *Chronology of Zhou Enlai (1898–1949) (Revised Edition)* (Beijing: Central Literature Publishing House, 1998), 341–342.
25. Pang Xianzhi, ed., *Chronicle of Mao Zedong (1893–1949) (Revised Edition)*, vol. 1 (Beijing: Central Literature Publishing House, 2012), 626.
26. *Selected Important Documents Since the Founding of the Party*, vol. 13 (Beijing: Central Literature Publishing House, 2011), 422–423.
27. The nine-point agreement is as follows: (1) Kung and Soong will form the Executive Yuan, clearing out pro-Japanese factions. (2) Central Army will withdraw and leave the northwest. (3) Chiang agrees to release patriotic leaders upon his return. (4) The Soviet government and the Red Army remain unchanged, with the two Soongs guaranteeing that Chiang will stop the "anti-Communist campaign" and Zhang Xueliang will support; the Red Army will change its designation and unite in command and action upon the outbreak of war. (5) Open up governance and convene a National Salvation Conference. (6) Release political prisoners in batches. (7) Upon the outbreak of war, the CPC will be publicly recognized. (8) Form an alliance with the Soviet Union and establish contact with Britain, the US, and France. (9) Upon his return, Chiang will issue a public apology and resign as Premier.
28. Jin Chongji, ed., *Biography of Mao Zedong (1893–1949)* (Beijing: Central Literature Publishing House, 2004), 435.

Chapter 6 The National War of Resistance and the Protracted War

1. Pang Xianzhi, ed., *Chronicle of Mao Zedong (1893–1949) (Revised Edition)*, vol. 2 (Beijing: Central Literature Publishing House, 2013), 2.
2. Qin Xiaoyi, ed., *Historical Materials of the Lugou Bridge Incident (Part One)*, in vol. 1 of *Revolutionary Documents* no. 106 (Taipei: The Party History Committee of the Central Committee of the Kuomintang, 1986), 3–4.
3. *History of the Chinese People's Liberation Army*, vol. 2 (Beijing: Military Science Press, 2010), 14.
4. Ibid., 19.
5. *Selected Works of Mao Zedong*, vol. 2 (Beijing: People's Publishing House, 1991), 363–364.
6. Military History Research Department of the Academy of Military Sciences, *War History of the Chinese People's Liberation Army*, vol. 2 (Beijing: Military Science Press, 1987), 8–9.
7. *Selected Works of Mao Zedong*, vol. 2 (Beijing: People's Publishing House, 1991), 353.
8. Ibid., 354.
9. Ibid., 354–356.
10. *Concise Reader of the History of the Chinese People's War of Resistance Against Japanese Aggression* (Beijing: People's Publishing House, 2015), 75.
11. Jin Chongji, ed., *Biography of Mao Zedong (1893–1949)* (Beijing: Central Literature Publishing House, 2004), 479.
12. Jin Chongji, ed., *Biography of Zhou Enlai (1898–1949)* (Beijing: People's Publishing House, 1989), 371.
13. Pang Xianzhi, ed., *Chronicle of Mao Zedong (1893–1949) (Revised Edition)*, vol. 2 (Beijing: Central Literature Publishing House, 2013), 22–23.
14. Ibid., 23.
15. Ibid.
16. Ibid., 22.
17. *Concise Reader of the History of the Chinese People's War of Resistance Against Japanese Aggression* (Beijing: People's Publishing House, 2015), 96.
18. *Selected Works of Mao Zedong*, vol. 2 (Beijing: People's Publishing House, 1991), 387–388, 390–391, and 394.
19. Wang Ming (Chen Shaoyu), "Report at the Political Bureau of the Central Committee Meeting (December 9, 1937)," in Jin Chongji, ed., *Biography of Mao Zedong (1893–1949)* (Beijing: Central Literature Publishing House, 2004), 522–523.
20. Mao Zedong, "Speech at the Political Bureau of the Central Committee Meeting (November 13, 1943)," in Jin Chongji, ed., *Biography of Mao Zedong (1893–1949)* (Beijing: Central Literature Publishing House, 2004), 525.
21. Wang Ming (Chen Shaoyu), Zhou Enlai, Bo Gu (Qin Bangxian), and Ye Jianying, "Telegram to Luo Pu (Zhang Wentian), Mao Zedong, and the Political Bureau of the Central Committee (December 21, 1937)," in Jin Chongji, ed., *Biography of Zhou Enlai (1898–1949)* (Beijing: People's Publishing House, 1989), 393.
22. Jin Chongji, ed., *Biography of Mao Zedong (1893–1949)* (Beijing: Central Literature Publishing House, 2004), 526–527.
23. *Ta Kung Pao*, editorial, April 25, 1938, "The current situation is a critical juncture for the future of the War of Resistance. If we achieve victory in this battle, the tangible and

intangible impacts will have a decisive effect." Another editorial on April 26, 1938, added, "This battle is certainly not the final decisive battle, but it serves as a quasi-decisive battle. For the Japanese militarists, this battle represents their last struggle."

24. Pang Xianzhi, ed., *Chronicle of Mao Zedong (1893–1949) (Revised Edition)*, vol. 2 (Beijing: Central Literature Publishing House, 2013), 70.
25. *Selected Works of Mao Zedong*, vol. 2 (Beijing: People's Publishing House, 1991), 462–463.
26. The quotes from *On Protracted War* are found in *Selected Works of Mao Zedong*, vol. 2 (Beijing: People's Publishing House, 1991), 478, 503, and 511–512.
27. *Selected Works of Mao Zedong*, vol. 2 (Beijing: People's Publishing House, 1991), 501.
28. Ibid., 405, 407, and 433–434.

Chapter 7 Independent and Autonomous Guerrilla Warfare Behind Enemy Lines

1. *Concise Reader of the History of China's War of Resistance Against Japanese Aggression* (Beijing: People's Publishing House, 2015), 107.
2. *Selected Works of Wang Jiaxiang* (Beijing: People's Publishing House, 1989), 138 and 141–142.
3. *Selected Important Documents Since the Founding of the Party (1921–1949)*, vol. 15 (Beijing: Central Literature Publishing House, 2011), 592 and 601–602.
4. Pang Xianzhi, ed., *Chronicle of Mao Zedong (1893–1949) (Revised Edition)*, vol. 2 (Beijing: Central Literature Publishing House, 2013), 203–204.
5. *Concise Reader of the History of China's War of Resistance Against Japanese Aggression* (Beijing: People's Publishing House, 2015), 150–151.
6. *Autobiography of Peng Dehuai* (Beijing: People's Publishing House, 1981), 235.
7. *Concise Reader of the History of China's War of Resistance Against Japanese Aggression* (Beijing: People's Publishing House, 2015), 152.
8. *Autobiography of Peng Dehuai* (Beijing: People's Publishing House, 1981), 238.
9. Pang Xianzhi, ed., *Chronicle of Mao Zedong (1893–1949) (Revised Edition)*, vol. 2 (Beijing: Central Literature Publishing House, 2013), 207.
10. Ibid., 208.
11. *Selected Works of Mao Zedong*, vol. 2 (Beijing: People's Publishing House, 1991), 773–776.
12. *Selected Works of Soong Ching-ling*, vol. 1 (Beijing: People's Publishing House, 1992), 321–322.
13. Pang Xianzhi, ed., *Chronicle of Mao Zedong (1893–1949) (Revised Edition)*, vol. 2 (Beijing: Central Literature Publishing House, 2013), 264–267.
14. Jin Chongji, ed., *Biography of Mao Zedong (1893–1949)* (Beijing: Central Literature Publishing House, 2004), 619.
15. *Selected Works of Mao Zedong*, vol. 2 (Beijing: People's Publishing House, 1991), 778–779.
16. Ibid., 781–783.
17. *Selected Works of Mao Zedong*, vol. 3 (Beijing: People's Publishing House, 1991), 892.
18. *Collected Works of Mao Zedong*, vol. 2 (Beijing: People's Publishing House, 1993), 385–386.
19. Ibid., 141.
20. According to Xie Juezai's diary entry from June 4, 1941: "Yesterday afternoon, during heavy rain, lightning struck the county magistrate's meeting room. Eight people were hit, and the

acting magistrate of Yanchuan County (currently head of the fourth section) Li Caiyun was killed instantly. This morning, his coffin was transported back by car." See *Diary of Xie Juezai*, vol. 1 (Beijing: People's Publishing House, 1984), 314.
21. *Collected Works of Mao Zedong*, vol. 3 (Beijing: People's Publishing House, 1996), 338.
22. Ibid., 339.
23. Second Historical Archives of China, ed., *Compilation of Archival Materials on the History of the Republic of China*, series 5, vol. 2, Military (5) (Jiangsu: Jiangsu Ancient Books Publishing House, 1998), 979.
24. Israel Epstein, *Unsealing the Blockade to Visit Yan'an* (Beijing: People's Daily Publishing House, 1995), 27–28.
25. *Selected Important Documents Since the Founding of the Party (1921–1949)*, vol. 21 (Beijing: Central Literature Publishing House, 2011), 471.
26. Pang Xianzhi, ed., *Chronicle of Mao Zedong (1893–1949) (Revised Edition)*, vol. 2 (Beijing: Central Literature Publishing House, 2013), 540.
27. *Selected Important Documents Since the Founding of the Party (1921–1949)*, vol. 21 (Beijing: Central Literature Publishing House, 2011), 488.
28. Ibid., 505.
29. Pang Xianzhi, ed., *Chronicle of Mao Zedong (1893–1949) (Revised Edition)*, vol. 2 (Beijing: Central Literature Publishing House, 2013), 556–557.
30. Ibid., 557–558.
31. Pang Xianzhi, ed., *Chronicle of Mao Zedong (1893–1949) (Revised Edition)*, vol. 2 (Beijing: Central Literature Publishing House, 2013), 558.
32. *Selected Works of Mao Zedong*, vol. 3 (Beijing: People's Publishing House, 1991), 1102–1103.
33. Ibid., 1030.
34. Ibid., 1077.

Chapter 8 Marxism Must Also Be Adapted to China

1. When this article was compiled into *Selected Works of Mao Zedong (Type A)* in 1964, Mao Zedong changed the title to "Oppose Bookism." Later, it was included in the second edition of *Selected Works of Mao Zedong* published by People's Publishing House in June 1991.
2. Pang Xianzhi, ed., *Chronicle of Mao Zedong (1893–1949) (Revised Edition)*, vol. 1 (Beijing: Central Literature Publishing House, 2013), 306.
3. *Selected Works of Mao Zedong*, vol. 1 (Beijing: People's Publishing House, 1991), 111–112.
4. *Selected Works of Mao Zedong*, vol. 1 (Beijing: People's Publishing House, 1991), 115 and 109.
5. *Collected Works of Mao Zedong*, vol. 1 (Beijing: People's Publishing House, 1993), 268.
6. *Selected Works of Mao Zedong*, vol. 1 (Beijing: People's Publishing House, 1991), 116 and 110.
7. *Selected Works of Mao Zedong*, vol. 3 (Beijing: People's Publishing House, 1991), 179.
8. *Collected Works of Mao Zedong*, vol. 8 (Beijing: People's Publishing House, 1999), 308.
9. *Selected Important Documents Since the Founding of the Party (1921–1949)*, vol. 12 (Beijing: Central Literature Publishing House, 2011), 51 and 53.
10. *Collected Works of Mao Zedong*, vol. 8 (Beijing: People's Publishing House, 1999), 263.
11. Ibid., 299.

12. *Mao Zedong's Military Manuscripts Since the Founding of the People's Republic of China*, vol. 2 (Beijing: Military Science Press and Central Literature Publishing House, 2010), 241.
13. *Collected Works of Mao Zedong*, vol. 8 (Beijing: People's Publishing House, 1999), 184.
14. Mo Wenhua, *Memoirs of Mo Wenhua* (Beijing: Chinese People's Liberation Army Publishing House, 1996), 380–381.
15. *Mao Zedong's Military Manuscripts Since the Founding of the People's Republic of China*, vol. 2 (Beijing: Military Science Press and Central Literature Publishing House, 2010), 113–114.
16. Pang Xianzhi, ed., *Chronicle of Mao Zedong (1893–1949) (Revised Edition)*, vol. 1 (Beijing: Central Literature Publishing House, 2013), 576.
17. *Selected Letters of Mao Zedong* (Beijing: Central Literature Publishing House, 2003), 68.
18. *Mao Zedong's Military Manuscripts Since the Founding of the People's Republic of China*, vol. 2 (Beijing: Military Science Press and Central Literature Publishing House, 2010), 241.
19. *Complete Works of Lenin*, vol. 39 (Beijing: People's Publishing House, 1986), 128.
20. *Selected Works of Mao Zedong*, vol. 1 (Beijing: People's Publishing House, 1991), 187.
21. These categories constitute the first to ninth sections of chapter five, "Strategic Defense," namely (1) Active Defense and Passive Defense, (2) Preparation for Counter-Encirclement and Suppression, (3) Strategic Retreat, (4) Strategic Counter-Offensive, (5) The Beginning of the Counter-Offensive, (6) The Problem of Concentrating Forces, (7) Mobile Warfare, (8) Quick-Decision Battle, and (9) Annihilation Battle.
22. Pang Xianzhi and Feng Hui, eds., *Chronicle of Mao Zedong (1949–1976)*, vol. 5 (Beijing: Central Literature Publishing House, 2013), 329.
23. *Mao Zedong's Philosophical Annotations* (Beijing: Central Literature Publishing House, 1988), 311–312.
24. Refers to the CPC Central Committee organ *Bolshevik*, first published on October 24, 1927.
25. Refers to Stalin's *Foundations of Leninism*.
26. Qu Qiubai, *History of the Russian Revolutionary Movement* (Beijing: New Youth Society, 1927).
27. *Selected Letters of Mao Zedong* (Beijing: Central Literature Publishing House, 2003), 22.
28. Ibid., 24.
29. Quoted in Gong Yuzhi, Pang Xianzhi, and Shi Zhongquan, *Mao Zedong's Reading Life* (Beijing: SDX Joint Publishing Company, 2010), 28.
30. *Mao Zedong's Philosophical Annotations* (Beijing: Central Literature Publishing House, 1988), 9.
31. This was the second section of chapter two of the "Dialectical Materialism (Lecture Outline)" that Mao Zedong prepared for lectures at the Resistance Against-Japanese Military and Political University, written in July 1937.
32. This was the first section of chapter three of the "Dialectical Materialism (Lecture Outline)," written in August 1937, originally titled "The Law of Contradiction."
33. *Mao Zedong's Military Manuscripts Since the Founding of the People's Republic of China*, vol. 2 (Beijing: Military Science Press and Central Literature Publishing House, 2010), 114.
34. National Defense University of the Chinese People's Liberation Army, *History of the Resistance Against-Japanese Military and Political University of the Chinese People* (Beijing: National Defense University Press, 2000), 37.
35. *Selected Works of Mao Zedong*, vol. 1 (Beijing: People's Publishing House, 1991), 282.

36. *Collected Works of Mao Zedong*, vol. 8 (Beijing: People's Publishing House, 1999), 321.
37. The above quotations from "On Practice" are from *Selected Works of Mao Zedong*, vol. 1 (Beijing: People's Publishing House, 1991), 284, 288, 290–292, and 296.
38. *Selected Works of Mao Zedong*, vol. 1 (Beijing: People's Publishing House, 1991), 299.
39. Ibid., 319–320.
40. *Selected Important Documents Since the Founding of the Party (1921–1949)*, vol. 15 (Beijing: Central Literature Publishing House, 2011), 651.
41. Ibid., 650.
42. Pang Xianzhi, ed., *Chronicle of Mao Zedong (1893–1949) (Revised Edition)*, vol. 2 (Beijing: Central Literature Publishing House, 2013), 237.
43. *Selected Works of Mao Zedong*, vol. 3 (Beijing: People's Publishing House, 1991), 795, 796–797, 801, 800.
44. Hu Qiaomu, *Hu Qiaomu's Recollections of Mao Zedong (Revised Edition)* (Beijing: People's Publishing House, 2014), 192–193.
45. *Selected Works of Mao Zedong*, vol. 3 (Beijing: People's Publishing House, 1991), 791, 792.
46. Pang Xianzhi, ed., *Chronicle of Mao Zedong (1893–1949) (Revised Edition)*, vol. 2 (Beijing: Central Literature Publishing House, 2013), 469.
47. Hu Qiaomu, *Hu Qiaomu's Recollections of Mao Zedong (Revised Edition)* (Beijing: People's Publishing House, 2014), 48.
48. *Selected Works of Mao Zedong*, vol. 3 (Beijing: People's Publishing House, 1991), 812, 814, and 817.
49. These 18 rectification documents are as follows: (1) Mao Zedong's report at the Party School on February 1, 1942; (2) Mao Zedong's report at the Yan'an Cadre Conference on February 8, 1942; (3) two reports by Kang Sheng; (4) Central Committee's decision on strengthening Party spirit; (5) Central Committee's decision on investigation and research; (6) Central Committee's decision on Yan'an Cadre School; (7) Central Committee's decision on on-the-job cadre education; (8) Mao Zedong's speech at the Border Region Council; (9) Mao Zedong's report on reforming study; (10) Mao Zedong's essay on opposing liberalism; (11) two prefaces to Mao Zedong's *Rural Surveys*; (12) six concluding remarks from the history of the Communist Party of the Soviet Union; (13) Stalin's twelve points on Bolshevization of the Party; (14) chapters 2, 3, 4, and 5 of Liu Shaoqi's essay on Communist Party member self-cultivation; (15) Chen Yun's essay on how to be a Communist Party member; (16) Red Fourth Army's Ninth Congress on incorrect tendencies within the Party; (17) publicity guide pamphlet; and (18) Central Publicity Department's decision on discussing Central decisions and Mao Zedong's reports on the rectification of the three styles in Yan'an.
50. The newly added 19th to 22nd rectification documents are Stalin's essay on leadership and inspection; Lenin, Stalin, and others on Party discipline and Party democracy; Stalin on egalitarianism; Dimitrov on cadre policy and cadre education policy.
51. *Selected Important Documents Since the Founding of the Party (1921–1949)*, vol. 19 (Beijing: Central Literature Publishing House, 2011), 329–330.
52. *Selected Important Documents Since the Founding of the Party (1921–1949)*, vol. 20 (Beijing: Central Literature Publishing House, 2011), 173.
53. Pang Xianzhi, ed., *Chronicle of Mao Zedong (1893–1949) (Revised Edition)*, vol. 2 (Beijing: Central Literature Publishing House, 2013), 460.

54. *Collected Works of Mao Zedong*, vol. 3 (Beijing: People's Publishing House, 1996), 262.
55. *Selected Important Documents Since the Founding of the Party (1921–1949)*, vol. 22 (Beijing: Central Literature Publishing House, 2011), 390.
56. *Selected Works of Liu Shaoqi*, vol. 1 (Beijing: People's Publishing House, 1981), 335.

Chapter 9   Confrontation and Negotiation

1. Harry S. Truman, *Memoirs (Chinese Translation)*, vol. 2 (Beijing: World Affair Press, 1965), 70–71.
2. Mao Zedong, *Selected Works of Mao Zedong*, vol. 4 (Beijing: People's Publishing House, 1991), 1130, 1132.
3. Pang Xianzhi, ed., *Chronicle of Mao Zedong (1893–1949) (Revised Edition)*, vol. 3 (Beijing: Central Literature Publishing House, 2013), 13.
4. Mao Zedong, *Selected Works of Mao Zedong*, vol. 4 (Beijing: People's Publishing House, 1991), 1153–1154.
5. Quoted in Yang Tianshi, *In Search of the Real Chiang Kai-shek: The Diaries of Chiang Kai-shek Decoded*, vol. 2 (Taiyuan: Shanxi Publishing Group and Shanxi People's Publishing House, 2008), 430.
6. Quoted in Zhang Xiuzhang, *The Diaries of Chiang Kai-shek Revealed*, vol. 2 (Beijing: Unity Press, 2007), 730.
7. Pang Xianzhi, ed., *Chronicle of Mao Zedong (1893–1949) (Revised Edition)*, vol. 3 (Beijing: Central Literature Publishing House, 2013), 17.
8. *Collected Works of Mao Zedong*, vol. 4 (Beijing: People's Publishing House, 1996), 20–22.
9. Pang Xianzhi, ed., *Chronicle of Mao Zedong (1893–1949) (Revised Edition)*, vol. 3 (Beijing: Central Literature Publishing House, 2013), 21.
10. *Selected Important Documents Since the Founding of the Party (1921–1949)*, vol. 22 (Beijing: Central Literature Publishing House, 2011), 677–678.
11. Jin Chongji, ed., *Biography of Zhou Enlai (1898–1949)* (Beijing: People's Publishing House, 1989), 599–600.
12. Ibid., 599.
13. Quoted in Yang Tianshi, *In Search of the Real Chiang Kai-shek: The Diaries of Chiang Kai-shek Decoded*, vol. 2 (Taiyuan: Shanxi Publishing Group and Shanxi People's Publishing House, 2008), 441.
14. *Collected Works of Mao Zedong*, vol. 4 (Beijing: People's Publishing House, 1996), 25.
15. Quoted in Yang Tianshi, *In Search of the Real Chiang Kai-shek: The Diaries of Chiang Kai-shek Decoded*, vol. 2 (Taiyuan: Shanxi Publishing Group and Shanxi People's Publishing House, 2008), 441.
16. *Collected Works of Mao Zedong*, vol. 4 (Beijing: People's Publishing House, 1996), 31.
17. Mao Zedong, *Selected Works of Mao Zedong*, vol. 4 (Beijing: People's Publishing House, 1991), 1159.
18. Quoted in Pang Xianzhi, ed., *Chronicle of Mao Zedong (1893–1949) (Revised Edition)*, vol. 3 (Beijing: Central Literature Publishing House, 2013), 35–36.
19. Party History Research Office of the CPC Central Committee, *Ninety Years of the Communist Party of China* (Period of New Democratic Revolution) (Beijing: Party History Publishing House and Party Building Books Publishing House, 2016), 279.
20. Pang Xianzhi, ed., *Chronicle of Mao Zedong (1893–1949) (Revised Edition)*, vol. 3 (Beijing: Central Literature Publishing House, 2013), 97.

21. *Collected Works of Mao Zedong*, vol. 3 (Beijing: People's Publishing House, 1996), 454.
22. Military History Research Department of the Academy of Military Sciences, *History of the Chinese People's Liberation Army*, vol. 3 (Period of the National Liberation War) (Beijing: Military Science Publishing House, 1987), 46.
23. Mao Zedong, *Selected Works of Mao Zedong*, vol. 4 (Beijing: People's Publishing House, 1991), 1187–1188.
24. Ibid., 1195.
25. Ibid., 1184–1185.
26. Ibid., 1198–1199.
27. Military History Research Department of the Academy of Military Sciences, *History of the Chinese People's Liberation Army*, vol. 3 (Period of the National Liberation War) (Beijing: Military Science Publishing House, 1987), 97.
28. Shi Zhe, *Beside the Historical Giant* (Beijing: Central Literature Publishing House, 1991), 337–338.
29. Pang Xianzhi, ed., *Chronicle of Mao Zedong (1893–1949) (Revised Edition)*, vol. 3 (Beijing: Central Literature Publishing House, 2013), 176.
30. Military History Research Department of the Academy of Military Sciences, *History of the Chinese People's Liberation Army*, vol. 3 (Period of the National Liberation War) (Beijing: Military Science Publishing House, 1987), 102–106.
31. *Collected Military Works of Mao Zedong*, vol. 4 (Beijing: Military Science Publishing House and Central Literature Publishing House, 1993), 68.
32. Mao Zedong, *Selected Works of Mao Zedong*, vol. 4 (Beijing: People's Publishing House, 1991), 1230.
33. Ibid., 1235.
34. Ibid., 1243, 1244, 1248, 1250, 1253, and 1255–1256.
35. Ibid., 1298.

Chapter 10 Carrying the Revolution to the End

1. Party History Research Office of the CPC Central Committee, *Ninety Years of the Communist Party of China* (New Democratic Revolution Period) (Beijing: Party History Publishing House and Party Building Books Publishing House, 2016), 284.
2. Mao Zedong, *Selected Works of Mao Zedong*, vol. 4 (Beijing: People's Publishing House, 1991), 1224–1225.
3. Pang Xianzhi, ed., *Chronicle of Mao Zedong (1893–1949) (Revised Edition)*, vol. 2 (Beijing: Central Literature Publishing House, 2013), 249.
4. Mao Zedong, *Collected Military Works of Mao Zedong*, vol. 4 (Beijing: Military Science Press and Central Literature Publishing House, 1993), 459.
5. Pang Xianzhi, ed., *Chronicle of Mao Zedong (1893–1949) (Revised Edition)*, vol. 2 (Beijing: Central Literature Publishing House, 2013), 272.
6. Mao Zedong, *Collected Military Works of Mao Zedong*, vol. 4 (Beijing: Military Science Press and Central Literature Publishing House, 1993), 459.
7. Mao Zedong, *Selected Works of Mao Zedong*, vol. 4 (Beijing: People's Publishing House, 1991), 1346.
8. Military History Research Department of the Academy of Military Sciences, *History of the Chinese People's Liberation Army (War of Liberation Period)*, vol. 3 (Beijing: Military Science Press, 1987), 233.

9. Mao Zedong, *Collected Military Works of Mao Zedong*, vol. 4 (Beijing: Military Science Press and Central Literature Publishing House, 1993), 391.
10. Mao Zedong, *Selected Works of Mao Zedong*, vol. 4 (Beijing: People's Publishing House, 1991), 1335–1336.
11. Mao Zedong, *Collected Military Works of Mao Zedong*, vol. 5 (Beijing: Military Science Press and Central Literature Publishing House, 1993), 37.
12. Mao Zedong, *Selected Works of Mao Zedong*, vol. 4 (Beijing: People's Publishing House, 1991), 1351.
13. Pang Xianzhi, ed., *Chronicle of Mao Zedong (1893–1949) (Revised Edition)*, vol. 2 (Beijing: Central Literature Publishing House, 2013), 358.
14. Party History Research Office of the CPC Central Committee, *History of the Communist Party of China*, vol. 1, pt. 2 (Beijing: Party History Publishing House, 2011), 330.
15. Mao Zedong, *Collected Military Works of Mao Zedong*, vol. 5 (Beijing: Military Science Press and Central Literature Publishing House, 1993), 231.
16. Military History Research Department of the Academy of Military Sciences, *History of the Chinese People's Liberation Army (War of Liberation Period)*, vol. 3 (Beijing: Military Science Press, 1987), 271.
17. Mao Zedong, *Collected Military Works of Mao Zedong*, vol. 5 (Beijing: Military Science Press and Central Literature Publishing House, 1993), 209.
18. Ibid., 230–231.
19. Mao Zedong, *Selected Works of Mao Zedong*, vol. 4 (Beijing: People's Publishing House, 1991), 1361.
20. Mao Zedong, *Collected Military Works of Mao Zedong*, vol. 5 (Beijing: Military Science Press and Central Literature Publishing House, 1993), 401.
21. Ibid., 410.
22. Mao Zedong, *Selected Works of Mao Zedong*, vol. 4 (Beijing: People's Publishing House, 1991), 1365.
23. Mao Zedong, *Collected Military Works of Mao Zedong*, vol. 5 (Beijing: Military Science Press and Central Literature Publishing House, 1993), 239.
24. Mao Zedong, *Selected Works of Mao Zedong*, vol. 4 (Beijing: People's Publishing House, 1991), 1364–1366.
25. Ibid., 1365.
26. These eight conditions are as follows: (1) Punish war criminals. (2) Abolish the pseudo-constitution. (3) Abolish the pseudo-legal system. (4) Reorganize all reactionary armies according to democratic principles. (5) Confiscate bureaucratic capital. (6) Reform the land system. (7) Abolish traitorous treaties. (8) Convene a political consultative conference without reactionaries and establish a democratic coalition government, taking over all power from the Nanjing KMT government and its subordinate governments.
27. Mao Zedong, *Selected Works of Mao Zedong*, vol. 4 (Beijing: People's Publishing House, 1991), 1438–1439.
28. Mao Zedong, *Selected Writings of Mao Zedong (Part Two)* (Beijing: Central Literature Publishing House, 2003), 2128.
29. Pang Xianzhi, ed., *Chronicle of Mao Zedong (1893–1949) (Revised Edition)*, vol. 2 (Beijing: Central Literature Publishing House, 2013), 470.
30. *Selected Important Documents Since the Founding of the Party (1921–1949)*, vol. 26 (Beijing: Central Literature Publishing House, 2011), 235.

31. Pang Xianzhi, ed., *Chronicle of Mao Zedong (1893–1949) (Revised Edition)*, vol. 2 (Beijing: Central Literature Publishing House, 2013), 472.
32. He Yingqin, Yu Youren, Ju Zheng, and Tong Guanxian were then serving as Premier of the Executive Yuan, President of the Control Yuan, President of the National History Museum of the Presidential Office, and President of the Legislative Yuan, respectively.
33. Pang Xianzhi, ed., *Chronicle of Mao Zedong (1893–1949) (Revised Edition)*, vol. 2 (Beijing: Central Literature Publishing House, 2013), 478.
34. Ibid.
35. Ibid., 482.
36. Mao Zedong, *Selected Works of Mao Zedong*, vol. 4 (Beijing: People's Publishing House, 1991), 1451.
37. Mao Zedong, *Collected Works of Mao Zedong*, vol. 5 (Beijing: People's Publishing House, 1996), 343–345.
38. Ibid., 350.

Chapter 11   The World Has Changed

1. Bo Yibo, *Memoirs of Several Major Decisions and Events (Revised Edition)*, vol. 1 (Beijing: People's Publishing House, 1997), 83–84.
2. Quoted in *Chronicle of Chen Yun (1905–1995)*, vol. 2 (Beijing: Central Literature Publishing House, 2000), 40.
3. Mao Zedong, *Selected Works of Mao Zedong*, vol. 1 (Beijing: People's Publishing House, 1991), 31.
4. *Selected Important Documents Since the Founding of the People's Republic of China*, vol. 1 (Beijing: Central Literature Publishing House, 1992), 336.
5. Mao Zedong, *Selected Works of Mao Zedong*, vol. 1 (Beijing: People's Publishing House, 1991), 35.
6. Institute of Contemporary China Studies, *A History of the People's Republic of China*, vol. 1 (1949–1956) (Beijing: People's Publishing House and Contemporary China Publishing House, 2012), 115.
7. Ibid., 119.
8. Pang Xianzhi and Feng Hui, eds., *Chronicle of Mao Zedong (1949–1976)*, vol. 1 (Beijing: Central Literature Publishing House, 2013), 422.
9. Bo Yibo, *Memoirs of Several Major Decisions and Events (Revised Edition)*, vol. 1 (Beijing: People's Publishing House, 1997), 157–158.
10. *Selected Diplomatic Works of Zhou Enlai* (Beijing: Central Literature Publishing House, 1990), 48–50.
11. Mao Zedong, *Collected Works of Mao Zedong*, vol. 6 (Beijing: People's Publishing House, 1999), 2.
12. *Beside the Historical Giant: Memoirs of Shi Zhe* (Beijing: Central Literature Publishing House, 1991), 434.
13. Pang Xianzhi and Jin Chongji, eds., *Biography of Mao Zedong*, vol. 3 (Beijing: Central Literature Publishing House, 2011), 998.
14. Ibid., 995.
15. Ibid., 998.
16. Pang Xianzhi and Feng Hui, eds., *Chronicle of Mao Zedong (1949–1976)*, vol. 1 (Beijing: Central Literature Publishing House, 2013), 53.

17. Quoted in Pang Xianzhi and Jin Chongji, eds., *Biography of Mao Zedong*, vol. 3 (Beijing: Central Literature Publishing House, 2011), 996.
18. Ibid., 998.
19. Ibid.
20. Ibid., 1000.
21. Ibid., 997.
22. Pang Xianzhi and Feng Hui, eds., *Chronicle of Mao Zedong (1949–1976)*, vol. 1 (Beijing: Central Literature Publishing House, 2013), 61–62.
23. Ibid., 62.
24. Ibid., 62–63.
25. Ibid., 63.
26. *Selected Important Documents Since the Founding of the People's Republic of China*, vol. 1 (Beijing: Central Literature Publishing House, 1992), 95.
27. Ibid., 96.
28. *People's Daily*, January 3, 1950.
29. Pang Xianzhi and Jin Chongji, eds., *Biography of Mao Zedong*, vol. 3 (Beijing: Central Literature Publishing House, 2011), 1003.
30. Ibid., 998.
31. Ibid., 1007.
32. *Selected Important Documents Since the Founding of the People's Republic of China*, vol. 1 (Beijing: Central Literature Publishing House, 1992), 118.
33. Ibid., 121.
34. Li Jiagu, ed., *Compilation of Historical Materials on Sino-Soviet Relations (1933–1945)* (Beijing: Social Sciences Literature Press, 1997), 645.
35. *Selected Important Documents Since the Founding of the People's Republic of China*, vol. 1 (Beijing: Central Literature Publishing House, 1992), 121.
36. Li Jiagu, ed., *Compilation of Historical Materials on Sino-Soviet Relations (1933–1945)* (Beijing: Social Sciences Literature Press, 1997), 647.
37. *Selected Important Documents Since the Founding of the People's Republic of China*, vol. 1 (Beijing: Central Literature Publishing House, 1992), 122–123.
38. Li Jiagu, ed., *Compilation of Historical Materials on Sino-Soviet Relations (1933–1945)* (Beijing: Social Sciences Literature Press, 1997), 648–649.
39. Pang Xianzhi and Jin Chongji, eds., *Biography of Mao Zedong*, vol. 3 (Beijing: Central Literature Publishing House, 2011), 1008.
40. *Selected Important Documents Since the Founding of the People's Republic of China*, vol. 1 (Beijing: Central Literature Publishing House, 1992), 122.
41. Pang Xianzhi and Jin Chongji, eds., *Biography of Mao Zedong*, vol. 3 (Beijing: Central Literature Publishing House, 2011), 1014.
42. Pang Xianzhi and Feng Hui, eds., *Chronicle of Mao Zedong (1949–1976)*, vol. 1 (Beijing: Central Literature Publishing House, 2013), 112.
43. Mao Zedong, *Collected Works of Mao Zedong*, vol. 3 (Beijing: People's Publishing House, 1996), 146–147.
44. Ibid., 143.
45. Chen Yun, *Selected Works of Chen Yun*, vol. 2 (Beijing: People's Publishing House, 1995), 91.

46. Mao Zedong, *Collected Works of Mao Zedong*, vol. 6 (Beijing: People's Publishing House, 1999), 24.
47. Ibid., 67–68 and 70.
48. Ibid., 75–76.
49. Party History Research Office of the Central Committee of the CPC, *The Ninety Years of the Communist Party of China (The Period of Socialist Revolution and Construction)* (Beijing: Party History Publishing House and Party Building Books Publishing House, 2016), 411 and 414–414.
50. Mao Zedong, *Collected Works of Mao Zedong*, vol. 5 (Beijing: People's Publishing House, 1996), 305–306.
51. Pang Xianzhi, ed., *Chronicle of Mao Zedong (1893–1949) (Revised Edition)*, vol. 2 (Beijing: Central Literature Publishing House, 2013), 264.
52. Mao Zedong, *Collected Works of Mao Zedong*, vol. 6 (Beijing: People's Publishing House, 1999), 168.
53. Pang Xianzhi, ed., *Chronicle of Mao Zedong (1893–1949) (Revised Edition)*, vol. 2 (Beijing: Central Literature Publishing House, 2013), 153.
54. Quoted in *Beside the Historical Giant: Memoirs of Shi Zhe* (Beijing: Central Literature Publishing House, 1991), 380.
55. Mao Zedong, *Collected Works of Mao Zedong*, vol. 8 (Beijing: People's Publishing House, 1999), 336–337.

Chapter 12   Resisting US Aggression and Aiding Korea to Protect the Homeland

1. *Mao Zedong's Military Manuscripts Since the Founding of the People's Republic of China*, vol. 1 (Beijing: Military Science Press and Central Literature Publishing House, 2010), 154.
2. Ibid., 158.
3. Pang Xianzhi and Hui Feng, eds., *The Chronicle of Mao Zedong (1949–1976)*, vol. 1 (Beijing: Central Literature Publishing House, 2013), 161n1.
4. *Mao Zedong's Military Manuscripts Since the Founding of the People's Republic of China*, vol. 1 (Beijing: Military Science Press and Central Literature Publishing House, 2010), 160.
5. Ibid., 158–159.
6. Ibid., 179.
7. Ibid., 168.
8. Military History Research Department of the Academy of Military Sciences, *The History of the War to Resist US Aggression and Aid Korea*, vol. 1 (Beijing: Military Science Press, 2000), 60.
9. *Selected Military Works of Peng Dehuai* (Beijing: Central Literature Publishing House, 1988), 466.
10. *Selected Works of Mao Zedong*, vol. 6 (Beijing: People's Publishing House, 1999), 92–94.
11. *Mao Zedong's Military Manuscripts Since the Founding of the People's Republic of China*, vol. 1 (Beijing: Military Science Press and Central Literature Publishing House, 2010), 196, 199, and 205.
12. Li Ping and Ma Zhishun, eds., *The Chronicle of Zhou Enlai (1949–1976)*, vol. 1 (Beijing: Central Literature Publishing House, 1997), 67; see also Pang Xianzhi and Jin Chongji, eds., *Biography of Mao Zedong*, vol. 3 (Beijing: Central Literature Publishing House, 2011), 1075.

13. Military History Research Department of the Academy of Military Sciences, *History of the War to Resist US Aggression and Aid Korea*, vol. 1 (Beijing: Military Science Press, 2000), 125.
14. *Selected Military Works of Zhou Enlai*, vol. 4 (Beijing: People's Publishing House, 1997), 56–57.
15. Ibid., 58.
16. *Selected Diplomatic Works of Zhou Enlai* (Beijing: Central Literature Publishing House, 1990), 24.
17. Pang Xianzhi and Feng Hui, eds., *The Chronicle of Mao Zedong (1949–1976)*, vol. 1 (Beijing: Central Literature Publishing House, 2013), 200.
18. Military History Research Department of the Academy of Military Sciences, *History of the War to Resist US Aggression and Aid Korea*, vol. 1 (Beijing: Military Science Press, 2000), 149.
19. *Selected Diplomatic Works of Zhou Enlai* (Beijing: Central Literature Publishing House, 1990), 27.
20. *Mao Zedong's Military Manuscripts Since the Founding of the People's Republic of China*, vol. 1 (Beijing: Military Science Press and Central Literature Publishing House, 2010), 225.
21. Ibid., 226–227.
22. Ibid., 227.
23. Pang Xianzhi and Feng Hui, eds., *The Chronicle of Mao Zedong (1949–1976)*, vol. 1 (Beijing: Central Literature Publishing House, 2013), 201 n. 1.
24. Pang Xianzhi and Jin Chongji, eds., *Biography of Mao Zedong*, vol. 3 (Beijing: Central Literature Publishing House, 2011), 1080.
25. Ibid.
26. *The Autobiography of Peng Dehuai* (Beijing: People's Publishing House, 1981), 257.
27. The two Xiaos refer to Xiao Jinguang and Xiao Hua, who at the time were the Deputy Commander and Deputy Political Commissar of the Northeast Border Defense Army, respectively, and also served as Commander of the Navy and Deputy Director of the General Political Department of the Military Commission.
28. *Mao Zedong's Military Manuscripts Since the Founding of the People's Republic of China*, vol. 1 (Beijing: Military Science Press and Central Literature Publishing House, 2010), 199.
29. Pang Xianzhi and Feng Hui, eds., *The Chronicle of Mao Zedong (1949–1976)*, vol. 1 (Beijing: Central Literature Publishing House, 2013), 204–205.
30. *The Autobiography of Peng Dehuai* (Beijing: People's Publishing House, 1981), 258.
31. *Mao Zedong's Military Manuscripts Since the Founding of the People's Republic of China*, vol. 1 (Beijing: Military Science Press and Central Literature Publishing House, 2010), 237.
32. Li Ping and Ma Zhishun, eds., *The Chronicle of Zhou Enlai (1949–1976)*, vol. 1 (Beijing: Central Literature Publishing House, 1997), 85.
33. *Literature of the Communist Party of China*, no. 6 (1995): 87.
34. These issues refer to that (1) the Soviet Union can fully meet our requests for planes, artillery, tanks, etc., but it is unclear whether it will be through a lease-lend arrangement or require payment; and (2) as long as the Soviet Union can deploy volunteer air forces to help us fight in Korea within two to two and a half months and also provide air cover for Beijing, Tianjin, Shenyang, Shanghai, Nanjing, and Qingdao, we are not afraid of comprehensive air attacks.

35. *Selected Works of Mao Zedong*, vol. 6 (Beijing: People's Publishing House, 1999), 104.
36. Li Ping and Ma Zhishun, eds., *The Chronicle of Zhou Enlai (1949–1976)*, vol. 1 (Beijing: Central Literature Publishing House, 1997), 87.
37. *Mao Zedong's Military Manuscripts Since the Founding of the People's Republic of China*, vol. 1 (Beijing: Military Science Press and Central Literature Publishing House, 2010), 257.
38. Ibid., 261.
39. Ibid., 258–259.
40. Ibid., 266.
41. Wang Yan, ed., *The Chronicle of Peng Dehuai* (Beijing: People's Publishing House, 1998), 444.
42. *Mao Zedong's Military Manuscripts Since the Founding of the People's Republic of China*, vol. 1 (Beijing: Military Science Press and Central Literature Publishing House, 2010), 268–270.
43. US Information Service, June 12, 1951, quoted in Pang Xianzhi and Jin Chongji, eds., *Biography of Mao Zedong*, vol. 3 (Beijing: Central Literature Publishing House, 2011), 1117.
44. Pang Xianzhi and Feng Hui, eds., *The Chronicle of Mao Zedong (1949–1976)*, vol. 1 (Beijing: Central Literature Publishing House, 2013), 355.
45. Ibid., 356–357.
46. *History of the Chinese People's Liberation Army*, vol. 4 (Beijing: Military Science Press, 2011), 208.
47. *Mao Zedong's Military Manuscripts Since the Founding of the People's Republic of China*, vol. 2 (Beijing: Military Science Press and Central Literature Publishing House, 2010), 174–175.

Chapter 13 Establishing a Socialist System

1. Party History Research Office of the CPC Central Committee, *History of the Communist Party of China*, vol. 2 (1949–1976), pt. 1 (Beijing: Party History Publishing House, 2011), 184.
2. Ibid.
3. Pang Xianzhi and Feng Hui, eds., *Chronicle of Mao Zedong (1949–1976)*, vol. 2 (Beijing: Central Literature Publishing House, 2013), 116.
4. *Selected Important Documents Since the Founding of the People's Republic of China*, vol. 2 (Beijing: Central Literature Publishing House, 1992), 354.
5. Pang Xianzhi and Jin Chongji, eds., *Biography of Mao Zedong*, vol. 3 (Beijing: Central Literature Publishing House, 2011), 1307.
6. *Collected Manuscripts of Liu Shaoqi Since the Founding of the People's Republic of China*, vol. 3 (Beijing: Central Literature Publishing House, 2005), 528.
7. Bo Yibo, *Reflections on Some Major Decisions and Events (Revised Edition)*, vol. 1 (Beijing: People's Publishing House, 1997), 197–198.
8. *Collected Manuscripts of Liu Shaoqi Since the Founding of the People's Republic of China*, vol. 4 (Beijing: Central Literature Publishing House, 2005), 526.
9. *Selected Important Documents Since the Founding of the People's Republic of China*, vol. 4 (Beijing: Central Literature Publishing House, 1993), 222 and 227.

10. Pang Xianzhi and Feng Hui, eds., *Chronicle of Mao Zedong (1949–1976)*, vol. 2 (Beijing: Central Literature Publishing House, 2013), 121–122.
11. Ibid., 122.
12. *Collected Works of Mao Zedong*, vol. 6 (Beijing: People's Publishing House, 1999), 289.
13. Ibid., 499.
14. Contemporary China Research Institute, *History of the People's Republic of China*, vol. 1 (1949–1956) (Beijing: People's Publishing House, Contemporary China Publishing House, 2012), 199.
15. Ibid., 202.
16. *Selected Works of Liu Shaoqi*, vol. 2 (Beijing: People's Publishing House, 1985), 207 and 218–219.
17. Contemporary China Research Institute, *History of the People's Republic of China*, vol. 1 (1949–1956) (Beijing: People's Publishing House, Contemporary China Publishing House, 2012), 181, 185, and 187.
18. *Collected Works of Mao Zedong*, vol. 7 (Beijing: People's Publishing House, 1999), 1–2.
19. Ibid., 12.
20. Ibid., 170–171.
21. *Selected Important Documents Since the Founding of the People's Republic of China*, vol. 4 (Beijing: Central Literature Publishing House, 1993), 17.
22. The actual completion date was around February 17.
23. The "third reading draft" was actually completed on February 25.
24. The first meeting of the Constitution Drafting Committee of the People's Republic of China was held on March 23.
25. On June 14, 1954, the 30th meeting of the Central People's Government Committee passed the "Draft *Constitution of the People's Republic of China*" and the "Decision to Publish the Draft *Constitution of the People's Republic of China*." On the same day, the draft constitution was published and submitted for nationwide discussion and feedback.
26. *Collected Works of Mao Zedong*, vol. 6 (Beijing: People's Publishing House, 1999), 320–321.
27. Refers to the "Nineteen Articles" promulgated by the Qing government in November 1911.
28. The *Provisional Constitution of the Republic of China* was promulgated in March 1912 in the name of Sun Yat-sen, the Provisional President of the Republic of China. It was abolished by Yuan Shikai in May 1914.
29. Refers to the "Temple of Heaven Draft Constitution" drafted by the Yuan Shikai government in October 1913 and the *Constitution of the Republic of China* promulgated in May 1914, as well as the *Constitution of the Republic of China* promulgated by the Cao Kun government in October 1923 and the "Draft Constitution" drafted by the Duan Qirui executive government in December 1925.
30. The *Provisional Constitution During the Tutelage Period* was promulgated by the KMT government in June 1931.
31. Refers to the *Constitution of the Republic of China* manipulated by the KMT government and passed by the National Assembly in December 1946.
32. *Collected Works of Mao Zedong*, vol. 6 (Beijing: People's Publishing House, 1999), 325–326.

33. Pang Xianzhi and Jin Chongji, eds., *Biography of Mao Zedong*, vol. 3 (Beijing: Central Literature Publishing House, 2011), 1280–1281.
34. Zhejiang Province Mao Zedong Thought Research Center and the Party History Research Office of the Zhejiang Provincial Committee, eds., *Mao Zedong and Zhejiang* (Beijing: Party History Publishing House, 1993), 1279.
35. Pang Xianzhi and Jin Chongji, eds., *Biography of Mao Zedong*, vol. 3 (Beijing: Central Literature Publishing House, 2011), 5.
36. Pang Xianzhi and Feng Hui, eds., *Chronicle of Mao Zedong (1949–1976)*, vol. 2 (Beijing: Central Literature Publishing House, 2013), 225, n. 1.
37. Ibid., 221–222.
38. Ibid., 222.
39. This was the name in the initial draft of the constitution, later confirmed as the Standing Committee of the National People's Congress.
40. Pang Xianzhi and Jin Chongji, eds., *Biography of Mao Zedong*, vol. 3 (Beijing: Central Literature Publishing House, 2011), 1284–1285 and 1287–1289.
41. Pang Xianzhi and Feng Hui, eds., *Chronicle of Mao Zedong (1949–1976)*, vol. 2 (Beijing: Central Literature Publishing House, 2013), 227.
42. Ibid., 247–248.

Chapter 14 "Using the Soviet Union as a Reference"

1. Pang Xianzhi and Feng Hui, eds., *Chronicle of Mao Zedong (1949–1976)*, vol. 4 (Beijing: Central Literature Publishing House, 2013), 418–419.
2. *Selected Works of Mao Zedong*, vol. 8 (Beijing: People's Publishing House, 1999), 260–261.
3. *Selected Important Documents Since the Founding of the People's Republic of China*, vol. 8 (Beijing: Central Literature Publishing House, 1994), 46.
4. Bo Yibo, *Recollections of Several Major Decisions and Events (Revised Edition)*, vol. 1 (Beijing: People's Publishing House, 1997), 482.
5. Pang Xianzhi and Feng Hui, eds., *Chronicle of Mao Zedong (1949–1976)*, vol. 2 (Beijing: Central Literature Publishing House, 2013), 560.
6. Wu Lengxi, *New Explorations and Rectification Against the Right: Memoirs of Wu Lengxi (Part One)* (Beijing: Central Literature Publishing House, 2016), 14.
7. The above quotations from Mao Zedong's interjections and discussions can be found in Pang Xianzhi and Jin Chongji, eds., *Biography of Mao Zedong*, vol. 4 (Beijing: Central Literature Publishing House, 2011), 1434, 1439–1440, 1435–1438, and 1442.
8. See Pang Xianzhi and Jin Chongji, eds., *Biography of Mao Zedong*, vol. 4 (Beijing: Central Literature Publishing House, 2011), 1438.
9. Yang Shengqun and Yan Jianqi, eds., *Chronicle of Deng Xiaoping (1904–1974)*, vol. 2 (Beijing: Central Literature Publishing House, 2009), 1273.
10. Pang Xianzhi and Jin Chongji, eds., *Chronicle of Mao Zedong (1949–1976)*, vol. 2 (Beijing: Central Literature Publishing House, 2013), 545.
11. Ibid., 549–550.
12. Wu Lengxi, *Ten Years of Sino-Soviet Debate—Memoirs on Sino-Soviet Relations 1956–1966* (Beijing: Central Literature Publishing House, 2014), 15.
13. Leng Rong and Wang Zuoling, eds., *Chronicle of Deng Xiaoping (1975–1997)*, vol. 1 (Beijing: Central Literature Publishing House, 2004), 68.

14. Pang Xianzhi and Feng Hui, eds., *Chronicle of Mao Zedong (1949–1976)*, vol. 3 (Beijing: Central Literature Publishing House, 2013), 311.
15. *Selected Works of Mao Zedong*, vol. 7 (Beijing: People's Publishing House, 1999), 44.
16. Pang Xianzhi and Jin Chongji, eds., *Biography of Mao Zedong*, vol. 4 (Beijing: Central Literature Publishing House, 2011), 1446.
17. *Selected Works of Mao Zedong*, vol. 7 (Beijing: People's Publishing House, 1999), 23 and 44.
18. Ibid., 25–27.
19. Ibid., 24 and 29–31.
20. Ibid., 41–42.
21. Ibid., 42.
22. *Selected Important Documents Since the Founding of the People's Republic of China*, vol. 9 (Beijing: Central Literature Publishing House, 1994), 342.
23. Yang Shangkun, *The Diaries of Yang Shangkun*, vol. 1 (Beijing: Central Literature Publishing House, 2001), 251.
24. Party History Research Office of the CPC Central Committee, *Ninety Years of the Communist Party of China (Period of Socialist Revolution and Construction)* (Beijing: Party History Publishing House, Party Building Books Publishing House, 2016), 483.
25. Pang Xianzhi and Jin Chongji, eds., *Biography of Mao Zedong*, vol. 4 (Beijing: Central Literature Publishing House, 2011), 1576.
26. Huang Yanpei, at the time Chairman of the China National Democratic Construction Association and Vice Chairman of the Standing Committee of the National People's Congress.
27. *Selected Works of Mao Zedong*, vol. 7 (Beijing: People's Publishing House, 1999), 164–165.
28. The above quotations from "On the Correct Handling of Contradictions Among the People" are from *Selected Works of Mao Zedong*, vol. 7 (Beijing: People's Publishing House, 1999), 205–207, 209, 211, and 213–216.
29. *Selected Works of Mao Zedong*, vol. 7 (Beijing: People's Publishing House, 1999), 228.
30. Ibid., 310.

Chapter 15   The Great Leap Forward

1. Party History Research Office of the Central Committee of the CPC, *History of the Communist Party of China*, vol. 2 (1949–1978), pt. 1 (Beijing: Party History Publishing House, 2011), 417.
2. Out of 156 projects, 150 were actually under construction, with 146 of them being undertaken during the period of the First Five-Year Plan.
3. Party History Research Office of the Central Committee of the CPC, *History of the Communist Party of China*, vol. 2 (1949–1978), pt. 1 (Beijing: Party History Publishing House, 2011), 414.
4. Ibid., 418–419.
5. Pang Xianzhi and Feng Hui, eds., *Chronicle of Mao Zedong (1949–1976)*, vol. 3 (Beijing: Central Literature Publishing House, 2013), 220.
6. *Selected Important Documents Since the Founding of the People's Republic of China*, vol. 11 (Beijing: Central Literature Publishing House, 1995), 294–295.
7. Party History Research Office of the Central Committee of the CPC, *Ninety Years of the Communist Party of China (Socialist Revolution and Construction Period)* (Beijing: Party History Publishing House and Party Building Books Publishing House, 2016), 493.

8. In fact, representatives from 68 Communist and Workers' Parties attended this meeting, with four parties not publicly reported.
9. *Collected Works of Mao Zedong*, vol. 7 (Beijing: People's Publishing House, 1999), 321.
10. Pollitt and Gollan were respectively the Chairman of the Central Executive Committee of the Communist Party of Great Britain and the General Secretary of the Central Committee of the Communist Party of Great Britain at that time.
11. *Collected Works of Mao Zedong*, vol. 7 (Beijing: People's Publishing House, 1999), 325–326.
12. Ibid., 326.
13. Pang Xianzhi and Feng Hui, eds., *Chronicle of Mao Zedong (1949–1976)*, vol. 3 (Beijing: Central Literature Publishing House, 2013), 261–262.
14. Refers to the June 20, 1956, editorial in *People's Daily*, "Oppose Conservatism and Rashness."
15. Pang Xianzhi and Feng Hui, eds., *Chronicle of Mao Zedong (1949–1976)*, vol. 3 (Beijing: Central Literature Publishing House, 2013), 266.
16. Ibid., 276–279.
17. Ibid., 281.
18. Refers to Zhou Enlai's Government Work Report at the Fourth Session of the First National People's Congress on June 26, 1957.
19. Bo Yibo, *Reflections on Several Major Decisions and Events (Revised Edition)*, vol. 2 (Beijing: People's Publishing House, 1997), 663–664.
20. *Selected Important Documents Since the Founding of the People's Republic of China*, vol. 11 (Beijing: Central Literature Publishing House, 1995), 303–304.
21. The Beidaihe Conference refers to the expanded meeting of the Political Bureau of the Central Committee chaired by Mao Zedong from August 17 to 30, 1958, at the Central Rehabilitation Center in Beidaihe. The conference adopted the "Resolution on the Establishment of People's Communes in Rural Areas" and 40 other documents, significantly promoting the Great Leap Forward and the People's Commune Movement.
22. Under Mao Zedong's direct leadership, starting on August 23, 1958, the People's Liberation Army launched a military operation shelling the KMT-held Jinmen Island. Mao Zedong established the principle of "directly targeting Chiang, indirectly targeting the US" and timely issued a letter to Taiwan compatriots, developing the struggle into an international battle against the US conspiracy of "One China, One Taiwan" or "Two Chinas."
23. Zhang Chunqiao was then Deputy Minister of Publicity for the Shanghai Municipal Party Committee.
24. Pang Xianzhi and Feng Hui, eds., *Chronicle of Mao Zedong (1949–1976)*, vol. 3 (Beijing: Central Literature Publishing House, 2013), 468.
25. Ibid., 469
26. Ibid., 491 and 496.
27. *Collected Works of Mao Zedong*, vol. 7 (Beijing: People's Publishing House, 1999), 437.
28. Pang Xianzhi and Feng Hui, eds., *Chronicle of Mao Zedong (1949–1976)*, vol. 3 (Beijing: Central Literature Publishing House, 2013), 494–495 and 497–498.
29. *Collected Works of Mao Zedong*, vol. 7 (Beijing: People's Publishing House, 1999), 432.
30. Pang Xianzhi and Feng Hui, eds., *Chronicle of Mao Zedong (1949–1976)*, vol. 3 (Beijing: Central Literature Publishing House, 2013), 526–527.

31. *Collected Works of Mao Zedong*, vol. 8 (Beijing: People's Publishing House, 1999), 9–12.
32. Ibid., 14.
33. The original text at this point also includes the phrase "observers and accountants belong to this category." On September 16, 1961, while reviewing a cadre study material containing this passage, Mao Zedong deleted this sentence.
34. *Collected Works of Mao Zedong*, vol. 7 (Beijing: People's Publishing House, 1999), 457.
35. *Selected Works of Chen Yun*, vol. 3 (Beijing: People's Publishing House, 1995), 134.
36. The actual steel production in 1959 was 13.87 million tons. See Su Xing, *Economic History of New China (Revised Edition)* (Beijing: Party School Press of the Central Committee of CPC, 2007), 355.
37. Pang Xianzhi and Feng Hui, eds., *Chronicle of Mao Zedong (1949–1976)*, vol. 4 (Beijing: Central Literature Publishing House, 2013), 70.
38. This expanded meeting of the Political Bureau of the Central Committee and the subsequent Eighth Plenary Session of the Eighth Central Committee from August 2 to 16, 1959, are collectively known as the Lushan Conference.
39. *Collected Works of Mao Zedong*, vol. 8 (Beijing: People's Publishing House, 1999), 76 and 80.
40. Peng Dehuai was then a member of the Political Bureau of the Central Committee, Vice Premier of the State Council, and Minister of National Defense.
41. *Selected Important Documents Since the Founding of the People's Republic of China*, vol. 12 (Beijing: Central Literature Publishing House, 1996), 443–445.
42. Huang Kecheng was then Chief of General Staff of the People's Liberation Army; Zhang Wentian was then Vice Minister of Foreign Affairs; Zhou Xiaozhou was then First Secretary of the Hunan Provincial Committee of the CPC.
43. Pang Xianzhi and Feng Hui, eds., *Chronicle of Mao Zedong (1949–1976)*, vol. 4 (Beijing: Central Literature Publishing House, 2013), 113–114.
44. Ibid., 131 and 143.

Chapter 16   Reflections After Calming Down

1. *Collected Works of Mao Zedong*, vol. 7 (Beijing: People's Publishing House, 1999), 432–433.
2. Ibid., 435.
3. Pang Xianzhi and Feng Hui, eds., *Chronicle of Mao Zedong (1949–1976)*, vol. 3 (Beijing: Central Literature Publishing House, 2013), 498–499.
4. *Selected Works of Marx and Engels*, vol. 3 (Beijing: People's Publishing House, 2012), 671.
5. *Collected Works of Stalin*, vol. 2 (Beijing: People's Publishing House, 1979), 546.
6. Ibid., 547.
7. *Collected Works of Mao Zedong*, vol. 7 (Beijing: People's Publishing House, 1999), 435 and 438–439.
8. Pang Xianzhi and Feng Hui, eds., *Chronicle of Mao Zedong (1949–1976)*, vol. 3 (Beijing: Central Literature Publishing House, 2013), 518.
9. Ibid., 521.
10. This meeting of the Political Bureau of the Central Committee of the CPC was held in Hangzhou, presided over by Mao Zedong, and primarily discussed the 1960 national economic plan and Sino-Soviet and Sino-Indian relations.
11. Referring to the book, chapters 20–36.

12. Zhejiang Mao Zedong Thought Research Center and Party History Research Office of the Zhejiang Provincial Committee of the CPC, eds., *Mao Zedong and Zhejiang* (Beijing: Party History Publishing House, 1993), 116.
13. Quoted in Pang Xianzhi and Jin Chongji, eds., *Biography of Mao Zedong*, vol. 5 (Beijing: Central Literature Publishing House, 2011), 2001.
14. *Collected Poems of Mao Zedong*, referring to *Chairman Mao's Nineteen Poems* (Beijing: Cultural Relics Press, September 1958), a vertical edition in traditional binding.
15. Recollections of Deng Liqun, see Pang Xianzhi and Jin Chongji, eds., *Biography of Mao Zedong*, vol. 5 (Beijing: Central Literature Publishing House, 2011), 2001–2003.
16. *Collected Works of Mao Zedong*, vol. 8 (Beijing: People's Publishing House, 1999), 116.
17. Ibid.
18. Ibid., 302.
19. Ibid., 11–120, 130–131, 133, and 140.
20. Ibid., 109.

Chapter 17 The Struggle with Khrushchev

1. On June 28, 1958, based on the recommendations of Soviet military advisers, China requested technical assistance from the Soviet Union for the development of nuclear submarines for the Chinese Navy. On July 21, Soviet Ambassador to China Yudin conveyed to Mao Zedong a proposal from Khrushchev and the Presidium of the CPSU to establish a joint nuclear submarine fleet between the Soviet Union and China. Due to the adverse impact on China's sovereignty, China withdrew its request for Soviet assistance in developing nuclear submarines.
2. In August 1959, Indian troops invaded Langju in Xizang, China, triggering the first armed conflict along the Sino-Indian border since the founding of the People's Republic of China. Subsequently, Indian troops repeatedly crossed the actual control line on both the western and eastern sectors of the Sino-Indian border, continuously provoking border incidents and establishing military posts within Chinese territory. The Chinese government lodged strong protests with the Indian government multiple times and suggested resolving the border issues through negotiations, but the Indian side consistently refused.
3. The Far Eastern Republic, also known as the Chita Republic, was a nominally independent state established by Soviet Russia east of Lake Baikal in 1920. In reality, it served as a buffer zone between Soviet-controlled areas and Japanese-occupied territories. In October 1922, Japanese troops were forced to withdraw from Siberia, and in November of the same year, the Chita Republic was incorporated into Soviet Russia.
4. *Collected Works of Mao Zedong*, vol. 8 (Beijing: People's Publishing House, 1999), 358–359.
5. Ibid., 370.
6. Ibid., 231.
7. Pang Xianzhi and Feng Hui, eds., *Chronicle of Mao Zedong (1949–1976)*, vol. 3 (Beijing: Central Literature Publishing House, 2013), 396.
8. *Declaration of the Communist and Workers' Parties at the Moscow Meeting* (Beijing: People's Publishing House, 1958), 13.
9. *The Polemic on the General Line of the International Communist Movement* (Beijing: People's Publishing House, 1965), 96–97.
10. Wang Yan, ed., *Chronicle of Peng Dehuai* (Beijing: People's Publishing House, 1998), 681.

11. Ibid.
12. *Mao Zedong's Military Manuscripts Since the Founding of the People's Republic of China*, vol. 2 (Beijing: Military Science Press and Central Literature Publishing House, 2010), 380.
13. *Collected Works of Mao Zedong*, vol. 7 (Beijing: People's Publishing House, 1999), 395.
14. Ibid., 385 and 390–392.
15. Pang Xianzhi and Feng Hui, eds., *Chronicle of Mao Zedong (1949–1976)*, vol. 3 (Beijing: Central Literature Publishing House, 2013), 396.
16. Ibid., 351.
17. Ibid., 373.
18. Jin Chongji, ed., *Biography of Zhou Enlai*, vol. 4 (Beijing: Central Literature Publishing House, 2011), 1574.
19. Quoted in Wu Lengxi, *Ten Years of Polemics: A Memoir on Sino-Soviet Relations* (Beijing: Central Literature Publishing House, 1999), 277.
20. Wang Taiping, ed., *A Diplomatic History of the People's Republic of China*, vol. 2 (1957–1969) (Beijing: World Affairs Press, 1998), 236.
21. Pang Xianzhi and Feng Hui, eds., *Chronicle of Mao Zedong (1949–1976)*, vol. 4 (Beijing: Central Literature Publishing House, 2013), 431.
22. Ibid., 434 and 436.
23. Ibid., 452.
24. Wang Taiping, ed., *A Diplomatic History of the People's Republic of China*, vol. 2 (1957–1969) (Beijing: World Affairs Press, 1998), 236.
25. Publication details of the other seven articles are as follows: September 13, 1963, "On the Question of Stalin" (Second Commentary); September 26, 1963, "Is Yugoslavia a Socialist Country?" (Third Commentary); October 22, 1963, "Apologists of Neo-Colonialism" (Fourth Commentary); November 19, 1963, "Two Different Lines on the Question of War and Peace" (Fifth Commentary); December 12, 1963, "The Differences Between Comrade Togliatti and Us" (Sixth Commentary); February 4, 1964, "The Leaders of the CPSU are the Greatest Splitters of Our Time" (Seventh Commentary); March 31, 1964, "Proletarian Revolution and Khrushchev's Revisionism" (Eighth Commentary).

Chapter 18 Launching the "Great Cultural Revolution"

1. Refers to the big slogans and big-character posters that appeared at that time.
2. Pang Xianzhi and Feng Hui, eds., *Chronicle of Mao Zedong (1949–1976)*, vol. 5 (Beijing: Central Literature Publishing House, 2013), 595.
3. Pang Xianzhi and Jin Chongji, eds., *Biography of Mao Zedong*, vol. 6 (Beijing: Central Literature Publishing House, 2011), 2387.
4. Pang Xianzhi and Feng Hui, eds., *Chronicle of Mao Zedong (1949–1976)*, vol. 5 (Beijing: Central Literature Publishing House, 2013), 579.
5. Ibid., 593.
6. Tao Zhu, Chen Boda, Kang Sheng, and Li Fuchun were added to the Standing Committee of the Political Bureau of the Central Committee.
7. Pang Xianzhi and Feng Hui, eds., *Chronicle of Mao Zedong (1949–1976)*, vol. 3 (Beijing: Central Literature Publishing House, 2013), 193.
8. *Declaration of the Meeting of Communist and Workers' Parties of Socialist Countries* (Beijing: People's Publishing House, 1958), 11.

9. *Selected Important Documents Since the Founding of the People's Republic of China*, vol. 20 (Beijing: Central Literature Publishing House, 1998), 21.
10. Ibid., 65–67.
11. Pang Xianzhi and Feng Hui, eds., *Chronicle of Mao Zedong (1949–1976)*, vol. 6 (Beijing: Central Literature Publishing House, 2013), 45–46.
12. Pang Xianzhi, ed., *Chronicle of Mao Zedong (1893–1949) (Revised Edition)*, vol. 2 (Beijing: Central Literature Publishing House, 2013), 611.
13. The "four olds" refer to old ideas, old culture, old customs, and old habits.
14. The "three supports" refer to supporting industry, supporting agriculture, and supporting the leftists. The "two militaries" refer to military control and military-political training.
15. Pang Xianzhi and Feng Hui, eds., *Chronicle of Mao Zedong (1949–1976)*, vol. 6 (Beijing: Central Literature Publishing House, 2013), 130–132.
16. Ibid., 11.
17. Li Ping and Ma Zisun, eds., *Chronicle of Zhou Enlai (1949–1976)*, vol. 3 (Beijing: Central Literature Publishing House, 1997), 386–387; Pang Xianzhi and Feng Hui, eds., *Chronicle of Mao Zedong (1949–1976)*, vol. 6 (Beijing: Central Literature Publishing House, 2013), 320.
18. Pang Xianzhi and Feng Hui, eds., *Chronicle of Mao Zedong (1949–1976)*, vol. 6 (Beijing: Central Literature Publishing House, 2013), 322.
19. Ibid., 327.
20. Ibid., 329–331.
21. Ibid., 389.
22. Ibid., 417.
23. Refers to the title "Great Leader."
24. Pang Xianzhi and Feng Hui, eds., *Chronicle of Mao Zedong (1949–1976)*, vol. 6 (Beijing: Central Literature Publishing House, 2013), 419.
25. Ibid., 424.
26. Ibid., 458.
27. Party History Research Office of the Central Committee of the CPC, *The Ninety-Year History of the Communist Party of China* (Socialist Revolution and Construction Period) (Beijing: Party History Publishing House, 2016), 614.
28. Pang Xianzhi and Feng Hui, eds., *Chronicle of Mao Zedong (1949–1976)*, vol. 6 (Beijing: Central Literature Publishing House, 2013), 552.
29. Ibid., 557.
30. Ibid.
31. In April 1975, the Central Committee of the CPC removed the rightist label from Zhang Naiqi.
32. Pang Xianzhi and Feng Hui, eds., *Chronicle of Mao Zedong (1949–1976)*, vol. 6 (Beijing: Central Literature Publishing House, 2013), 562–563.
33. Ibid., 564.
34. *Selected Works of Deng Xiaoping*, vol. 2 (Beijing: People's Publishing House, 1994), 12.
35. Pang Xianzhi and Feng Hui, eds., *Chronicle of Mao Zedong (1949–1976)*, vol. 6 (Beijing: Central Literature Publishing House, 2013), 593.
36. Ibid., 614–615.
37. Ibid., 619.

38. On January 8, 1976, Zhou Enlai passed away. Around Qingming Festival (April 4), a mass movement commemorating Zhou Enlai and opposing the "Gang of Four" and the criticism of Deng Xiaoping erupted in Beijing and many other cities. The "Gang of Four" tried to suppress these revolutionary activities. On April 5, large crowds at Tiananmen Square protested. At the time, the Political Bureau of the Central and Mao Zedong mistakenly labeled the incident as counter-revolutionary, resulting in Deng Xiaoping's removal from all his positions. In December 1978, the Third Plenary Session of the Eleventh Central Committee of the CPC decided to revoke the erroneous documents concerning the "Counterattack the Right-Deviationist Reversal-of-Verdicts Trend" campaign and the Tiananmen Incident and formally redressed the Tiananmen Incident.
39. Lei Jieqiong, inscription for Mao Zedong's former residence in Shaoshan, Hunan, May 1994.

Chapter 19 Opening the Door to Normalizing China-US Relations

1. *People's Daily*, July 16, 1971, 1.
2. Pang Xianzhi and Feng Hui, eds., *Chronicle of Mao Zedong (1949–1976)*, vol. 6 (Beijing: Central Literature Publishing House, 2013), 203.
3. *Collected Military Manuscripts of Mao Zedong Since the Founding of the People's Republic of China*, vol. 2 (Beijing: Military Science Press and Central Literature Publishing House, 2010), 349–351.
4. Pang Xianzhi and Feng Hui, eds., *Chronicle of Mao Zedong (1949–1976)*, vol. 6 (Beijing: Central Literature Publishing House, 2013), 237.
5. *Collected Military Manuscripts of Mao Zedong Since the Founding of the People's Republic of China*, vol. 2 (Beijing: Military Science Press and Central Literature Publishing House, 2010), 367.
6. Ibid., 346.
7. Pang Xianzhi and Feng Hui, eds., *Chronicle of Mao Zedong (1949–1976)*, vol. 6 (Beijing: Central Literature Publishing House, 2013), 441.
8. *Collected Military Manuscripts of Mao Zedong Since the Founding of the People's Republic of China*, vol. 2 (Beijing: Military Science Press and Central Literature Publishing House, 2010), 356.
9. Pang Xianzhi and Feng Hui, eds., *Chronicle of Mao Zedong (1949–1976)*, vol. 6 (Beijing: Central Literature Publishing House, 2013), 230.
10. Military Science Academy, ed., *Chronicle of Ye Jianying (1897–1986)*, vol. 2 (Beijing: Central Literature Publishing House, 2007), 983.
11. Party History Research Office of the CPC Central Committee, *History of the Communist Party of China*, vol. 2 (1949–1978), pt. 2 (Beijing: Party History Publishing House, 2011), 886. Xiong Xianghui, *My Life in Intelligence and Diplomacy* (Expanded Edition) (Beijing: Party History Publishing House, 2005), 195.
12. "Memorandum of Conversation" (October 25, 1970), in Tao Wenzhao, ed., *Documents on US China Policy (1949–1972)*, vol. 3, pt. 2 (Beijing: World Affairs Press, 2005), 1060–1062.
13. Li Ping and Ma Zisun, eds., *Chronicle of Zhou Enlai (1949–1976)*, vol. 2 (Beijing: Central Literature Publishing House, 1997), 410–411.
14. Tao Wenzhao, ed., *Documents on US China Policy (1949–1972)*, vol. 3, pt. 2 (Beijing: World Affairs Press, 2005), 1068. Wang Taiping, ed., *Diplomatic History of the People's Republic of China*, vol. 3 (1970–1978) (Beijing: World Affairs Press, 1999), 351.

15. *Collected Works of Mao Zedong*, vol. 8 (Beijing: People's Publishing House, 1999), 436–437.
16. Richard Nixon, *The Memoirs of Richard Nixon*, vol. 2, trans. Qiu Ke'an et al. (Beijing: World Affairs Press, 2001), 657.
17. Tao Wenzhao, ed., *Documents on US China Policy (1949–1972)*, vol. 3, pt. 2 (Beijing: World Affairs Press, 2005), 1069–1070.
18. Pang Xianzhi and Feng Hui, eds., *Chronicle of Mao Zedong (1949–1976)*, vol. 6 (Beijing: Central Literature Publishing House, 2013), 373.
19. Prior to this, China had invited both the Canadian and England table tennis teams, who participated in the 31st World Table Tennis Championships, to visit China. Members of the US table tennis team, including the Chairman of the US Table Tennis Association's International Committee, Lafford Harrison, expressed their desire to visit China to the Secretary-General of the Chinese table tennis team, Song Zhong. Xiong Xianghui, *My Life in Intelligence and Diplomacy* (Expanded Edition) (Beijing: Party History Publishing House, 2005), 239.
20. Pang Xianzhi and Feng Hui, eds., *Chronicle of Mao Zedong (1949–1976)*, vol. 6 (Beijing: Central Literature Publishing House, 2013), 373.
21. Ibid., 383.
22. Richard Nixon, *The Memoirs of Richard Nixon*, vol. 2, trans. Qiu Ke'an et al. (Beijing: World Affairs Press, 2001), 658.
23. Li Ping and Ma Zisun, eds., *Chronicle of Zhou Enlai (1949–1976)*, vol. 2 (Beijing: Central Literature Publishing House, 1997), 451.
24. Ibid., 452–453.
25. Wang Taiping, ed., *Diplomatic History of the People's Republic of China*, vol. 3 (1970–1978) (Beijing: World Affairs Press, 1999), 352–353.
26. Ibid., 353.
27. Party History Research Office of the CPC Central Committee, *History of the Communist Party of China*, vol. 2 (1949–1978), pt. 2 (Beijing: Party History Publishing House, 2011), 889–890.
28. Richard Nixon, *The Memoirs of Richard Nixon*, vol. 2, trans. Qiu Ke'an et al. (Beijing: World Affairs Press, 2001), 661.
29. Wang Taiping, ed., *Diplomatic History of the People's Republic of China*, vol. 3 (1970–1978) (Beijing: World Affairs Press, 1999), 353–354.
30. Richard Nixon, *The Memoirs of Richard Nixon*, vol. 2, trans. Qiu Ke'an et al. (Beijing: World Affairs Press, 2001), 662–663.
31. Tao Wenzhao, ed., *Documents on US China Policy (1949–1972)*, vol. 3, pt. 2 (Beijing: World Affairs Press, 2005), 1069–1086. Nixon's letter was dated June 4, 1971. See Wang Taiping, ed., *Diplomatic History of the People's Republic of China*, vol. 3 (1970–1978) (Beijing: World Affairs Press, 1999), 354.
32. Pang Xianzhi and Feng Hui, eds., *Chronicle of Mao Zedong (1949–1976)*, vol. 6 (Beijing: Central Literature Publishing House, 2013), 385–386.
33. Military Science Academy, ed., *Chronicle of Ye Jianying (1897–1986)*, vol. 2 (Beijing: Central Literature Publishing House, 2007), 997.
34. Wang Taiping, ed., *Diplomatic History of the People's Republic of China*, vol. 3 (1970–1978) (Beijing: World Affairs Press, 1999), 354–356.

35. Ibid., 357–358. Li Ping and Ma Zisun, eds., *Chronicle of Zhou Enlai (1949–1976)*, vol. 2 (Beijing: Central Literature Publishing House, 1997), 490–491.
36. Wang Taiping, ed., *Diplomatic History of the People's Republic of China*, vol. 3 (1970–1978) (Beijing: World Affairs Press, 1999), 359.
37. Pang Xianzhi and Feng Hui, eds., *Chronicle of Mao Zedong (1949–1976)*, vol. 6 (Beijing: Central Literature Publishing House, 2013), 422.
38. Ibid., 423.
39. Wang Taiping, ed., *Diplomatic History of the People's Republic of China*, vol. 3 (1970–1978) (Beijing: World Affairs Press, 1999), 359–360.
40. Richard Nixon, *The Memoirs of Richard Nixon*, vol. 2, trans. Qiu Ke'an et al. (Beijing: World Affairs Press, 2001), 672.
41. *People's Daily*, February 17, 1972, 1.
42. Richard Nixon, *The Memoirs of Richard Nixon*, vol. 2, trans. Qiu Ke'an et al. (Beijing: World Affairs Press, 2001), 673–674.
43. For the content of these discussions, see Xiong Xianghui, *My Life in Intelligence and Diplomacy* (Expanded Edition) (Beijing: Party History Publishing House, 2005), 261–262, 265, 267, and 280–281; Pang Xianzhi and Feng Hui, eds., *Chronicle of Mao Zedong (1949–1976)*, vol. 6 (Beijing: Central Literature Publishing House, 2013), 427–428.
44. Richard Nixon, *The Memoirs of Richard Nixon*, vol. 2, trans. Qiu Ke'an et al. (Beijing: World Affairs Press, 2001), 476 and 677.
45. *People's Daily*, February 28, 1972, 1.

Chapter 20 Unfulfilled Aspirations

1. Pang Xianzhi and Feng Hui, eds., *Chronicle of Mao Zedong (1949–1976)*, vol. 2 (Beijing: Central Literature Publishing House, 2013), 197.
2. Ibid., 210.
3. Ibid., 256–257.
4. Ibid., 257–258.
5. On August 11, 1954, Zhou Enlai delivered a diplomatic report at the 33rd meeting of the Central People's Government Council, declaring: "Liberating Taiwan is China's sovereign right and internal affair, and will not allow foreign interference."
6. On August 22, 1954, various democratic parties and people's organizations issued a *Joint Declaration for the Liberation of Taiwan*.
7. Pang Xianzhi and Feng Hui, eds., *Chronicle of Mao Zedong (1949–1976)*, vol. 2 (Beijing: Central Literature Publishing House, 2013), 262–264.
8. This treaty was abolished after the establishment of diplomatic relations between the United States and China. On December 15, 1978, the US government issued a statement announcing that the US-Taiwan "Mutual Defense Treaty" would be terminated, effective January 1, 1980.
9. *History of the Chinese People's Liberation Army*, vol. 5 (Beijing: Military Science Press, 2011), 72–73; *Collected Military Manuscripts of Mao Zedong Since the Founding of the People's Republic of China*, vol. 2 (Beijing: Military Science Press and Central Literature Publishing House, 2010), 193.
10. Pei Jianzhang, ed., *Diplomatic History of the People's Republic of China (1949–1956)* (Beijing: World Affairs Press, 1994), 339.

11. *Selected Diplomatic Works of Zhou Enlai* (Beijing: Central Literature Publishing House, 1990), 134.
12. *People's Daily*, April 17, 1957, 1. The headline of the report reads: "Chairman Voroshilov Toasts at the Banquet Hosted by Premier Zhou: May All People on Earth Live in Peace, and Chairman Mao Says: We Are Ready for the Third Cooperation Between the KMT and the CPC."
13. *History of the Chinese People's Liberation Army*, vol. 5 (Beijing: Military Science Press, 2011), 214–215.
14. *Collected Military Manuscripts of Mao Zedong Since the Founding of the People's Republic of China*, vol. 2 (Beijing: Military Science Press and Central Literature Publishing House, 2010), 370.
15. *History of the Chinese People's Liberation Army*, vol. 5 (Beijing: Military Science Press, 2011), 215.
16. *People's Daily*, July 1, 1958, 1.
17. Party History Research Office of the CPC Central Committee, *History of the Communist Party of China*, vol. 2 (1949–1978), pt. 2 (Beijing: Party History Publishing House, 2011), 635.
18. *History of the Chinese People's Liberation Army*, vol. 5 (Beijing: Military Science Press, 2011), 219–220.
19. Pang Xianzhi and Feng Hui, eds., *Chronicle of Mao Zedong (1949–1976)*, vol. 3 (Beijing: Central Literature Publishing House, 2013), 440–441.
20. These five suggestions are as follows: First, the Chinese government declares that Taiwan and the Penghu Islands are Chinese territory, and Jinmen, Mazu, and other offshore islands are inland islands of the Chinese mainland. The Chinese government has the right to take appropriate measures at an appropriate time to liberate these territories of China, which is an internal affair of China and does not permit foreign interference. Second, the US government guarantees to withdraw all its armed forces from Taiwan, the Penghu Islands, and the Taiwan Strait. Third, the Chinese government declares that the offshore islands of Jinmen, Mazu, etc., occupied by KMT troops and directly threatening the ports of Xiamen and Fuzhou, must be recovered. If the KMT troops are willing to withdraw from these islands voluntarily, the Chinese government will not pursue them. Fourth, the Chinese government declares that after recovering the offshore islands of Jinmen and Mazu, it will strive to peacefully liberate Taiwan and the Penghu Islands and avoid using force to achieve the liberation of Taiwan and the Penghu Islands for a certain period of time. Fifth, the Chinese and US governments agree that the freedom and safety of navigation and flight in the international waters and airspace of the Taiwan Strait must be guaranteed.

    See Han Nianlong, ed., *Contemporary Chinese Diplomacy* (Beijing: China Social Sciences Press, 1988), 107–108.
21. Wang Taiping, ed., *Diplomatic History of the People's Republic of China*, vol. 2 (1957–1959) (Beijing: World Affairs Press, 1998), 431.
22. Ibid.
23. Pang Xianzhi and Feng Hui, eds., *Chronicle of Mao Zedong (1949–1976)*, vol. 3 (Beijing: Central Literature Publishing House, 2013), 456–457.
24. *Selected Diplomatic Works of Zhou Enlai* (Beijing: Central Literature Publishing House, 1990), 265.

25. Xikang Province was abolished in 1955.
26. *Collected Works of Mao Zedong*, vol. 7 (Beijing: People's Publishing House, 1999), 420–421.
27. Ibid., 425.
28. Quoted in Pang Xianzhi and Jin Chongji, eds., *Biography of Mao Zedong*, vol. 4 (Beijing: Central Literature Publishing House, 2011), 1847.
29. *Collected Works of Mao Zedong*, vol. 7 (Beijing: People's Publishing House, 1999), 427–429.
30. Pang Xianzhi and Feng Hui, eds., *Chronicle of Mao Zedong (1949–1976)*, vol. 3 (Beijing: Central Literature Publishing House, 2013), 464–466.
31. Li Ping and Ma Zisun, eds., *Chronicle of Zhou Enlai (1949–1976)*, vol. 2 (Beijing: Central Literature Publishing House, 1997), 524.
32. Party History Research Office of the CPC Central Committee, *History of the Communist Party of China*, vol. 2 (1949–1978), pt. 2 (Beijing: Party History Publishing House, 2011), 639.
33. *Collected Works of Mao Zedong*, vol. 8 (Beijing: People's Publishing House, 1999), 89–90.
34. Pang Xianzhi and Feng Hui, eds., *Chronicle of Mao Zedong (1949–1976)*, vol. 6 (Beijing: Central Literature Publishing House, 2013), 427.
35. Ibid., 380.
36. Ibid., 578.
37. Ibid., 649 n. 1.

Index

A

agreements
- Agreement Between the Central People's Government and the Local Government of Xizang on Measures for the Peaceful Liberation of Xizang, 225. *See also* Agreement on the Peaceful Liberation of Xizang
- Agreement Between the United States of America and the Republic of China for the Disposition of Lend-Lease Supplies, 179
- Agreement on the Peaceful Liberation of Xizang, 225
- Domestic Peace Agreement, 204–5
- Double Tenth Agreement, 192
- Korean Armistice Agreement, 249, 253, 394
- Military Assistance Agreement, 400
- Mutual Defense Assistance Agreement, 394
- October 10 Agreement, 180
- Package Agreement, 220
- Political Consultative Conference Agreement, 180, 192
- Sino-Soviet Agreement on the Chinese Eastern Railway, Lüshun, and Dalian, 218–20. *See also* Package Agreement
- Sino-Soviet Loan Agreement to the People's Republic of China, 218
- US-Taiwan Military Agreement, 400
- Yalta Agreement, 215, 218

agricultural mutual aid movement, 253, 255, 258
agricultural production cooperatives, 254, 278
anti-Communist, 34, 36, 98, 102, 128, 130–34, 142, 160
Anti-Dühring, 77, 154
anti-rightist struggle, 298
armed separation of workers and peasants, 47, 145
armies
- Chen-Su Army, 187
- Chen-Xie Group, 186–87
- Chinese People's Volunteer Army, 232, 237, 241–42, 244–47
- Eighteenth Group Army, 170, 172
- Eighth Route Army, 106, 108, 110–14, 120, 126–31, 133, 135, 137, 151, 170. *See also* Eighteenth Group Army
- Eight-Power Allied Forces, 4
- Field Army, 182, 184–87, 194, 196–202, 206
- Fourth Red Army, 46–47, 49–53, 55–59, 61–64, 74, 89

Front Army, 64–65, 67, 69–70, 72–74, 86–87, 89–94, 96–99, 103
KMT Army, 58, 113, 116, 120, 128, 130, 178–81, 183, 185–86, 191, 200, 202, 206–7
Korean People's Army, 229, 232–36, 247
Left Route Army, 92
Liu-Deng Army, 183, 186–87
National Revolutionary Army, 44, 106
New Fourth Army, 106, 108, 126–28, 130–31, 133–34
North China Area Army, 111, 113
Northeast Army, 96, 98, 100, 102, 152
Northeast Border Defense Army, 229–35, 240
Northwest Army, 100
People's Liberation Army (PLA), 183–84, 187–88, 191–92, 195, 197–98, 201–2, 204–5, 207, 224–25, 227, 236, 244, 356, 393–94, 397–98, 402, 407
Red Army, 6, 43, 45–53, 55–59, 61–69, 71–76, 79–102, 106–7, 110–11, 113, 120, 146, 148–50, 152–54, 174, 416
Right Route Army, 92–93
Workers' and Peasants' Revolutionary Army, 41, 44, 48–49
Art of War, The, 149–52
atomic bomb, 233, 285, 342–43, 346–47, 373
atrocities in modern and contemporary China
April 12 Massacre, 173
February 7 Massacre, 28
Nanjing Massacre, 116

B
backstage battlefield, 130
Bai Chongxi, 195, 206
base areas
central revolutionary base area, 71
Jin-Cha-Ji base area, 185
Jinggang Mountains base (area), 48–49, 53–54, 78
resistance base area, 99, 128
Shaanxi-Gansu base area, 94
Shaanxi-Gansu-Ningxia base area, 111
Beiyang Government, 19–20
Bo Gu, 72, 76, 80–83, 85, 89, 92, 116, 157, 162. *See also* Qin Bangxian
bookishness, 146–47
Bo Yibo, 240, 253–54, 261, 275, 303
Braun, Otto, 81
bureaucratic capital, 252, 257
bureaucratism, 212, 289

C
Cai Hesen, 3, 10, 12–13, 24–25, 27
Cai Tingkai, 69, 71
Cai Yuanpei, 9, 12–13, 24
Cao Juren, 393, 408, 410
Ceaușescu, Nicolae, 376, 379
Central Bureau, 27–28, 44, 67–68, 73–74, 149
Central Bureau of the Soviet Area, 67–68, 73
Central Committee of the CPC, 29, 33–35, 40, 42–44, 47, 49, 52–56, 58–59, 61–63, 67, 72, 74, 78, 80–81, 83, 85, 87, 89, 91–96, 99–103, 108, 110, 115, 123–29, 132, 134, 137–39, 141, 147–49, 154, 158–66, 171, 174, 177, 179–80, 183–85, 187, 192–95, 203–4, 212, 214–17, 221–22, 227, 231–32, 234, 236, 239, 241–43, 245, 252–53, 255, 257, 262, 266–67, 270, 274–75, 279–81, 283, 287–88, 293, 297–98, 301, 304, 306–7, 309–3, 315, 318–19, 325–26, 328–29, 335–36, 338–39, 342–43, 345–47, 349–51, 353–56, 359–62, 365–70, 376, 380–81, 394–95, 404–5, 410
Central Military Commission, 63, 73, 80, 131, 134, 171, 182, 185, 193–94, 196–97, 200, 202–4, 229–31, 237, 338–39, 342, 356, 366, 369, 401
Central People's Government, 209, 211, 219, 222, 225, 228, 233, 249, 261, 263, 270
Central Publicity Department, 108, 154, 163–64

INDEX

Central Secretariat, 165, 171, 175, 237, 239, 241
Central Soviet Area, 66, 68, 70–73, 76, 79–80, 146–48, 154
Chang Tso-lin, 12–13
Chen Boda, 261, 265–67, 269–70, 281, 307, 316, 326–27, 329, 359–63, 365
Chen Changhao, 91–92
Chen Cheng, 70–71, 172, 410
Chen Duxiu, 10–11, 27–29, 32, 34, 39, 44, 147, 160
Chen Geng, 74, 186
Cheng Qian, 206, 261, 408
Chen Shaoyu, 67, 115–16, 125, 159, 162
Chen Shunong, 10, 26
Chen Yi, 48, 50, 52, 57–59, 61–63, 131, 187, 194, 197, 204, 206, 359, 365–66, 373, 375, 394, 403
Chen Yun, 82, 84–85, 116, 126, 171, 210, 222, 240, 261, 278, 287, 311, 313–14
Chen Zhengren, 75
Chiang Ching-kuo, 172
Chiang Kai-shek, 32, 34, 36, 40, 43, 50, 57, 64–66, 69–70, 80, 86–87, 90, 93–102, 106–7, 110–11, 116–17, 123, 127–28, 130–33, 138, 140–41, 160, 169–84, 186–89, 191–92, 195–200, 202, 205, 207, 224–25, 263–64, 334, 342, 375, 383, 388–89, 393, 395–96, 399–400, 403–4, 406–2
China Democratic League, 192
China-US Relations, 371, 439
China-US talks, 380–81, 399
Chinese People's Political Consultative Conference (CPPCC), 207, 221, 236, 261, 287, 355, 368, 395
Chinese United Front Against Japanese Aggression, 94, 124, 126–27, 146, 158
Chinese Workers' and Peasants' Revolutionary Committee, 64, 67
Chongqing negotiations, 140, 171, 175, 177–78
class struggle, 30, 318, 347, 353
Clausewitz, Carl von, 150–52

On War, 151–52
Collected Poems of Mao Zedong, 328
Comintern, 27, 40–41, 47, 67, 79–80, 84, 115, 124–26, 146–47, 158
Communist Manifesto, The, 20–21, 280
Communist Party of China (CPC), 3, 10, 12, 27–37, 39–41, 43–45, 47, 57–58, 62, 66–67, 72, 74, 83, 91, 95–96, 100–101, 103, 106–1, 114–16, 120, 123–26, 128, 130–33, 137–42, 145–47, 149, 152–54, 158–60, 163–64, 166–67, 169, 172–78, 180, 184, 187, 189, 192–93, 202–5, 209–1, 216, 222, 227, 232, 251–53, 255, 257–59, 261, 266, 269–70, 272, 275–76, 279–81, 284, 287–88, 293, 297–98, 304–6, 309–10, 312–13, 318, 325–26, 328–29, 335, 337, 341–47, 349–54, 356, 359–61, 370, 376, 380–81, 394–95, 400, 404–5, 407, 410
Communist Party of the Soviet Union (CPSU), 214, 279–81, 334–39, 342–47
Communists, 35–37, 40, 96, 102, 114, 123, 127, 132–33, 165, 170, 173, 182, 203, 210, 276
"Communist Wind," 311–12, 317, 319, 323, 325
CPC's battles of resistance against external and internal enemies
  Agrarian Revolutionary War, 149, 212
  Battle of Dabaidi, 51, 53
  Battle of Menglianggu, 186
  Battle of Panlong, 184
  Battle of Pingxingguan, 113
  Battle of Shajiadian, 184
  Battle of Shanghai, 114
  Battle of Tai'erzhuang, 116
  Battle of Wuhan, 118, 123
  Battle of Zhiluo Town, 94–95
  Chengdu Campaign, 207
  Dingtao Campaign, 182
  Eastern Henan Campaign, 194
  Handan Campaign, 178
  Hengyang-Baoqing Campaign, 206

Huaihai Campaign, 196–98, 200, 202, 211
Hundred-Regiment Campaign, 129
Jinmen Artillery Battle, 342, 401
Liaoshen Campaign, 196–97, 200
Pingjin Campaign, 196, 200–202
Xiangfan Campaign, 194
Yangtze River Crossing Campaign, 204–6
CPC's uprisings
　Autumn Harvest Uprising, 39–42, 44–45, 49, 54, 103
　Guangzhou Uprising, 49
　Nanchang Uprising, 40, 48–49, 52, 74
Cultural Book Society, 25–26

D

Dabie Mountains, 183, 186–87
Dachen Islands, 394, 397–98
declarations
　Cairo Declaration, 136
　China-US Joint Communiqué, 391
　Communist and Workers' Parties of the Socialist Countries Conference in Moscow, 337. *See also* Moscow Declaration
　Moscow Declaration, 337–38
Democratic League, 171, 178, 192
Deng Fa, 73, 82
Deng Liqun, 326–29
Deng Xiaoping, 76, 82, 126, 171, 182, 186, 194, 197, 204, 206, 240, 261–62, 267, 281, 283, 287, 329, 346, 366–67, 369–70, 395
Deng Zihui, 131, 240, 261
domestic conferences
　Bandung Conference, 399–400
　Beidaihe Conference, 306, 310, 353
　Central Work Conference, 330, 353, 359
　Chengdu Conference, 303
　December Meeting, 115–16, 125, 185
　Gutian Conference, 62, 64
　Hangzhou Conference, 300–301
　Luochuan Conference, 111, 115
　Lushan Conference, 316, 318, 321, 326, 364
　Nanning Conference, 301–3
　Ningdu Conference, 76
　Supreme State Conference, 289
　Zhengzhou Conference, 308-2, 316, 322–23
　Zunyi Conference, 82, 84–86, 145, 147–49, 157, 160
domestic political movements
　Anti-rash Progress Campaign, 301–4
　Anti-Rightist Campaign, 352
　Criticize Deng, Counter the Right-Deviationist Reversal-of-Verdicts Trend Campaign, 370
　Criticize Lin and Criticize Confucius Campaign, 366
　"Great Cultural Revolution," 258, 347, 349–52, 354–56, 358–60, 364, 366, 369–70, 378, 437
　Great Revolution, 33–36, 40, 44, 47, 77, 103, 145, 149, 160, 211
　May Fourth Movement, 10, 15–17, 21, 26, 30
　New Culture Movement, 10–11
　Xinhai Revolution, 5–7, 21, 34
　(Yan'an) Rectification Movement, 135, 163, 165–66, 286, 297
Dong Biwu, 116, 123, 184, 240, 261, 267, 368
Du Yuming, 197, 199–200, 202

E

Eisenhower, Dwight D., 334, 342–43, 397–98, 403
encirclement and suppression (campaigns), 47, 49–51, 58, 65–75, 79–80, 82, 85, 94, 96, 129, 153, 157
extreme left, 366
extreme right, 366

F

Far Eastern Republic, 334
"February Adverse Current," 359, 364–65
February Letter, 53, 55

Feng Yuxiang, 64
Five-Year Plan
    First, 259, 295–96
    Second, 276, 282, 287, 299–300
    Third, 300
"four crossings of the Chishui River," 87
Fu Lianzhang, 74–76
Fu Zuoyi, 195–96, 200–202

G
"Gang of Four," 368–70
    Jiang Qing, 350–51, 359–60, 366–70
    Wang Hongwen, 367–68
    Yao Wenyuan, 368
    Zhang Chunqiao, 306, 359, 368
Gao Gang, 231–32, 234, 237, 240, 242, 244, 261
general line, 253, 260–61, 267, 269, 302, 304, 317, 346
Geneva Conference, 371, 394–95
Great Leap Forward, 295, 298, 300, 303, 306, 308, 310–11, 315–17, 321–23, 327, 330, 352–53, 433
great-power chauvinism, 337, 341
Guan Feng, 359, 365
Guo Huazong, 68–69

H
Han Deqin, 71
Hao Mengling, 68, 71
He Changgong, 41, 48, 50
He Jian, 50, 55
He Kequan, 82. *See also* Kai Feng
He Long, 126, 206
He Shuheng, 10, 15, 22, 26
He Xiangning, 132, 261
He Yingqin, 65, 69–70, 173, 205
He Zizhen, 50, 75, 77, 84, 88
Hong Kong, 225–26, 408
Huang Wei, 197–99
Huang Yanpei, 137, 215, 261, 289, 355
Hunan autonomy movement, 24–25
Hu Qiaomu, 161, 163, 240, 261, 267, 281, 302, 311, 316, 329
Hu Sheng, 281, 326–29
Hu Shi, 10, 17, 23

Hu Zongnan, 89–90, 93, 184–85, 207

I
incidents in modern and contemporary China
    April 12 Incident, 133
    Lin Biao Incident, 364
    Lugou Bridge Incident, 105–6, 114, 156
    May 30 Incident, 30
    September 18 Incident, 89
    Southern Anhui Incident, 130–32
    Sun Liren Incident, 400
    Tiananmen Incident, 370
    Wu Guozhen Incident, 400
    Xi'an Incident, 100–103, 150, 176
    Zhenbao Island Incident, 374–75
    Zhongshan Warship Incident, 32

J
Jiang Guangnai, 71
Jiang Hua, 50, 57, 328
Jinggang Mountains, 46–54, 59, 78, 153
Jinmen, 306, 342, 393–94, 397–98, 400–410

K
Kai Feng, 82, 149. *See also* He Kequan
Kang Sheng, 116, 164, 359–61
Kang Youwei, 10, 21
Khrushchev, Nikita, 279–82, 299, 333–36, 339–47, 350, 353, 373, 436
Kim Il Sung, 234–36, 242, 244, 246, 249
Kissinger, Henry, 371, 377, 380–85, 387–88
KMT Government, 65, 106, 124, 127, 137–40, 156, 173, 175, 179, 199, 204–5, 213–14, 217–19, 222, 225
Kung Hsiang-hsi, 101, 188
Kuomintang (KMT), 28–34, 36–37, 39–41, 49, 51–52, 57–58, 65, 67–68, 75, 81, 86–90, 100, 106–6, 120, 124, 127–28, 130–34, 137–42, 145, 149–50, 153–54, 156, 158, 160, 170–87, 191–200, 202, 204–7, 210, 212–15, 217–19, 222, 225, 256, 394, 398–404, 407, 412

L

Lai Chuanzhu, 50, 131, 230
land reform, 49, 142, 188, 193, 211, 223–24, 252, 254, 278
laws
   Common Program, 261, 268–69
   Constitution of the People's Republic of China, 251, 261, 267, 269–71
   Constitution of the Republic of China, 192, 264
   Land Reform Law of the People's Republic of China, 211
   Provisional Constitution of the Republic of China, 264
leftist, 36, 67, 73–75, 77, 79, 114, 147, 149, 157–60, 162–63, 193, 253, 308–10, 312, 314, 317–19, 351, 353–54, 359, 366, 369, 373
Liang Qichao, 6, 9–10, 21
Liang Shuming, 192, 368
Liaoluo Bay, 402
Liao Yaoxiang, 196
liberated areas, 142, 172, 174–77, 179–80, 182–84, 186–87, 193
liberating Taiwan, 216, 227, 394, 396–97
Li Da, 27
Li Dazhao, 11–12, 27, 44
Li De, 81, 83, 92. *See also* Braun, Otto
Li Fuchun, 82, 240, 282, 303, 359, 373, 375
Li Jinxi, 8, 20, 23–24
Li Jishen, 137, 202, 214, 261, 408
Li Mi, 198, 200, 202
Lin Biao, 50, 56–57, 62, 82, 94, 97, 195–96, 200, 204, 206, 224, 240–41, 352, 359–66, 368, 378
Lin Boqu, 126, 139, 204, 240, 261, 305
Li Shizeng, 12–13
Liu Angong, 55–56, 59
Liu Bing, 370
Liu Bocheng, 82, 86–87, 92, 171, 182, 186, 194, 197, 204, 206
Liu Ding, 152
Liu Lantao, 253–54

Liu Shaoqi, 82, 116, 126, 131, 135, 165, 167, 171, 174, 184, 204, 214–15, 218, 240, 253–54, 258, 261, 266–67, 269, 271, 275, 281, 287, 303–4, 326, 336, 352, 359, 368, 400
Liu Shiyi, 52
Liu Yazi, 132, 137
Liu Zhi, 195, 197–98
Li Weihan, 10, 159, 204, 252, 255, 261–62, 267
Li Xiannian, 301, 303, 359, 370, 373, 375
Li Zongren, 64, 116, 202, 205
local people's congresses, 261, 271
Long March, 76, 79–80, 82, 84, 86–89, 94–96, 146–47, 149, 154, 350. *See also* westward expedition
Lu Deming, 42, 44
Luo Ming, 75–76
Luo Pu, 72. *See also* Zhang Wentian
Luo Ronghuan, 50, 62, 126, 195, 200, 206, 224, 240
Luo Zhanglong, 10, 13, 25
Luo Zhuoying, 70–71

M

Ma Bufang, 206
MacArthur, Douglas, 227–28, 236, 246
Macau, 226
Malinovsky, Rodion, 338, 340–41
Mao Anqing, 29, 32–33
Mao Anying, 29, 32–33, 245
Mao's works and documents
   Analysis of the Classes in Chinese Society, 19, 31–32
   "Bombard the Headquarters—My First Big-Character Poster," 351
   Class Basis of Chao Hêng-t'i and the Tasks Before Us, The, 32
   "Concentrate Superior Forces to Annihilate the Enemy in Detail," 182
   "Current Situation and Border Area Issues," 129
   Current Situation and Tasks, 188

"Draft Resolution on Several Issues Concerning the People's Commune," 309–10
"Economic and Financial Problems in the War of Resistance Period," 165
"Extensively Absorb Intellectuals," 165
"Gutian Conference Resolutions," 62
"Letter from the Central Committee to Comrades on Implementing the Northward Policy," 93
"Notice on the September Meeting from the Central Committee," 194
"On Coalition Government," 142
"On Contradiction," 78, 155, 157–58, 283, 288, 321, 332
"On Investigation Work," 146
"On New Democracy," 150, 165
"On Practice," 78, 155–58, 321, 332
"On Protracted War," 117–18, 120, 150
"On the People's Democratic Dictatorship," 21
"On the Question Whether Imperialism and All Reactionaries Are Real Tigers," 312
"On the Tactics Against Japanese Imperialism," 94
"On the Ten Major Relationships," 273–74, 282–85, 292–93, 304
"Oppose Stereotyped Party Writing," 163
Peasant Issues Series, 33
"Preface to *The Communist*," 165
"Problems of Strategy in China's Revolutionary War," 72, 79, 150, 152
"Proclamation of the Chinese PLA," 187
"Rectify the Party's Style of Work," 165
"Rectify the Style of Study, the Party, and Writing," 163
"Reform Our Study," 160, 162–63, 165
"Report on an Investigation of the Peasant Movement in Hunan," 34, 212

"Resolutions of the Ninth Congress of the Fourth Red Army of the CPC," 62. *See also* "Gutian Conference Resolutions"
Rural Surveys, 162–63, 165
Since the Sixth Congress, 162–63
"Smash Chiang Kai-shek's Offensive Through Self-Defense War," 180
"Some Estimates on the Current International Situation," 181
"Some Issues Concerning Methods of Leadership," 165
"Strive to Mobilize All Forces to Win the War of Resistance," 108
"Struggle for a Fundamental Improvement in the National Financial and Economic Situation," 222
"Summary of the Second Anti-Communist Campaign," 165
"Talks at the Yan'an Forum on Literature and Art," 145, 165
"The Major Changes in China's Military Situation," 199
"The Party's Tasks After Japan's Surrender," 180
"The Policy, Methods, and Prospects of Resisting Japan's Invasion," 108
"The Situation and Tasks of the War of the Resistance After the Fall of Shanghai and Taiyuan," 114
"The Struggle in the Jinggang Mountains," 47
"The Urgent Tasks After the Establishment of the United Front of the KMT and the CPC," 107
"Where Do Correct Ideas Come From?," 157
Mao Yichang, 24
Mao Zetan, 48, 76, 100
Marxism, 11, 21, 24–26, 78, 124, 145–46, 153–54, 157–59, 161, 164–67, 281–82, 318, 322, 364, 420
Marxism-Leninism, 124, 153–54, 157, 159, 161, 164, 166, 281–82, 364

Ma Xulun, 202, 261
Mikoyan, Anastas, 217, 226, 279
Molotov, Vyacheslav, 214, 217, 245
Montargis meeting, 26
"mopping-up" operations, 128, 130, 133
mutual aid teams, 252–54

N

Nanjing, 13, 15, 55, 101–2, 114, 116, 152, 179, 191–92, 198–99, 204–6, 300
National Assembly, 138–39, 173, 175–76, 178, 191–92
national bourgeoisie, 192, 210–11, 221, 223, 290
National Congress of the CPC
  First, 27, 275
  Third, 28, 44
  Seventh, 125, 142, 166
  Eighth, 258, 275–76, 284, 287–88, 293, 304–6, 352, 400
  Ninth, 360
National Government, 32, 40, 140–41, 178. *See also* KMT Government
nationalism, 268, 334, 340
National People's Congress, 261–62, 268, 270–71, 301, 355, 360, 366–69
National Political Council, 126, 132–33
news agencies
  Agence France-Presse, 378
  Associated Press, 378, 403
  Citizen News Agency, 20
  Kyodo News, 378
  TASS, 217, 334, 343
  Xinhua News Agency, 131, 178, 192, 199, 276, 281
Nie Rongzhen, 82, 97, 204, 206, 229, 231, 359, 373, 375
Nixon, Richard, 371–73, 376–91, 411
Ni Zhiliang, 235–36, 240, 242

O

October Revolution, 11–12, 17, 22, 25–26, 280, 298
"One Guideline, Four Objectives," 410

P

Party Constitution, 166–67, 287, 360
party's cooperation
  cooperation between the KMT and the CPC (KMT-CPC cooperation), 29, 31, 36, 39–40, 107, 109, 145, 149, 400
  intra-party cooperation, 28
  multi-party cooperation, 272
peasant movement, 30, 33–34, 44
Peking University, 12–13, 15, 349, 351
Peng Dehuai, 50–51, 64, 73, 77, 82, 91–94, 97, 106, 112, 116, 129, 171, 184, 206, 232, 240–47, 261, 316–18, 339–40, 342, 363, 405, 407
Peng Huang, 15, 26
Peng Pai, 33, 35
Peng Zhen, 126, 171, 240, 267, 281
People's Commune Movement, 306, 308, 310–12, 321, 323, 327, 330, 352–53
People's Republic of China (PRC), 63, 67, 209–3, 218–21, 235–36, 251, 253, 261, 266–67, 269–72, 293, 310, 342, 360, 370–71, 377, 379–85, 387, 391, 393, 405–6
periodicals
  Chinese Youth, 32
  Eighth Route Army Military and Political Magazine, 135
  Free China, 409
  Journal of the New Citizen, 6
  Liberation, 120
  Liberation Daily, 138–39
  Nanyang Siang Pau, 408
  New Youth (*Youth Magazine*), 10
  Peasant Monthly, 32
  Peking University Daily, 24
  People's Daily, 229, 281, 289, 301–2
  Poetry Periodical, 66
  Political Weekly, 32
  Red China, 75
  Red Flag, 154, 225, 327, 347
  Republic Daily, 55
  Ta Kung Pao, 16, 24, 117
  Time, 137

Weekly Review, 17
Xiangjiang Daily News, 6
Xiangjiang Review, 16, 18
Xinhua Daily, 177
"Ping-Pong diplomacy," 378, 411
plenary sessions of the CPC
   Second Plenary Session of the Seventh Central Committee, 202–3
   Second Plenary Session of the Eighth National Congress, 352
   Second Plenary Session of the Ninth Central Committee, 360–61
   Second Plenary Session of the Tenth Central Committee, 369
   Third Plenary Session of the Seventh Central Committee, 222
   Third Plenary Session of the Eleventh Central Committee, 360
   Expanded Fourth Plenary Session of the Sixth Central Committee, 67, 72
   Expanded Sixth Plenary Session of the Sixth Central Committee, 124–25
   Sixth Plenary Session of the Sixth Central Committee, 124–25, 128, 158–59, 161
   Sixth Plenary Session of the Eighth Central Committee, 309–10, 312–13
   Seventh Plenary Session of the Sixth Central Committee, 138, 141, 166
   Seventh Plenary Session of the Eighth Central Committee, 313
   Eighth Plenary Session of the Eighth Central Committee, 318
   Tenth Plenary Session of the Eighth Central Committee, 353
   Eleventh Plenary Session of the Eighth Central Committee, 351, 354
   Expanded Twelfth Plenary Session of the Eighth Central Committee, 359
Political Bureau of the Central Committee (Political Bureau), 42–43, 72, 81–85, 87, 89, 91, 93–94, 100, 102, 108, 110, 115, 117, 124–29, 147, 149, 154, 160–62, 165–66, 171, 177, 193–94, 214–15, 221, 227, 232, 239–43, 245, 253, 255, 262, 266–67, 275, 280–81, 283, 287, 301, 309–1, 315, 325–29, 345, 350–52, 360–61, 366–67, 369, 380–81, 394–95, 404, 410
political tendencies
   adventurism, 54, 75, 85, 147, 155, 160, 342
   capitulationism, 32, 114, 147, 158, 344
   dogmatism, 73, 146–47, 153, 155–60, 162–64, 167, 281, 286, 302, 334
   opportunism, 54, 95, 114, 318
political thoughts
   Mao Zedong Thought, 166–67, 361
   Three Principles of the People, 174, 409
Production Campaign, 135–36, 311–12
Provisional Central, 72–75, 77, 83

Q

Qi Benyu, 359, 365
Qin Bangxian, 72, 80, 157, 162
Qiu Qingquan, 198–200, 202
Qu Qiubai, 35, 37, 41, 147

R

railways
   Chengdu–Chongqing Railway, 225
   Chinese Eastern Railway, 215, 217–21
   Datong–Puzhou Railway, 111
   Jinpu Railway, 110, 198, 232
   Pinghan Railway, 109, 132
   Pingsui Railway, 110, 112
   Pingzhang Railway, 201
   Sichuan–Hankou Railway, 225
Rao Shushi, 240, 261
Red Guards, 354–55, 357, 359
Ren Bishi, 73, 113, 124, 135, 165, 171, 184, 204, 240
Republic of China, 7, 136, 179, 192, 219–20, 264
rightists, 32, 298, 300, 302, 317, 350–51, 355, 389
Roshchin, Nikolai, 239
Ruijin, Jiangxi Province, 52, 55, 72–73, 76

S

semi-colonial and semi-feudal economy, 252
"Seventeen Articles on Agriculture," 274–75
Seventh Fleet, 227, 393, 397
Shao Lizi, 172, 174–75, 177, 204
Shaoshan Chong, 3, 5
Shaoshan, Hunan Province, 1, 3, 5, 29–30, 314, 349
shelling of Jinmen, 306, 342, 403, 406–7, 410
Shen Junru, 202, 215, 261
Shi Zhe, 214
Sino-Soviet Polemics, 333, 344, 346–47, 353
"Sixteen-Character Formula," 49, 72, 78
Snow, Edgar, 5, 7–8, 11, 15, 377, 387
socialist system, 260, 271, 291, 304
socialist transformations. *See also* Three Major Transformations
   agriculture, of, 253–54
   capitalist industry and commerce, of, 254–58
   handicrafts, of, 258
Soong Ching-ling, 132, 261, 368
Soong Mei-ling, 101–2
Soviet Republic of China, 73, 77, 99
Soviet Union (Soviet), 32, 55, 58, 64, 66–68, 70–73, 76, 78–82, 89–90, 93, 96–98, 132, 134, 136, 146–50, 152, 154, 160, 162, 171, 175, 177, 179, 181–82, 213–22, 226, 228, 231, 234–35, 238–39, 241–43, 245, 252, 254–55, 262–65, 271, 273, 276–82, 284–86, 299, 305–6, 309, 321–26, 328–30, 333–47, 353, 372–76, 380, 383, 385–86, 397, 400, 404, 432
Stalin, 78, 115, 159, 161, 164, 203, 213–18, 220, 226, 231, 236–37, 239, 241–42, 245, 248, 262, 265, 280–81, 291, 309, 321–26, 335, 337
   Economic Problems of Socialism in the USSR, 309, 321–24, 326

State Council, 20, 268, 271, 275–76, 282–83, 301, 304, 354, 356, 361, 366, 368–70
state-owned economy, 188, 252
Strong, Anna Louise, 169, 181
Sun Liren, 400, 409
Sun Yat-sen, 7, 21, 31, 36, 132
Sun Yuanliang, 198–99
Su Yu, 182, 187, 193–94, 197, 206, 229–31, 240

T

Taiwan question, 334, 342, 376–77, 383–86, 388, 391, 393–97, 399, 404–7, 409–1
Taiwan Strait, 227, 342, 380–81, 383, 391, 393, 399–400, 403, 406
Tan Daoyuan, 65, 69
Tan Yankai, 20, 25
Tan Zhenlin, 50, 57, 62, 76, 182, 197, 206, 265, 359
Tao Yi, 22, 26
Teng Daiyuan, 50–51
38th parallel, 228–29, 232, 234–36, 238–41, 243–44, 246–48
Three Major Transformations, 254, 265
Tian Jiaying, 267, 281, 307, 316, 326–29
total resistance against Japanese aggression by the whole nation, 123–24, 154, 158
treaties
   Mutual Defense Treaty, 395, 397, 399–400, 402
   Sino-Soviet Treaty of Friendship, Alliance, and Mutual Assistance, 218–19, 221
   Treaty Banning Nuclear Weapon Tests in the Atmosphere, in Outer Space, and Under Water, 346
   Warsaw Pact, 336
Truman, Harry S., 169, 227–28

U

United Nations Security Council, 227, 229, 398

W

Wan Fulin, 98
Wang Jiaxiang, 73–74, 79–85, 92, 94, 124–26, 162
Wang Jingwei, 32, 40, 101, 127
Wang Jinyu, 68–69
Wang Li, 359, 365
Wang Ming, 67, 72–73, 75, 79–80, 84, 89, 115–16, 125–27, 146–47, 149, 158–60, 162. *See also* Chen Shaoyu
Wang Ruofei, 171–72, 174–75, 177
Wang Shijie, 172, 174, 177
warfare strategies
   guerrilla warfare, 49, 64–65, 75, 78, 110–16, 118, 120–22, 126–28, 134, 179, 182, 334
   protracted war, 110, 116–18, 136, 148, 181, 189, 235, 248
wars at home and abroad
   civil war, 85, 96, 100–103, 107, 113, 120, 125, 132, 150, 153–54, 162–63, 169–73, 175, 177–79, 181–82, 187, 192, 337, 356, 393, 396
   Cold War, 228, 238, 372
   Eastern Expedition, 96–97, 99
   Guadalcanal Campaign, 136
   Korean War, 222–23, 227–28, 231–39, 246, 248–49, 251, 261, 393, 396, 399–400
   North African Campaign, 136
   Northern Expedition, 33, 36
   Pacific War, 130, 134
   Resist US Aggression and Aid Korea, 223, 232, 237–38, 240–42, 245–47, 249. *See also* Korean War
   Sino-Japanese War, 4, 120
   Southern Henan Campaign, 132
   Soviet-German War, 134
   War of Liberation, 122, 203, 208, 224, 242
   War of Resistance, 99–100, 102–3, 105, 107–10, 113, 117–18, 120, 122–23, 125–26, 128, 134–35, 142–43, 150, 160, 165, 169–70, 173–74, 179–80, 182, 242, 258, 418
   War of Resistance Against Japanese Aggression, 99–100, 103, 107, 109, 117, 120, 122, 126, 134, 150, 169–70, 173, 180, 242, 258. *See also* War of Resistance
   Xuzhou Campaign, 117
Warsaw talks, 375–77
Wedemeyer, Albert C., 173, 248
Wei Lihuang, 195–96
westward expedition, 82, 84
Wu Guozhen, 172, 400
Wu Lengxi, 276, 281, 302, 307, 316

X

Xi'an, 100–103, 150, 152, 176, 180, 206, 241
Xiangtan, 1, 9, 34, 314, 350
Xiang Ying, 67–68, 73, 116, 126, 130, 365
Xiang Zhenxi, 29, 32–33
Xiao Hua, 229–30
Xiao Zisheng, 10, 12, 105
Xibaipo, 193, 203–4, 226
Xinmin Institute, 10, 12–13, 15, 22, 25–26
Xiong Xianghui, 384–85
Xu Teli, 8–9, 74
Xu Xiangqian, 91–93, 206, 359, 373, 375

Y

Yahya Khan, 376, 380, 382
Yan'an, 9, 96, 101, 103, 112, 115–17, 124, 127, 129, 135, 137–42, 145, 147, 151, 154, 156, 163–66, 170, 172, 174, 177, 181, 183, 185, 194, 286, 355
Yang Changji, 8–10, 12–14, 24, 26
Yang Hucheng, 94, 96, 100, 102
Yang Kaihui, 14, 24, 26, 29, 32–33, 67–68, 100
Yang Shangkun, 82, 116, 126, 240
Yan Xishan, 64, 112, 177
Ye Fei, 401–2
Ye Jianying, 91, 106, 116, 123, 152, 204, 359, 364–65, 373, 375, 385

Ye Ting, 106, 130–31
Yijiangshan Island, 397–98
Yi Lirong, 10, 26
Yuan Shikai, 7

Z
Zeng Guofan, 9
Zeng Zhi, 50, 57
Zhang Guotao, 27, 89, 91–93, 123
Zhang Huizan, 65–66, 69
Zhang Jichun, 267
Zhang Jingyao, 18–20, 22, 24, 28, 30
Zhang Lan, 137, 214, 261
Zhang Naiqi, 368
Zhang Qun, 172, 174–75, 177
Zhang Shizhao, 24, 68, 204, 408–9
Zhang Wentian, 72, 79–85, 92, 97, 99, 101, 115–16, 126, 159, 162, 240, 317
Zhang Xueliang, 94, 96–102
Zhang Zhizhong, 172, 174–75, 177, 204–5, 408, 410
Zhou Enlai, 37, 40, 59, 61, 67, 72–74, 81–86, 89–92, 94, 96–98, 100–102, 106, 111, 116, 123, 126, 135, 140–41, 171–72, 174–77, 184, 204–5, 207, 215–18, 229–30, 234–37, 240–45, 261, 271, 274, 279, 281, 287, 300–301, 303, 326, 339, 342–43, 356, 359–61, 364–68, 371, 374, 376–88, 395, 398–99, 404–5, 408, 410–11
Zhou Shizhao, 22, 26
Zhou Yili, 75
Zhuang Zedong, 378
Zhu De, 46, 48–53, 55, 57–58, 61–64, 67, 73–74, 81–86, 91–92, 99, 106, 111, 113, 116, 126, 135, 140, 171, 184, 204–5, 215, 240, 261, 271, 287, 329, 368